Praise for *Planetary Solidarity*

"An excellent, challenging, inspiring book! Anyone who thinks social justice, climate change, and Christian doctrine are separate issues will be enlightened to see how inseparable they actually are as women's voices uncover the deep connections. Even more valuable, anyone who unthinkingly takes all three to be gender-neutral will be stimulated to realize the opposite. The approach through a gender lens lifts up insights from poor women struggling for life amid ecological damage, women politically active to protect the earth, both connected with women wrestling with the meaning of inherited Christian belief in an ecologically disintegrating world. A breathtaking contribution that cannot be ignored."
Elizabeth Johnson, Distinguished Professor of Theology, Fordham University, New York City

"We are standing at the end of the modern age, and at the beginning of the ecological future of our world if our world is to survive. *Planetary Solidarity* is a gateway to the green reformation of Christian theology, ethics, and spirituality. In solidarity we hear the cry of the poor and the cry of the earth, and see the earth is still taking care of us. Leading feminist theologians from around the world address issues of women and climate, climate crimes, and the dying earth. This rich book is an eye-opener and a 'must' for theologians and ecologists."
Jürgen Moltmann, Professor Emeritus of Systematic Theology, University of Tübingen

"This is a pathbreaking book exposing the challenges for women in the face of climate catastrophe around the planet. From an evolutionary context to ethical responses, *Planetary Solidarity* offers women's perspectives for a more inclusive ecotheology and a more engaged eco-justice. These voices are inspiring and life-transforming in the hands of the gifted women writers assembled here. This is an engaging book; a must read."
Mary Evelyn Tucker, founder and director of the Forum on Religion and Ecology at Yale

"An insightful, pathbreaking, and timely collection of female voices on the impact of climate justice on the ways we understand and articulate the fundamental Christian beliefs. The survival not only of humanity but also of the entire planet depends on how this vision of 'planetary solidarity' is put into practice. What an awesome challenge this book lays before us, believers and nonbelievers alike!"
Dr. Peter C. Phan, Georgetown University

"Solidarity involves more than taking a stance (like Martin Luther did) or marching for a cause (like Martin Luther King Jr. did). As the editors astutely observe, it entails building stronger communities where power is shared and relationships are fostered. In the context of climate injustice such solidarity has to be planetary in scope. It is tested where powerful interests are at stake and when love grows cold. It comes as no surprise that women are taking the lead in understanding what solidarity with the victims of climate change entails. In this volume, such solidarity prompts reflection—on nothing less than the deepest convictions that support Christian forms of solidarity. The varied voices included in this volume should be echoed all around the world. "
Ernst M. Conradie, University of the Western Cape

"A magnificent choir of women's voices rises up on behalf of a shared future: across a powerful diversity of theological feminisms, cultures, creatures, and doctrines, this energizing cantata sings its solidarity in the face of climate change and in the key of courage."
Catherine Keller, George T. Cobb Professor of Constructive Theology, Drew Theological School. Author of *Cloud of the Impossible: Negative Theology and Planetary Entanglement*

"The editors are to be congratulated on mobilizing a major response both to the challenge of climate justice and to Pope Francis's influential encyclical *Laudato Si'*. Importantly, they do so through an array of women theologians—including major names such as Eaton, Gebara, and McFague—all of them contributing important insights from a whole range of contexts. They address the crucial point that planetary insecurity resulting from climate change falls especially heavily on

women, but these reflections are important well beyond feminist and womanist circles. I expect to draw on this book very extensively in both research and teaching."
Christopher Southgate, Associate Professor in Interdisciplinary Theology, University of Exeter, UK

"Climate change is affecting all of us and especially poor women around the globe. How Christians think theologically deeply impacts the way we view climate change. With strong vision and a prophetic mission, Kim and Koster have put together an important collection of how we need to work toward *Planetary Solidarity*. This is a challenging and provocative book that is urgently needed."
Serene Jones, President and Johnston Family Professor for Religion and Democracy, Union Theological Seminary

Planetary Solidarity

Planetary Solidarity

Global Women's Voices on Christian Doctrine and Climate Justice

Grace Ji-Sun Kim and Hilda P. Koster, editors

Fortress Press
Minneapolis

PLANETARY SOLIDARITY
Global Women's Voices on Christian Doctrine and Climate Justice

Cover image: Mother Root © Jan Richardson. janrichardson.com
Cover design: Tory Herman

Hardcover ISBN: 978-1-5064-3262-5
eBook ISBN: 978-1-5064-0893-4

To our precious children and to the countless women around the globe who have taken up the struggle for ecojustice, often at great risk to their own lives. We are immensely indebted to their courage and vision and stand with them in solidarity. May this book contribute to creating a just and loving planetary community in which all may flourish.

Contents

Notes on Contributors

Sharon A. Bong is associate professor in gender and religious studies at the School of Arts and Social Sciences, Monash University Malaysia. She graduated with a PhD in religious studies (2002) and an MA in women and religion (1997), University of Lancaster, UK. She has authored *The Tension between Women's Rights and Religions: The Case of Malaysia* (2006) and edited *Trauma, Memory and Transformation in Southeast Asia* (2014). She was former coordinator of the Ecclesia of Women in Asia and a forum writer for the Catholic Theological Ethics in the World Church.

Rosemary P. Carbine holds a masters and doctoral degree in theology from the University of Chicago Divinity School and is currently associate professor of religious studies at Whittier College. She specializes in historical and constructive Christian theologies, and focuses on comparative feminist, womanist, and Latina/mujerista theologies, theological anthropology, and public/political theologies. She has coedited and contributed chapters to three books, *The Gift of Theology: The Contribution of Kathryn Tanner* (2015), *Theological Perspectives for Life, Liberty, and the Pursuit of Happiness: Public Intellectuals for the Twenty-First Century* (2013), and *Women, Wisdom, and Witness: Engaging Contexts in Conversation* (2012), as well as published numerous essays in anthologies and articles in *Journal of the American Academy of Religion, Journal for the Academic Study of Religion, Journal of Feminist Studies in Religion, Teaching Theology and Religion*, and *Harvard Theological Review*. Carbine has served as cochair of the Feminist Theory and Religious Reflection Group within the American Academy of Religion and as co-convener of the Women's Consultation on Constructive Theology in the Catholic Theological Society of America.

Meehyun Chung is professor of systematic theology at the United Graduate School of Theology of Yonsei University, Seoul, and an ordained minister in the Presbyterian Church in the Republic of Korea (PROK). She holds a doctorate degree in theology from Basel University in Switzerland. In 2006, Chung received the Karl Barth Prize from the Union of Protestant Churches within the EKD for her doctoral thesis. She was awarded the Marga Bührig Award in 2013 for her book *Reis und Wasser*. Prior to her current position, Chung served as vice president for the Ecumenical Association of Third World Theologians (EATWOT) and worked as the head of the Women and Gender Desk at Mission 21, Protestant Mission Basel, Switzerland, between 2005 and 2013.

Celia Deane-Drummond is professor of theology at the University of Notre Dame. In 2015, she was appointed director of the Center for Theology, Science and Human Flourishing at Notre Dame. She holds two doctorates, one in plant physiology and one in systematic theology. Her books include *Ecology in Jürgen Moltmann's Theology* (2nd ed., 2016), *The Wisdom of the Liminal: Human Nature, Evolution and Other Animals* (2014), *Re-Imaging the Divine Image: Humans and Other Animals* (Goshen Lectures 2014), and the coedited volumes *Religion in the Anthropocene* (2017), *Technofutures, Nature and the Sacred* (2015), *Animals as Religious Subjects* (2013), and *Religion and Ecology in the Public Sphere* (2011).

Wanda Deifelt is professor of religion at Luther College. She studied at the Faculdade de Teologia, Escola Superior de Teologia, São Leopoldo, Brazil, and received her doctorate from Garrett Evangelical Theological Seminary, Evanston, Illinois. She was awarded a ThD Honoris Causa by the University of Oslo in 2005. Deifelt is a member of the Lutheran-Roman Catholic Commission on Unity, appointed by the Lutheran World Federation and the Pontifical Council for Promoting Christian Unity, and of the Board of the Institute for Ecumenical Studies in Strasbourg. She also served as theological advisor to the Council of the Lutheran World Federation, Standing Committee of Ecumenical Affairs, Geneva, 1998–2003. Deifelt's research interests are contextual, liberation, and feminist theologies; ecumenical and interfaith issues; and Reformation studies.

Heather Eaton is full professor at Saint Paul University, Ottawa. She has authored and edited many books, including *Advancing Nonviolence and Social Transformation: New Perspectives on Nonviolent Theories* (2016), *The Intellectual Journey of Thomas Berry: Imagining the Earth Community* (2014), *Ecological Awareness: Exploring Religion, Ethics and Aesthetics* (2011),

Introducing Ecofeminist Theologies (2005), and *Ecofeminism and Globalization: Exploring Religion, Culture, Context* (2003). She is on the board of the journal *Worldviews: Global Religions, Environment and Culture*, the steering committee of the Religion and Ecology session of the American Academy of Religion, and past president of the Canadian Theological Society.

Ivone Gebara is a Brazilian feminist philosopher and theologian. She taught for several years in the Institute of Theology of Recife in Brazil and gave alternative theological formation to the leaders of Christian communities and social movements. Presently, she is living in São Paulo and is invited for lectures and workshops by universities and religious centers in Brazil and across the world. She is the author of over thirty books and numerous articles published in Portuguese, Spanish, French, English, and German. Among her major publications translated into English are *Out of Depths: Women's Experiences of Evil and Salvation* (2002) and *Longing for Running Water: Ecofeminism and Liberation* (1999).

Arnfríður Guðmundsdóttir is a professor of systematic theology and academic dean of the Faculty of Theology and Religious Studies at the University of Iceland. She received her PhD from Lutheran School of Theology at Chicago in 1996. She is the author of *Meeting God on the Cross: Christ, the Cross and the Feminist Critique* (2010). Guðmundsdóttir is an ordained minister within the Evangelical Lutheran Church of Iceland.

Melanie L. Harris received her PhD and MA from Union Theological Seminary in the City of New York and an MDiv from Iliff School of Theology in Denver, Colorado. She is the Founding Director of African American and Africana Studies and a full professor of Religion and Ethics at Texas Christian University. A graduate of the Harvard Leadership Program, her research focuses on Womanist Ethics, Ethical Leadership and Ecology. Dr. Harris is the author of *Gifts of Virtue, Alice Walker and Womanist Ethics* (2010), *Ecowomanism: African American Women and Earth Honoring Faiths* (2017), and coeditor with Kate M. Ott of *Faith, Feminism and Scholarship* (2011). Dr. Harris is an ordained minister in the African Methodist Episcopal Church and an American Council of Education Fellow with the University of Denver.

Grace Ji-Sun Kim received her PhD from the University of Toronto and is an associate professor of theology at Earlham School of Religion,

Richmond, Indiana. She is the author and editor of twelve books, most recently *Mother Daughter Speak* (2017), *Embracing the Other* (2015), and *Contemplations from the Heart* (2014). Kim is on the American Academy of Religion's (AAR) Board of Directors as an at-large director, she on the AAR's Program Committee, and has served on the Research Grant's Jury Committee. She is a co-chair of AAR's steering committee "Women of Color Scholarship, Teaching and Activism Unit." Kim is a regular *Huffington Post* blogger and is an ordained minister of word and sacrament within the Presbyterian Church (USA) denomination.

Hilda P. Koster is associate professor of religion at Concordia College, Moorhead in Minnesota. A native of the Netherlands, she holds a BA and an MDiv from the University of Groningen in the Netherlands, a ThM from Princeton Theological Seminary, and a doctorate in theology from the Divinity School of the University of Chicago. Koster's publications on theology, ecofeminism, and environmental ethics have appeared in *Theology Today*, *The Journal of Religion*, *Anglican Theological Review*, *Scriptura*, and the edited collection *Christian Doctrines for Global Gender Justice* (2015). She is the coeditor of *The Gift of Theology: The Contribution of Kathryn Tanner* (2015). At Concordia, Koster has directed the Environmental Studies Program (2012–16) and is involved in campus sustainability initiatives.

Sallie McFague is Distinguished Theologian in Residence at the Vancouver School of Theology, the E. Rhodes and Leona B. Carpenter Professor of Theology Emerita at Vanderbilt University (1980–2000), and former dean of Vanderbilt Divinity School (1975–1980). McFague's work has explored the relationship between faith and action: how what we believe influences how we act. She has been especially concerned with how the ways that we think of God and of ourselves influence our actions toward justice and sustainability for the planet. Her major works include *Blessed Are the Consumers: Climate Change and the Practice of Restraint* (2013), *A New Climate for Theology: God, the World and Global Warming* (2008), *Life Abundant: Rethinking Theology and Economy; For a Planet in Peril* (2000), *The Body of God: An Ecological Theology* (1993), *Models of God* (1987), and *Metaphorical Theology* (1982).

Joyce Ann Mercer is professor of practical theology and pastoral care at Yale Divinity School. She is the editor of the journal *Religious Education* and the current president of the Association of Practical Theology. Her recent publications include the coedited volume *Conundrums in Practical Theology* (2016) and a chapter on Indonesia's 1965–67 anti-communist massacre in the forthcoming *Practicing Ubuntu: Practical Theological Perspectives on Injustice, Personhood and Human Dignity* (LIT Verlag).

Cynthia Moe-Lobeda is author of *Resisting Structural Evil: Love as Ecological-Economic Vocation* (2013), *Public Church: For the Life of the World* (2004), *Healing a Broken World: Globalization and God* (2002), and numerous articles and chapters. She is coauthor of *Saint Francis and the Foolishness of God* (1993, 2015) and *Say to this Mountain: Mark's Story of Discipleship* (1996). Moe-Lobeda was appointed theological consultant to the presiding bishop of the Evangelical Lutheran Church in America and has served as a health worker/church worker in Honduras and as director of the Washington, DC, office of Augsburg College's Center for Global Education. She is full professor of Christian ethics at Pacific Lutheran Theological Seminary, Church Divinity School of the Pacific, and the Graduate Theological Union in Berkeley, California. Moe-Lobeda holds a doctoral degree in Christian ethics from Union Theological Seminary.

Fulata Lusungu Moyo is the World Council of Church's program executive for A Just Community of Women and Men, moving the Gender Advisory Group toward a process of gender justice policy and its connection to gender advocacy training using international tools like CEDAW and UNSCR1325 for the deference of women's human rights. She has served as a visiting scholar at Harvard Divinity School, developing an ethic of care in response to human trafficking and sexual violence. Moyo has guest edited two journals, the *Ecumenical Review* 64, no. 3 (2014) and *International Review of Mission* 104 (April 2015); she is the coeditor of *Women Writing Africa: Eastern African Region* (2007). Her other publications include several book chapters as well as journal articles on gender justice and religion. She earned a PhD from the School of Religion and Theology, University of KwaZulu-Natal in South Africa, with a focus in gender and sexual ethics.

Isabel Mukonyora is professor of religion at Western Kentucky University and publishes on the religious and theological dimensions of the Masowe Apostles. Among her many publications are numerous book chapters addressing contemporary problems of displacement in Global Christianity. She is the author of the book *Wandering a Gendered Wilderness* (2007). Mukonyora holds a Master of Letters degree from the University of Aberdeen in Scotland and a DPhil from Oxford University.

Her teaching and research is based on her extensive reading of the history of Christian theology, religious studies, and anthropology.

Jea Sophia Oh is assistant professor of philosophy at West Chester University of Pennsylvania. She has developed a comparative postcolonial ecotheology and pursues ongoing research in comparative theology, process theology, environmental ethics, postcolonialism, and feminism. Her book *A Postcolonial Theology of Life: Planetarity East and West* (2011) is the first approach to bridge postcolonialism and ecological theology with the use of Asian spirituality.

Nancy Pineda-Madrid is associate professor of theology and Latina/o ministry at Boston College. Her published works include *Suffering and Salvation in Ciudad Juarez* (2011) and the coedited *Hope: Promise, Possibility and Fulfillment* (2013) and *The Holy Spirit: Setting the World on Fire* (2017) as well as numerous articles. She is a former president of the Academy of Catholic Hispanic Theologians of the United States (ACHTUS) and a former vice president of the International Network of Societies of Catholic Theology (INSeCT). Currently, she is working on a book on Guadalupe. She lives in Boston with her spouse, Larry Gordon.

Barbara R. Rossing is professor of New Testament at the Lutheran School of Theology at Chicago. Rossing received her MDiv from Yale University Divinity School and ThD from Harvard University Divinity School. Rossing has served on the executive committee and council of the Lutheran World Federation (2003–10) and chaired the Lutheran World Federation's theology and studies committee. She chairs the Ecological Hermeneutics section of the Society of Biblical Literature. Her publications include *The Rapture Exposed: The Message of Hope in the Book of Revelation* (2004), *The Choice between Two Cities: Whore, Bride and Empire in the Apocalypse* (1999), two volumes of the *New Proclamation* commentary (2000, 2004), the nine-session Bible study *Journeys through Revelation: Apocalyptic Hope for Today* (2010), and articles and book chapters on the Apocalypse and ecology. Her media appearances include "Living the Questions," CBS "Sixty Minutes," and The National Geographic Channel.

Theresa A. Yugar is a professor at California State University, Los Angeles in the Liberal Studies, Chicana(o) and Latina(o) Studies, and Women's, Gender, and Sexuality Studies departments. She has a PhD in women's studies in religion from Claremont Graduate University and a Master's degree in feminist theology from Harvard University. In the past, she has been Chair for both the American Academy of Religion's Women's Caucus, National and Western. She is the author of the book *Sor Juana Inés de la Cruz: Feminist Reconstruction of Biography and Text* (2014).

Acknowledgments

A book is the end result of struggle, perseverance, and a committed community who helped us publish something meaningful, thoughtful, and helpful. To that end, there are many people we would like to acknowledge.

We are both grateful to our individual institutions, Concordia College and Earlham School of Religion, who have given support and encouragement for this book. The faculty and deans at both institutions are committed to the work of gender justice and climate justice, and it is wonderful to be supported by such a compassionate community of colleagues.

We are grateful to Dr. Jenny Daggers, who worked with Grace Ji-Sun Kim on the first two volumes of this book series. Daggers and Kim's vision and commitment to theology, doctrine, and gender justice led to the emergence of two important volumes. It was Hilda Koster who initiated this third volume to continue the work of focus on doctrine and gender justice. Koster was a contributor to volume 2, and her work on ecological theology allowed us to focus volume 3 on climate change. Climate change is one of the most important issues of our time; it affects women and children around the globe, but especially in the Global South, in specific and often dramatic ways.

We are thankful to Dr. Celia Deane-Drummond for her generous and thoughtful foreword to our book. She is a leader in the field of ecological theology and ethics, and it is an honor to have her write the foreword. We are grateful to each of our writers who made important contributions to doctrine, gender justice, and climate justice. Each scholar came from her own social location to make this book a global project to fight against climate change, sexism, and environmental racism. The unique and deep insights into church doctrine, gender justice, and climate change make this a pivotal book for our time.

We are deeply appreciative to our Fortress Press editor, Michael Gibson, who was keen and excited about this project right from the beginning and helped us through to its completion. His dedication to the project has made it easier for us to work, edit, and complete it on time.

We are also indebted to our families. Grace is thankful to her husband, Dr. Perry Lee, who always jumped in to fill the gap in parenting their three children. His faithful support has made it easier to work on this book. She is also thankful for the interest her three children, Theo, Elisabeth, and Joshua, have in environmental justice, as they are the future generation and will inherit the problems from earlier generations' mistakes. It is her children who give her hope that a better future is possible here on earth. Finally, Grace thanks her research assistants, Bruce Marold and Sue Kern, for helping with editing some of the manuscript. She is also thankful to her dean, Dr. Jay Marshall, for his support in her work in the World Council of Churches' (WCC) working group on climate change. Her involvement in the WCC has provided an avenue to understand the tremendous global impact of climate change and the urgent need to work toward climate justice.

Hilda is grateful to her husband, Dr. Jan Pranger, and her daughter, Emma, for supporting her work on this project by accommodating her being away from the family. Her husband's research on churches' responses to the oil boom and bust in western North Dakota and to the ways Native communities are impacted has importantly informed her own research on sex trafficking in the Dakotas. Hilda is thankful, too, for the support of the Collegeville Institute at St. John's University, which offered her the opportunity to work on editing this book and writing her own chapter during the fall of 2016. She thanks Dr. Don Ottenhof, the director of the Collegeville Institute, for his careful feedback on this project and the Collegeville Institute staff, especially Carla Durand, for creating such a welcoming community. Hilda gives special thanks also to her fellow scholars at the Institute for their support, especially Anita Amstutz, Jessica Coblentz, Sarah Lane Cawte, Brendon McInerny, and Shirly Showalther, and to the members of the St. Ben's and St. John's communities, especially Sister Theresa Schumacher, Sister Ann Marie Biermaier, and Dr. Elizabeth Gailbraith. Her time at the Institute was greatly enriched by the Benedictine hospitality at St. Ben's and St. John's.

Foreword

Celia Deane-Drummond

The theological perspectives represented in this book attest to the challenge of working across national, cultural, and disciplinary boundaries.[1] It would be foolish to imagine that the diversity of women's voices represented here from Canada, Brazil, Malaysia, Iceland, Switzerland, Zimbabwe, and Korea, in addition to the many essays from those living in the United States, cover *all* the possible ecofeminist theological perspectives interrogating a very wide array of Christian doctrines. But there is good representation across continents, and there are also important strands binding this book together as a whole. These strands will convince the reader that gender considerations are critical when dealing with complex sociocultural questions arising from climate change and other environmental harms. As a contextual approach, this in turn impacts the specific constructive feminist theological proposals. The first, most obvious strand, as the title implies, is that of solidarity, that is, the need to pay close attention to the real lives of unrepresented women and their struggles in the face of environmental injustices. Solidarity is more than simply deeper knowledge and understanding of such contexts, important though that is; it also carries a political and social component expressed in demands for structural reform. A second strand is the importance of gender issues

---

1. I am grateful to the editors for the invitation to contribute to this volume and to Michelle Marvin for editorial support.

in down-to-earth, lived situations and struggles. The specific case studies illustrated here are fascinating.

Some of the most heart wrenching stories come to the surface in Joyce Mercer's ethnographic work among women who are environmental activists in the Philippines as she works toward a different theological understanding of what it means to be a church community. For example, Mercer's interview with one woman activist named Glacy Macabale witnesses to how the combined lives of those who make their living through fishing and marine life are under threat through reclamation development projects in Manila Bay. But activism also carries a grim, formidable toll: thirty-three environmental activists were murdered in the Philippines in 2015 alone. Macabale herself has suffered death threats. Such stories of what has to amount to bold self-sacrifice for the sake of the most vulnerable people and ecosystems are bound to challenge those who read this book. Western, middle-class ecofeminists may seem, by comparison, lukewarm in their commitment. How many of us would be prepared to put our own lives literally on the line for the sake of protecting the planet? Feminist theologians have in general rejected any positive readings of suffering or sacrifice for the sake of their faith commitments, but cases like this challenge a deeper solidarity.

In my own experience, one of the most powerful influences in recent years came while I was on a year release (2009–10) from my academic position at Chester, UK, in order to work as a theological accompanier with the Catholic Fund for Overseas Development (CAFOD). My brief was to develop teaching materials on climate justice. Part of my experience included a visit to a group of Mosero women, a particularly vulnerable Maasai tribe living at the border of Kenya and Tanzania. Those who were part of this project were deliberately selected because of their extreme vulnerability. This community had no access to clean water, so they, along with their animals, faced total devastation. Using the steam that naturally vents from the volcanic ground, the CAFOD project employed a simple distillation technology to solve the water inaccessibility problem. We talked to the Mosero women's group through a local interpreter who was responsible for the project on the ground. When a Mosero woman named Mary Kair spoke up about her experiences, she spoke not just for herself but also on behalf of the whole women's community. The sense of intense solidarity between the women in this group was palpable and so striking that I began to consider what it means to have a collective conscience. Indeed, this group had much to teach me not just through their solidarity but by their belief in the direct results of God's actions in their midst and through their witness to the very real presence of the risen Jesus. I wrote about this encounter in an article that was published shortly afterwards.[2] I was also struck by their overwhelming gratitude that we had come and visited them and their desire to show solidarity *with us*. This was a humbling experience for me: I had so much to learn. The articulate, intelligent, and generous warmth of these women, who were some of the most impoverished in the world, and their generous gifts of beads and even their very selves made me realize that those living in the West have far more to learn about what it means to live well and be human compared with our own current meager offerings of solidarity. As many authors in this volume point out, it is not enough just to speak in theory; careful, respectful listening followed by action is part and parcel of what entering into solidarity is all about.

At the time when I was involved in this project, both Pope John Paul II and Pope Benedict XVI had made significant moves in the direction of encouraging environmental activism. Many authors in this volume engage with Pope Francis's most recent encyclical *Laudato Si'*. While recognizing his call for solidarity with those suffering the deepest impacts of climate change, along with a sharp critique of modernity's contribution to climate change and environmental harms, the bulk of contributors to this volume clearly still remain frustrated with his message. There are two main sources of this frustration. The first is that Pope Francis fails to take proper account of the disproportionate impacts on women: environmental justice is globally gendered. Men and women are spoken about in the encyclical in terms that imply both are equally affected. Yet, even the most basic social science overview shows that this is not the case. Allied to this issue are those unaddressed questions associated with population growth, which again impact primarily women. Second, Pope Francis reiterates traditional Catholic dogmas on the place of the family, Christian eschatology, the role of the Virgin Mary, and so on in a way that is narrowly conservative from a feminist perspective. In addition, suspicion that Pope Francis is still at root highly anthropocentric stems from some texts that still rely on an elevated place of humanity in relationship with the natural world. I have some sympathy with these criticisms, especially those critiques related to what could be termed gender neutrality in practical environmental contexts. Given the extent of advice received from a whole host of scientists, it is disappointing that the social sciences were not given greater acknowledgement by Pope Francis.

---

2. Celia Deane-Drummond, "A Case for Collective Conscience: Climategate, COP-15 and Climate Justice," *Studies in Christian Ethics* 24, no. 1 (2011): 5–22.

Yet, insofar as he has at least initiated a discussion in favor of women deacons in the Roman Catholic Church, I think it is important to see that he is up against huge internal political obstacles in bringing about change, even if many committed feminists will see this as too little, too late. He is also deliberately trying not to align with perceivably ideological views that would then fail to carry traditional Catholics toward taking environmental questions seriously. After all, this crisis is serious enough to attempt, at least, to be inclusive. How far he really is on a trajectory of reform regarding the role of women in the Catholic Church more broadly remains to be seen. The second main critique relates to his perceived anthropocentrism and other traditional and essentialist views on the human person, including women. I think Pope Francis is ambiguous in this respect, and perhaps confusingly so. He is somewhat contradictory in his philosophical presuppositions, which means he holds together a strong affirmation both of the intrinsic worth of all creatures *and* the worth of interconnectedness between all life forms, with allowance to use other animals, but not indiscriminately. Such ambivalence may reflect a desire to engage in dialogue. It is noticeable that he has shifted official teaching in the direction of affirming the intrinsic value of all creatures. What was previously at the periphery of official Catholic teaching has now come into the center. But he could have gone further in taking account of views emerging from his own lived context. As Theresa Yugar points out, Pope Francis's universalist portrayal of the Virgin Mary as mother of nature is challenged by the variety of practices found in Latin American popular devotion to her, as one who has absorbed some of the characteristics of the indigenous goddesses Tonantzin and Pachamama.

In reading this book, I was also struck by the significance of evolutionary narratives in theological method in many cases, featuring especially in Heather Eaton's chapter, which is intended to set the methodological stage for the chapters that follow. This is particularly intriguing since evolution is treated as a grand cosmic narrative that serves to frame theological parameters rather than the other way around. Nonetheless, as Ivone Gebara is only too acutely aware, it is important to recognize that science, like theology, tells its own powerful stories. Evolutionary science, at least that associated with the evolution of life, is more or less wedded to a materialist naturalist philosophy, and debates in the science of cosmological evolution are only weakly similar to those evolutionary discussions emerging from the life sciences. Science in general questions the credibility of traditional Christian beliefs, including belief in the resurrection and future hope. For earlier feminist theologians, such as Daphne Hampson, traditional Christian views were no longer persuasive due to their patriarchal structure.[3] Her post-Christian view emerged from her own jaded experience of the church. For many of the contributors to this volume, that patriarchal anxiety may still be present, but it is joined by an insistence that it is only *this* life and death that is of crucial theological significance, not the next. There are challenging systematic theological questions as well as ethical issues that arise following such a move. For example, affirming death as a prelude to life could just as easily slide into its acceptance rather than political resistance.

It is important, further, not to confuse different problems. Recognition of the vulnerability, fragility, and mortality that living creatures experience in this world, alongside the immanence of God in God's creation, is quite compatible with belief in the bodily resurrection of not just humans but other creatures as well. For classic Christian eschatology speaks not necessarily of a rejection of our bodies or a rejection of this creaturely world but rather of its renewal and restoration. Such expanded traditional beliefs in redemption, of course, are inevitably a step of reasoned faith arising out of religious experience, and one that liberal Protestant theologians from Rudolf Bultmann onward have also rejected in the name of current science. Yet, historical and philosophical analysis of that science shows that the sciences in all their plurality are not value free; indeed, they are caught up in a particular Western history that is itself culturally situated. I can understand those who do decide to cross the Rubicon, leaving traditional Christian doctrines such as God's transcendence or resurrection hope behind as no longer providing meaning. I align with Sallie McFague and Cynthia Moe-Lobeda, who are among those ecofeminists in this volume who resist that move.

How far and to what extent specific theological doctrinal elements can be adapted or changed, given the context of environmentally conscious feminism and in the light of different cultural contexts, is what is worked out in this book. Not all the authors in this book agree on where lines need to be drawn. But those who delve carefully into the theologies represented in this book will be provoked, challenged, and above all jolted into a sharper realization of the theological and explicitly doctrinal importance of the intersection between global women's experience, ecology, and climate justice.

3. Daphne Hampson, *Theology and Feminism* (Oxford: Blackwell, 1990).

Introduction: Global Women's Voices on Christian Doctrine and Climate Justice

Grace Ji-Sun Kim and Hilda P. Koster

Climate change is real and impacts the entire planet. The devastating effects of climate change are unfathomable, however, to many who live in the wealthy Western world, who are shielded from the most brutal aspects of its reality. Women and children, the poorest and the most vulnerable people in the world, are the ones who bear the brunt of and are most especially affected by the consequences of climate change. Climate change puts poor women and children at risk and deprives them of the lives they had known.

Stories like that of Jahanara Khatun are common among women in places where climate change is destroying the lives of the poor. A devastating storm in 2009 destroyed her home in Dakope, Bangladesh. She lost her husband to the storm and had to sell her son and daughter into bonded servitude. She spends her days gathering cow dung for fuel and trying to grow vegetables in soil that is now poisoned by saltwater due to the high tides driven by the storm. Climate change may make the sea levels rise further, and the next storm may wipe out her current attempt at rebuilding her life.[1] Khatun's story is but one of countless stories of women and children brutalized by climate change.

---

1. Read more of this story in Gardiner Harris, "Borrowed Time on Disappearing Land," *New York Times*, March 28, 2014, https://tinyurl.com/laec4ms.

At such a consequential time, the choice is stark: the world's wealthy people and nations may sit back and watch this tragic story unfold, or we can work toward climate justice. Climate justice is the understanding that global warming is not just an environmental matter but also a moral, political, sociological, and religious concern. Climate justice is often seen as a human rights issue. It stems from the observation that climate change will have the most adverse effects on the livelihood and health of people with the least political and economic power. In his encyclical *Laudato Si': On Care for Our Common Home*, Pope Francis observes that "a true ecological approach *always* becomes a social approach; it must integrate questions of justice in debates on the environment, so as to hear *both the cry of the earth and the cry of the poor.*"[2] By highlighting the need for justice, the pope calls our attention to the fact that the world's poor—especially in the Global South—have done the least to cause the problem of anthropogenic climate disruption but are the first to suffer its catastrophic effects. Pope Francis's call for climate justice is shared by the World Council of Churches, the National Council of Churches in the United States, the South African Council of Churches, and many other national and international church bodies.[3] Like *Laudato Si'* these ecumenical organizations remind us that from a Christian perspective, God's justice is an expression of love and, hence, never a mere weighing of interest against interest. It involves passionate advocacy for those who do not have a voice.

Climate Justice and Women

This book brings together leading Latina, womanist, Asian, Asian American, South American, European, and African theologians on the issues of doctrine, women, and climate justice. We believe that a focus on women is warranted because theological and ecclesial documents too often do not spell out the ways climate change affects poor and indigenous women around the globe. Indeed, the voices of women are

---

2. Francis, *Laudato Si': On Care for Our Common Home* (Huntington, IN: Our Sunday Visitor, 2015), 45.
3. The South African Council of Churches conducted one of the most comprehensive church-based studies on climate change: South African Council of Churches Climate Change Committee, "Climate Change—A Challenge to the Churches in South Africa," South African Council of Churches, November 2009, PDF, http://tinyurl.com/mfdknsm. For the National Council of Churches USA, see "Creation Justice Ministries Faith Principles on Climate Change," Creation Justice Ministries, http://tinyurl.com/m6qxwvq. See also the forward-looking study on climate change by the Presbyterian Church USA, "The Power to Change, U.S. Energy Policy and Global Warming," Advisory Committee on Social Witness Policy, 2008, PDF, accessed September 8, 2016, http:// tinyurl.com/k39hz93. The latter two studies focus their discussion of climate change on climate justice. The World Council of Churches publishes many books, booklets, and pamphlets on climate change. Most recent is their publication *Making Peace with the Earth* (2016), edited by Grace Ji-Sun Kim.

conspicuously absent from *Laudato Si'*. Nor does the encyclical draw on the insights and experiences of women environmental activists working to mitigate the negative effects of climate change and fossil fuel extraction on their communities, let alone include the rich theological writings by feminist/womanist/*mujerista* theologians in the field of ecotheology.

Climate change affects everyone. Yet, because women make up the majority of the world's poor and tend to be more dependent on natural resources for their livelihoods and survival, they are at a higher risk. In the exploited world, poor women are often the primary caregivers of their families and hence play an important role in securing household water, food, and fuel. In times of drought, women must walk farther and spend more of their time collecting water. Girls may have to drop out of school to help their mothers with these tasks, continuing a cycle of poverty and gender inequity.[4] Moreover, as the story of Jahanara Khatun so painfully illustrates, because poor women in the Global South often have very little access to education and hence trustworthy employment and income, they are vulnerable when rural families are forced to migrate due to rising seawaters or desertification. Dislocated young girls, moreover, often end up in domestic servitude or the sex trade.

Women are further at increased risk because of lack of independence and decision making power, which significantly constrains their ability to adapt to climate change. Not only do women often lack control over family finances and assets, they are underrepresented in community politics and thus have little influence over community strategies as to how to adapt to changing weather patterns in ways that supports their rights and priorities. It is not surprising, therefore, that many environmental grassroots movements—such as the Chipko movement in India, the Greenbelt Movement in Kenya, and the women's collective *Conspirando* in Latin America—not just originated with women but organized primarily around the plight of (rural) women and the need for their empowerment. While these movements may not have arisen in response to the effects of climate change, per se, they understand that the degrading of the natural environment and the world's climate is a women's issue.

By focusing on the plight of women, we are not suggesting that

---

4. The connections between the effects of climate change on poor women are widely reported. See, for instance, World Health Organization, *Gender, Climate Change and Health* (Geneva: World Health Organization, 2014). See also, United Nations Population Fund (UNFPA), *State of the World Population: Women, Population and Climate Change* (New York: UNFPA, 2009). A very helpful documentary is *Weathering Change*, a movie by Population Action International that documents stories about climate and family from women around the world, see www.weatheringchange.org.

women are innately more attuned to the natural world. While the oppression of women and the oppression of nature often intersect, assertions that women have a special relation to nature and/or are more virtuous when it comes to environmental responsibility have rightly been criticized as essentialist.[5] This line of argument tends to lock women into fixed roles based on traditional divisions of labor and their childbearing capacities. We also do not intend to unduly victimize women and suggest that they are always necessarily more negatively affected by climate change. Studies from around the globe show that women are often tremendously resourceful and resilient in finding ways to adapt to a changing climate.[6] Moreover, as Seema Arora-Johnson has pointed out, while poverty often is an indicator of increased vulnerability to the negative effects of climate change, there are other factors, most notably those of power, class, race, and religion, that play a significant and, in some cases, determining role when it comes to women's ability to negotiate the challenges posed by climate change.[7] Finally, by calling attention to the plight of poor and indigenous women, we do not want to reinscribe the binary dichotomy between the Global South and the Global North. The debates on climate change, gender, and development tend to cast the Global South as culturally backward when it comes to equality between women and men. This dynamic not only overlooks the various ways women do exercise agency in the exploited world, it also conveniently ignores the climate-related suffering due to social and economic inequities in countries in the Global North.

Doctrinal Reimagining

The women theologians writing for this book are much attuned to the intricate ways questions of climate justice and gender intersect with those of class, race, and ethnicity, which are prevalent in both the Global South and North. While they come from a wide range of denominational and ecclesial backgrounds, they all write as feminist/womanist/*mujerista* theologians. What this means is that they critically analyze the myriad ways constructions of gender, race, class, and ethnicity inform church doctrine and practice. As Serene Jones reminds

---

5. For this criticism, see Melissa Leach, "Earth Mother Myths and other Ecofeminist Fables: How a Strategic Notion Rose and Fell," *Development and Change* 38, no. 1 (2007): 67–85. See also Joyce Mercer's chapter in this volume.

6. See, for instance, the excellent case studies in Irene Dankelman, *Gender and Climate Change: An Introduction* (London: Earthscan, 2010).

7. Seema Arora-Johnson, "Virtue and Vulnerability: Discourses on Women, Gender and Climate Change," *Global Environmental Change* 21, no. 2 (2011): 744–51.

us, feminist theology "explores how Christian faith grounds and shapes women's experiences of hope, justice, and grace, as well as instigates and enforces women's experiences of oppression, sin and evil."[8] Thus, the theologians writing for this book are critical of the ways Christian teaching has been both anthropocentric, as well as androcentric, heterosexist and Eurocentric. And as theologians committed to ecojustice, they criticize Christianity's earth-fleeing, anti-body spirituality, which they believe energizes the interlocking of oppression of nature with suppression of women.

Our book further reflects a "subfield" of feminist theology, first coined by Jones, which takes Christian doctrine as an important interlocutor for feminist theology.[9] Doctrines are teachings—for instance, teachings on God, creation, sin and grace, and Christ and redemption—which have been passed on throughout church history. While doctrines often have been used to stifle change, they also form the theological threads that weave communities of faith together. Doctrines provide the basic outline for what Christians do and do not believe, and, hence, they regulate the broadest parameters within which the Christian life can take shape. According to Jones, therefore, doctrines are much more than propositional statements or static rules; instead, they serve as "imaginative lenses through which to view the world."[10]

The purpose of engaging doctrine, then, is to open up fresh possibilities for life together—with one another and with the Earth. Yet, in order for this to happen, it is imperative to rework interpretations of doctrines that have reinforced colonialism, patriarchy, climate change, racism, and other injustices. The theological work of creative reimaging with doctrine must therefore always include critical retrieval, reformation, and reconstruction.

Planetary Solidarity follows in the footsteps of two earlier volumes edited by Grace Ji-Sun Kim and Jenny Daggers: *Reimagining with Christian Doctrines: Responding to Global Gender Injustices*[11] and *Christian Doctrines for Global Gender Justice*.[12] *Planetary Solidarity* is the third volume

---

8. Serene Jones, *Feminist Theory and Christian Theology: Cartographies of Grace* (Minneapolis: Fortress, 2000), 14.

9. For more discussion, please see Serene Jones, "Feminist Theology and the Global Imagination," in *The Oxford Handbook of Feminist Theology*, ed. Sheila Briggs and Mary McClintock Fulkerson (Oxford: Oxford University Press, 2012); and Jones, *Feminist Theory*, ch. 1.

10. Jones, *Feminist Theory*, 16.

11. Grace Ji-Sun Kim and Jenny Daggers, *Reimagining with Christian Doctrines: Responding to Global Gender Injustices* (New York: Palgrave Macmillan, 2014). *Reimagining with Christian Doctrines* began the creative imagining of traditional doctrines as a "subfield" of feminist theology.

12. Jenny Daggers and Grace Ji-Sun Kim, *Christian Doctrines for Global Gender Justice* (New York: Palgrave Macmillan, 2015). *Christian Doctrines for Global Gender Justice* continued the constructive work of using Christian doctrines to achieve global gender justice. The premise of both volumes is that

in this series and answers the question of how Christian doctrine may be put to work toward both gender and climate justice.[13] The book answers the call of *Laudato Si'* to work toward climate justice and connects this to the struggle for gender justice by having women theologians from around the globe speak in their own voices. As with the previous volumes, it is the purpose of the book to take forward the struggle for gender justice in our society and churches in solidarity with justice struggles in our wider world.

Planetary Solidarity

The title of our book reflects our deeply held conviction that the daunting task of working toward climate justice must be done in solidarity with those who suffer most from injustice and who will benefit from change. As both an ideal and an objective of political engagement, solidarity draws from politics, economics, religion, and every other one of our vocations.[14] Whereas solidarity generally includes notions of political activity, it is more than alliances of common interests or objectives. As Heather Eaton observes in her chapter in this book, solidarity, in the political sense, is about social justice and movements for transformation with a responsibility to the common good. Solidarity expresses a realization and analysis of inequities and patterns of injustice, and a commitment to social change to remedy these inequalities.

As a theological concept, solidarity refers to the (Catholic) notion of *koinonia* (the communion of saints).[15] It is about building stronger communities where power is shared and relationships are formed.[16] Solidarity advocates a re-centering of power and privilege around building community. It is a commitment to be with others in a most radical way. There should not be a vantage point from which we look at others as other in the sense of objects of charity. Instead, solidarity springs from the acknowledgement that all are equal participants in community and have a contribution to make.[17]

---

received doctrines can be reconceived in light of a correction in the traditional roles and understandings of the spiritual capacities of women.

13. With the other volumes in this set, it feeds the work of feminist/womanist/*mujerista* theological reimagining but extends its frame of analysis to include reflection on the ways climate change intersects with the sufferings of women. Yet, while this book was conceived in connection to the previous volumes, it very much stands on its own. It is further important to note that while the immediate impulse for this volume has been the release of *Laudato Si'*, it is not meant as a systematic reflection on the encyclical.

14. Joerg Rieger and Rosemarie Henkel-Rieger, *Unified We Are a Force: How Faith and Labor Can Overcome America's Inequalities* (St. Louis: Chalice, 2016), xii.

15. Anselm Min, *The Solidarity of Others in a Divided World* (New York: T&T Clark, 2004), 141.

16. Rieger and Henkel-Rieger, *Unified*, 32.

17. Min, *Solidarity of Others*, 82.

Solidarity does not mean, however, that we are the same or that our differences do not matter. Rather, it means just the opposite as it allows us to deal with our differences more constructively and put them to work for a common cause.[18] Solidarity requires attention to differences in suffering while extending preferential treatment to those who suffer more. And like with its political interpretation, solidarity as a theological category asks that we be advocates for those who are disadvantaged, resist injustice, and work for change. In community, we are in solidarity with each other. We stand with the most vulnerable and do not stay silent. We speak out so the rest of the world can see the injustices caused by the wealthy nations against the Earth.

Solidarity, then, connotes double resistance: resistance to individualism and resistance to totalitarianism. It is otherness in togetherness, not in isolation or competition.[19] In an age of anthropogenic climate change, it is pertinent, moreover, that we broaden and deepen our solidarity to include the nonhuman world and the planetary systems and processes on which all life depends. Theology and doctrine have focused on humanity and made the "rest of creation" external to the story of God with human beings. Climate change brings home that there is no such externality. Climate change affects atmospheric patterns, ocean currents, fresh water quality and quantity, soil fertility, food stability, and, of course, the living ecosystems that are at the basis of all living communities. Planetary solidarity requires that we give voice to these interconnected systems of life. It asks for nothing less than a bio-cracy, in which all life forms have a vote. It is from this Earth-centric stance that the authors in this book work toward gender and climate justice.

Outline of the Book

The contributors to *Planetary Solidarity* each focus their reflections around one of the following doctrines: the triune God, creation, anthropology, sin, redemption, Christ, cross and redemption, the Holy Spirit, the church, and eschatology. Many contributors write from their specific geographical, sociocultural, political, and economic location; others contextualize their writing within an ongoing doctrinal discussion in ecofeminist theology.

The book is divided into two main parts. Part 1 is entitled "Reimagining" and gathers chapters that reflect on the theological ramifications

18. Rieger and Henkel-Rieger, *Unified*, 54.
19. Ibid., 141.

of a commitment to planetary solidarity. Part 2, "Doctrines and Situations," consists of chapters that discuss a particular doctrine in relation to gender and climate justice. Three of the chapters in part 1, chapters 2, 3, and 4, explicitly relate their reflections to *Laudato Si'*. Readers interested in ecofeminist responses to various parts of the pope's encyclical should note these chapters especially.

Heather Eaton's opening chapter, "An Earth-Centric Theological Scaffold for Planetary Solidarity," helpfully develops the concept of planetary solidarity in great detail. She gives special consideration to what we might mean by the term "planetary" and argues that climate change is more than a simple question of justice; it is a matter of disregarding the finite conditions of life. If we are to flourish, it is within specific boundaries. Her essay is critical of prominent themes within Christianity such as resurrection, paradise, individual restoration, and immortality, which she argues indicate a commitment to surmounting what is most unmistakable in human existence: vulnerability, mortality, and finitude. Drawing on concepts from ecofeminist thinkers Ivone Gebara, Anne Primavesi, and Sallie McFague, Eaton builds a theological scaffold—reflective of much of the ecofeminist work done in this book—that sets the parameters for an ecofeminist theology that embraces, not denies, the finite conditions of life as a premise for creaturely flourishing in an era of climate change.

In chapter 2, North American, Catholic feminist theologian Rosemary P. Carbine discusses different theologies and practices of the Catholic public church—found in Pope Francis's environmental encyclical on the one hand and in US nuns' eco-activism on the other hand—from the perspective of feminist hermeneutics. How do these different expressions of the Catholic public church enable and energize an integral ecology that attends to and addresses the intersections of ecological, sociopolitical, and gender justice? In the initial three sections, this chapter brings a critical ecofeminist and public theological analysis to bear on recent examples of the Catholic public church. The concluding section opens up new possibilities for understanding different Catholic theological and activist responses to our ecological crises. Extending Elisabeth Schüssler Fiorenza's feminist hermeneutical method to interpret these examples of Catholic eco-public theologies, Carbine shows how Catholic practices of public engagement for ecojustice envision a more complex notion of the common good—or, in other words, incarnate an integral ecology.

In chapter 3, "Women Suffering, Climate Injustice, God, and Pope Francis's Theology: Some Insights from Brazil," Brazilian ecofeminist theologian Ivone Gebara addresses the dilemma Latin American ecofeminist liberationists like herself face when it comes to Pope Francis's encyclical. While the pope champions liberationist concerns and deserves support in his conflict with the Vatican's conservative forces, his encyclical does not reflect the real-life situations and sufferings of poor women in Latin America and upholds a nostalgic and patriarchal theology. The latter, Gebara argues, is ultimately inadequate to address the real possibilities of the world today. The first half of Gebara's chapter gives an analysis of the ways climate-change-induced suffering intersects with other evils that cripple the lives of poor women, such as domestic violence, poor living conditions, poverty-induced illness, cultural dependence, and abandonment. Instead of easing the many levels of suffering, traditional God-talk often exacerbates it insofar as it keeps women dependent on a male savior. The second part of the chapter gives a critical reading of *Laudato Si'*, especially of its abstract, idealized notion of womanhood by way of its portrayal of Mary and its support for a patriarchal symbolic vision, which at most leads to a paternalistic benevolence to marginalized groups but does little to dismantle hierarchies of power and oppression.

Whereas Gebara's reflections stem from her experiences as a Latin American theologian, Sharon Bong analyzes the theological anthropology operative in *Laudato Si'* from a South Asian perspective. Her chapter (chapter 4) reads the encyclical in light of three high-impact documents on human rights issued by the United Nations that demonstrate the connection between climate change and gender justice.[20] Bong argues that these documents, which were all available prior to the encyclical's publication, put the encyclical's silence on the plight of poor women in sharp relief. She further juxtaposes *Laudato Si'* with the theologizing of the Ecclesia of Women in Asia. The latter contextualizes theological reflections on humanity within the lived realities of women, who are neither represented as passive nor seen as victims, and reclaims the erotic in deeper appreciation of the cosmos. This way of viewing humanity, Bong argues, should be put to work toward a more inclusive notion of climate justice.

Part 2, "Doctrines and Situations," is organized around the major doctrines that make up the Christian story, yet all aim at retelling parts of that story from the perspective of the intersection of climate and gender justice. In chapter 5, "Reimagining the Triune God for a

---

20. United Nations, "Addis Ababa Action Agenda of the Third International Conference on Financing for Development (Addis Ababa Action Agenda)," A/RES/69/313, United Nations General Assembly, July 27, 2015, 1–2, http://tinyurl.com/knkhhpl; United Nations, "Sustainable Development Goals," September 25, 2015, http://tinyurl.com/lrkafoq; UN News Centre, "Assembly President: Unity over Paris Climate Accord Should Not Be Forgotten," United Nations, December 15, 2015, http://tinyurl.com/jwwkzmw.

Time of Global Climate Change," ecofeminist theologian Sallie McFague discusses how the picture of God as an all-powerful lord and king has encouraged the human domination of nature and marginalized humans. Drawing on Jesus's life and death, McFague instead defends a kenotic model for thinking about divine power; an understanding based in the story of self-emptying love. She argues that what we learn from the story of Jesus is that the power of the triune God is a power of *empowerment* through self-emptying of one for the other in a cycle of giving and receiving. This leads to a radically different picture of our place on our planet—namely, one that stresses our fragility and radical dependence on all that is and calls us to a life of sacrificial love for others. McFague argues that this picture has the further advantage of resonating in a profound way with the insight of the so-called "new materialism" of postmodern science—namely, that we are animals, bodies dependent on other bodies, incarnational beings at the mercy of the many sources of power on our planet, among them, climate change.

In chapter 6, "And G*d Saw That It Was Good—*Imago Dei* and Its Challenge to Climate justice," Wanda Deifelt addresses the question of humanity being made in the image of God and the consequences of this claim. While maintaining that the concept of *imago Dei* continues to be valid, particularly in the context of disenfranchised individuals and communities who have their human dignity denied, the concept also needs to be revisited in order to curb anthropocentric theology and practice. Human activity has been a destructive influence on climate and the environment in the past two hundred years, and this is often justified through religious discourse. Deifelt argues that in order to put the concept of *imago Dei* toward critical use, it is necessary to read the first chapter of Genesis and its creation narrative in its original context of the Babylonian creation poem, the *Enûma Elish*. Whereas according to the latter, human beings are created for servitude and are at the whims of the gods, in Genesis 1:1–2:4a human beings are made in the dignity of God's likeness and are called to share in God's rule. In other words, the "dominion" clause is meant not to dominate or control but to elevate an enslaved and exiled people. How may we use this emancipatory potential of the *imago Dei* for an age of climate injustice?

Reflecting on the effects of climate change in her native Iceland, Arnfríður Guðmundsdóttir's (chapter 7) argues in favor of the doctrine of sin as a useful way to address the serious consequences of global climate change. Sin is a relational concept. It signifies a broken relationship to God, our neighbor, nature, and even ourselves. For when we forget that we are stewards of God's good creation, when we forget about others and we ourselves become the center of our universe, we become twisted and ingrown. To be exclusively preoccupied with ourselves is what it means, theologically, to be caught in sin. Using this understanding of sin, Guðmundsdóttir discusses the visible signs of climate change in Iceland—the rapid melting of its glaciers and the threat to its coastal areas by rising sea levels—against the backdrop of a political struggle to preserve Iceland's inland from the development of power plants used to provide energy for multinational corporations. The latter not only will increase CO_2 emissions and, hence, contribute to the threats posed by a warming climate, it also stands in stark contrast to Iceland's bounty of "green" energy.

In chapter 8, Hilda P. Koster uses Christian sin-talk to reflect on the increase of sex trafficking and other forms of gender-based violence in the wake of the oil boom in western North Dakota, which especially affects indigenous women and girls. Drawing on studies by James Martin-Schramm and Susan B. Thistlethwaite, her chapter presents both fracking and sex-trafficking as issues of climate justice and argues that they come from the same place, namely a disrespect for the earth and a denial of our vulnerability as embodied beings. Yet, in order not to reiterate Christianity's long-standing tendency to see women's sexuality as the source of sin or condemn the victims of sex trafficking as sinners, this chapter relies on the social statement on gender based violence by the Evangelical Lutheran Church of America, which is the largest Protestant denomination in the Dakotas, and the work on structural evil by feminist Lutheran ethicist Cynthia Moe-Lobeda. Koster argues that when understood as structural evil, the language of sin not only allows us to see sex trafficking as an intrinsic part of the predatory practices of the extraction industry—an industry with little to no regard for the integrity of women's bodies, human (indigenous) communities, and the Earth—but also exposes the intricate ways the rest of us, through our addiction to fossil fuels, are implemented in these practices and the economic structures supporting them. While divesting ourselves from these structures might be hard, seeing connections is the first step in developing the moral vision needed to resist and stand in solidarity with its victims. This chapter thus uses the doctrine of sin as a "social diagnostic" of what ails us in order to envision a remedy.

Chapters 9 and 10 relate a concern for climate justice to Christology and the doctrine of the incarnation. In chapter 9, Malawian theologian Fulata Moyo explores an Earth-centered understanding of the incarnation by way of the African indigenous ritual of burying the umbilical cord. Moyo argues that by way of this ritual, ecofeminists/womanist theologians can assert the connection of a mother to her newborn child and the Earth and, hence, as the most organic imperative to activism for ecological justice. Indeed, she believes that because the cultural practice of burying the umbilical cord is shared by many indigenous communities around the world, elevating this practice as a way to talk about incarnation would make the mother-child relationship an intrinsic expression of mutual survival of ecosystems and marginalized human communities.

In chapter 10, Isabel Mukonyora constructs an African Christology for climate justice from the lived understanding of Christ by female followers of the Masowe Apostles, an African-initiated church popular among the Shona people of Zimbabwe. Building on her extensive fieldwork, Mukonyora argues that the Masowe interpret Christ by way of the high God Mwari, who in traditional Shona society is connected with knowledge and wisdom related to fertility, ecosystems, and the continuation of the tribe and is often worshiped by way of feminine images, especially that of African motherhood. Might this interpretation of Christ be a source for an African eco-Christology that connects salvation with Earth healing and empowers poor and marginalized women in their struggle to find life in a land stricken by drought?

Exploring an Earth-centric theology of the cross, Jea Sophia Oh (chapter 11) examines the paradox that life comes from death. Jesus compared his death on the cross to a seed that falls to the ground and dies. A seed has a potential to bear fruit because it contains life. The secret of life is in its hybrid process of disintegration and proliferation as numerous grains come from a kernel of wheat that has fallen to the ground and dies. Nonetheless, if it remains only a single seed, it eventually loses its life. This process of life out of death can be found in all living organisms. The Christian account of cross and resurrection—and, hence, salvation—is thus deeply intertwined with evolutionary and ecological processes of the renewal and continuation of life. Yet, its salvific power will not breed new life in isolation. We are called to be part of the generative power signified in Jesus's death and resurrection by committing ourselves to the integrity of earthly life of which we are a part.

In chapter 12, "Salvation for All! Cosmic Salvation for an Age of Climate Injustice: A Korean Perspective," Korean theologian Meehyun Chung argues in favor of an inclusive and this-worldly doctrine of salvation in order to correct an overly anthropocentric, individualistic, and otherworldly soteriology that she argues has dominated Korean Christianity. While most Western ecotheologies have also defended an earthly and inclusive understanding of salvation, Chung contextualizes her eco-soteriology within the history of Christian mission in colonial and postcolonial Korea. Her chapter gives special attention to the role of women and gender within Korean Christianity. Writing from a primarily historical perspective, Chung skillfully demonstrates the ambivalent role Christianity played in both challenging and reinforcing Korea's patriarchal hierarchies. Against this background, her chapter shows a way forward for a Korean ecofeminist soteriology centered around the concept of healing binary oppositions between human and nature, man and woman, and Christian and indigenous religiosity. It is her hope that by way of such a soteriology, Korean Christianity might become a more positive force in overcoming the religious, social, political, and military divisions that plague the Korean Peninsula and hinder an effective response to the challenges posed by climate change and its injustices.

Womanist ethicist Melanie L. Harris takes up the doctrine of the divine Spirit in "Ecowomanist Wisdom: Encountering Earth and the Spirit." Her chapter (chapter 13) develops ecowomanism as a distinct yet integral part of African American women's spiritual experience and, hence, womanist theologizing. Ecowomanism is born out of the realization that for poor black women in North America, air pollution and lack of access to safe drinking water and wholesome food are part of a daily struggle for survival and reflect the multilayered oppressions suffered by women of color. For Harris, therefore, spiritual ecology focuses on the spiritual base of the day-to-day struggle of black women for sustenance. It is framed by themes of spirit, sacredness of the Earth, and interconnectedness.

In chapter 14, Cynthia Moe-Lobeda, a Euro-American theologian and ethicist, continues discussing pneumatology in the context of climate justice. Her chapter starts with the observation that the climate crisis—the crucible of existence for high-consuming people today—creates a haunting contradiction. God created a world that God declared "*tov*" (a goodness that is life-furthering). While we are called to serve God's purposes in the world, we are doing the opposite: we are undoing Earth's capacity to further life. The contradiction runs deeper. Called to love one's neighbor as God loves, we are causing death and destruction for "climate-vulnerable" people the world over. Hundreds of millions may be displaced or killed by climate change. Wherein lies the moral-spiritual power to reverse this trajectory of horror? Scripture and theology teach that the Holy Spirit empowers human creatures to participate in God's healing and liberating work. Moe-Lobeda's chapter probes that claim by exploring three questions: According to Scripture, what does the Spirit's morally empowering role look like? What might

13

get in the way of our capacity to receive, trust, and heed the Spirit's power in us? What are the implications of these findings for high-consuming societies in the midst of escalating climate catastrophe?

In chapter 15, Latina scholar Theresa Yugar offers an ecofeminist and postcolonial reading of Mary in the Americas. Whereas Mary's intercessory role in Catholic Europe is anthropocentric, in Latin and South America, Mary's intervention includes the Earth and the cosmos. The latter is due in part to the fact that in the Americas, Mary has absorbed the qualities of indigenous goddesses such as Tonantzin and Pachamama, who in the Mesoamerican-Inca world view were identified with Mother Earth. Yugar's chapter further suggests that the cosmic reach of Marian devotion in the Americas may offer a correction to Pope Francis's idealized portrayal of Mary as the queen of the universe. She argues that the retrieval of Mary's Latin and South American roots opens up an alternative route for articulating the cosmic reach of Marian devotion: an approach not at odds with the concrete realities and lived experiences of women and all other Earth creatures.

Chapter 16 continues the discussion on ecclesial and devotional practice. Working from a practical theological perspective, Joyce Ann Mercer addresses issues of ecological justice in the Philippines, starting with the work of women environmental activists. She listens as these women describe, in their own words, what is most urgent among environmental issues in their context. Through their narratives, a picture emerges of the close relationship between ecological degradation and economic neocolonialism in the Philippines. Women involved in climate-justice work in the Philippines often risk their safety and even lives while standing in solidarity with poor and indigenous communities. Relating these experiences to ecclesiology, Mercer argues in favor of an image of the church as a community of witness and empowerment for an ailing ecosphere, and of women as leaders called to a ministry of care in which human flourishing is bound to that of the Earth.

The final two chapters of the book, chapters 17 and 18, discuss eschatology and hope. In Chapter 17, "¡Somos Criaturas de Dios!—Seeing and Beholding the Garden of God," Latina theologian Nancy Pineda-Madrid observes that in the corpus of contemporary theological writings, there is no dearth of works exploring what it means for human beings to be children of God. Rarely, however, do these texts connect this notion with our creaturely nature. In many Latinx communities the common Spanish expression, somos criaturas de Dios, does call forth this appreciation. We are children of God precisely as creatures. What this means is that we cannot be known without reference to God. This reference lies not with the distinctiveness of the human but with the connectedness of creation. Drawing on this insight, Pineda-Madrid's chapter argues for the primacy of religious symbols that mediate eschatological hope as they urge us to consider our creaturehood.

The book ends with Barbara Rossing's chapter, "Reimagining Eschatology toward Healing and Hope for a World at the *Eschatos*." Her chapter seeks to reimagine the constellation of doctrines that have come to be labeled eschatology through a feminist liberation lens of healing. Two Scripture verses—Mark 5:23 and Revelation 22:2—suggest a trajectory that has been largely overlooked in eschatological thinking but one that we need today for ourselves and for our world: the trajectory of healing. In the Gospels, eschatology and healing are deeply connected in ways we have not always seen. "My daughter is at the *eschatos*," the synagogue leader Jairus implores Jesus (Mark 5:23). "Come heal her!" *Eschatos* means the edge, the edge of life and death, the brink. We are the daughter at the brink—the *eschatos*—and we need healing!

* * *

As coeditors of *Planetary Solidarity*, we hope that this book will be a catalyst to reimagine church doctrine toward global gender justice in light of climate change. Our inherited notions of God and doctrines have perpetuated the ideas of domination, subordination, and subjugation. These threads have infiltrated the church's views of the Earth. Ever since the Mesopotamians and the Greeks, the Earth has been understood as feminine and as something to be conquered and used. We are to "dominate" over the Earth. Therefore, masculine and patriarchal church doctrines need to be challenged, reimagined, and reunderstood for future generations of the church.

With a common urgency and responsibility to adequately address our current climate disaster, we need to rework our patriarchal notions of the divine and work toward an inclusive, just, and life-giving understanding of the Creator who brought forth and sustains all life. We do this by working in solidarity with women around the globe who want both climate justice and gender justice so that future generations can live sustainably in a more just Earth community.

PART I

Reimagining

1

———

An Earth-Centric Theological Framing
for Planetary Solidarity

Heather Eaton

What is Evolution? Evolution is not merely an idea, a theory or a concept, but is the name of a process of nature.

—Ernst Mayr[1]

Planetary solidarity in the context of climate change is a desirable, albeit daunting, image. It is desirable because climate change is a planetary phenomenon requiring a commensurate response. It is daunting because there is little functioning solidarity among the varied human communities, cultures, and nation states of the planet. Seemingly simple as a summons and objective, the call for planetary solidarity is neither facile nor straightforward.

This chapter is divided into two sections. The first considers several meanings to the terms *planetary* and *solidarity*. Together, these could be

1. Ernst Mayr, *What Evolution Is* (New York: Basic Books), 275.

considered an Earth-centric framing. The second section looks at theological considerations of salvation, with reference to the work of Ivone Gebara on the subject of life and its limits and conditions.

Planetary Solidarity

In this era where life and life systems of the planet are threatened, and where inequities and injustices across and within human communities are stark, the image of planetary solidarity is ethically and ecologically appealing. Yet, both *planetary* and *solidarity* are multifaceted and will be examined in greater depth in order to render more definition and detail to this image.

Planetary

Of the many ways to ponder *planetary*, the most obvious characteristic of the planet is the biosphere: this interactive, infinitely dynamic, complex sphere of life that characterizes planet Earth. While the origins of life remain shrouded in the past, what is known of the emergence and evolution of life tells a tale of immense creativity, stunning elegance, and immeasurable complexities. Much of life's history and processes are inaccessible to human perception and knowledge. Nevertheless, some parameters are becoming recognized.

For example, life is intensely differentiated and entangled and can thrive in many, dissimilar ecosystems. Yet, life exists within defined limits: a small temperature range, precise atmospheric activities and oxygen levels, dynamic ecosystems, and an intricate hydrologic cycle. Life can adapt to changes, if gradual. Life is individual, collective, interconnected, and relational. All life forms, as individuals, die. Life, collectively as interdependent species within vibrant, interlinked ecosystems, thrives or perishes together.

The first, and primary, meaning of *planetary* is the biosphere. It is important to perceive this sphere of life as differentiated and dynamic, yet deeply integrated. Earth sciences support the concept that the Earth's processes are entangled, intermingled, and mutually dependent: a self-regulating organism as the Gaia Hypothesis suggests. Earth's organic and inorganic matter reciprocally regulates the biosphere and the conditions of life. The planet, including the biosphere, lithosphere (rock), hydrosphere, and atmosphere interact dynamically, continuously, and cannot be understood as discrete processes. Planetary processes—climate systems, hydrologic cycle, ocean currents, and biomass distribution—are distinct from bioregions or ecosystems, yet are interactive. A useful metaphor is to consider the Earth as a verb, not a noun.

There is a mounting evidence that the Earth's biosphere is entering a new era, the Anthropocene: anthropogenic ecological impacts on a geological scale. Various meanings of an Anthropocene age are debated. Here, it implies that the ecological consequences of *Homo sapiens* are such that the Cenozoic era is collapsing, and most planetary processes, ecosystems, evolutionary trajectories, and climate and hydrological systems are disturbed or deteriorating. Earth sciences have concluded that the current ecological impact is anthropogenic and planetary, albeit differentiated.[2]

This meaning of *planetary* is apparent with a cursory look at climate change. As mentioned, geodynamics such as the hydrologic cycle, biosphere, and climate systems are interconnected and mutually influential. Climate change affects atmospheric patterns, ocean currents, fresh water quality and quantity, soil fertility, food stability, and, of course, the living ecosystems that are at the basis of all living communities. Climate systems follow planetary cycles and structures, bioregions, and ecosystems as well as plate tectonics. They have nothing to do with political boundaries or nation states: the standard planetary map.

The denial of climate change science, the protectionist stances, the economic fears, and the ongoing gridlock around responses are directly related to the social and economic organization of nation states. Climate change action requires, at least, a functioning image of a global human community. Some resist this image because it can erase differences among, as well as the structured inequities within and between, cultures. Moreover, in pondering the meaning of *planetary*, it is evident that ecological planetary systems do not dovetail, in any manner, with political configurations. To see the planet as a composite of nation states, or as a global human community, impedes an ecological planetary awareness. Thus, responding to climate change is forcing new political alignments and new ecological perceptions of planetary realities.

In effect, one of the only "global" systems is economic: elaborate phenomena comprised of global financial and governance institutions, with endless mind-bending propaganda and advertising that reshape the social imagination and cultural priorities. Many, if not most, humans work to serve this global system, noting that the benefits and burdens are not equally shared. Such "globalization" contains subtle

---

2. Ecological issues occur at many levels (ecosystem, bioregion, planetary) and are distinct in innumerable ways.

and blatant forms of cultural imperialism and colonization that have restructured cultural patterns virtually around the world. This global map also does not intersect with planetary systems, although it relies entirely on ecological health.

The juxtaposition of the three images—planetary biosphere, nation states, and economic globalization—reveals the stark differences between, and consequences of, these configurations. Planetary solidarity can be interpreted within each trope. The emphasis here is to accentuate how world views of the planet Earth as a global community (of humans), or nation states, or economic imbroglios are dissimilar to a planetary, ecologically based image. These are planetary maps. Often, climate change debates and disputes are about the compromises needed to bridge the gaps between the maps. Yet, they are not equivalent. Humans live on a thin layer of culture over a vast expanse of nature. The natural world, ecological vitality, and biospheric integrity are the *determining* planetary features. Thus, whatever planetary solidarity can mean, it should begin with ecological literacy about, and protection of, planetary dynamics and the biosphere. There is no other way forward.

Another facet of *planetary* is that of an Earth community. Of course, it is popular to claim that the Earth is our home and that we belong here, often accompanied with the iconic image of the Earth from space. It can, however, be based in a superficial understanding of *planetary*, in two ways. First, to consider the planet as *home* is insufficiently accurate and comprehensive. The notion of the planet as *home* can simply mean as a house, a dwelling place: it is "where we live" and does not address the dynamics of life. It often maintains a partition between ourselves and planetary processes. Second, it ignores the larger communities of life with whom we cohabitate. To explain these, I will begin with the importance of integrating evolution into the notion of planetary.

Evolution

Evolution describes the biospheric processes of the natural world, from the origins of life to the present.[3] It explains the dynamics between a common genetic base of life and the mechanisms of species change over generations—or descent with modification.[4] The term *evolution*

---

3. For an expanded version of the science and theological significance of evolution, see Heather Eaton, "The Revolution of Evolution," *Worldviews* 11, no. 1 (2007): 6–31.
4. For a detailed explanation of the multiple meanings of evolution see Stephen C. Meyer and Michael Keas, "The Meanings of Evolution," in *Darwinism, Design and Public Education*, ed. John Angus Campbell and Stephen C. Meyer (East Lansing: Michigan State University Press, 2003), 135–56.

represents a multidisciplinary mosaic incorporating immense quantities of data from geology and plate tectonics to biochemistry, genetics, and more. The overwhelming agreement is that evolution is not a hypothesis, meaning a guess; it is the developing descriptions of the dynamic and organic processes and conditions of life on Earth. Evolution indicates that "nature" is living and dynamic, not orderly or mechanistic, neither random nor determined. It is patterned but not predictable. Life evolves. Evolution is a planetary process.

The planet has generated several periods of life expansion and complexifications, interspersed with several mass extinctions. The last massive extinction was sixty-five million years ago, with the demise of the impressive dinosaurs. Evolutionary processes generated life again, but the recovery of biodiversity was chaotic.[5] Millions of years were required to regenerate and innovate pathways for the emergence of life for this era, the Cenozoic: the age of birds, fish, flowers, and mammals.

Diversity and complexity are characteristics of the Cenozoic. Mammals thrived, developing bonding patterns, social structures, and forms of consciousness. Twenty-three million years ago, there is evidence of the first hominids, evolved from bonobos and chimpanzees (98.77 percent of DNA base pairs are identical between humans and chimpanzees). This animal was bipedal four million years ago, with a shift from *Homo erectus* to *Homo sapiens* (as we call ourselves) three to four hundred thousand years ago. Here is a creature with technological savvy, greater memory, elaborate brain functions, symbolic representation, culture, adaptability, language, and self-consciousness. *Homo sapiens* are emergent from and part of evolutionary expansions of the Cenozoic era of Earth.

To deliberate evolution can induce a revolution of awareness of the meaning of human embeddedness in planetary processes. All our attributes and sensibilities have evolved from planetary processes. This changes all our customary reference points. Evolution provides us with a planetary timeline, of histories that do not involve us, of our kinship with other animals, and of our radical dependency on innumerable organisms for basic survival. Evolution bends the mind, expands the horizon, and reverses the reference points. The planet is not our context, and we are not the key reference point. Although Earth is our home, it is not as an occupant or as a global citizen. This is a significant conceptual shortcoming in promoting the image of the Earth as

---

5. See Peter Wilf, Conrad C. Labandeira, Kirk R. Johnson, and Beth Ellis, "Decoupled Plant and Insect Diversity after the End-Cretaceous Extinction," *Science* 313, no. 5790 (2006): 1112–15.

our home without any ecological or evolutionary literacy. Earth is our source, origin, and basis for everything that makes and keeps us alive. Evolution beckons us to become scientifically literate and to situate ourselves in larger planetary processes.

We begin to see ourselves as more than living "with nature," or succumbing to the forces of nature. We emerged from, and are entangled in, immense life projects. My purpose here is to accentuate the depth of continuity between the planetary processes and ourselves. This does not override differentiations or ignore the innumerable distinctions between humans and other animals, nature, and culture (the social constructions of nature) or that our lives are replete with mediated experiences.

To persistently speak of humans and "the environment" as discontinuous or separate is absurd in the face of interrelated planetary dynamics. Yet, everyday language is replete with these demarcations. Consideration of evolution invites attentiveness to connection and continuity—that we, too, are a planetary process. All human vitality is dependent upon the natural world, in every way. Innovative theories of emergent complexity, ingenuity, entanglement, relationality, and new materialism are grappling with these evolutionary and planetary insights perceiving countless interconnected systems and relations intertwined throughout the biosphere. They are transforming the meaning of *planetary* in ways I consider to be crucial for a viable future. They are the foundation of planet solidarity.

Connections between Humans and Other Animals

The last meaning of *planetary* to be explored is the plethora of connections between humans and other animals. The insistence on human distinction from and superiority to other animals has obstructed our ability to see the similarities and kinship. Claims that humans' distinctiveness due to emotional sensitivities, empathy, decision making processes, intelligent thought, moral capacity, communication, and language do not hold up in the face of animal research in cognitive ethnology, social neurosciences, and evolutionary biology.[6] Many animals, including mice, display these abilities. Most animals negotiate

---

6. The area of animal studies is now substantial. For influential works see Marc Bekoff and Jessica Pierce, *Wild Justice: The Moral Lives of Animals* (Chicago: University of Chicago Press, 2009); Marc Bekoff, *The Emotional Lives of Animals: A Leading Scientist Explores Animal Joy, Sorrow, and Empathy—and Why They Matter* (Novato, CA: New World Library, 2007); Marc Bekoff, *Animal Passions and Beastly Virtues: Reflections on Redecorating Nature* (Philadelphia: Temple University Press, 2005); Frans de Waal, *Primates and Philosophers: How Morality Evolved*, ed. Stephen Macedo and Josiah Ober (Princeton: Princeton University Press, 2006).

their lives with companions, often friends, in social orders with ethical codes and with myriad communication systems. Studies on virtually all animals are revealing unexpected capacities and consciousness. For example, crows, dogs, primates, octopi, and rodents have been studied for their exceptional problem solving skills and moral codes. Octopi are now recognized as "highly intelligent, capable of tenderness, playfulness, happiness and friendship."[7] The activities of animals, their social forms and interactions, ingenuity, responsiveness, and what can only be called their thoughts, feelings, and personalities are now studied intensively. This knowledge is occurring in tandem with entering the sixth era of massive extinctions.[8]

In many Euro-Western contexts, people are awakening to animals and issues of hunting, farming, food sources, animal testing and research, companion animals, shelters, and zoos. Concerns about animal welfare are rising. However, what is deeply troubling about this is that from a larger perspective, animals are severely threatened and in a catastrophic decline. All large mammals are endangered to varying degrees, as are innumerable insects, birds, fish, and plants. The planet is entering a new period of extinction with scientists warning that species all over the world are "essentially the walking dead."[9] Most of the demise and disappearance of animals is silent. They simply die off from habitat loss, pollution, or food shortages. In other instances, they are pushed off their land for human development or killed for food, skins, tusks, horns, or trophy hunting. Climate change impacts on animals are difficult to measure. At times, it is heartbreaking. As I write this chapter, hippopotami are being culled, as in shot, in Kruger Park South Africa because the drought is causing them to die a slow death.[10] The drought is due to climate changes. Although there are multiple causes, overall it is anthropogenic activities and pressures causing this extinction—again, a planetary phenomenon.

The suffering and loss of animals is, at times, seen to be an extraneous concern for those focused on social injustices. It is a cause carried by the affluent, ecotourists, animal rights activists, or those not in dire need of food, land, or capital. This is fundamentally shortsighted for ecological and ethical reasons. While not the central topic here, animal

---

7. Ben East, "*Soul of an Octopus* by Sy Montgomery Review—A Fond Study of the Elusive 'Alien,'" *The Guardian*, July 5, 2016, http://tinyurl.com/lmrnbmh.

8. Elizabeth Kolbert, *The Sixth Extinction: An Unnatural History* (New York: Henry Holt, 2014).

9. Gerardo Ceballos, Paul R. Ehrlich, Anthony D. Barnosky, Andrés García, Robert M. Pringle, and Todd M. Palmer, "Accelerated Modern Human-Induced Species Losses: Entering the Sixth Mass Extinction," *Science Advances* 1, no. 5 (June 5, 2015): e1400253, http://tinyurl.com/qc5apmq.

10. Rudzani Tshivhase, "Kruger Park Considers Culling Hippos," SABC News, March 11, 2016, http://tinyurl.com/mfqdyao.

rights is a subject requiring global attention and, in my view, in tandem with human rights.

Thus, the term *planetary* must include the animals with whom we live and an acute concern for their welfare and right to thrive. Euro-Western world views have developed without a consideration of an evolutionary framework and with an emphasis on demarcations between humans and other animals. We begin to see how limited our horizon has been in understanding ourselves, other planetary life, and our place within the scheme of things. *Planetary* cannot mean simply international, worldwide, new cosmopolitanism, or global citizen. It cannot be an understanding of "humans and the Earth" or a superficial notion of Earth as home. To take seriously *planetary* is to integrate an evolutionary framework, to be ecologically literate, to see humans as one species among many, and to appreciate the other life forms of the Earth community. Planetary as home can be a useful image, if situated within this larger framework, which also includes the community of beings who also emerged from and belong to these immense, ingenious, and subtle planetary processes.

Planetary also means to be aware that all this is deteriorating. Further, when planetary systems such as climate patterns are in crisis, then the future of life is uncertain—all life. To understand this with precision and insight requires both a planetary conscience and consciousness. A way forward must expand into a deep solidarity, which will be explored next.

Solidarity

Solidarity is a rich concept.[11] It forms the basis of ideas and ideals of social cohesion and is the impetus for movements of social change and justice. Much has been researched and written about solidarity as a vision, an ideal, an objective and political engagement. Here, planetary solidarity is an appeal, with several facets.

Solidarity generally includes notions of political activity. It is more than alliances of common interests or objectives. Solidarity, in the political sense, is about social justice and movements for transformation with a responsibility to the common good. It means awareness and analyses of inequities and patterns of injustice, and commitments to

11. Solidarity is a widespread yet overall ambiguous, theoretically under-defined, casually used concept with unclear presuppositions. I am attempting to not define it precisely but point to some issues with its use. See Michael Hoelzl, "Recognizing the Sacrificial Victim: The Problem of Solidarity for Critical Social Theory," *Journal for Cultural and Religious Theory* 6, no. 1 (December 2004): 45–64.

social change to remedy these inequalities. Solidarity requires particular attentiveness to those who benefit least within the social imagination and sociopolitical praxis. Plus, solidarity means active resistance to oppression and constructive efforts for justice and equality.

Climate Justice

Solidarity with respect to climate justice must therefore include a comprehensive approach integrating scientific analysis with political, economic, and ethical considerations. Most often, climate justice resides in the discourses of and efforts for human rights, noting that climate change is and will affect those with the least political and economic power to mitigate the effects. Climate justice is attentive to governance and to oppressive patterns of ethnicity, gender, and poverty. It looks at the modalities of power, national security, political transparency, food, land, and water sovereignty and encourages community-led solutions. Thus, climate justice is concerned with efforts to reduce climate changes, or adapt to them, tethered to human rights.

The research on and appeals for climate justice are gaining traction around the world. Myriad publications and centers promote climate justice. One such effort summarizes the focus:

> Climate justice links human rights and development to achieve a human-centred approach, safeguarding the rights of the most vulnerable people and sharing the burdens and benefits of climate change and its impacts equitably and fairly. Climate justice is informed by science, responds to science and acknowledges the need for equitable stewardship of the world's resources.[12]

While fully supportive of this focus for climate justice, I find it limited from the planetary perspectives mentioned above. Climate justice is virtually always anthropocentric. Often, there will be mention of "the environment," but one is hard-pressed to find anything on climate justice that is not anthropocentric. When there is mention of the efforts to have water considered as a right, it is always a human right; plants and other animals are not privy to such rights. Considerable work is occurring in environmental rights, which are again mostly anthropocentric and about humans' right to healthy "environments" and resources.

Climate justice is grounded in theories of human rights. A question to ask is if it is beneficial to expand the notion of rights to a planetary

---

12. For example, the Mary Robinson Foundation offers a good summary of the principles of climate justice. See http://tinyurl.com/l98yxtb.

perspective. For example, the Great Apes Project argues that non-human hominids should have the right to life, freedom, and not to be tortured.[13] In 2000, animals, plants, and other organisms had their rights to dignity accepted by the Constitution in Switzerland, although the implications remain undefined. At the 2010 World People's Conference on Climate Change in Bolivia, the *Universal Declaration of Rights of Mother Earth* was drafted, bestowing legal rights on vital Earth processes, water, and air. This is currently under review at the United Nations. These represent an ecological expansion of the rendering of "rights."

The image of ecological rights is both potent and problematic.[14] Rights are constructed on dissimilar platforms. Anthropocentric and bio- or eco-centric rights differ. The relationships among rights, justice, responsibilities, worth, dignity, subjectivity, and intrinsic value are controversial. For example, if the natural world has only instrumental or utilitarian worth, not inherent worth, then it has no dignity, no subjectivity, and no rights. Does water have rights, or do humans have rights to water? Do plants and other animals have rights? Although evocative and persuasive to summon "rights," it requires an enriched moral and ecological imagination to equip rights for a planetary solidarity.

Beyond Justice

Planetary solidarity requires a larger framework than rights, justice, and an equitable sharing of resources. It requires ecological and evolutionary literacy to inform the notion of solidarity, in a biospheric sense. Such solidarity comes from an understanding of human belonging in a planetary more so than a political sense. In a factual manner, human futures depend on ecological stability, sustainability, and vitality. There is no viable future for humans on an ecologically devastated, or even deteriorated, planet. This "fact" has a great deal of difficulty penetrating Euro-Western world views that construe identity as individual, familial, ethnic, or national. For planetary solidarity to have traction, there needs to be a shift from personal and political identity formations to planetary citizenship.

For those whose primary framework is human rights, justice, and

---

13. Great Apes Project, http://www.projetogap.org.br/en/.
14. An expanded version of this topic can be found in Heather Eaton, "Where Do We Go from Here? Methodology, Next Steps, Social Change," in *Christian Faith and the Earth: Current Paths and Emerging Horizons in Ecotheology*, ed. Ernst M. Conradie, Sigurd Bergmann, Celia Deane-Drummond, and Denis Edwards (London: Bloomsbury, 2014), 195–218.

political solidarity, this shift seems imprudent. To consider ecosystems, animals, and planetary processes as a defining framework is to obscure, if not erase, issues of inequities and injustice. Yet, this is shortsighted. A planetary framework that is ecologically literate offers a way forward that incorporates and enlarges discerning patterns of injustices. Injustices within and across human communities are multiple, mutually reinforcing, socially embedded, ideologically structured, and materially manifested. Injustices inflicted on other animals, life-forms, ecosystems, waterways, and climate processes are also, if not equally, complex and offensive. One could argue that they are more consequential because ecological ruin affects all related life communities, as well as intensifying social injustices.

Solidarity, in the planetary sense I am proposing, is more than an expansion of justice and rights. Solidarity must be enlarged to include the community of other animals and life forms who participate in stabilizing Earth life. In effect, all planetary activities could be included in such solidarity, since the whole is required for the parts to thrive. It is crucial to grasp that the biosphere functions in intimately entangled ways; thus, planetary solidarity needs to be commensurate with these. Such solidarity opposes the segregation of humans from the planet, other animals, ecosystems, and the biosphere. This invented yet believed human/Earth apartheid is manifestly one cause of the decline of ecological health and the ideological and political impasse in responding. The counterpoint is the blend of meanings of planetary and solidarity explored above, which could become the foundation for an Earth-centric theological framing.

An Earth-Centric Theological Framing

Ecotheology implies comprehensive reform, novel interpretations, and transformed praxes of Christian traditions.[15] Ecological issues have seeped into all aspects of theology, sparking varied responses from apologetics and minor modifications to systemic critiques, radical revisions, and political activism. While there is a range of ecotheology methods, disciplines, and topics, the overall aim is to orient elements of Christianity toward ecological sustainability and to transform the traditions and their social milieu. Ecotheologies are operational, worldwide, and are gaining traction. Their ecological impacts are not easy to measure.

---

15. Ernst M. Conradie, "Contemporary Challenges to Christian Ecotheology: Some Reflections on the State of the Debate after Five Decades," *Journal of Theology for Southern Africa* 147 (2013): 106–23.

For present purposes, I am glossing over multiple distinctions to deliberate on the normative framework upon which Christian world views are built. I am using the metaphor of the framing of a building: the supporting framework upon which is constructed the basic architecture, or presuppositions, of most Christian world views. These include the character of the phenomenal order (good, corrupt, chaotic), human anthropology (sinful, incomplete, blessed), a human/nature/divine nexus, and the need for salvation. The metaphor of a building frame renders obvious the starting points and essential building materials. For example, for most ecotheologies, the starting point, and ultimate reference point, is Christianity. In my view, this is no longer a viable approach for theological reflection. Before delving into this seeming paradox, I will expose three key supports of the Christian theological architecture that act as obstacles to planetary solidarity. The first is creation.

Christian Architecture: Creation

To address planetary solidarity in conversation with Christianity requires examining notions of creation.[16] Historically, there have been two ontological options.[17] The most prevalent emphasized the limits, imperfections, or sinfulness of creation. These were secured to concepts about evil, sin, suffering, death, and fall-redemption.[18] Overall, the supposition is that creation is not as God intended it, due to various failings: fallen angels, original or other sins, corrupt or transitory nature of matter, uncontrolled natural forces, human death, and so on. The divine is absent, obscured, or imperceptible in creation. Salvation means to be saved from this debased creation and from mortality and the failings of one's body. Humans will be saved to another dimension: redeemed, healed, and (re)united with God in an afterlife. It is impor-

---

16. Early works in ecotheology examined the theological meaning of creation, and many jettisoned this approach for a scientific account of cosmology and evolution. For example, see Sallie McFague, *The Body of God: An Ecological Theology* (Minneapolis: Fortress, 1993); Anne Primavesi, *From Apocalypse to Genesis: Ecology, Feminism and Christianity* (Minneapolis: Fortress, 1991) and *Gaia's Gift: Earth, Ourselves and God after Copernicus* (London: Routledge, 2003); Rosemary Radford Ruether, *Gaia and God: An Ecofeminist Theology of Earth Healing* (San Francisco: HarperOne, 1994); John Haught, *God after Darwin: A Theology of Evolution* (Boulder, CO: Westview, 2001); Thomas Berry *The Dream of the Earth* (Berkeley, CA: Counterpoint, 2015, orig. edition 1988).
17. See Heather Eaton, "Creation: God, Humans and the Natural World," *Concilium* 4 (2012): 56–66.
18. The classic Christian doctrine of creation was that of *creatio ex nihilo*: that God freely created everything in form and being out of nothing. There are countless tomes: why God created, God's freedom, divine self-emptying (kenosis), if and how God influences creation, and if God suffers with or because of creation, as well as related notions of a fall, salvation, divine action, providence, and a host of other topics. For centuries, this speculative approach to creation has governed.

tant to grasp that life and existence are interpreted to be inadequate and flawed and judged as unacceptable.

The alternative was to consider creation to be ontologically good, albeit imperfect or incomplete. Hildegard von Bingen and Thomas Aquinas studied cosmological and Earth sciences and built a theological edifice on the precept that creation is wholesome and permeated with divine presence. Life and existence are worthy, and God is present. The natural world is a place of divine revelation, as primary, secondary, or parallel to the customary Christian notions of revelation. Those now known for their "creation spirituality," including Meister Eckhart, Francis of Assisi, and Julian of Norwich, enriched their theologies based on revelations of the divine in the natural world. However, this path was never well travelled, until recently.

Although severely abridged, the synopses of these two ontologies reveal opposing beliefs. They unite on the conviction that life is inadequate, which became the basic architecture for Christian world views. Terrestrial life has been judged to be defective throughout Christian histories, although the reasons vary. This negative assessment of creation competed with scientific evidence about the universe, the planet, and the biosphere over centuries.[19] It greatly affected Christian anthropology. Theology became situated predominantly within a moral sphere, resulting in an intense focus on sin and the need for salvation from sin, nature, death, and the planet.

Although the contemporary emphasis has changed, and creation is now viewed as "good," Christian anthropology is replete with beliefs about humans as ontologically other than, separate from, and superior to the natural world. The natural world is the backdrop to the human and divine drama. At best, the planet is a set of resources for human stewardship and earthly prosperity. The emphases on human distinction from and transcendence over the natural world are the studs and cross braces of Christian theological framing. They are the supportive structures for the doctrines of revelation, salvation, Christologies, and Trinitarian theologies. Although Christian theologies and world views can be divergent on many aspects, the ideas that human origins, nature, and destiny are distinct from planetary processes remain the governing and operative beliefs across cultures and traditions.[20]

The negative ontology about creation has been discussed, debated, and by and large dropped by ecotheologians. The hierarchical dualisms

---

19. For example, Galileo and Copernicus revealed a heliocentric not geocentric universe, evoking enormous theological resistance. Evidence of evolution is currently challenging many theological views.
20. Renowned exceptions were Alfred North Whitehead and Pierre Teilhard de Chardin.

woven throughout this view have been exhumed and eschewed. However, I want to emphasize that the ontological distinctions between humans and the natural world linger or live on in Christian world views, including in some ecotheologies. They remain central planks of a Christian theological building framing. It is readily seen in the pervasive Christian anthropocentrism, a second obstacle to planetary solidarity.

Anthropocentrism

In general, Christian world views separated the natural world from spiritual imagery, religious experiences, and sacred presence. The result is a stalwart anthropocentric bias.[21] Anthropocentrism differs across Christian traditions, yet unites in claiming that humans are the sole or essential *imago Dei*. Humans are spiritually superior to, and transcend, the natural world. It cannot be overstated how powerfully anthropocentrism functions. It is emphasized explicitly in Christian doctrines and operates insidiously throughout Euro-Western world views and practices. Ecotheologians have had to contend with this tenacious anthropocentrism and the Christian emphasis on humanity's transcendence over the natural world.[22] Anthropocentrism precludes planetary solidarity.

The antidote is an Earth-centric approach, which does not diminish *Homo sapiens'* uniqueness and superiority as a technologically savvy and dominant species. It does, however, at a minimum, impose good stewardship and an ethic of living within the rhythm and limits of the natural world. However, for an authentic planetary solidarity, stewardship is insufficient. Of course planetary stewardship is necessary. However, the image of stewardship implies that humans are in a caretaking role of planetary processes when, in fact, humans are unable to understand these processes in depth. Stewardship implies an ontological separation between humans and the natural world and maintains a strong anthropocentrism with an understanding that together with God, we will take care of God's garden. The stewardship image is replete with ecological and theological hubris. As an ethic of restraint, stewardship is essential. As a theological model, it is detrimental. An Earth-centric approach would mean the ecological and ethical primacy of a functioning biosphere. In this framing, the Earth community has rights and

---

21. Although anthropocentrism can range from strong to weak, from Lynn White forward it is readily recognized that the governing Christian theologies and operative world views promoted a strong anthropocentrism.
22. Clive Pearson, "On Being Public about Ecotheology," *Ecotheology* 6, no. 1–2 (July 2001): 51.

humans have obligations toward planetary solidarity inclusive of the whole planet.

Yet, anthropocentrism is not easy to resolve from a theological perspective. One of the key difficulties in reinterpreting Christianity for planetary solidarity is that the theological tenets are inter-supporting—hence the architectural framing image. They stand or fall together. The anthropocentrism of Christianity is fastened to core teachings on creation, salvation, Christology, resurrection, and eternal life. Obviously, these are complex theological doctrines interpreted differently within and across Christian traditions. Nevertheless, a central plank connecting them within the Christian edifice is the certitude of a bodily resurrection affixed to an otherworldly afterlife destiny, or salvation ideology—a third obstacle to planetary solidarity.

Salvation Ideology

Every religious world view interprets, albeit distinctly, that life does not end with death. However, the Christian tradition has extreme claims and has built a fortress around them: salvation from earthly life, a bodily resurrection, eternal life, and a belief in the ultimate and infinite worth of humans. Saved humans are destined to live forever, reunited elsewhere in everlasting blessedness. These teachings, beliefs, and doctrines, interpreted with minimal variations, are promoted, proclaimed, and promised every day, everywhere around the world. Such interpretations of salvation and eternal life are subsumed in the meanings given to resurrection. Together, these frame the Christian theological structure upon which everything else rests.

The Christian assessment is that terrestrial life is insufficient. Death, as our finale, is unacceptable. Christian ideology emphasizes transcending death and promises salvation from the precariousness and fragility of life as lived. Christianity has developed an extreme opposition to, even refusal of, the conditions of life. Regardless, death is inescapable and a condition of life.

As a result, Christianity supports attempts to escape, resist, or control life's requisites.[23] Furthermore, because of the refusal to accept the conditions of life, Christianity has and is involved in domination. Here, Ivone Gebara offers valuable insights. She suggests that at the basis of

---

23. Much research has exposed the intimate relationships between Christianity and hierarchical dualisms, which contain a division between spiritual and material, and eternal and temporal spheres. The set of dualisms have been embedded in Christian ideologies and practices of social and ecological domination. See Heather Eaton, *Introducing Ecofeminist Theologies* (London: T&T Clark, 2005).

domination in Christian cultures is a flight from life's provisos: vulnerability, finitude, and mortality. The consequences are escapist spiritualities, and praxes of domination: of land, animals, and peoples.[24] The commitment to be redeemed from life as given and promises of otherworldly eternal life are antithetical to vulnerability, finitude, and mortality. Refusing the conditions of life is the beginning of sin, which leads to a fall into domination.

This rejection of life's limits, which becomes a flight from reality, has created distortions throughout theological assertions. The Christian tradition constantly tries to "lift" humanity above the Earth and the existential limits. Gebara proposes we need an alternative understanding of sin, redemption, revelation, creation, nature, humanity, and the divine that could provide a new framing for theology.[25] For example, Gebara suggests our salvation is found in returning to our embodied selves and refusing escapism and domination. We can embrace with joy and sorrow the genuine limitations, richness, and struggles of life in community and in solidarity with all life. Death is an inherent part of the human reality, not that from which we are to be saved. We will die, and that could be the end. This would sharpen our appreciation for existence as given. It could heighten our awareness of an indwelling spirit or sacred presence—one in which we live and have our being—perceiving we live in a divine milieu, an Earth community saturated with divine presence.

Gebara does not develop this theology in detail, which is unfortunate as she is an original thinker and her views are challenging and insightful. If domination were considered to be the result of refusing the conditions of life—meaning vulnerability, mortality, and finitude—then a way forward is to embrace them, difficult as that is. (This does not mean accepting conditions of injustices or inequalities.) If sin originates in a repudiation of life's provisos—exacerbated by the Christian claim that another life, elsewhere, enduing forever will be perfect—and that these claims orient psychically and materially Christian cultures, then the enormity of the challenges becomes clear. Theological distortions are revealed. All facets of the classic fall-redemption theology are dismantled. The emphasis on salvation from sin shifts to salvation being found in living this life with grace, gratitude, and planetary solidarity.

Gebara sees the need to reframe the whole of theology: notions of

---

24. Found in Rosemary Radford Ruether, "Ecofeminism: The Challenge to Theology," in *Christianity and Ecology: Seeking the Well-Being of Earth and Humans*, ed. Dieter T. Hessel and Rosemary Radford Ruether (Cambridge, MA: Harvard University Press, 2000), 105.
25. Ivone Gebara, *Longing for Running Water: Ecofeminism and Liberation* (Minneapolis: Fortress, 1999).

sin, redemption, revelation, creation, anthropology, and the Divine.[26] She disputes otherworldly afterlife theologies, defies hierarchy, and confronts christofacism.[27] Her proposal supports interreligious collaboration, biospheric consciousness, and justice and liberation efforts. The challenges and oppositions to the fall-redemption theological system are stark, and the consequences are far-reaching. Underlying Gebara's intimations are the beginnings of an alternative theological framing that can support a planetary solidarity.

Evil, Sin, and Suffering

A few words about evil, sin, and suffering may clarify further the limits of a fall-redemption theology. The term *evil* is more than slippery. Given the cultural differentiations on what is judged to be evil, and that it is both a religious and secular term, what is meant by evil? To study the history of the concept of evil yields a perplexing assortment: natural disasters; anthological orientations, impulses, and practices of "wrong-doing"; depravity; grave crimes coupled with a lack of remorse; and, to use the term of Hannah Arendt, extreme culpable wrongdoing. Studies on evil suggest the need for thick and thin categories and a conceptual pluralism.[28] For others, it is a concept "too confused by old arguments that have been overtaken by events."[29] Evil is ostensibly a necessary word in the moral lexicon, but a precise definition is elusive.

The word sin is also ambiguous. Usually, sin has a religious connotation, such as turning away from God or transgressing a divine moral law. However, again, interpretation is everything, and again, there are no stable definitions. Much is debated and contested. Discussions about sin related to a "fall" have ebbed, and the emphasis is on moral actions. For ecotheologians, the sources and activities of sin are complex when evolution is considered. For example, the undeniable kinship between humans and other animals raises new questions. Do animals sin?[30] The

26. Gebara did this with her book *Out of the Depths: Women's Experience of Evil and Salvation* (Minneapolis: Fortress, 2002).
27. Dorothee Soelle saw the rise of the Christian right as a soft fascism, a highly seductive form of evangelization that supports militarism, racism, misogyny, abolishment of state-support health and welfare, and so forth. See Dorothee Soelle, "Christofacism," in *The Window of Vulnerability: A Political Spirituality* (Minneapolis: Fortress, 1990), 133–40.
28. Luke Russell, *Evil: A Philosophical Investigation* (Oxford: Oxford University Press, 2014).
29. Rollo Romig, "What Do We Mean by 'Evil'?" *The New Yorker*, July 25, 2012, http://tinyurl.com/l79lv8e.
30. J. Wentzel van Huyssteen, "Primates, Hominids, and Humans—From Species Specificity to Human Uniqueness? A Response to Barbara J. King, Gregory R. Peterson, Wesley J. Wildman, and Nancy R. Howell," *Zygon* 43, no. 2 (June 2008): 505–25; Celia Deane-Drummond, "Shadow Sophia in Christological Perspective: The Evolution of Sin and the Redemption of Nature," *Theology and Science*

answers vary depending on the meaning of sin and morality. Over-all, if there is an emphasis on the continuities between humans and other animals, then moral responsiveness originated within evolution-ary processes. Human differences with other animals are matters of degree and not of kind.[31] For ethnographers, mammals (some birds, rodents, octopi, and so on) are often goal directed, make choices, and have social codes and mechanisms of moral education and chastise-ment. Morality is about survival, kinship, conflict resolution, and com-munal cohesion. It is associated with emotional and social sensibilities and the dynamics of hierarchies and taboos. Incipient and proto-morality are terms used to denote the evolution of social codes, sen-timents, and cognitive abilities underlying human morality. Although aspects of free will are operative in most mammals, sin is not a service-able concept. Few animals transgress, and their modes of nonviolent conflict negotiation and resolution are often effective. What is star-tling is how rare any wanton violence occurs within and among ani-mals; when it does, it is virtually always serving the survival needs of the individual and species.[32]

If the discontinuities are emphasized, the differences between human and other animals are of kind, not degree. Other animals are thought to operate with instinct or limited moral awareness or free-dom and, hence, are incapable of sin. For humans, morality and sin are related to free will and/or aberrant anthropological propensities, and morality engages conceptual, rational processes. Thus, stressing con-tinuities or discontinuities, the notion of sin belongs to human rather than planetary or other animal activities. In this frame, if only humans sin, then only humans require redemption and salvation.

If morality means a priority of the weak, and if sin is associated with a lack of flourishing, then sin permeates the biosphere, as suggests Michael Northcott. All of creation has fallen and is in need of redemp-tion, although sin is endemic to humanity. For Northcott, in order to flourish biologically and morally, life needs to attend to embodi-ment and vulnerability. Yet, these will be conquered with salvation. He writes, "For it is through the 'folly of the Cross' and the vindication of the resurrection that embodied vulnerability and weakness are divinely exalted as the means to overcoming evil and redeeming cre-

6, no. 1 (2008): 13–32; Michael S. Northcott, "Do Dolphins Carry the Cross? Biological Realism and Theological Ethics," *New Blackfriars* 84, no. 994 (2003): 540–53.

31. Waal, *Primates and Philosophers.*

32. Marc Bekoff and Jessica Pierce, "Wild Justice Redux: What We Know about Social Justice in Ani-mals and Why It Matters," *Social Justice Research* 25, no. 2 (2012): 122–39. Frans B. M. de Waal, Patri-cia Smith Churchland, Telmo Pievani, and Stefano Parmigiani, eds., *Evolved Morality: The Biology and Philosophy of Human Conscience* (Leiden: Brill, 2014).

ation."[33] The starting point, presuppositions, and telos are the fall-redemption-resurrection-salvation theology mentioned above. As I would not start there, I do not share his framework or viewpoint.

There are anthropological and theological presuppositions woven throughout many positions about sin that are presumed to be "true." They are left unexamined and undefended except by Scripture, or fall-redemption theological beliefs. Morality (and hence discussions about evil and sin) rarely include a scientific evolutionary perspective, and if so, there are *a priori* theological commitments. I suggest such premises and assumptions require interrogation.

When sin is related to extreme culpable wrongdoing and violence, then only humans are involved. In fact, the aggression and violence of *Homo sapiens* is staggering. Other animals never display anything like the persistent viciousness of humans. Yet, the observation of human violence requires qualification: it is predominantly male violence. Studies on sin as reckless and overt violence rarely explicitly and publicly confront the reality that virtually all direct manifestations of violence—aggression, cruelty, sexual assaults, murder, torture, serial killings, massacres, and war crimes—are committed by men—not *Homo sapiens* as a species. Most of the conceptual dimensions of violence—thinking, planning, arming, and financing of war activities—are performed by men. Men, usually against other men, coordinate societal security systems. If we add violence against women, killing animals for sport, combat competitions, forcing animals to fight, even vehicle accidents, it is more than fair to claim that male aggression dominates *Homo sapiens* violence. I am not claiming women are incapable of such activities. However, women rarely do them, in any culture. Women do participate in myriad familial, indirect, and structural violence that are detrimental to individuals, kin groupings, and social cohesion. Still, I find it offensive and disingenuous to debate if animals sin when the global pandemic of male violence is a principal threat to human and other animal societies.[34] Thus, the theological stance of salvation from sin is rickety at best.

From the viewpoint of suffering, the image of planetary solidarity can seem to ignore the extreme unevenness of suffering within and across human communities. Planetary perspectives are accused of overlooking vast inequities and human misery caused by systematic injustices, and of focusing instead on the planet, stars, evolution, and a

33. Northcott, "Dolphins Carry," 544.
34. The topic of male violence is almost impossible to address publicly. We can discuss violence against women, domestic violence, gun culture, war, torture, and unending violent conflicts without ever specifying the perpetrators, who are overwhelmingly men.

grand metaphysical, but irrelevant, scheme of things. Nothing could be farther from the truth. Injustices, suffering, human diminishment, and ethnic and gender discrimination are social profiles and human experiences in many contexts. The point is to develop a notion of planetary solidarity that is mindful of suffering and accentuates justice beyond the human community. Many animals suffer greatly, most often due to *Homo sapiens*. The goal is to transform the interpretative framework for planetary solidarity to include and go beyond morality and ethical theories.

Theological Framings for Planetary Solidarity

Three theological framing options are now discernable. When salvation is related to moral restitution, flawed existence, or otherworldly eternal life, and the need is to be saved from life's conditions, then the framing of Christian theology is the customary salvation narrative as described above. This otherworldly longing and construal of salvation is operative across all Christian traditions. Furthermore, it can be appealing in periods of decline and cultural powerlessness. A popular form of this salvation ideology is on T-shirts or bumper stickers, with the iconic image of the Earth from space and the slogan "*Jesus—don't leave earth without him.*"

A second framing option comes from ecotheologians who study evolution and/or ecological dynamics. They recognize that the biosphere is the primary planetary system. Continuities are unmistakable between humans, other animals, and planetary processes. Individual lives may not flourish, and species come and go, but the biosphere establishes dynamics to support life within patterns of emerging complexities. Consequentially, the ontological divides between humans, other animals, and the planet's processes must be radically revised. This dismantles some of the previous framing of salvation.

However, for many the assurance of a personal, bodily, glorious afterlife is core to their interpretation of salvation and resurrection. The human person is to be fulfilled only in the future and is destined for eternal life with God. This life remains a shadow, fragment, propensity, or potential. Salvation can mean a natural continuation of God's activities and promises now unto eternity. Divine presence is not only immanent but is embedded and active in "creation." In this framing, salvation is a fulfillment of, rather than rescue from, planetary life.

Jürgen Moltmann, a proponent of this interpretation, is certainly a leading, learned, and creative ecotheologian. Over decades, he has studied contemporary sciences and advanced an innovative, yet fairly classical ecotheology. Noting the diligence and density of his theological proposal, a glimpse at his salvific and eschatological vision is worthwhile. In *God in Creation*, he writes: "It is only the eschatological annihilation of death, the redemption of the body on a new earth and under a new heaven, which will consummate the 'becoming' process of human beings, thereby fulfilling their creaturely being."[35] In a similar theological vein almost thirty years later, now inclusive of Earth, he claims: "God will 'indwell' his creation on earth as in heaven and, in the presence of the eternally living God, death will be no more; all things will participate in the eternal livingness and righteousness of God."[36] On the relevance of current existence, Moltmann writes: "Creation 'in the beginning' opens up the prospect of history which arrives at its goal only in the new creation of all things. The perfected creation does not lie behind us in a primal state but ahead of us in a final one. We await the consummated creation and, together with the cosmos, are now existing in its prehistory."[37]

This framing is appealing to many as it is both scientifically literate and theologically normative. Of concern is that, once again, current existence is a temporary, incomplete, and inadequate version of a future form. We are in "prehistory." I find this theological framing increasingly unacceptable for three reasons. First is the assertion of an eternal, otherworldly, embodied afterlife. This is a belief functioning like knowledge. Yet, it is a claim, desire, act of faith, or a conviction. It may or may not be true. It is not verifiable.[38] The second objection is the judgment that this life is inferior to a superior, imagined future one. Surely there are many reasons for this negative judgment. There is no question that "life" is unfair. Many humans, as well as other life forms, do not survive, suffer maladies and injustices, cannot flourish, rarely reach their potential, and die young. The precariousness of life overwhelms, and we reject the conditions. But these are the conditions: vulnerability, mortality, and finitude. The normative Christian world view is based on the stance that these are unacceptable: somehow wrong, not as it should be. Christianity's verdict that there must be more and other—some reality where we are indispensable and impervious to suffering and death—is a belief, fantasy, delusion, conviction, or commitment. It is not a fact. How can it be spiritually truthful and

---

35. Jürgen Moltmann, *God in Creation: An Ecological Doctrine of Creation*, trans. M. Kohl (London: SCM, 1985).

36. Jürgen Moltmann, "Is the World Unfinished? On Interactions between Science and Theology in the Concepts of Nature, Time and the Future," *Theology* 114, no. 6 (2011): 410.

37. Ibid.

38. I am extremely aware that this is deemed verifiable through faith, Scripture, tradition, revelation, doctrine, etc. However, when examined carefully, these are tautological arguments.

mature that an imaginary future be judged superior to an actual present?

A third objection is that this Christian salvation narrative rests on the claim that humans are of infinite value. But perhaps we are not as significant as we assume, envision, or desire to be. In fact, it may be the height of arrogance to imagine we have eternal life. It may be the height of ignorance to believe our lives continue after death, given all of the scientific evidence of the life cycle. An effective planetary solidarity is not possible within this framing of human prominence. What we know about the Earth processes does not affirm human centrality or continuity. How can we be so convinced of our ultimate importance in the scheme of things? Few theologians tackle the fact that *Homo sapiens* are simply not the reference point for the amplitude of reality. Perhaps we have the privilege of conscious life for an instant, in a dynamic universe and a magnificent and ingenious biosphere. That is the gift.

In my view, fall-redemption theologies and the customary beliefs about a post-death bodily resurrection, an otherworldly afterlife, and eternal life need to be abandoned. Apart from their epistemological frailty and verification limits, these beliefs prevent awareness of and gratitude for the privilege of existence within life's provisos. They prevent appreciating the planet's dynamics and the astonishing and creative evolution of life. They prevent seeing the whole community of life, and especially the magnificent animals that should be able to live and thrive. These views prevent the delicacy of life from permeating our spiritual awareness. I consider the belief that our destiny is elsewhere to be an affront to the divine gift of life, here and now. Furthermore, the anthropocentric emphasis impedes recognizing the priority of planetary dynamics and evolution—from which we originated and are immersed—that reveal a depth of divine presence and activity that dazzles the spiritual sensibilities beyond belief.

From a different angle, these Christian cultural promises of a superior world elsewhere permeate the psychic orientation and expectations in Euro-Western contexts. Although Christianity has reduced cultural power, the commitments to a different, better, and other world do not diminish. Euro-Western societies are oriented toward transcending the conditions of life, which results in an alienation of humans from the Earth, with attitudes and actions that repeatedly disrupt the integrity of the natural world.

My proposal is for an Earth-centric theological framing for a planetary solidarity that requires understanding evolution. This is the third and final option. Evolutionary processes govern the universe, the Earth, the biosphere, and human emergence and development. Theology needs to be reframed and unified with these cosmological, evolutionary, and Earth sciences. This requires that we understand, in depth, that humans originate from, are embedded in, dependent upon, and entangled with evolutionary and biospheric processes. There is no other possibility for an empirical and ecological framing of planetary solidarity. Ecological literacy should be the foundation for religious education. Religious experiences and knowledge, including theological doctrines, need to be revised *starting* with an evolutionary framework.

To begin, theological reflection with understanding of the basis and basics of evolution changes the references points. Of the many ways to intersect religion and evolution, I am privileging one that integrates religion into an evolutionary framework, rather than the reverse. The level and type of consciousness out of which religions have come should be considered as an evolutionary process. Religions are a part of the evolutionary and cultural development of humans as a symbolic species, an emergent phenomenon within human consciousness and a later cultural formation. Such an approach affirms that religions, and what they represent in terms of consciousness, are more, rather than less, inherent to humans as a species. When evolution, rather than religion, is the starting point, then religion is situated in much larger processes. An evolutionary perspective requires that we think more about the nature of religion and less about the perennial truths of specific texts, doctrines, and beliefs. Given the multitude of religions that have come and gone within human symbolic histories, it is reasonable to assume current ones will also disappear. Starting with evolution would entail a focus on religious consciousness and what experiences and knowledge are represented by religious sensibilities, which would transform Christian theologies.[39] However many of these theological challenges that evolution poses have not been addressed.

Ecotheology has expanded and shifted, often focusing on social ethics, justice, and stewardship. Excellent work in ecotheology is occurring around the world, promoting whatever supports an integral ecology approach in each ecotheologian's Christian tradition. The papal encyclical *Laudato Si'* is an admirable example of a Catholic approach. Here too, however, the thorny questions around otherworldly salvation are evaded. Still more ecotheologians do not address either the otherworldly, afterlife salvation ideology or evolution in depth.

Salvation is a worthy concept, and one that requires a fresh

---

39. A comparison can be made between how religions interpret each other. From a Christian viewpoint, some emphasize Christian supremacy, or a theology of world religions, or religious pluralism. Religious pluralism, not supremacy, is empirically sound, not ideologically driven.

approach. I agree with Gebara that salvation is about how life is lived here and now. Salvation is about embracing the uncertainty of life with is vulnerability, finitude, and mortality. Salvation involves fundamental concepts of and commitments to a common good, with commensurate ethics and expanded and effective mechanisms of justice within a biospheric view. Such an image of planetary solidarity signifies that we must reassess ourselves beyond ethnic communities and nation states. From bioregional to planetary ecosystems, ecological knowledge is developing and must be embedded in a vision, social imaginary, or world view to orient humanity in this Anthropocene era. Questions about salvation must be dealt with, unless we decide that debating which framework and orientation is inconsequential for responding and adapting to escalating ecological degradation. Of course, thinking through the implications, grappling with choices and decisions, and planning for the consequences are the difficult tasks.

Planetary solidarity has to be more than a global solidarity of human communities, with a perfunctory mention of "the environment." It must be a form of solidarity wherein human communities are intimately intertwined with one another, within larger communities of life, and within the natural systems of the planet. As Edgar Morin suggests in *Homeland Earth*, solidarity means conscious participants in the complex web of a planetary era.[40] This is not an uncritical optimism. It requires a monumental effort.[41] This is salvation. Ivone Gebara writes:

> This salvation, this dreaming toward justice and beauty, is a historical and spiritual process that requires our participation. It is a process that begins again and again in the daily life of each believer. Yet it is much bigger than our individual lives. Our salvation demands both the massive overhaul of institutional structures and the practice of small, daily actions of vision and hope.[42]

Outside of ecotheology, notions of a planetary community and solidarity are increasing with the realization that new visions are needed to respond to ecological dilemmas in a culturally diverse, yet global world and interconnected Earth.[43] Terms such as bio, ecological, or

---

40. Edgar Morin and Anne Brigitte Kern, *Homeland Earth: A Manifesto for the New Millennium* (Cresskill, NJ: Hampton, 1999).
41. This is well described in Sam Mickey, *Whole Earth Thinking and Planetary Coexistence: Ecological Wisdom at the Intersection of Religion, Ecology, and Philosophy* (New York: Routledge, 2015), 55.
42. Ivone Gebara, "Yearning for Beauty: What Do Beauty and Justice Have to Do with Our Salvation? Everything," *The Other Side* 39, no. 4 (July–August 2003): 24.
43. For a discussion of the emergence of planetary thinking, see Heather Eaton, "Global Visions and Common Ground: Biodemocracy, Postmodern Pressures and the Earth Charter," *Zygon* 49, no. 4 (December 2014): 917–37. See also Sam Mickey, *On the Verge of a Planetary Civilization: A Philosophy of*

green democracy; global ecological citizenship; biospheric egalitarianism; ecological-cosmopolitanism; ecological civilization; and planetary society or global consciousness are regularly used. In spite of suspicions of what lurks behind "global," and the tensions between global-local and planetary-contextual issues, many ecological postmodernists realize that a unifying path must be found for a viable planetary future. The Earth Charter is one among many initiatives responsive to postmodern pressures and seeks a global vision and common ground for an emerging world community.[44] There is a growing desire for common ground, an integral vision, and shared principles upon which to build a viable collective future. Here is where the image of planetary solidarity has traction.

Conclusion

Planetary solidarity is crucial for a viable future. However, if we assume that planetary life, or creation, is not as it should be—which is the Christian claim—then we believe we should have a redemption, resurrection, and afterlife. However, I think it is the initial assumption that should be interrogated. It is the height of hubris to judge that "creation as a whole is subject to futility—that is, it does not function in the way originally intended."[45] Who are we to suggest this? Life is fraught with suffering, vulnerabilities, mortality, and finitude. These are the conditions of planetary life: beautiful, terrible, fragile, and vulnerable. Life functions collectively, deeply entangled, in a biosphere. Christian ideology does not accept these conditions. I agree with Gebara that this refusal is the source of much injustice and domination. I would add that these beliefs prevent us from seeing the extraordinariness of life: the delicacy, ingenuity, exquisiteness, creativity, and overwhelming magnificence of planetary life. It is increasingly recognized that we know very little of the deep realities of the Earth and its 4.4 billion year geo-genesis. Reverence and gratitude would be an appropriate spiritual response.

An Earth-centric framing for planetary solidarity is a different pathway of perceiving, interpreting, and living. It could provide an alternative theological framing. It is not straightforward, especially when

Integral Ecology (Lanham, MD: Roman & Littlefield, 2014); Kingsley L. Dennis, "Is There a Coherent Purpose for Planetary Consciousness?," *World Future Review* 7, no. 2/3 (2015): 296–305; Araan Gare, "The Grand Narrative of the Age of Re-Embodiment: Beyond Modernism and Postmodernism," *Cosmos and History* 9, no. 1 (2013): 327–57.

44. Earth Charter Commission, "The Earth Charter," Earth Charter Initiative, 2000, PDF, http://tiny url.com/masgopz.

45. Deane-Drummond, "Shadow Sophia," 27.

considering detailed ethics. However, it is not based on a denial of the fundamental conditions of life. A dedication to reality as encountered rather than a fantasy of another life elsewhere might be a better place from which to develop planetary solidarity.

From a different angle, Christian hubris is stark. A 2013 study using light wavelengths indicated that there are 225 billion galaxies in the observable universe.[46] In 2016, South African's radio telescope, MeerKAT, detected 1,300 galaxies in a tiny corner of universe where only seventy were known, at a quarter of its eventual capacity.[47] The truth is we, as *Homo sapiens*, have almost no clue about the dynamics, dimensions, and boundaries of reality: planetary or cosmic. Some humility in front of this *divine milieu* is vital.

Humans are but one recent evolutionary moment of Earth, maybe even a glorious one, in a drama of 4.5 billion years of planetary activities. And Earth is but one planet, in one solar system, in one galaxy, in a universe with inestimable billions of galaxies, dominated by dark matter and dark energy, within an expanding fabric of space and time, of approximately 13 billion years and counting. Is it conceivable that Christianity has the measure of this universe? Is it credible that Christianity is an accurate reference point of, and can account for, all this reality?

46. Maria Temming, "How Many Galaxies Are There in the Universe?," *Sky and Telescope*, July 18, 2014, http://tinyurl.com/p2tr9hk.
47. "South African Super-Telescope Reveals Distant Galaxies and Black Holes," *The Guardian*, July 16, 2016, http://tinyurl.com/ho6rebg.

Re-Imaging with Laudato Si'

2

———

Imagining and Incarnating an Integral Ecology: A Critical Ecofeminist Public Theology

Rosemary P. Carbine

In his landmark encyclical *Laudato Si'* on the environment, issued in June 2015,[1] Pope Francis portrays our global environmental crises in similar ways to ecofeminist theologies that interconnect the exploitation, degradation, and deterioration of the environment with the subjugation of women.

> Our common home is like a sister with whom we share our life and a beautiful mother who opens her arms to embrace us. . . . This sister now cries out to us because of the harm we have inflicted on her by our irresponsible use and abuse of the goods with which God has endowed her. We have

---

1. Francis, *Laudato Si': On Care for Our Common Home* (Huntington, IN: Our Sunday Visitor, 2015). Cited hereafter in parentheses by paragraphs.

come to see ourselves as her lords and masters, entitled to plunder her at will. . . . The earth herself, burdened and laid waste, is among the most abandoned and maltreated of our poor. (1–2)

From the encyclical's opening paragraphs, Francis implicitly situates ecological and social justice in struggles against patriarchy/kyriarchy or imbalanced power relations among humans and between humans and other-than-human life that arise from and affect other kinds of sociocultural and theological mastery.[2] Sins against the sacramentality of creation as the incarnation of divine love and hope (84–86)—for instance, decreasing biodiversity, increasing climate change, defor-estation, destruction of wetlands, and pollution of water, soil, land, and air by manufacturing, agribusiness, nuclear, and other industries (8, 12, 20, 23–24)—can then be construed as sins of eco-injustice against poor and marginalized peoples, especially indigenous peoples (146) and women. As Francis states, "The human environment and the nat-ural environment deteriorate together. . . . In fact, the deterioration of the environment and of society affects the most vulnerable people on the planet" (48). Here, the pope echoes but does not cite Brazilian lib-eration theologian Leonardo Boff when he contends that "a true eco-logical approach always becomes a social approach; it must integrate questions of justice in debates on the environment, so as to hear both the cry of the earth and the cry of the poor" (49; see also 93).[3] Thus, an integral ecology embodies "an integrated approach to combating poverty, restoring dignity to the excluded, and at the same time pro-tecting nature" (139).

Drawing on ecofeminist theologies and feminist public theologies, this chapter explores recent examples of the Catholic public church with reference to whether its different global and US expressions

---

2. Patriarchy is an analytical concept in feminist critical theory that problematizes sociocultural and political constructions of privileged and marginalized status. Rather than a sex/gender sys-tem of universal male dominance, *patriarchy* refers to multiple interconnections among gender, race, class, culture, sexuality, geopolitical identity, religion, and so on that all justify hierarchical ranked power relations, as well as ultimately idealize an elite, white, male, Western, Christian, heterosexual paradigm of personhood. To better capture this complex, multilayered system of dominance, Elisabeth Schüssler Fiorenza renames patriarchy as kyriarchy (rule of the master or lord), in order to avoid any literal misinterpretation of patriarchy (rule of the father) that falsely prioritizes women's struggles with sexism and with hierarchical gender dualisms. For Schüssler Fiorenza, kyriarchy emphasizes "the multiplicative interstructuring of the pyramidal hierarchi-cal structures of ruling which affect women in different social locations differently." Elisabeth Schüssler Fiorenza, *But She Said: Feminist Practices of Biblical Interpretation* (Boston: Beacon, 1992), 115. Kyriarchy better communicates what feminist theorists and theologians intend by patri-archy—that men and women are relatively advantaged and marginalized in different sociohistori-cal contexts through related and mutually reinforcing interconnections among our social identity markers. Ibid., 123.

3. Leonardo Boff, *Cry of the Earth, Cry of the Poor* (Maryknoll, NY: Orbis, 1997).

enable and energize an integral ecology that attends to and addresses the intersections of ecological, sociopolitical, and gender justice. Rather than framed solely by feminist public theology that focuses on the church's public engagement, this chapter reads different global and US theologies and practices of the Catholic public church—found in Pope Francis's environmental encyclical on the one hand and in US nuns' eco-activism on the other hand—from the perspective of feminist hermeneutics. In the initial three sections, this chapter brings a critical ecofeminist and public theological analysis to bear on recent examples of the Catholic public church and in the concluding section takes a feminist hermeneutical perspective in order to open up new possibilities for understanding different Catholic theological and activist responses to our ecological crises. Extending Elisabeth Schüssler Fiorenza's feminist hermeneutical method to interpret these examples of Catholic eco-public theologies illuminates how and to what degree Catholic practices of public engagement for ecojustice envision and enflesh a more complex notion of the common good[4]—or, in other words, incarnate an integral ecology.

Defining Public Theology

Public theology represents a polyvalent field of Christian thought and practice regarding the mutual interplay between religious and public life, between church and world, between the body of Christ and the body politic. As I have argued elsewhere,[5] public theology refers to the practices that religious actors (for instance, institutional or clerical leaders, religious orders and communities, theologians, laity in parish organizations, activists in social movements, etc.) utilize to address various publics or audiences—namely the church, the academy, and society at large—about contemporary pressing social issues and concerns from religious perspectives in order to influence public discourse and policy en route to creating a more just common life. Based on Catholic conciliar and feminist as well as womanist theologies, public

---

4. Schüssler Fiorenza is regarded as a public intellectual, but her theological categories have yet to be actualized for their feminist theopolitical implications. See Ronald F. Thiemann, "Faith and the Public Intellectual," in *Walk in the Ways of Wisdom: Essays in Honor of Elisabeth Schüssler Fiorenza*, ed. Shelly Matthews, Cynthia Briggs Kittredge, and Melanie Johnson-DeBaufre (Harrisburg, PA: Trinity Press International, 2003), 88–105.

5. This and the next paragraph draw on Rosemary P. Carbine, "Creating Communities of Justice and Peace: Sacramentality and Public Catholicism in the United States," *Journal for the Academic Study of Religion* 29, no. 2 (2016): 182–202; and Rosemary P. Carbine, "Public Theology: A Feminist Anthropological View of Political Subjectivity and Praxis," in *Questioning the Human: Toward a Theological Anthropology for the Twenty-First Century*, edited by Lieven Bove, Yves De Maeseneer, and Ellen Van Stichel (New York: Fordham University Press, 2014), 148–63.

theology can be construed, in my view, in terms of the church's sacramental and eschatological significance in the public sphere, that is, in terms of its ability to signify and create community, to stand as an albeit incomplete and imperfect sign of a not yet fully realized good society. From a feminist vantage point, public theology has less to do with making religious claims more intelligible to a wider society via shared norms and practices of rational public discourse, or introducing faith-based views into current civic debates to reshape public discourse and policy. Rather, public theology employs a rich range of theopolitical community-building praxes that evoke and witness to new possibilities for a more just, loving, and peaceful world, for a more interdependent, interconnected sense of solidarity that seeks justice.

Whether through rhetorical, symbolic, or prophetic practices, public theology aims to critically participate in and transform public life so as to forge solidarity with marginalized groups and thereby better embrace and begin to enhance this life together. Rhetorical practices include a variety of aesthetic genres that give voice to and urge solidarity with marginalized peoples often denied political subjectivity and agency. These practices educate about institutionalized injustices, contest the contours of commonly held constitutive values of US and geopolitical life that feed these injustices, and pave an alternative path for empathy and solidarity.

Symbolic practices reflect on the sociopolitical significance and implications of central religious symbols in order to construct a transcendent normative moral framework of shared rights and responsibilities in public life. Rather than sacralize a theocratic nation-state, justify a certain sociopolitical order, or demand confessional conformity to a Christian theological imaginary, symbolic practices draw on or extend Christianity's organizing symbols, especially God-talk, in order to craft a shared political space of moral discourse and practice about the meaning of *human being* and the mutual obligations of human beings to one another and to the world. In other words, symbolic practices reinterpret a religious symbol system to redirect our sociopolitical moral imaginary toward justice.

Finally, prophetic practices in keeping with scriptural traditions challenge injustices in public life and simultaneously engage in practices that both imagine and perform more just future alternative possibilities. These practices mediate the present and future reality or point the way toward a more just common life by dramatizing injustice and attempting to partly actualize an alternative possibility to that injustice through different forms of collective action. Taken together, rhetorical, symbolic, and prophetic practices of public theology express and embody—discursively, theologically, and politically—different forms of public participation that reach toward a reshaped shared sense of the common good. These practices contribute to a constructive theology of world making or

> envisioning and enacting worlds—that is critiquing and deconstructing oppressive worlds, on the one hand, and noticing, constructing, or creating more liberative alternate worlds, on the other. . . . Theology in this vein involves ways of fusing religion and politics to "remake the world" by criticizing the injustices so present . . . in both our civil and global public life and by actualizing (imagining and partly incarnating) an alternative, more just, and liberative shared common life. . . . World making constitutes one way of doing theology, of negotiating among inherited traditions and crafting out of them innovative ways of being and living in our concrete contexts for more liberative purposes, that is, for more humane worlds of meaning and action.[6]

On my reading, *Laudato Si'* especially exemplifies rhetorical, to a certain degree symbolic, and somewhat prophetic practices of Catholic public theology. The letter is addressed to all people (3) and encourages international political, economic, religious, and scientific dialogue (chapter 5). Moreover, the encyclical outlines a cogent and compelling interpretation of various environmental crises (chapters 1 and 3) and emphasizes the contribution of Christian claims and practices to address those crises (chapter 2). However, as elaborated in the next section below, it offers mixed religiopolitical messages about reimagining religious symbols—especially in the case of God-talk—that in turn only somewhat transform status quo public discourse, politics, and economics in the pursuit of ecojustice. Only some of these symbols prompt a religiopolitical prophetic praxis of ecological virtues and education (chapter 6) that stress civic and political attitudes and actions for enhancing the common good that encompasses human and other-than-human life alike.

Reading *Laudato Si'* from a Critical Ecofeminist and Public Theology Perspective

In *Laudato Si'*, Pope Francis articulates an integral ecology that weaves

---

6. See Laurel C. Schneider and Stephen G. Ray Jr., eds., *Awake to the Moment: An Introduction to Theology* (Louisville: Westminster John Knox, 2016), 108–9; see also ibid., 105–11. For a rich array of practices of world making beyond the rhetorical, symbolic, and prophetic practices outlined in this chapter, see also ibid., 111–73.

together concerns about environmental crises and social justice. Francis calls for an ecological conversion to our common home by interlinking economic and ecological problems, especially but not only with attention to the Global South. For example, he understands the Earth's climate and water as common goods that enable and support the flourishing all life, human and other-than-human, and that require distributive justice of sustainable supplies for the respect of basic human rights that create the "condition for the exercise of other human rights" (23, 28, 30, 95, 156–57). Minoritized communities in the global economy are gravely affected by climate change, as their ecosystems degrade or disappear, causing further disasters such as resource-based conflicts and the refugees from them (25, 48, 57). Also, "water poverty," according to Francis, "especially affects Africa where large sectors of the population have no access to safe drinking water or experience droughts which impede agricultural production" (28). Rapid climate change and increasingly limited as well as unsafe water detract from and damage civil society or our mutual interdependence with and obligations to one another for the common good (25, 42). Indeed, the world itself stands as a common good that encompasses our obligations to the sustainability of present and future generations, thereby prompting the Portuguese bishops to urge not only solidarity with the present-day poor, a kind of intragenerational solidarity, but also intergenerational solidarity (159, 162).

As a rhetorical practice of eco-public theology, *Laudato Si'* relies on worldwide Catholic bishops' statements to effectively locate climate and other environmental crises within global contexts of economic injustice and inequality. African bishops urge universal human and planetary solidarity with respect to aquifers (14, 38). Latin American bishops resist the internationalization of the Amazon's rainforests in order to protect national sovereignty from transnational economic interests but also to preserve forest ecosystems and indigenous economies from the rise in ranching (38). Filipino Catholic bishops lament pollution from deforestation, agriculture, fishing, and other industries that deplete marine and ocean life, particularly coral. These "underwater cemeteries" no longer foster the million species that undergird the economies of world majority peoples (41). Backed up by this chorus of global Catholic bishops, an integral ecology inspires new international relations that recognize the "ecological debt" that the Global North owes the Global South for its disproportionate consumption of and consequent harm to natural resources and local cultures (51, 95, 143–44). Francis's brother Argentine bishops emphasize that this harm occurs primarily through the deregulation of multinational corporations who operate in the Global South but leave in their wake unemployment and unsustainable infrastructure as well as polluted and depleted resources (51).

Continuing to invoke the patriarchal/kyriarchal theological and symbolic framework for ecojustice that opened the encyclical, Francis observes that "these situations have caused sister earth, along with all the abandoned of our world, to cry out, pleading that we take another course" (53). Latin American and Caribbean bishops reiterate this lament by expressing deep concerns about the ways in which powerful Global North economic interests offset and outweigh growing ecological sensibilities (54, 56), at times expressed in world summits on the environment that, in the pope's view, lack political force and efficacy (166–67, 169). Thus, in coalition with the US bishops, Francis recommends "differentiated responsibilities" and practices to restore civil society in an economic and ecological way: limited consumption by developed nations of the Global North (52, 104–5), sovereignty as well as sustainable development in nations of the Global South (172), and robust, legally binding norms and regulations to protect ecosystems and curb the "techno-economic paradigm" or our globalized logic of control and consumption of the world's resources, including peoples and cultures, for immediate interests and infinite profits at the expense of the poor (53, 106, 109, 145, 170, 210).

As a symbolic practice of eco-public theology, Francis highlights salient creation-centered theologies to revive the links between religious convictions and ecological commitments "that everything is interconnected, and that genuine care for our own lives and our relationships with nature is inseparable from fraternity, justice, and faithfulness to others" (70). In particular, he stresses the universal goodness, interrelatedness, and mutual responsibilities of all creation, too often disregarded, disrupted, and distorted by the sins of dominion and anthropocentrism (65–67), which are "manifest in all [their] destructive powers in wars, the various forms of violence and abuse, the abandonment of the most vulnerable, and attacks on nature" (66). As an antidote to these consumerist sins against our created and fundamentally Trinitarian web of relationships with God, one another, and all life (240), Francis reinterprets biblical Sabbath traditions as well as a Christian theology of work to restore these relational balances for the fulfillment of all life (71, 125–28). Encouraging the contemplation of creation's sacramentality or suffusion with divine presence, Brazilian bishops align with Francis's ecological theology of creation by linking the indwelling of the Spirit in all life with the cultivation of ecological ethics (88).

Francis's eco-pneumatology parallels but does not mention Catholic ecofeminist theologian Elizabeth Johnson's theology of the Spirit, which she develops from an innovative combination of evolutionary theory and Christian theology to affirm both scientific evolutionary theory and religious belief in a creator God. For Johnson, the ineffable but active indwelling of the Spirit points to divine love that creates and continues to give life, that stands in compassionate solidarity with all suffering and extinct life, and that empowers and enables all living and dying life toward a future eschatological transfiguration.[7]

> Infinite mystery of self-giving love, the Creator Spirit calls the world into being, gifts it with dynamism, and accompanies it through the by-ways of evolution, all the while attracting it forward toward a multitude of "endless forms most beautiful." We glimpse here bounteous personal love that pours itself out in empowerment of a creation that is transient and vulnerable yet resilient and generative, a creation that without this love would be literally nothing at all. As such unbounded love will do, the Spirit of God unleashes autonomy in the beloved rather than seeking to control the other by any form of power-over, even if benevolently exercised. Sheer overflowing goodness, the Creator respects the freedom and independence of the world such divine bountifulness lets loose, and works through its dynamisms and interlocking evolutionary processes.[8]

In his encyclical, the pope apparently translates this tacit ecofeminist pneumatology into a practice of ecological citizenship and its associated civic and political virtues of loving care, responsibility, and solidarity (210–11, 219–20, 229, 231), out of which a new "shared identity" and "social fabric emerges" (232). For instance, Paraguayan bishops observe that a radically egalitarian sacramentality demands equal dignity and security of all people, both urban elites and rural campesinos alike (94).

Pope Francis proposes Jesus as the theological paradigm for rejecting all sorts of anthropocentric dualisms and domination between heaven/Earth, spirit/matter, soul/body, and leisure/labor (98). Against the christological backdrop of the incarnation, which unifies divinity and humanity and thus reconciles all sorts of false dualisms (100), Francis opposes subject-object relations between human and other-than-human earthly life (11). Objectifying other-than-human life for its instrumental value to human life and needs trades on a flawed Christian anthropology of dominion and mastery (116), thrives on a "throw-

---

7. Elizabeth A. Johnson, *Ask the Beasts: Darwin and the God of Love* (London: Bloomsbury, 2014), 16–17, 143.
8. Ibid., 178–79.

away culture" (22), and negatively stereotypes and impacts marginalized peoples as dominated and disposable (82, 106).

In a similar vein but unstated in the encyclical, ecofeminist theologian Sallie McFague takes the incarnation, or the embodiment of God in Jesus's feeding and healing ministry with poor, oppressed, and other marginalized peoples, as a theological starting point for an evolutionary ecological world view that urges a love of nature in and for itself as well as a universal love of all natural bodies, human and nonhuman alike, as subjects in their own right. McFague analyzes how theological symbols and models of a transcendent, imperial, and judgmental God influence and structure human-nature/subject-object relations. She demythologizes medieval mechanistic and modern consumerist views of nature that objectify, operationalize, and commodify the world's resources to serve and satisfy certain privileged human desires and needs. Rather than a hierarchical, dualist, and instrumentalist view of the triangulated God-human-world relationship in which patriarchy/kyriarchy, capitalism, and Christianity combine to manipulate nature for our own purposes and as a path or vehicle to the divine, McFague's metaphorical God-talk for the world as the body of God reveres nature as a sacramental sign of the divine without collapsing God and the world and consequently treats all bodies as sacramental subjects, rather than objects, within God.[9]

Extending the focus on bodies from the personal to the political to the earthly and ultimately to the cosmic, Brazilian ecofeminist theologian Ivone Gebara, also absent from the encyclical, supports a similar ecological holistic world view, what she calls a biocentric, unitary world view, through God-talk. For Gebara, all life is embraced by, dwells within, and co-constitutes one same Sacred Body of the divine.[10] Within this Sacred Body, relatedness encompasses and characterizes our earthly, human (including sex/gender, ethnic, social/cultural, and sexual), ethical, religious, and even cosmic condition, so much so that "we are all both created within and creators of this relatedness. We are of its substance and it is of our substance. . . . Within that rediscovery we are reborn in God; we are reborn to the Earth, to the cosmos, to history, and to service to one another in the construction of human relationships grounded in justice and mutual respect."[11] Rather than only earthly or ecological citizenship, Gebara underscores cosmic citizen-

9. See Sallie McFague, *Super, Natural Christians: How We Should Love Nature* (Minneapolis: Fortress, 1997), 1–9, 12–16, 20–22, 24–25, 32–39, 164–75.

10. See Ivone Gebara, *Longing for Running Water: Ecofeminism and Liberation* (Minneapolis: Fortress, 2002), 82, 91, 94, 97, 105, 155.

11. Ibid., 103, 151; see also 75, 84–92, 140–41.

ship to overcome all sorts of sexist, racist, and nationalist exclusions as well as other prevalent forms of xenophobia in our world.[12]

For both ecofeminist theologians and Pope Francis, then, treating species, plant, and all *other* life as resources only facilitates and furthers objectification and engenders global patterns of inequality (33, 81–82), leading to environmental racism, modern-day slavery, and sexual exploitation, for example (45–46, 123). By contrast, recognizing the radically incarnational and sacramental subjectivity of all life assigns intrinsic rather than instrumental worth to all life as profoundly inter-related, whether inhabiting social ecologies or natural ecosystems (140).

As a prophetic practice of eco-public theology, *Laudato Si'* identifies the idolatry of current economic models as sins against a creator God as well as against vulnerable peoples and environments (56, 75) but does not grapple sufficiently with how ecological crises most nega-tively affect women, in particular global poor and indigenous women most susceptible to anthropogenic climate change and other eco-injus-tices wrought by the Global North. In other words, this encyclical fails to realize an integral ecology with respect to gender justice for various theological reasons. The encyclical's blind spot to fully elaborating its own eco-public theology emerges most prominently in its lack of prophetic God-talk and praxis. Different models of God emerge within *Laudato Si'* that correlate more or less with the intersections of gender, social, and ecojustice. Pope Francis employs God-talk in the encyclical in ways that both challenge and reinforce patriarchal/kyriarchal sys-tems of imbalanced power relations among humans and between humanity and all creatures to the detriment of women. For example, he foregrounds paternal language for an all-powerful creator God as a theological symbol to reject absolute anthropocentric domination and simultaneously to create common bonds among humans and between humans and other-than-human life (89). However, the relational inter-dependence of all life is guaranteed by a dominating father God "who alone owns the world" (75), which thereby reinscribes and prescribes the very same social, political, economic, and even ecological struc-tures that ironically the encyclical aims to undercut and undo.[13]

By contrast, as Johnson observed, an eco-public theology rooted in a theology of the Spirit resists any patriarchal/kyriarchal model of God: "Neither overriding monarch nor absent deist God, the Spirit of

---

12. Ibid., 158.
13. See Catherine Keller, "Encycling: One Feminist Theological Response," in *For Our Common Home: Process-Relational Responses to* Laudato Si', ed. by John B. Cobb Jr. and Ignacio Castuera (Anoka, MN: Process Century, 2015).

God moves the extravagant divine generosity to create and sustain the conditions that have enabled the biodiverse community of life to become so interesting and beautiful. The unimaginable epochs of time over which this has occurred are themselves a gift of opportunity for nature's emergent freedom to work."[14] Prioritizing Jesus's paternal God-talk in the encyclical (96) not only silences numerous biblical and gospel maternal and other feminized metaphors for the divine but also, and more importantly, replicates patriarchal/kyriarchal theologies of God as monarchical sovereign king and lord of creation as well as their concomitant social, political, economic, and ecological implications. As Catholic ecofeminist theologian Rosemary Radford Ruether demonstrated in her trailblazing feminist theology nearly thirty-five years ago, patriarchal/kyriarchal God-talk with its underlying dualisms functions to legitimate unjust religious, sociopolitical, economic, and ecological structures.

> An ecological-feminist theology of nature must rethink the whole Western theological tradition of the hierarchical chain of being and chain of command. This theology must question the hierarchy of human over non-human nature as a relationship of ontological and moral value. It must challenge the right of the human to treat the nonhuman as private property and material wealth to be exploited. It must unmask the structures of social domination, male over female, owner over worker that mediate this domination over nonhuman nature. Finally, it must question the model of hierarchy that starts with non-material spirit (God) as the source of the chain of being and continues down to nonspiritual "matter" as the bottom of the chain of being and the most inferior, valueless, and dominated point in the chain of command.[15]

In other words, hierarchical gender, race, class, and other dualisms provide the theological symbolic and cultural system that fuels, perpetuates, and reifies hierarchical human-earthly relations. For these reasons, the encyclical's patriarchal/kyriarchal God-talk—even when an absolute dominating father God is characterized as affectionate and compassionate (73, 77, 96, 220, 226)—contradicts and therefore cannot prophetically galvanize an integral ecology founded on the Spirit.

Toward a Feminist Integral Ecology: The Plowshares Movement

In the concluding chapter of *Laudato Si'*, Pope Francis recognizes that

14. Johnson, *Ask the Beasts*, 179.
15. Rosemary Radford Ruther, *Sexism and God-Talk: Toward a Feminist Theology* (Boston: Beacon, 1983), 85.

"Christian spirituality proposes an alternative understanding of the quality of life, and encourages a prophetic and contemplative lifestyle" (222). Indeed, US Catholic women religious engage in prophetic eco-activism that more fully realizes an integral ecology by interlinking sociopolitical justice and ecological solidarity in our increasingly globalized and militarized world. Since the 1970s, US Catholic nuns and laywomen within the Plowshares Movement have charted alternate peaceful paths to the death-dealing convergence of US militarism and nuclearism, the exploitation of land and labor, and religious, sociocultural, and economic oppression, including the feminization not only of poverty but also of ecocide.[16]

The Plowshares Movement confronts and contests primarily nuclear war with nonviolent protest actions.[17] The Plowshares Movement inaugurated its nonviolent direct actions of nuclear inspection and disarmament on September 9, 1980, when the Plowshares Eight walked into General Electric in King of Prussia, Pennsylvania, and poured blood and hammered on nuclear blueprints and missile nose cones to dismantle and disarm such state symbols of violence, death, and war.[18] Since the Plowshares Eight, nearly one hundred Plowshares symbolic disarmament actions have taken place at global nuclear weapons facilities, leading to trials, fines, and lengthy jail sentences for activists.[19]

Women in the Plowshares Movement incisively combined militarism

16. Renewed attention to Plowshares activist nuns through the character Sister Jane Ingalls on the Netflix hit series *Orange Is the New Black* prompted me to revisit and modify my prior work on this movement, found in Rosemary P. Carbine, "Claiming and Imagining: Practices of Public Engagement," in *Prophetic Witness: Catholic Women's Strategies for Reform*, ed. Colleen M. Griffith (New York: Crossroad, 2009), 176–85. See Jamie Manson, "The Nun and the Actress Behind 'Orange Is the New Black,'" *National Catholic Reporter*, June 10, 2015, https://www.ncronline.org/blogs/grace-margins/nun-and-actress-behind-orange-new-black.
17. Major scholarly studies of the Plowshares Movement include Sharon Erickson Nepstad, *Religion and War Resistance in the Plowshares Movement* (New York: Cambridge University Press, 2008); Sharon Erickson Nepstad, "Disciples and Dissenters: Tactical Choice and Consequences in the Plowshares Movement," in *Authority in Contention*, ed. Daniel J. Meyers and Daniel M. Cress (Amsterdam: Elsevier, 2004), 139–59; Jason C. Bivins, *The Fracture of Good Order: Christian Antiliberalism and the Challenge to American Politics* (Chapel Hill: University of North Carolina Press, 2003); Murray Polner and Jim O'Grady, *Disarmed and Dangerous: The Radical Lives and Times of Daniel and Philip Berrigan* (Boulder, CO: Westview, 1998); Patricia F. McNeal, *Harder Than War: Catholic Peacemaking in Twentieth-Century America* (New Brunswick, NJ: Rutgers University Press, 1992); Fred A. Wilcox, *Uncommon Martyrs: The Berrigans, the Catholic Left, and the Plowshares Movement* (Reading, MA: Addison-Wesley, 1991); and Charles A. Meconis, *With Clumsy Grace: The American Catholic Left, 1961–1975* (New York: Seabury, 1979).
18. Philip Berrigan with Fred A. Wilcox, *Fighting the Lamb's War: Skirmishes with the American Empire: The Autobiography of Philip Berrigan* (Monroe, ME: Common Courage, 1996), 183–85, 191.
19. Paul Magno, "The Plowshares Anti-Nuclear Movement at 35: A Next Generation?," *Bulletin of the Atomic Scientists* 72, no. 2 (2016): 85–88; Ardeth Platte and Susan Crane, "Plowshares Movement History 1980–2009," YouTube video, 15:12, posted by "disarmnowplowshares," August 1, 2012, https://www.youtube.com/watch?v=KqzsL-Z2kI4; Arthur J. Laffin, *The Plowshares Disarmament Chronology, 1980–2003* (Marion, SD: Rose Hill, 2003); and Arthur J. Laffin and Anne Montgomery, eds., *Swords into Plowshares: Nonviolent Direct Action for Disarmament* (San Francisco: Harper & Row, 1987).

with patriarchy and global ecological crises, and thus are largely credited with expanding the Plowshares agenda and actions beyond anti-nuclear-war protests. For example, in July 1969, women antiwar activists called the New York 5 staged and led a draft board raid in midtown Manhattan to explicitly link militarism and patriarchy. The New York 5 challenged women's roles in patriarchal militarist societies and in anti-militarist movements. According to their statement, Plowshares leaders reinforced a patriarchal pacifism and an antifeminist patriarchal Catholicism, to the detriment of the movement and its goals.[20] Their pioneering protest slowly shifted the gears in the movement.

More than thirty years later, three Dominican nuns, Carol Gilbert, Jackie Hudson, and Ardeth Platte, broke into one Minuteman III missile silo in Colorado on October 6, 2002, at which reactivated first-strike nuclear missiles laid beneath thousands of miles of ranch and farmland.[21] Dressed in white hazmat suits labeled "Disarmament Specialist" and "Citizen Weapons Inspections Team," the nuns exercised their Dominican charism as a religious order of preachers and intended, according to Gilbert, to expose and symbolically disarm this weapon of mass destruction. They cut through two sets of gates, poured their own blood from baby bottles in the shape of crosses on and around the silo entrance, and hammered on the silo's 110-ton concrete lid. Then, they performed a liturgy of prayers for peace and awaited arrest. They called their symbolic disarmament action Sacred Earth and Space Plowshares to show, according to Gilbert, that nuclear weapons kill not only people "but also Mother Earth herself, the species, the trees, anything living." Moreover, as Platte observed, "we are all part of a loving nonviolent circle, the family of God. . . . We are one, one body, one blood, and . . . we must learn how to live on Planet Earth together." As indicated by this action, Plowshares activists break into military facilities, hammer on and pour their own blood on nuclear weapons, and risk jail along with fines (between 2.5 and 3.5 years for the nuns along with over $3,000 in fines for injury to and obstruction of national defense[22]) to expose the all-too-often invisible immorality and illegality of nuclear war and to witness to an alternative political reality—to

20. See Marian Mollin, "Communities of Resistance: Women and the Catholic Left of the Late 1960s," *Oral History Review* 31, no. 2 (2004): 29–51, esp. 40–51; and Marian Mollin, *Radical Pacifism in Modern America: Egalitarianism and Protest* (Philadelphia: University of Pennsylvania Press, 2006).
21. *Conviction: A Documentary Film*, directed by Brenda Truelson Fox (Boulder, CO: Zero to Sixty Productions, 2006), DVD, 43 min.
22. In May 2015, an appellate court overturned the conviction of Sister Megan Rice and two other activists similarly charged with sabotage for performing a Plowshares action at the Y-12 National Security Complex in Oak Ridge, Tennessee. See William J. Broad, "Sister Megan Rice, Freed from Prison, Looks Ahead to More Anti-Nuclear Activism," *The New York Times*, May 26, 2015, https://

the always in-breaking but not yet fully instantiated world without war.

Plowshares activists and actions founded on these theological underpinnings constitute a form of community building, of world making. They seek to upend a patriarchal, militarist sociopolitical order and, at the same time, to create an alternative community to it. Jonah House, a nonviolent resistance and pacifist community started in Baltimore in 1973, signifies such an alternative community.[23] Community building in the Plowshares Movement takes place at Jonah House because it provides material, affective, and spiritual support for Plowshares activists, both in and out of jail.[24]

During their trials, which charge them with damaging federal property with intent to injure and obstruct the national defense, Plowshares activists relied on rhetorical practices, such as courtroom testimony, to interrupt a prevailing irrational civic discourse about war[25] and to reassert and reclaim religiopolitical resistance actions as a legitimate form of political participation.[26] Plowshares activists incorporated a broad range of defenses for their disarmament actions, relying on historical, legal, and religious defenses. On historical grounds, the Catonsville Nine, for example, situated nonviolent direct action within a longstanding US democratic tradition of gaining public voice through protest politics.[27]

www.nytimes.com/2015/05/27/science/sister-megan-rice-anti-nuclear-weapons-activist-freed-from-prison.html.

23. See Berrigan, *Fighting the Lamb's War*, 166–68, 170–72, 175.
24. Ibid., 166–67, 219. See also Sharon Erickson Nepstad, "Persistent Resistance: Commitment and Community in the Plowshares Movement," *Social Problems* 51, no. 1 (2004): 43–60, esp. 50–59; and Bivins, *Fracture of Good Order*, 128–39, 145–51.
25. Berrigan rejected the role of a priest in perpetuating such irrational public discourse: "As a priest, I stood square in the middle of the power pyramid. . . . My job was to interpret the capitalist, expansionist, war-driven paradigm of America's military-industrial complex, making it appear rational, when in fact it is destructively irrational." Berrigan, *Fighting the Lamb's War*, 36.
26. Bivins, *Fracture of Good Order*, 139–45.
27.   Yes, I came
        to the conclusion
        that I was in direct line
        with American democratic tradition
        in choosing civil disobedience.

        . . .
        There have been times in our history
        when in order to get redress
        in order to get a voice *vox populi*
        arising from the roots
        people have so acted.
        From the Boston Tea Party.

        . . .
        through the civil rights movement
        we have a rich tradition
        of civil disobedience. (Berrigan, *Fighting the Lamb's War*, 106, see also 85)

Drawing on this range of defenses, Plowshares activists repeatedly confront and resist the law of the state, which authorizes and legitimates violence, with the law of Christ, which promotes nonviolence, love, and justice.[30] Courtroom testimony affords Plowshares activists a rhetorical practice to give voice to global suffering as well as to critically engage in and reshape US public discourse about war. After 9/11, the nuns involved in Sacred Earth and Space Plowshares intended to check the US government's warrior nation mentality and its threats to use first-strike nuclear weapons against Iraq or other Axis of Evil nations. The trial judge disregarded or placed extensive gag rules on such defenses in the nuns' trial, effectively eliminating thirty categories of testimony derived from appeals to God, religion, morality/ethics, political policy and wisdom regarding the MinuteMan III missile system, international treaties and laws pertaining to nuclear nonproliferation since 1968, war crimes, UN charters, the Geneva Convention, and so on. Despite the judge's limits on the nuns' defenses, Platte affirms that they were led by the Spirit of God to this work to make a better world for future generations, which Hudson considers a call to be the people of God, to do service for the world, a service that Gilbert understands as fidelity to the gospel of nonviolence and to intergenerational solidarity. Even limited testimony enables Plowshares activists to educate about the atrocities of war and their faith-based reasons for participating in antiwar actions, thereby creating and enacting, even if briefly, a counter-rhetoric and counter-public to militarism, poverty, and ecocide.

Religious symbols add an explicitly theological dimension to Plowshares practices of public engagement. Plowshares activists turn to symbolic practices to provide a theological basis for their nonviolent direct active interference with the US military industrial complex. A Plowshares theology of political activism rests on reinterpreting major Christian symbols, especially hammers and blood. These activists take their religious directive to disarm and destroy weapons of war-making from the prophet Isaiah 2:4 "to beat their swords into plowshares, and their spears into pruning hooks; nation shall not lift up sword against nation, neither shall they learn war anymore."[31] Blood signifies the

---

On legal grounds, Plowshares activists argued a necessity defense, which elaborates the responsibilities of citizens to prevent imminent harm to human life.[28] On religious grounds, the Griffiss Plowshares labeled nuclearism (nuclear weapons and their associated military and other structures) an established civil religion, which not only bordered on idolatry but also infringed upon the constitutional disestablishment as well as free exercise of religion.[29]

28. Ibid., 187.
29. Ibid., 193–95; Philip Berrigan and Elizabeth McAlister, *The Time's Discipline: The Beatitudes and Nuclear Resistance* (Baltimore: Fortkamp, 1989), 133.
30. Berrigan, *Fighting the Lamb's War*, 201–2.

death-dealing purposes of the weapons as well as a sharp contrast between militarist societies and the new society, the new family of God initiated in the life-ministry, death, and resurrection of Jesus as well as remembered and reconstituted through Eucharist celebrations. Through blood, Sacred Earth and Space Plowshares underscores that militarism means the end of all human and earthly life. Pushing blood symbolism beyond solely antiwar protest, beyond resistance to nuclear war and its impending ecological disaster, the nuns also use blood to resignify the missile silo and the surrounding farmland as a site for sustaining rather than annihilating full earthly flourishing. As Hudson claims, "our interconnectedness with all of creation means that our every thought, word, and action determines the direction of the universe." Sacred Earth and Space Plowshares thus enabled an imitation of Christ and emulated the purpose of Jesus's life and ministry: to establish a more interdependent, interconnected sense of community with all of life.

The Plowshares Movement pivots around nonviolent direct actions of civil disobedience that reflect the twofold dynamic of public theology's prophetic practices: to denounce an oppressive war-making state on the one hand, and announce and prefigure an alternative possibility to it on the other hand.[32] Nonviolent direct action performs both "divine disobedience" to a militarist state and divine obedience to a gospel of life, epitomized in the resurrection of Jesus, that provides "a vision of life by which to interpret and to confront the works of death."[33] Nonviolent direct action thereby provides a major "means for making this vision real" and for "recreat[ing] the political order."[34] In other words, Plowshares protest actions together with the activists' subsequent prison terms embody prophetic practices because they evoke and engender an alternative possibility for our common life, that is, a more just counter-public to a militarist society. Indeed, jail should be considered among the repertoire of Plowshares prophetic practices to subvert a war-making society. While prison is designed to undermine community through alienation and isolation, Plowshares activists tried to create community through jail.[35] Moreover, Plowshares activists often interpret jail as prophetic witness to a different

---

31. On the sociopolitical and historical context and interpretations of Isaiah, see Daniel Berrigan, *Testimony: The Word Made Fresh* (Maryknoll, NY: Orbis, 2004), 3–22.
32. Sharon Erickson Nepstad, "Disruptive Action and the Prophetic Tradition: War Resistance in the Plowshares Movement," *U.S. Catholic Historian* 27, no. 2 (2009): 97–113.
33. Berrigan, *Fighting the Lamb's War*, 175, 188, quote at 180.
34. Ibid., 211.
35. Ibid., 164–67; see also Nepstad, "Persistent Resistance," 49.

world, based on biblical and theological themes of the desert and wilderness as sites of profound marginality and also social change.[36]

Reinterpretation of Christian symbols informed and influenced Plowshares prophetic practices in that the movement relied on religious symbols to criticize the predominant sociopolitical order as well as to propel collective action that imagined and attempted to actualize a more just, more peaceful this-worldly order. Plowshares protest actions imitate a nonviolent revolutionary Christ, a Christ who used subversive public acts (such as living among the outcast and oppressed, overturning the money changers' tables, dying a criminal's death on the cross) to confound and confront all forms of social, religious, and imperial domination.[37] For example, the Good Friday Plowshares of Holy Week 1995 in Washington, DC,[38] politically dramatized Christ's last days during Holy Thursday, Good Friday, and Holy Saturday, pouring blood at the World Bank and Pentagon as well as staging die-ins at the White House to symbolically oppose the sanctions then imposed on Iraq, all of which resignified how Christ defied Roman imperialism, colonialism, and militarism with nonviolence.

To envision and enflesh a counter-public to a militarist society that is bent on sustaining rather than destroying life, Plowshares activists draw on theological symbols from Christian eschatology to articulate in theological terms an alternative pacifist vision of the good society that rests on love, justice, equality, and peace, or the "kin-dom" of God.[39] Lacking its original imperialist meanings, the kin-dom of God, much like the theological image of the body of Christ (1 Corinthians 12) invoked by the nuns, underscores the interrelation and interdependence of all life in the reality of God. Plowshares actions get and give us a this-worldly glimpse of this good society in their actions, trials, and jail time, so that the kin-dom of God might become an intrahistorical reality—especially with regard to women and to the Earth.

This analysis of Plowshares actions has held these practices of public theology in creative and dynamic tension—without reifying or drawing sharp distinctions among them—to demonstrate multiple ways in which religious resources propel participation in and transformation of US public life. Plowshares activists testified, using their symbolic as well as prophetic protest politics to educate in their words, symbols, and actions about US imperial militarism and an alternative life-giving

36. Berrigan, *Fighting the Lamb's War*, 96–97, 225–26. See also Rosalie G. Riegle, ed., *Doing Time for Peace: Resistance, Family, and Community* (Nashville: Vanderbilt University Press, 2012).
37. Berrigan, *Fighting the Lamb's War*, 98, 109, 169.
38. Ibid., 204–5.
39. Ibid., 96, 209–11.

sociopolitical order to it. They articulated and attempted to live out a Christian symbol of the good society, the kin-dom of God. By seeking to realize the kin-dom of God, they did not coerce conformity to Christianity and thereby eschew religious pluralism. Rather, they rethought central Christian symbols for their political meanings, in order to prophetically reconfigure and remake a more just, more emancipatory body politic, which includes honoring all the bodies of Mother Earth.

Insights from Feminist Hermeneutics

This chapter has aimed to explicate the strengths and shortcomings of global and US Catholic eco-public theologies from a feminist perspective. In conclusion, then, a critical feminist hermeneutics will particularly help summarize and spotlight some of the most significant religiopolitical benefits and limits of these theologies.

According to Elisabeth Schüssler Fiorenza, feminist hermeneutics involves (1) the criticism of Christian texts and communities that were generated in and that still continue to justify as well as prescribe a patriarchal/kyriarchal religious and political order, as well as (2) the reconstruction of Christian texts and communities to better account for and empower women's significant contributions to Christian history and theology, both past and present.[40] Feminist hermeneutics consists of several steps,[41] which admit and affirm multiple voices, encourage egalitarian debate about alternate views, and foster solidarity among women's religiopolitical struggles. Schüssler Fiorenza enumerates the rhetorical practices of feminist hermeneutics as rhetorics of liberation (demystifying patriarchy/kyriarchy), of differences (affirming multiple voices/perspectives), of equality (egalitarian process), and of vision (investigating religious resources that support such equality).[42] Diverse voices engaged in more inclusive and participatory interpretive debate both challenge a prevailing status quo that opposes such diversity and debate *and* enable the reshaping of religiopolitical norms and practices for the purpose of achieving solidarity toward liberation. Seeking more than simply adding marginalized women's

---

40. This paragraph traces some core contours of feminist biblical hermeneutics, outlined in Rosemary P. Carbine, "Ekklesial Work: Toward a Feminist Public Theology," *Harvard Theological Review* 99, no. 4 (2006): 433–55, esp. 445–53.

41. Schüssler Fiorenza, *But She Said*, 52–76.

42. Ibid., 131–32. In later works, a rhetoric of liberation is redefined as *conscientization*, a term drawn from Brazilian educator Paulo Freire that means raising awareness regarding oppression, in this case about political and religious forms of patriarchy/kyriarchy. Schüssler Fiorenza continues to explore feminist strategies of biblical interpretation as a primary means to sharpen such awareness alongside other rhetorical practices in *Wisdom Ways: Introducing Feminist Biblical Interpretation* (Maryknoll, NY: Orbis, 2001), 93–98, 151–61.

voices into existing hermeneutical methods, and by implication into Christian texts and communities, feminist hermeneutics carves out a rhetorical counter-public with this set of distinctive practices, so that different religious and political realities enshrined in historical and contemporary Christian texts and communities might be reimagined, re-debated, and ever transformed in a critical and constructive effort to build community among women's and men's struggles for broader religiopolitical and social change. Feminist hermeneutics thus inspires and inculcates a rich array of virtues, such as imagination, empowerment, transformation, and hope, which contribute to recreating and sustaining more participatory, egalitarian, and just communities.[43]

On my reading, the Vatican's most recent venture into global eco-public theology through the encyclical *Laudato Si'* does not fulfill the twofold purpose of feminist hermeneutics—namely, to criticize Christian traditions that continue to prescribe patriarchy/kyriarchy and to constructively engage with Christian traditions so as to foreground and foster women's innovative and salient contributions. Pope Francis's God-talk as an absolute dominating father retains a patriarchal/kyriarchal theology of power, which consequently creates a theological lacuna that leads him to tackle gender justice insufficiently as well as contradicts the promising eco-pneumatology that enlivens the encyclical's integral ecology. Moreover, Francis's ecological theology of the Spirit completely disregards and therefore invisibilizes longtime salutary feminist theological work in this field; indeed, this chapter reincorporated the ecofeminist theologies of Rosemary Radford Ruether, Sallie McFague, Ivone Gebara, and Elizabeth Johnson into this papal example of global Catholic eco-public theology to better actualize the encyclical's own proposals. Based on the fourfold rhetorical practices of feminist hermeneutics, then, the encyclical converses with and gives equal priority (a rhetoric of equality) to multiple different voices (a rhetoric of differences) from the Global South especially to chronicle our current environmental crises as well as offer concrete religiopolitical strategies and ethics to alleviate them. However, as demonstrated above, the encyclical's weak rhetoric of vision and therefore of liberation do not adequately critique and reconstruct religious resources

43. Schüssler Fiorenza, *Wisdom Ways*, 179. Feminist theologians at times criticize Christian hope as repressive and as a denial of human finitude. An otherworldly hope in an absolute future (i.e., in an afterlife) can postpone a pragmatic hope about actually changing our real historical future. Moreover, hope in an ultimate afterlife, modeled on the personal death and resurrection of Jesus, may downplay our very earthly lives and obscure the responsibilities and obligations that we owe one another and the Earth. See Margaret Farley, "Feminism and Hope," in *Full of Hope: Critical Social Perspectives on Theology*, ed. Magdala Thompson (New York: Paulist Press, 2003), 20–40, esp. 25–27. For more recent constructive theologies of hope, see Richard Lennan and Nancy Pineda-Madrid, *Hope: Promise, Possibility, and Fulfillment* (New York: Paulist Press, 2013).

within Christian traditions to illuminate and challenge the ways in which patriarchy/kyriarchy functions as the taproot of our world's ecological conundrums.

By contrast, some Catholic activist laywomen and, more recently, nuns within the Plowshares movement articulate and act on a US-based eco-public theology that strives in good feminist hermeneutical fashion to sever the links between religion, militarism, and patriarchal/kyriarchal power on the one hand, and in doing so highlight women's groundbreaking Christian theological praxis in Catholic pacifist traditions on the other hand. Again, adhering to the fourfold rhetorical practices of feminist hermeneutics, Plowshares activist nuns use prophetic nonviolent direct action, courtroom testimony, and serving jail time to ensure that multiple different voices are heard (a rhetoric of differences), including the voices of children, of future generations, of different earthly creatures, and even of the Earth itself, in ongoing religiopolitical debates about waging the war on terror. These activists struggle for an equal voice (a rhetoric of equality) amid the din of the US military-industrial complex, which also controls and limits their courtroom testimony, ensuring an American exceptionalism to humanitarian and environmental national and international laws and treaties.[44] Moreover, their struggles against American imperialism and militarism reaching new heights under the populist US presidency of Donald Trump are bolstered by a critical and creative reinterpretation and reconstruction (a rhetoric of vision) of Christian theological claims, symbols, and practices that only catch a glimpse of a rhetoric of liberation, of the ever-present, ever-coming kin-dom of God.

44. Nadja Popovich and Tatiana Schlossberg, "Twenty-Three Environmental Rules Rolled Back in Trump's First 100 Days," *The New York Times*, May 2, 2017, https://www.nytimes.com/interactive/2017/05/02/climate/environmental-rules-reversed-trump-100-days.html.

3

Women's Suffering, Climate Injustice, God, and Pope Francis's Theology: Some Insights from Brazil

Ivone Gebara

The Earth groans in a plurality of pains.[1] Sufferings of many types are expressed without our being able to understand them in their entirety or to relieve them as we would like. As humans, we are conscious of sorrows and pain, as well as joys and happiness. All that is good and bad is interconnected, touching our human condition and shaping our perceptions of the world. We are the ones who suffer it in our flesh, feeling the pain of others and the suffering of the planet. In my book *Out of the Depths: Women's Experience of Evil and Salvation*, I tried to elucidate the problem of evil and the suffering experienced by women.[2] I stepped

1. Translation from the Portuguese by Wanda Deifelt, Professor of Religion, Luther College, Decorah, Iowa.
2. Ivone Gebara, *Out of the Depths: Women's Experience of Evil and Salvation* (Minneapolis: Fortress, 2002).

away from the general, often abstract debate and attempted to engage the sufferings and evils that stem from ownership, power, worth, skin color, and gender, as experienced in women's everyday lives. I tried to show how everyday life can reveal aspects of evil that somehow are not included in the theories enunciated by philosophy and religions. There, I opened paths for a feminist phenomenology of evil based on the narratives of women's experiences stemming from different situations and different cultures. I wanted to show aspects of the complexity of evil not only in its ontological aspect but in its many existential manifestations. In this text, I want to broaden this problem to include other current perspectives. Climate change, God, and Pope Francis's theology are some of the themes from which my reflection on the suffering of women will draw, and from this I draw new outlines and invite collective action in view of the common good.

Climate Injustice and Women's Suffering

What do we mean by *climate injustice*? Of course, we are not thinking that the climate of the planet commits injustices against us, as if climate were an entity or its actions a punishment from the gods. No doubt ancient myths and the deification or demonization of the forces of nature have had an important role in different cultures. We used to believe that strong winds and storms were manifestations of divine wrath against our sins. Today, however, our references and interpretations are different. Climate injustice is, first of all, an expression that indicates that nefarious changes are inflicted upon different ecosystems and, therefore, upon all living beings. These changes, however, which cause much loss of life and vital energy, are largely the result of a human lack of responsibility toward humanity itself and the ecosystems of the planet. In other words, human behavior in terms of our survival, production of goods, accumulation of wealth, and production of new technologies has, to some degree, changed the climate of our planet, causing drastic consequences to life as a whole. I say to some degree because ecosystems are living and changing realities in their own rights. In this sense, we do not have absolute control over their manifestations and vitality.

Since the second half of last century, the connection between all forms of life on our planet has been revealed to us in profound, impressive, and also disastrous manners. We found out that, just as the climate changes us and makes us culturally different, our decisions regarding the exploitation of the Earth directly influence the climate. In simple terms, if a forest is devastated, we have less water to drink. If we divert the course of a river, local agriculture will no longer be the same. Or, if we make small streams disappear and pave over their location to make for a large avenue, we will gradually feel the effects of our intervention. If we destroy bees, there is no flower pollination. If we produce chemicals and do not worry about the installation of filters in the industries, we cause lung disease in many people. If we throw toxic waste in rivers and oceans, they are rendered lifeless. There are many examples, and this list grows every day.

It is in this sense that the expression *climate injustice* relates to unjust human actions that gradually undermine the balance of our common home and makes us fear for the future of life on our planet. Climate injustice is an expression of the social, political, and economic injustice that we commit against each other. It is the result of our unawareness and ignorance, of our greed and selfishness. There are short and long-term consequences for our intervention in the natural world, and these can translate into suffering affecting multiple groups. This suffering is presented in different ways, depending on how geographic location, social and gender identities, ethnicity, and class make us more or less victims of the impact that greed has had on the environment.

It is along this line of thought that I address particular expressions of suffering as the most vulnerable groups of women are affected by the harmful consequences of current global climate change.

To speak of climate injustice from the perspective of the suffering of women is to highlight a different aspect of the specificity of women's suffering. It demonstrates how certain human groups, in particular women, live in precarious political and other vulnerable situations in different parts of the world. This politics of precariousness and vulnerability is the public reflection of the lesser value of one group vis-à-vis another. In this sense, the social value of female bodies, the care for their needs, and the public expression of their power is less than that of male bodies. And, by speaking of male bodies and female bodies, I already find myself in an increasingly complex and ambiguous terrain considering that, more than in the past, I am invited to leave behind a solely biological concept of bodies. I get closer to the multiple bodily identities that go beyond male and female categorization. It is not enough to only affirm the diversity of persons and groups in theoretical or superficial ways. We must go further and get in touch with the differences in our personal constitution despite the many biological similarities. Undoubtedly, biology builds similarities between us, but differences are what mark our way of being in the world, how we feel, think, and experience our emotions, feelings, and mutual attractions. Difference frames references and plural understandings of life.

But difference also creates many difficulties, particularly on the need to legislate how many groups coexist. There is always a temptation to ignore those groups and people who seem to disrupt national identity or cultural and religious purity.

Who establishes the hierarchy or equality of sexualities and differences? Who determines their roles? Who legislates over their rights and duties? From what criteria does science or theology try to organize them and judge them? What reasons do these institutions find to assert authority over them?

Not all suffering experienced by women is related to economic and social conditionings or patriarchal devaluation of female bodies, although we cannot escape these realities. We are confronted by a complex reality that unfolds before our eyes, a reality of unspoken and often unimagined suffering. We are faced with new situations of war, forced emigration, abandonment, social poverty, and cultural dependence that change the thought patterns and theories we had. We are faced with the complexity of human lives and, in particular in this reflection, with the complexity of the suffering of women's lives.

What is a woman's life? What characterizes it? What are the greatest pains affecting it nowadays? There are multiple variables necessary to outline answers to these questions, and from them, we cannot avoid the thorny issue of subjectivity. To speak of subjectivity in the specific case of women's suffering means to accept the fact that, faced with similar situations, the reaction to and the reach of an open wound are different. They are different because each person reacts according to the interior orders of their personality and the exterior orders in which they were educated. For example, a case of domestic violence can find reactions ranging from silence regarding the identity of the perpetrator to the delivery of that same information to the police or the public exposure of the violence suffered. The reactions to a lack of drinking water can vary from almost accepting this situation as God's will to organizing toward the construction of wells in a neighborhood or a rural area. The reactions to exposure to pesticides can range from acritical acceptance to the refusal to consume any food containing pesticides. Many examples could appear in this context. The important thing seems to be the realization that, given the diversity of people's situations, there is no common reaction to the violence they experience. Regarding the effects of climate injustice, we should bear in mind not only the ongoing domestic role of women and the struggle that ensues when facing problems such as water, air pollution, and food for the family, but also broader political variables. In general, decisions regarding the destruction of a forest, the diversion of a river, or the production of war weapons fall on male shoulders. It is male power that makes decisions and appears as a sovereign authority. Most often, women are forced to consent, ignoring the consequences of those actions.

There is no doubt that the social division of labor, of power, and therefore of the great social and political decisions are shaped by gender inequality. Male interests in general focus on decisions with little or no concern for the survival needs of families. The short and long term effect of these decisions is a burden on women's lives. It suffices to remember that women are the ones who have to worry about the basic hygiene of children and sick family members and to ensure the cleanliness of homes. In making this statement, I am already getting into the social class perspective that is the focus of my attention and concern: the poor women who actually carry out these activities. I am not referring directly to those women who have their material livelihoods guaranteed and, therefore, are not subjected to the difficulties of the daily search for survival, as others are. My main concern is with the majority of the female population that is vulnerable due to the difficulties of survival and the denial of their rights. In addition, my statements also bring in the women from black, indigenous, and minority groups, whose presence is often forgotten because they are considered "lesser than" white women. Hierarchies persist—including hierarchy among women—and they invite us to review values and concepts critically. The helplessness of many women is enormous. Who will extend them a hand as they seek protection, emancipation, and quality of life? Where will they summon strength to get out of the system of domination and silence that characterizes their lives?

The Male God and His Anti-Environmentalist and Antifeminist Stance

In this context of struggles experienced primarily by women, there is a character who although considered "pure spirit" appears in the history of women coated with a male symbolic identity. It is "him" that many women address and call, waiting, perhaps, for an expected or unexpected miracle to happen.

Deep down, and with few exceptions, most Christian women, poor and rich, continue to imagine God as a male authority that helps and protects them. In most cases, it is a projection contrary to the reality that they experience with the men around them. They receive and project an image of God that sustains them and understands their difficulties without realizing that often the key problem lies in everyday relationships, in the materiality of everyday life. Something close to a contradiction is outlined in this experience. If, on the one hand, their wishes for life improvement are organized around their female needs, on the other hand, culture leads them to believe in an entity capable of supporting and helping them but whose historical image is male. Culture is ingrained in our projections, and trying to go beyond it is a path that few have forged.

In a similar vein, we cannot forget that the vast majority of the representatives of God and Jesus Christ are male and therefore project—albeit with varying nuances—male behavior toward women. In other words, a male image is transformed into an image of a good and just God and becomes a regulator of women's wishes and initiatives. The God of religious and social officialdom continues to command and demand compliance, with obligations sometimes maladjusted to the current reality. In general, this God confirms the might of those who dominate the Earth with their exacerbated will-to-power and their portrayal that God is the same for everybody. However, while he gives an abundance of goods for some, he leaves a shortage for others. This disparity of gifts is explained as a divine mystery to which we have no access. It hides many things—above all, reasons that are beyond our understanding. We have to submit to the power of a superior force that organizes and commands the world and our lives. Those who live in abundance are asked to share what they have, and this is usually done through donations, which end up providing the giver with a good conscience, besides the obvious tax break when such gifts are more significant. Those who are impoverished are expected to have an increasing gratitude for the crumbs that fall from the table of the rich. They are supposed to always be grateful for what they receive because, deep down, misery itself indicates that they are less valuable than others, and gratitude seems to be a virtue that belongs to them more than it does to others. This is not a matter of rights but instead of favors (handouts), as if having rights was the privilege of others or those who already have power. There is a rather perverse religious logic that we have created for ourselves to justify poor distribution of goods, unjust social division of labor, unfair wages, and lack of rights to land, country, or a decent place to live, as well as other situations that cover the intricacies of established power. And God "the Father" presides over this social game, the ecological destruction and the helplessness of many in light of society's daily assaults against each other. Therefore, it is not enough to say that God does not want injustice when those announcing this ethic are the first ones to miss out on justice for women and those who are different in their flock.

We are astonished by the naturalization of violence in human relations, the segregation of people with no right to a dignified life, as well as the physical, spatial, health care, educational, and environment segregation, considering that the democratic discourse appears as the first agenda in the assertion of our rights both in political society and in the churches.

However, doubts plague my observations and make me realize a huge gap between the language used and the lived experience, between what is said because it was learned and what is believed that it should be, and between what is lived in the intimacy and the exteriority of life. The intimacy of life reveals itself as the place where violence lives in a privileged way, the violence that is done and the violence that is suffered, the violence that is externalized and that comes out of ourselves. Anger against oneself for living in shortage. Anger toward the poor for showing me what I do not want to see and revealing the hidden and perhaps cruel face of myself. The poor who disturb my privileges and make me flee their presence and, if possible, even deny it. Then there is guilt. Guilt for not getting the expected success and guilt for enjoying what has been achieved. Each person lives the limits of their situation in their own way.

We create contrivances to endure plural and often contradictory situations. Multiple emotions intersect in our being and frequently allow alienation and lies to win over the dose of truth that also lives within us. Truth would first and foremost be the ability to recognize ourselves as not being what we say we are and being capable of lying about what we are. The lies or deceptions about ourselves and others affect our bodies and minds and alienate us from ourselves. This process of alienation applies to all of us—white, indigenous, black, women and men, young and old—as we live our different identities and cultures.

These lies, more than the tricks we resort to in our social lives, are a cloak to show what I am not. It is to be blind to oneself and pretend to be what one is not. It means a voluntary, involuntary, psychological, emotional, cultural, and social cover-up that has different expressions and intensities. Gender lies to gender, class lies to class, and ethnic groups lie to ethnic groups.

That is why speeches on the need for goodness and just relationships tend not to work: because they are also surrounded by obscure relations. They enclose a personal and social order based on principles that claim to be normative because they proceed from God or nature or science. But they forget to disclose that we are the ones making these claims because we are all trying to control and seize lives. There is a circuit of actions, reactions, and emotions in the process of wanting to save one's own skin while condemning others. The instrument is always a lie, a cover-up, or the fear of appearing as we are. We lie about not having an overseas bank account, about appropriation of public funds, and that we are seriously ill so someone will pity us and support us at least temporarily. We accuse others of being corrupt and liars, of being idolatrous, sinful, impure, abnormal, and marginal.

No doubt the proportion and scope of lies are different and might not allow any quantitative or qualitative comparison. But the fact is that we cover up to seem good, just, and in solidarity with the poor, abandoned, dependent, and needy. We hide passions and emotions. We hide power and might. We deny the existence of lust inscribed in the majority of our actions.

What I am saying does not refer to the denial of an actual situation of need and injustice. I am just trying to identify what in us causes this collective lie and dares not show its face. What I seek, perhaps, is to report the astonishing threshold established in all our relationships, in our commitment, and even in our beliefs. Once again, I call this threshold a lie in the absence of a softer and perhaps more appropriate word. Could this be the search for truth? But what truth? Is truth the opposite of lies? Does it have a place in the broader public relations? What is really *the truth*, that value the gospels say will set us free?

With these reflections, would I not be conducting an analysis similar to the wrath of medieval preachers, who considered the human race as already precondemned or in mortal sin since its inception? Would I not be focusing on the negativity of lies instead of the mixture of bodies and the beautiful diversity of corporeality? Would I be wanting to purify feelings, emotions, and behaviors so that something different could emerge and finally bring about my desires and fantasies of just relationships? Why would they be just and why would they bring the share of happiness that all, including myself, could enjoy? Would this be purism or a new moral idealism?

I navigate through murky waters amid much material and immaterial pollution. I grasp the social and personal organization and disorganization as if we no longer had clarity about our ways, and our beliefs no longer gave account of the madness in which we find ourselves.

Would there be alternatives for us, solutions that could lead us to more brotherly and sisterly processes? After all, what do we want? As an intellectual eager to improve human relations, what am I proposing or looking for? With whom do I join efforts along this path? Beyond global words like social and environmental justice, beyond universal brotherhood and sisterhood, and beyond universal love—how can we rearticulate paths in the midst of the complex entanglement of voices and preachers disguised in sheep's clothing?

How do we find beauty and good in this violent contingency that turns into new contingencies and that seems impossible to escape? Even God seems to turn into a contingency within the multiplicity of our contingencies. Is it really so?

I do not preach and do not want to be pessimistic. I only note the murky waters in which we swim, the tide, the mud that destroys the green and kills so many lives. But, with many other people, I am still able to sing softly, "tomorrow is another day."

The Theology of Pope Francis

What does Pope Francis say about the unstable situation in the world today? No doubt those who hear his speeches, read his texts, and are interested in his actions have multiple and varied interpretations of his pontificate. My own are undoubtedly limited to my own perceptions and convictions.

I think there is an undeniable value in Pope Francis's positive attempt to reflect on the great challenges of today's world and especially the issue of global warming and its related problems. It draws our attention to joint social responsibility, so that we may feel like participants in the mission of caring for the planet. Since its beginning, the encyclical *Laudato Si'* reminds us that we are earth (Gen 2:7) and this fact cannot be forgotten.[3] However, the encyclical should be situated not only in the current context of the world but also in the current context of Vatican policy, the role of the Vatican in relation to the different nations, as well as the internal organization of the different services of the Roman Catholic Church. The pope is the head of the Roman Catholic Church and the head of state, and this situation entails many contradictions.

In the midst of the current internal conflicts in the Vatican between conservative and progressive forces, many liberation theologians call upon us to support the pope in governing the Roman Catholic Church. This fair convocation cannot obscure critical views regarding papal theology, since it is a matter of not only defending or supporting the pope but also helping advance a more Christian vision, one more adjusted to the desires of today's world. In spite of many courageous social and political positions, the pope maintains, as a reference, tra-

---

3. Francis, *Laudato Si': On Care for Our Common Home* (Huntington, IN: Our Sunday Visitor, 2015).

ditional theology and paternalistic benevolent stances toward many groups. As we know, this is forged from a patriarchal symbolic vision in which the male figure remains the center of the world's organization and of divine revelation. Clothed in white, he symbolically represents the figure of God the Father, who has good governmental plans for the world, who has a "fair and salutary" word for the improvement of human relations. It is in this context that some of the pope's attitudes and writings reveal an inadequate and ambiguous account of women's issues.

In *Laudato Si'*, women do not speak in their own voice about their life situations, their sufferings, and their demands. The pope speaks for them, following a romantic tradition that praises women by elevating them to level of unreal qualities and, thus, preventing any further reflection. It embarks in a circuit of illusionary or romanticized affections, a circuit of words that reflect little of everyday life and reality. This is not a game of spiteful words believing that they are actually kind to women; rather, it is a game that covers up reality and the power that it wishes to maintain. For instance, to state several times in public that "Mary is more important than the apostles" is, to a certain extent, a language artifice, an idealization of women, or an idea whose real consistency in church history is quite debatable. We know how the image of the Virgin Mary, despite its importance in popular devotion, has been used by the clergy and theologians to keep women in a dependent status. The image we have of her is not that of any mother burdened by sexual conflicts, blood, sometimes unwanted pregnancy, or the distress and anxiety for the care of sons and daughters. Rather, this is a virgin mother, pure, perfect, without original sin, and free from any existential macula. References to the mother of Jesus pay attention to Mary, the woman, and, in the dimension of the symbolic, honor the idealization of her virtues and her distinction from ordinary mortals. All of this highlights a structure to imitate a prefabricated model.

The pope seems to ignore that feminism, in its diversity, created cultural and social disruptions to male hegemony and idealized models of femininity. These disruptions have received neither space nor effective consideration within the Roman Catholic Church. There is no recognition of and willingness to pay attention and listen to real women regarding their lives and what they have to say. There is no distinction between powers or representations; there is no effective change in theologies or symbolisms.

What does it mean for women who live under the yoke of poor living conditions, who, on a daily basis, experience domestic violence, war, and assaults in the most unusual situations, that, "carried up into heaven, [Mary] is the Mother and Queen of all creation"? Or that "in her glorified body, together with the Risen Christ, part of creation has reached the fullness of its beauty"?[4]

Mary, Mother and Queen. Why? What do motherhood and royalty have in common? Why does only "part" of creation reach the fullness of its beauty? What is this "part"? What does this theology mean to concrete women and to different groups and their sexual identity?

At the end of the same paragraph, the pope explains the exaltation of Mary: "Hence, we can ask her to enable us to look at this world with eyes of wisdom."[5] The text requires us to move to another level, to forget the real pain and real dignity that we seek, and to immediately situate ourselves in another epistemological and ontological realm, a realm that revolves around an aesthetic of desire, of a poetry inspired by male ideals toward the female maternal figure of the Virgin. What would women's "eyes of wisdom" look like? There is no clear answer in the text.

In the next paragraph, Mary's glory is brought back to Earth, yet her dependence on the masculine figure is reiterated through Joseph: "Through his work and generous presence, he cared for and defended Mary and Jesus, delivering them from the violence of the unjust by bringing them to Egypt."[6] Again, in the same paragraph and in the same perspective, the reasons for mentioning Saint Joseph are clarified: "He too can teach us how to show care; he can inspire us to work with generosity and tenderness in protecting this world which God has entrusted to us."[7]

There is something artificial in referencing these figures and presenting them as ideals or examples for faithful humanity. It is as if Pope Francis persisted in revitalizing an interpretive tradition that is no longer supported by today's world. Perhaps, given the relevance of many of his analyses, we expected a biblical hermeneutics more in tune with modern times.

To criticize this interpretation is not a denial of the symbolic dimension of figures who are not historical and who have become exemplar; it is not a denial of the mythical-religious constructions that are part of a cultural tradition. Rather, it is to make room for other interpretations more suited to modern times.

Judith Butler, in the book *Giving an Account of Oneself*, refers to Adorno's critique of abstract universality reflecting analogically on

4. Francis, *Laudato Si'*, 241.
5. Ibid.
6. Ibid., 242.
7. Ibid.

abstract theological "truths" and their consequences.[8] Butler states that abstract universality can be violent when it "fails to be responsive to cultural particularity and fails to undergo a reformulation of itself in response to social and cultural conditions it includes in its scope of applicability."[9] In this sense, the often called "universal religious truths" can hide the reality of people in their different bodies and contexts.

It is not always possible to live according to universal precepts or according to figures turned into universal religious reference. When this happens, we make room for disputes or opportunities where indifference to social and individual conditions begets different kinds of violence. This universality, when applied to supposedly historical situations, such as the notion that Jesus only had male apostles in his innermost life circle, seems to be, indeed, a historical anachronism. In addition, it is a systematic exclusion of women from public religious representation. Nevertheless, this claim continues to be maintained as the will of Jesus in current Roman Catholic circles. This reveals an attitude and perception of male power incapable of accepting the challenges of our times and of dialoguing with different perceptions of the world.

We are living in a conflict between the good religious memories that stem from a rural and semirural world and the challenges arising from the new forms of violence affecting women and the multiplicity of people excluded from the right to merely be recognized as people. In this conflict, the pope's theology analyzes real situations but returns to a nostalgic and patriarchal theology, with inadequate examples to address the real possibilities of the world today.

My question is regarding the so-called theology of the pope—that is, the reference to God and to the historical figures portrayed as obedient to divine plans. These figures are confronted with statements that, in my view, are full of meaning, such as, "Compulsive consumerism is one example of how the techno-economic paradigm affects individuals."[10] Or, referring to the ability to go out of ourselves, the pope affirms that "disinterested concern for others, and the rejection of every form of self-centeredness and self-absorption, are essential if we truly wish to care for our brothers and sisters and for the natural environment."[11]

A single text reveals a sort of incongruity between the current analyses of the world and the theological claims. So, my final question is this:

8. Judith Butler, *Giving an Account of Oneself* (New York: Fordham University Press, 2005).
9. Ibid., 6.
10. Francis, *Laudato Si'*, 203.
11. Ibid., 208.

If, at least in his discourse, Pope Francis were to overcome the masculine self-referencing so prevalent in the church, would he not be educating us toward a covenant of humanity with itself and beyond the established powers? Would he not be more closely addressing the questions of social and climate justice? If the hierarchy of the church were, in fact, to put itself in the place of the faithful and reinterpret biblical texts in a less literal, patriarchal way, would it not open doors and windows for a new understanding of the Christian experience? If, instead of a rigid dogmatism, we were to foster a poetic of life with all its variations, would we not be closer to the human mystery that characterizes us? Would we not be closer to the Earth's groans, expressed in the suffering of so many creatures?

I do not want to close this reflection with a conclusion. I enter the debate of today's world, especially with the people concerned with making this planet a place of dignity and respect for all beings. May we be able to live a "new reverence toward life," renewed each day as "our bread," "our water," "our air," and "our love" that nourish and cheer us on from generation to generation.

4

———

Not Only for the Sake of Man: Asian Feminist Theological Responses to *Laudato Si'*

Sharon A. Bong

In this chapter, I foreground the voices of Asian Catholic feminist theologians and activists from the Ecclesia of Women in Asia (EWA), who value the intersection of climate justice and gender justice. I bring their voices into conversation with Pope Francis in his latest encyclical letter *Laudato Si'* on climate justice.[1] Although these voices are not a direct response to the encyclical, they nevertheless offer not only a gendered but, more importantly, a feminist counterpoint to the church's teachings on humanity (anthropology) and, more specifically, on the nature-human relationship that is intrinsic to an appraisal of a much-anticipated encyclical. To that end, this conversation aims to

---

1. Francis, *Laudato Si': On Care for Our Common Home* (Huntington, IN: Our Sunday Visitor, 2015); hereafter cited in parentheses as *LS*.

interrogate the doctrinal interpretation of nature "designed" for the sake of human beings as embedded in *LS*.

The significance of the title is thus twofold: nature is "designed" not only for the sake of humanity, and the category of *man* entails not only a feminist but also queer re-visioning of the exclusivity of man (used doctrinally in a generic sense and that therefore sidelines women) and the "human." To facilitate these conversational threads, the chapter flows from a gendered appraisal of *LS* in light of three rights-based conventions or agreements on climate and gender justice that marked 2015 as a "a critical year for humanity,"[2] followed by the theologizing of EWA as a successor epistemology[3] to ecofeminism[4] in critically reframing these teachings, which culminates in a "feminist cyborg spirituality" that decenters the human in creation.[5]

Laudato Si'

Pope Francis's text is lauded as it is the first encyclical letter devoted specifically to climate change and climate justice and builds on the ecological visions of Francis's predecessors, Saint John Paul II and Pope Benedict XVI (nicknamed "the green pope").[6] The text is timely as "2015 [was] a critical year for humanity," per Cardinal Turkson, the president of the Pontifical Council for Justice and Peace, in light of three high-impact meetings involving heads of states held that year to arrive at a global consensus about "international development, human flourishing and care for the common home we call planet Earth."[7]

2. FABC Central Secretariat and the Archdioceses of Bombay Press Office, "Press Release: Publication of Pope Francis' Encyclical *Laudato Si'*: On the Care of Our Common Home," June 18, 2015, http://tinyurl.com/luwbho8.

3. Sharon A. Bong, "The Ecclesia of Women in Asia: Liberating Theology," in *Feminist Catholic Theological Ethics: Conversations in the World Church*, ed. Linda Hogan and Agbonkhianmeghe E. Orobator (Maryknoll, NY: Orbis, 2014), 66–67.

4. Rosemary Radford Ruether, "Motherearth and the Megamachine," in *Womanspirit Rising: A Feminist Reader in Religion*, ed. Carol P. Christ and Judith Plaskow (New York: HarperOne, 1992), 43–52; and Mary Daly, "Gyn/Ecology: Spinning New Time/Space," in *The Politics of Women's Spirituality: Essays on the Rise of Spiritual Power Within the Feminist Movement*, ed. Charlene Spretnak (New York: Doubleday, 1982), 207–12.

5. Agnes M. Brazal, "A Cyborg Spirituality and Its Theo-Anthropological Foundation," in *Feminist Cyberethics in Asia: Religious Discourses on Human Connectivity*, ed. Agnes M. Brazal and Kochurani Abraham (New York: Palgrave Macmillan, 2014).

6. FABC, "Press Release."

7. Ibid.

Redefining Humanity's Commitment to Climate Justice and Gender Justice

The "three high-impact meetings" were the Addis Ababa Action Agenda (AAAA) of the Third International Conference on Financing for Development, which serves as a "global framework for financing development post-2015," that was adopted by the UN General Assembly;[8] the UN General Assembly's agreed-upon seventeen Sustainable Development Goals (SDGs), which build on the Millennium Development Goals (MDGs) that were unrealized;[9] and COP21, the Twenty-First Conference of the Parties to the United Nations Framework Convention on Climate Change (UNFCCC).[10] The outcomes of these meetings frame 2015 as a "critical year for humanity" in two ways: firstly, in upholding the principle of universality, and secondly, in integrating climate justice with gender justice.

Partnerships in the form of multilateralism were the defining triumph of the Paris Agreement on climate change, the outcome of COP21. According to the UN general secretary Ban Ki-Moon, "for the first time every country has pledged to curb their emissions, strengthen resilience and act internationally and domestically to address climate change" to support the 2030 agenda (of the seventeen SDGs).[11] The principle of universality is thus apparent as the goal of COP21 "to reach a new international agreement on climate that is universal (agreed by and applicable to all countries)," with the COP comprising 196 parties (195 states and the European Union), is realized.[12] The breakthrough of the Paris Agreement builds on the trajectory of climate negotiations and incremental consensus, from the 1992 Rio Earth Summit (which adopted the UNFCCC) to the 2005 Kyoto Protocol and 2015 Paris Agreement.[13] As such, the universal accord arrived at today foregrounds humanity's cognizance of "anthropogenic climate change"—human-caused global warming from the emission of greenhouses gases—at the level of state actors (however contested this may

8. United Nations, "Addis Ababa Action Agenda of the Third International Conference on Financing for Development (Addis Ababa Action Agenda)," A/RES/69/313, United Nations General Assembly, July 27, 2015, 1–2, http://tinyurl.com/knkhhpl; hereafter AAAA.
9. United Nations, "Sustainable Development Goals," September 25, 2015, http://tinyurl.com/lrkafoq.
10. COP21, "Press Kit," accessed February 24, 2016, http://tinyurl.com/mhc8arf.
11. UN News Centre, "Assembly President: Unity Over Paris Climate Accord Should Not Be Forgotten," United Nations, December 15, 2015, http://tinyurl.com/jwwkzmw.
12. COP21, "A Short Glossary," accessed February 24, 2016, http://tinyurl.com/mcmbmbb.
13. COP21, "Press Kit."

be among some members of the scientific community) and its overdue readiness to redress this.[14]

Secondly, integrated approaches in acting globally and locally involving state and non-state actors and civil society as well as across sectors (for instance, politically, economically, socially, and so on) have shifted from a gender-neutral or, worse, gender-blind to a now gender-inclusive approach. This means that men and women are not similarly impacted by climate change but rather differently and disproportionately affected, and these consequences are compounded by the intersection of age, class (and caste), ethnicity, nationalism, religious affiliations, and so on. For example, the gendered dimension in ensuring the realization of development that is sustainable, equitable, and just is explicitly stated in article 6 of the AAAA:

> We reaffirm that achieving gender equality, empowering all women and girls, and the full realization of their human rights are essential to achieving sustained, inclusive and equitable economic growth and sustainable development . . . and to eliminate gender-based violence and discrimination in all its forms.[15]

Other vulnerable communities are also identified and named, for instance children and youth (article 7), least-developed countries, landlocked developing countries, and small islands developing states (article 8), which reflects a recognition not only of the sovereignty of states but, more importantly, the differentiated needs of these states arising from a profound disparity of access to resources.[16] The particularism arising from the recognition of "differentiated needs"—between the haves and haves not—complements not only a universal approach but also a gendered one.

Also illustrative of a gender-inclusive approach are the SDGs that are the bases of the "2030 Agenda for Sustainable Development," with 169 specific targets to be achieved over the next fifteen years with five Ps involved: people, planet, prosperity, peace, and partnership.[17] These SDGs inclusively encompass not only climate justice (for example, no poverty, zero hunger, clean water and sanitation, affordable and clean energy, sustainable cities and communities, responsible consumption, production, and climate action) but also gender justice (SDG 5) that

14. Global Greenhouse Warming, "Anthropogenic Climate Change," accessed March 9, 2016, http://tinyurl.com/6hl5dcz.
15. United Nations, AAAA, 3.
16. Ibid., 3–4.
17. United Nations, "Transforming Our World: The 2030 Agenda for Sustainable Development," A/RES/70/1, United Nations General Assembly, September 25, 2015, http://tinyurl.com/od9mens.

intersects with other "isms" (reduced inequalities, SDG 10) and recognizes the multi-sectoral interventions needed (such as good health and well-being; quality education; decent work and economic growth; industry, innovation, and infrastructure; and peace, justice, and strong institutions). Quite significantly, the SDGs privilege "humanity and the planet" in recognizing the symbiosis of SDGs 14 and 15 (life below water and life on land) that culminate in "partnerships" (SDG 17).[18]

These three texts are, in turn, sustained by a human rights framework premised on SDGs and, given the explicit gender justice articulated (particularly in the AAAA), also encompass women's rights as human rights. These rights-based albeit secular texts complement LS, a universal albeit faith-based text that also marks 2015 as "a critical year for humanity."[19] What, then, are the common goals shared by LS and points of departure in relation to these texts that redefine humanity's commitment to climate justice and gender justice?

Common Goals and Points of Departure

Laudato Si' comprises six chapters and 246 articles. The papal letter opens by quoting from Saint Francis of Assisi's canticle, after which it is named. Thus, the papal letter invokes the creator God who, "through our Sister, Mother Earth . . . sustains and governs us" (*LS*, 1)[20]. In the same manner that the triumph of the Paris Agreement acknowledges the history of more than two decades of climate negotiations, Pope Francis affirms his predecessors' visions: Pope John XXIII's *Pacem in Terris*, more than five decades ago, exhorting world peace; Pope Paul VI's reference to "the ecological concern as 'a tragic consequence' of unchecked human activity"; Pope John Paul II's "call for a global ecological conversion . . . to 'safeguard the moral conditions for an authentic human ecology'"; Benedict XVI's recognition in *Caritas in Veritate* on "integral human development" that "'the book of nature is one and indivisible,' and includes the environment, life, sexuality, the family, social relations" (*LS*, 6). It further is a homage to Saint Francis of Assisi, who shows "how inseparable the bond is between concern for nature, justice for the poor, commitment to society, and interior peace" (*LS*, 10). This sets the tone for Pope Francis's confidence in humanity "in building our common home" (*LS*, 13) and is a recurrent trope signifying the symbiotic nature-human relationship throughout the six chapters that thematically structure the encyclical letter.

18. Ibid.
19. FABC, "Press Release."
20. Numbers in *LS* refer to paragraphs.

Thematically, in chapter 1, "What Is Happening to Our Common Home," Pope Francis provides a litany of ills that beset planetary life (articles 17–61). In chapter 2, "The Gospel of Creation," he offers the church's "theology of creation," which is anthropocentric in centering the human at the heart of creation (articles 62–100). Chapter 3, "The Human Roots of the Ecological Crisis" resonates with the reality of "anthropogenic climate change,"[21] and humanity is held accountable for the excesses of anthropocentrism (articles 101–36). In chapter 4, "Integral Ecology," he extends the rhetoric in the previous chapters and emphasizes the integrative account of the ecological crisis, particularly its human and social dimensions (articles 137–62). In chapter 5, "Lines of Approach and Action," the logical redress of the "human causes of environmental degradation" would be an integrated and concerted multi-sectoral and multilevel response by humanity holding itself accountable (articles 163–201), culminating in chapter 6, "Ecological Education and Spirituality," which spiritualizes the call to action or Christian praxis as a call to "ecological conversion" in recognizing the sacramental nature of nature premised on the covenant between God-human-nature (articles 202–46). The encyclical letter ends, as it starts, with a eulogy to creation vis-à-vis its Creator.

In considering the common goals shared by the secular-based texts (for instance, AAAA, SDGs, and the Paris Agreement) and religious-based *LS*, anthropocentrism as a principle of universality, within a Christian framework, is paramount. In drawing from biblical wisdom, Pope Francis reiterates the church's "theology of creation," which renders the human as *imago Dei*: "created out of love and made in God's image and likeness" (Gen 1:26). The human being is thus conferred "an infinite dignity" (*LS*, 65) as the human alone is created in "God's image and likeness." And given the uniqueness of human beings' capacity to reason, humans are thereby further distinguished from other species (*LS*, 81). The human person is, therefore, ontologically superior in relation to other species in creation. The hierarchically ordered relationship of God-human-nature finds theological legitimacy: "Creation is of the order of love" (*LS*, 77). The integrity of the whole (of creation) resting on the equal integrity of its parts (or each species) runs counter to "Christian thought [that] sees human beings as possessing a particular dignity above other creatures" (*LS*, 119). To illustrate, experimentation on animals "'is morally acceptable' within reasonable limits [especially when it] contributes to caring for or saving human lives" (*LS*, 130).[22]

21. Global Greenhouse Warming, "Anthropogenic Climate Change."
22. For a counterargument on animal rights, see Deborah Slicer, "Your Daughter or Your Dog? A Feminist Assessment of the Animal Research Issue," *Hypatia* 6, no. 1 (March 1991): 108–24.

This ethical restraint safeguards not only human dignity (in eschewing the needless suffering of animals) but also "the integrity of creation." That experimentation must be limited to other species is evident as human dignity is not defended through scientific experimentation on "living human embryos" (LS, 136).

A mechanistic world view ensues that regards creation as created for the use of humankind, a tangible gift from its transcendent Creator (LS, 77). To ensure the sustainability of the Earth for its use—beginning with the mandate to subdue nature as an "insensate order" (LS, 115)—humankind is then ambivalently called to "responsible steward-ship" (LS, 116), a duty of care that embodies "a universal communion." With regard to the original harmonious God-human-nature relation-ship now ruptured, that "rupture is sin," as it is legitimated by dis-torted interpretations of humans conferred with the "mandate to 'have dominion over the earth'" (Gen 1:28) (LS, 66). Humankind, in disre-garding its "duty to cultivate and maintain a proper relationship with . . . my own self, with others, with God and with the earth" (LS, 70), has led to "a tyrannical anthropocentrism" (LS, 68) and "a distorted anthropocentrism" (LS, 69) in laying claim to "absolute dominion over the earth" (LS, 74). Whilst the pope concedes to the fallibility of the church given that a "mistaken understanding of our own principles has at times led us to justify mistreating nature, to exercise tyranny over creation" (LS, 200), the church remains exonerated from genuine accountability in LS.

Throughout LS, anthropocentrism is insisted upon despite its excesses. In deliberating on the "human roots of the ecological crisis" the instrumental use of nature is emphasized, albeit with restraint. Thus, Pope Francis states, "The modification of nature for useful pur-poses has distinguished the human family from the beginning" (LS, 102). Anthropocentrism gone amok—humanity's "unrestrained delu-sions of grandeur" (LS, 114)—is the logical conclusion of humankind harnessing its "God-given human creativity," which manifests as "techno-science" (for instance, nuclear energy, biotechnology, and information technology), culminating in humankind's complete absorption of the "globalization of the technocratic paradigm" (LS, 107). The old dualism of (masculinized) culture versus (feminized) nature—which ecofeminists posit is glimpsed within this paradigm of "modern anthropocentrism"[23]—when nature is treated as an "insen-sate order" (LS, 115) and humanity as an extension not only of anthro-pocentrism but also androcentrism, exercises concomitant "dominion"

---

23. Vandana Shiva, *Staying Alive: Women, Ecology and Development* (London: Zed, 2002).

or domination over the universe rather than "responsible steward-ship" (*LS*, 116). Yet, human dominance over nature is extolled despite the excesses of anthropocentrism, as, ironically, a "misguided anthro-pocentrism" is one that yields to "biocentrism"—as embraced by some ecofeminists[24]—where "the human person is considered as simply one being among others" rather than one above other species, as divinely ordained (*LS*, 118).

The next common goal would be the symbiosis of climate justice and social justice. In *LS*, this finds expression in two ways. Firstly, it echoes the biblical preference for the poor. Pope Francis consolidates the expansive concept of climate justice, consonant with the SDGs, where "a true ecological approach *always* becomes a social approach; it must integrate questions of justice in debates on the environment, so as to hear *both the cry of the earth and the cry of the poor*" (*LS*, 49). He rumi-nates on the "decline in the quality of human life" (e.g., the dignity of the poor is violated as they are deprived of a basic and universal right to accessible and drinkable water) and the "breakdown of society." And in so doing, he draws a parallel to ecological erosion and deems this as "symptomatic of real social decline" (*LS*, 46) where humanity has for-gotten "how to live wisely, to think deeply and to love generously" (*LS*, 47). The pope affirms the dignity of indigenous peoples as an example of one of the world's most disenfranchised peoples, as they inhabit the fragile interstices of climate justice and social justice. In recognition that "human ecology" encompasses "cultural ecology," he calls for the preservation of their "cultural treasures," which are constantly threat-ened by the avaricious "consumerist vision of (non-indigenous) human beings" (*LS*, 144), and the right of indigenous peoples to self-determi-nation by insisting upon "the constant and active involvement of local people *from within their proper culture.*"

Secondly, the pope alludes to *"differentiated responsibilities . . .* [among] one single human family" (*LS*, 52). This is consonant with the principle of "common but differentiated responsibilities" of COP21 that "underpins the collective efforts to tackle climate change by differen-tiating between countries according to their historical responsibility and their capabilities."[25] These *"differentiated responsibilities"* toward cli-mate justice and social justice among sovereign states are impacted by the "ecological debt" between the Global North and South that "com-pels us to consider an ethics of international relations" (*LS*, 51). This

---

24. See Carol J. Adams, "Ecofeminism and the Eating of Animals," *Hypatia* 6, no. 1 (March 1991): 125–45, which argues for a more inclusive ecofeminist discourse that accords equal importance to the "domination of animals" as it does the "domination of nature."
25. COP21, "A Short Glossary."

new ethics of "*one world with a common plan*" (*LS*, 164) resonates with the breakthrough of the Paris Agreement in terms of its "universal" acceptance in re-visioning what a "global commons" entails especially for poor countries (*LS*, 174). The related "principle of subsidiarity, which grants freedom to develop the capabilities present at every level of society, while also demanding a greater sense of responsibility for the common good from those who wield greater power" (*LS*, 196), complements the principle of "differentiation" of COP21. This new ethics potentially accords agency to "intermediate groups" and ensures "distributive justice" (*LS*, 157) and "preferential treatment for the poorest of our brothers and sisters" (*LS*, 158).

Yet, other than these secular documents, *LS* does not synergize climate justice with gender justice. From a gendered perspective, *LS* disappointingly comes across as a predominantly gender-neutral or worse, gender-blind text. Whilst "*differentiated responsibilities*" (*LS*, 52) among nation-states are noted and noteworthy, differentiated and disproportionate gendered impacts of climate injustice and gender injustice are not noted, though they are noteworthy. A gender-neutral approach that presupposes an undifferentiated impact ensues; where "preferential treatment for the poorest" is called upon, there is no distinction made between "our brothers and sisters" (*LS*, 158) or other differences that matter inter- and intragroup, for instance, age, class, caste, ethnicity, religious affiliation, and so on. This myopia elides hard-won victories made not only by ecofeminist theologians but also by activists such as WEDO, who were present at, among others, the 1992 Rio Summit and 2015 COP21,[26] by whose intergenerational visions and praxis gender justice for the past three decades has become indispensable in any rights discourse including climate justice.

Where *LS* is gendered in parts, it is no less problematic. The Earth is feminized as "sister earth" (*LS*, 53). And its need of masculine (as implied) protection is made apparent as the pope says, although "all creatures are moving forward with us and through us towards a common point of arrival, which is God" (*LS*, 83), this "does [not] imply a divinization of the earth which would prevent us from working on it and protecting it in its fragility" (*LS*, 90). The dualities that ecofeminists have departed from are rehearsed here: man versus woman aligned with culture versus nature and protector versus protected are essentializing (as these attributes are rendered as fixed and inviolable) and reductionist. The positioning of "sister earth" as fragile and therefore

26. Women's Environment & Development Organization, "Our Story," accessed March 19, 2016, http://tinyurl.com/mgqmvj7.

in constant need of (male) protection (from being violated) is made more docile as nature is not in itself divine. Contrary to the mystics (and spiritually grounded ecofeminists) for whom nature in itself is sacred, in *LS*, nature is made sacred through humanity's encounter with God, who becomes "a means of mediating supernatural life"—notably through the Eucharist (*LS*, 235), which "is the living centre of the universe [and] itself an act of cosmic love." In this way, nature in itself is not made divine but rather "is projected towards divinization . . . towards unification with the Creator himself" (*LS*, 236). This, in turn, strengthens the dualism of (masculinized) Creator versus (feminized) creation.

The more contestable gendering of *LS* arises from two aspects: its heterosexist assumptions and its negation of sexual and reproductive health and rights (SRHR) in relation to overpopulation. According to *LS*, human beings' dignity stems from a "sense of belonging, of rootedness, of 'feeling at home'" (*LS*, 151). This includes owning a home (*LS*, 152), which is the basis of "human ecology" as "[having] a home has much to do with a sense of personal dignity and the growth of families" (*LS*, 152), thereby alluding to the procreative imperative directed at humanity. The "sense of belonging, of rootedness, of 'feeling at home'" as such becomes heteronormative. In drawing from Pope Benedict XVI, "human ecology" tempered with moral law becomes more explicitly heterosexist: it extends to the "acceptance of our bodies as God's gift" rather than claiming "absolute power over our own bodies" (*LS*, 155), which risks cancelling out "sexual difference" between man and woman. Pope Benedict XVI thus emphasizes that the boundary of "femininity or masculinity is necessary if [we] are going to be able to recognize [ourselves] in an encounter with someone who is different."

On the second aspect, Pope Francis posits that weak responses to the cries of the (feminized) Earth include "certain politics of 'reproductive health'" aimed at overpopulation (*LS*, 50) or reducing the "presence of human beings" (*LS*, 60), and this is placed on par with systemic violations of climate and social justice such as "ecological debt" between the Global North and South (*LS*, 51), a "techno-economic paradigm" (*LS*, 53), and a "deified market" (*LS*, 56). To reclaim the covenantal bond between God-human-nature, an "environmental education" that instills in each of us an "ethics of ecology . . . to grow in solidarity, responsibility and compassionate care" (*LS*, 210) is needed. The mainstreaming of such education (for instance, in schools, families, media, catechesis, and so forth) would potentially create an "ecological citizenship" (*LS*, 211). In so doing, humanity would embrace the "culture of life" (with family at its heart) and reject the "culture of death"

(*LS*, 213), which implicitly refers to reproductive health policies that are aimed at redressing overpopulation, which is, once again, put on par with "self-interested pragmatism" and "the paradigm of consumerism" (*LS*, 215).

In summary, the faith-based encyclical letter is consonant with contemporary rights-based frameworks of the AAAA, SDGs, and the Paris Agreement in recognizing the urgency in halting the ecological crisis (as much of the damage is irreversible), its integrative approach of local and global levels, and the emphasis on the collective accountability of all but the differentiated responsibility of the poor and poorer nations. Universalism is here inflected by the particularism of differentiated needs that, in turn, not only offers a refreshing decolonizing turn but also makes for more effective strategizing as these aspirations on climate justice are grounded in lived realities. A faith-based approach draws from spiritual sources in recognizing the integrity of nature and dignity of humanity as creations of God and caring for the whole of creation and its parts as Christian praxis. The fruits of such an "ecological conversion" that *LS* exhorts include: "a prophetic and contemplative lifestyle," a return to a life of "simplicity" (*LS*, 222), "sobriety" (*LS*, 223), "humility" in avoiding "limitless mastery" and autonomy (*LS*, 224), "inner peace," and "a capacity for wonder" (*LS*, 225). These virtues are a safeguard against "the logic of violence, exploitation and selfishness" (*LS*, 230) and form the bases for a new ethics of care.

However, the centrality of the human in creation within a Christian framework as reinforced in *LS* remains an obstacle to "ecological conversion" *from within* the Christian faith, as anthropocentrism is fundamentally endorsed notwithstanding the calls to redefine "dominion." Espousing equal integrity for all species (for instance, animal rights on par with human rights) is tantamount to a "misguided anthropocentrism." A more glaring myopia is the lack of a gendered analysis of the ecological crisis except to reinforce heterosexism and denounce certain reproductive health policies aimed at addressing the population crisis—which *LS* remains silent on—that compounds the ecological crisis. This omission is all the more disappointing when benchmarked against the rights-based frameworks that have drawn from the critical resources of feminist epistemologies and the women's rights movements on climate justice, which are incomplete without gender justice. In following through the decolonizing zeal of *LS*, I now bring into dialogue Asian feminist theologians from EWA on climate justice and gender justice.

Asian Feminist Theologizing on Climate and Gender Justice

The Ecclesia of Women in Asia is an academic forum of feminist Catholic women theologizing from the context of Asia. One of EWA's aims is to "endeavor to build communities that are inclusive, equitable, sustainable, and just at local, regional, and global levels."[27] EWA's mission is to encourage and assist Catholic women in Asia to engage in research, reflection, and writing toward doing theology that "is inculturated and contextualized in Asian realities; builds on the spiritual experience and praxis of the socially excluded; promotes mutuality and the integrity of creation; and dialogues with other disciplines, Christian denominations and faiths."[28] This aim and mission are met primarily through a biennial conference that serves as a platform where Asian Catholic women's theologizing is not only heard (sometimes performed through dance, song, and art) and reflected on but also published. The past seven biennial conferences since its inception in 2001 have also afforded a space for dialogue among religious and laywomen, academic, pastoral, and grassroots women, as well as women from other faiths and beyond Asia, including partnerships with, among others, the Catholic Theological Ethics in the World Church (CTEWC).[29]

In seeking to "[promote] mutuality and the integrity of creation," the theologizing of EWA in the context of climate justice and gender justice offers three points of departure from *LS*: firstly, it is contextualized in the narratives of women who are represented as neither passive nor victims; secondly, it reclaims the erotic in deeper appreciation of the cosmos; and, thirdly, it decenters the human in creation.

Following the critical tradition of feminist epistemologies,[30] EWA's theologizing is situated knowledge: it starts from the lived realities of the "socially excluded" as articulated in its aim. The "socially excluded" in the following case study refers to female leaders in the Coalition to Save Mt. Kanlaon, "one of the Philippines' top ten biodiversity hot spots (as it hosts natural forest, flora and fauna, some of which

27. "About the Ecclesia of Women in Asia," Ecclesia of Women in Asia, accessed February 24, 2016, http://tinyurl.com/krb5n8h.
28. Ibid.
29. Andrea Vicini, Gina Wolfe, and Agnes Brazal, "Women's Theological Voices: A Conversation across Four Continents," Catholic Theological Ethics in the World Church, December 2, 2013, http://tinyurl.com/lmjus5z.
30. Donna Haraway, "Situated Knowledges: The Science Question in Feminism and the Privilege of Partial Perspective," in *Simians, Cyborgs and Women: The Reinvention of Nature* (London: Free Association, 1991), 183–201; Sandra Harding, *The Science Question in Feminism* (Milton Keynes, UK: Open University Press, 1986); Sandra Harding, *Whose Science? Whose Knowledge? Thinking from Women's Lives* (Milton Keyes, UK: Open University Press, 1991); and Nancy C. M. Hartsock, *The Feminist Standpoint Revisited and Other Essays* (Boulder, CO: Westview, 1998).

are 'either globally threatened or endangered' and headwater catchment of three major river systems)" situated in Negros Island. This area earmarked for conservation has been under grave threat, most notably from logging by the Energy Development Corporation (EDC), a fully privatized company seeking to further "widen its control and monopoly of the country's power industry."[31] Theologizing based on the narratives of these female activists, who comprise 80 percent of those who attend forums and mass mobilization gatherings, is aimed at reflecting how the "diocese practices peace based on justice and the integrity of creation and seeks to respond to the Philippine hierarchy's call for a theology of creation and the strengthening of the communities towards the creation of the Church of the Poor."[32] In eschewing a "Filipino piety" that is self-sacrificial and docile and is often perceived as ideally embodied by women,[33] taught as they are to imitate the "*kalooban* (spirit/soul/interiority) of Christ," these activists, in reflecting on their faith-based activism, engender an ecofeminist theology of liberation in Negros Island. The hallmarks of their ecofeminism are: it is holistic not dualistic, biocentric not anthropocentric, inclusive and participatory not androcentric, authority-centered, patriarchal, "missiological . . . prophetic, life-giving, liberating, and gives rise to creative expressions."[34]

This theology reclaims the essentialism of ecofeminism (which some feminists justly caution against)[35]—that not only makes visible the affinity between nature and woman but also invests both with integrity—as the women leaders in the Coalition embrace "inclusive notions of creation" they find analogous to "a close personal interrelationship (e.g., Earth as woman/mother and a source of blessing)."[36] Such an ecofeminist ethics of care extends the pope's observation that "a true ecological approach *always* becomes a social approach; it must integrate questions of justice in debates on the environment" (*LS*, 49), as "a social approach" is here appropriately gendered. In so doing, women "hear *both the cry of the earth and the cry of the poor*" (*LS*, 49), where the "earth" and the "poor" (such as, for instance, the activists as they remain disenfranchised) are not mere passive victims. Such an

---

31. Sophie Lizares-Bodegon and Andrea Lizares-Si, "No Mother Is for Sale: Practice towards an Ecofeminist Theology," in *Practicing Peace: Towards an Asian Feminist Theology of Liberation*, ed. Judette A. Gallares and Astrid Lobo-Gajiwala (Quezon City, PHL: Claretian, 2011), 242–44.

32. Ibid., 241.

33. Ibid., 251.

34. Ibid., 257.

35. Hilda P. Koster, "Ecological Evil, Evolution, and the Wisdom of God: Reimagining Redemption for Ecofeminist Religious Practice in an Age of Global Ecocide," in *Christian Doctrines for Global Gender Justice*, ed. Jenny Daggers and Grace Ji-Sun Kim (New York: Palgrave Macmillan, 2015), 55–56.

36. Lizares-Bodegon and Lizares-Si, "No Mother Is for Sale," 254.

ecofeminism liberates theology as it embraces the "traditional Filipino worldview of an integrated universe,"[37] and it is concretized by political action and avoids the pitfall of an uncritical essentialism where women and nature are represented and treated as docile objects of reproduction and resource. In other words, a *critical essentialism* is offered.

Secondly, reclaiming the erotic embedded in the feminine principle of *Sakti*, which draws from Tantric philosophy, is integral to reimagining the human-nature relationship in departure from a mechanistic and anthropocentric world view. *Sakti* is "the creative energy inherent in and proceeding from God. It is exemplified by the female principle, the female reproductive organs, or the goddess Sakti who is the wife of Shiva. As energy, Sakti is also viewed as the merging of powers emerging from each person. . . . Sakti is worshipped and cultivated as a power that can lead to spiritual liberation."[38] A "Sakti theology" that is centered on this "feminine principle" of creation is "constructed on women's experiences intersected by the variables of caste, class, gender, ethnicity . . . [and] will be empowering, embodied, *agapic*, context sensitive, and life generating. . . . It has consciousness raising and transformation as its goal." The "Asian woman" as such is not a monolithic category, and knowledge that is generated from the "crucible of women's day-to-day experience" becomes sound theology.[39] *Sakti* theology will be "life affirming and creation-centered instead of being anthropocentric."[40] *Sakti* theology as situated knowledge resonates with the sacramental joy of encountering God through creation (*LS*, 235) but extends this as erotic joy in encountering the feminine principle of creation that is not hierarchically ordered. In doing so, *Sakti* theology transcends dualisms that continue to define Christian thought.

Thirdly, the theologizing of EWA decenters the human in creation. From ecofeminist theologies of liberation that afford a radical ethics of care for creation, that are nurtured by the wellsprings of Asian spiritualities and rejuvenated by the power of the erotic, new metaphors for the organic continuum that is the cosmos emerge beyond the "common home." Notable among these is the "cyborg." Defined as "a creature in a post-gender world . . . [with] no origin story in the Western sense . . . [it] is resolutely committed to partiality, irony, intimacy, and

37. Ibid., 252.
38. Pushpa Joseph, "Revisioning Eros for Asian Feminist Theologizing: Some Pointers from Tantric Philosophy," in *Body and Sexuality: Theological-Pastoral Perspectives of Women in Asia*, ed. Agnes M. Brazal and Andrea Lizares-Si (Quezon City, PHL: Ateneo de Manila University Press), 38–39.
39. Ibid., 44.
40. Ibid., 51.

perversity. It is oppositional, utopian, and completely without inno-cence."[41] It engenders "three crucial boundary breakdowns": human and animal,[42] animal-human (organism) and machine,[43] and physical and nonphysical.[44] In a nonessential and performative sense, the cyborg is *queer* in dismantling boundaries between the parts of the whole of creation. *Queer* in this sense of boundary crossings that is emblematic of the cyborg "is always an identity under construction: a site of permanent becoming."[45] The fluidity of becoming is, in turn, embodied in the hyphenated identities of human-machine (for instance, use of prosthetics, cyber subjectivities as netizens) and human-animal-plants (for instance, genetically modified food, genetic mutations, and animal and human experimentation alluded to albeit with caution in *LS*, 133–36). Through the trope of the cyborg, the human in creation becomes decentered insofar as its relationality to other species in creation is foregrounded. Anthropomorphism con-structed as stable, fixed, and a given is thus deconstructed as identities become "multiple, contradictory, fragmented, incoherent, discipli-nary, disunified, unstable, fluid."[46] Where *queer* is more commonly associated with the fields of gender and sexuality studies, signifying non-heteronormative or transgressive subjectivities, in the field of ecofeminism, the cyborg is reminiscent of Vandana Shiva's "trans-gender," where she reminds us that the "feminine principle is not exclusively embodied in women, but is the principle of activity and cre-ativity in nature, women and men."[47]

The case for queer ecofeminisms can therefore be made considering that (1) queers and cyborgs are "not easily gendered or natured"[48] and therein lies possibilities of recognizing differences that matter but are not divisive; (2) "human sexual difference is parallel to the ecological notion of biodiversity," and not eliding differences that matter (includ-ing heterosexual versus LGBTIQ) "opens up the possibility of a radi-cal pluralism for the human species";[49] and (3) "liberating the erotic (as foundational for a "queer ecofeminism") requires reconceptualiz-

41. Donna Haraway, "A Cyborg Manifesto: Science, Technology, and Socialist-Feminism in the Late Twentieth Century," in *Simians, Cyborgs, and Women*, 150–51.
42. Ibid., 151–52.
43. Ibid., 152–53.
44. Ibid., 153–54.
45. Annamarie Jagose, *Queer Theory: An Introduction* (New York: New York University Press, 1996), 131.
46. Joshua Gamson, "Sexualities, Queer Theory, and Qualitative Research," in *Handbook of Qualitative Research*, ed. Norman K. Denzin and Yvonna S. Lincoln, 2nd ed. (London: Sage, 2000), 356.
47. Shiva, *Staying Alive*, 52.
48. Catriona Sandilands, "Mother Earth, the Cyborg, and the Queer: Ecofeminism and (More) Ques-tions of Identity," *NWSA Journal* 9, no. 3 (Autumn 1997): 19.
49. Danne Polk, "Ecologically Queer: Preliminaries for a Queer Ecofeminist Identity Theory," *Journal of Women and Religion* 19, no. 72 (July 2001): 84.

ing humans as equal participants in culture and nature . . . to build our common liberation."[50] A "common home" rings hollow when not all are welcome, given the heteronormativity and heterosexism inherent in *LS*.

Thus, the vision of a "feminist cyborg spirituality" recognizes "the presence of God's Spirit in all of creation, whether in humans, animals, non-sentient beings or human-made tools or technologies. The Spirit (Shekinah) indwells and embraces the whole of creation."[51] This redefinition of transcendence that begins with boundary crossings—as embodied in the hyphenated identities of animal-human-machine and physical-nonphysical—already includes post-humanists and transhumanists. The former believe that "there is no stable, fixed human essence" with regard to humans redesigning themselves and the latter that the "cyborg is an expression of a stage of the transformation of the human condition" within the continuum of human-machine.[52] This revisioning, indeed queering, of the human and, by extension, the dignity (hence superiority) of the human person leads the way to affirming the inherent sacredness of all creation, as therein lies the *imago Dei*—the likeness of God that is not exclusively embodied in the human person, especially when the human person is incrementally being de-essentialized and decentered.

Conclusion

An "ecological conversion" that embraces such inclusiveness and courage to reassess the full ethical implications of human culpability, capability, and compassion begins to realize the vision of "common home" where all species are different yet equal. In doing so, it fulfils the vision that all are one in Christ Jesus, who is queerly divine and human (Gal 3:28). In that time-space already carved out and indwelled by ecofeminists, we can then truly acclaim, "*Laudato Si*': Praise be to you."

---

50. Greta Gaard, "Toward a Queer Ecofeminism," *Hypatia* 12, no. 1 (Winter 1997): 132.
51. Brazal, "Cyborg Spirituality," 208.
52. Andrea Vicini and Agnes M. Brazal, "Longing for Transcendence: Cyborgs and Trans- and Posthumans," *Theological Studies* 76, no. 1 (2015): 156.

PART II

Doctrines and Situations

God, Creation, and Humanity

5

Reimagining the Triune God for a Time of Global Climate Change

Sallie McFague

Traditionally, Christian theology has emphasized both God's transcendence and immanence. For a doctrine of God to be effective, it must interpret both in a credible and powerful way. Transcendence has fared better here, though increasingly, while it is still powerful, it is no longer credible. Who can believe a supernatural, imperialistic, all-controlling super-person, imagined after a comic-book superhero? Yet, at one absurd end, this is the picture. Any powerful views of immanence, on the other hand, tend toward pantheism, in which all identity and distinctiveness of God and the world are lost.

We need a new basic model, paradigm, of the relationship of God and the world. Currently, in most Protestant circles, the prime model is not of God and the world but of God and the human being, specifically the male human being. While Roman Catholicism has had a doctrine of the world, since the Reformation, the Protestant focus has been narrowed to human individuals. This picture of two beings only marginally related, very independent, highly anthropocentric, is all about *who* has the power. It is a competitive model of two isolated monads, each vying for the gold medal, as in sports. The supposition is that God can intervene on behalf of individual human beings for their good (or not). At its most crude, the model is of two competitive human beings (males) vying for controlling power.

Therefore, *power* is the heart of the issue. Who has the most? The model we choose makes all the difference. But where do we get our models? The individualistic model is a combination of market capitalism and Enlightenment philosophy and anthropology. However, Christians believe Jesus is the face of God; Jesus's life, death, and teachings are a reflection of the "mind of God." A very different model emerges from this source—what can be called the "kenotic" model. Why accept one or the other? It is a jump, a leap of faith. There is no hard and fast evidence that one is better than the other. In terms of one's most basic, deepest commitment, one cannot be certain. The test (and it is only a test, not a certainty) is that one is "better" for oneself, the planet, and other creatures. Hence, Christians start with the story of Jesus. We move from there to talking about God and the world. We understand who God is (God's transcendence and immanence) and who we are because of Jesus. Does this mean literalism? Does it mean that Jesus is God and, therefore, we *know* what we Christians say is the "truth," that we need nothing else than the story of Jesus to say both who God is and who we are? No, but we do get some clear clues and directions from that story.

A kenotic theology is a story of self-sacrificing love, a model that upends the Enlightenment at its most vulnerable place. It is contrary to all we as Westerners value, expect, reward, and honor. But, what if the cross (dying to one's old life, trying to live a new, self-sacrificing love) *is* the way? What if we choose this as our model? How should we conceive of the transcendence/immanence of God and God's relation to the world if we take the life, death, and resurrection of Jesus as our model in a time of climate change? And what if some of the insights coming to us from postmodern philosophy, especially its anthropology, its understanding of how we fit into the scheme of things, have some interesting overlaps with the Christian kenotic picture? What if some of the novel insights into its basic "world view"—that is, the underlying assumptions about the human place in the world on issues of power, exceptionalism, responsibility, body, materialism, dependence, and so on—give us a very different picture than the traditional Protestant picture of two super-beings, God and man, struggling for dominance?

What if we might learn something about how to live a kenotic life from the very different picture of our place on our planet from an anthropology challenging us to face up to our radical dependence, fragility, and even weakness? The seeming absurdity of living a life of sacrificial love for others, which is at the heart of most religions, and certainly of Christianity, may find a partner in insights from postmodern science and philosophy in terms of its insistence that primarily and centrally we are animals, bodies dependent on other bodies, incarnational beings at the mercy of the many sources of power in our planet, among them, climate change. The focus on the body at the heart of the Christian story of the incarnation of God should make this tradition open to some of the distinctive insights of postmodernism: its profound materialism, its suspicion of "spirit," its call for a bio-cracy (in which all life-forms have a vote, unlike a democracy), its focus on human responsibility for our own actions, the call to love *this* world (not another), the insistence that we learn to face despair and death, the end of thinking in terms of "substance," its claim that agency (subjecthood) is not limited to human beings, and so on.

So, to return to our present dilemma: we might wish we could believe in an all-powerful, supernatural God who could solve all our problems, but that no longer is a persuasive argument. Why is the picture of this God no longer credible, no longer powerful? In part, it is because we no longer believe in ourselves as powerful individuals. Our whole picture of who we are and who God is has changed, so say the postmodernists. The individualistic, solitary, isolated human being who was a product of Enlightenment philosophy and Newtonian science has been undermined and with it, belief in a similar picture of God. The picture we have of ourselves and of God go together, and both have been undermined in the late twentieth and the twenty-first centuries. Let us look at what has happened to the happy picture of progress in the latter part of the nineteenth century at the hands of the three masters of suspicion: Freud, Darwin, and Nietzsche.

Freud, Darwin, and Nietzsche

Freud, Darwin, and Nietzsche undermined the sense of discovery, progress, and human control during the nineteenth century. The industrial revolution, the colonization of Africa and the East by Western powers, and advances in medicine and the other sciences combined to make human beings feel confident and, for the first time, in control of nature. This was to be short-lived, however. Freud destroyed the sense of clarity that people used to feel about their "insides," their motives and desire. Until Freud, things seemed relatively straightforward, but he opened up a vast internal swampy jungle, sowing seeds of doubt, mistrust, and deceit even in our most intimate secretive selves—our relations with parents and sexuality. One could no longer trust what people said about their motives, promises, or wishes. In fact, we didn't even know what our insides were telling us, and to the extent we did figure it out, we didn't like what we saw.

Whereas Freud generated an internal revolution—we could no longer trust our desires and our will to obey us (or even figure out *what* they were about)—Darwin worked on the "outside"—the world or cosmos and our place in it. Our industrial, scientific, and colonizing successes had led people in the West to believe in human centrality and exceptionalism. We were vastly different from all other animals—Descartes claimed we were unique because we could "think"; the rational mind set us off absolutely from all other creatures, making us the only subjects, and everyone and everything else became mere objects. Hence, it created a picture of human beings as rightful owners and users of the planet. *We* are living organisms and everything else is more like a machine with removable parts that can be used without damaging the whole.

It is difficult for us to imagine how it felt to be the hegemonic human being in such a world. By *hegemonic*, I mean the classic, desirable model of human being—Western, young, male, white-skinned, well-to-do, educated, confident, Protestant, able-bodied. To be sure, most people did not fit this model—women, children, all non-Westerners, physically or mentally challenged, old, colored skin, poor, uneducated, and so on. Immanuel Kant said that one owed such people as himself—the hegemonic human being—moral regard; that is, one should treat such people fairly and justly. This human being is the "neighbor" that the New Testament says we should "love." The rest—all the other human beings, all other animals and life-forms of any sort, and certainly plants, trees, mountains, the oceans, the land, and so on—fell outside of "moral concern."

What is left, of course, is a small elite of the planet's inhabitants, less than 1 percent. So, when Darwin claimed that we came from and are similar to—let alone completely dependent on—all other life-forms, this elite club of human beings felt threatened to the core. I recall my ancient New England matriarchal aunt saying that certainly *she* was not related to the apes! However, not only are we not at the top of the planet's creatures, we are the most vulnerable and least needed. If we were to disappear tomorrow from the planet, everything else would be better off (our pets would miss us for a few days until they adjusted!).

Climate change is an excellent example of how far we have fallen from our old status as the most powerful, brilliant, necessary animal on the planet to its worst enemy. Climate change, which we now know is the result of our greedy use of fossil fuels to energize our insatiable consumer market economy—our triumph, as it were, over the planet's resources—has boomeranged back on us as our greatest threat. What we thought we could control—the planet's energy to feed our insatiable desire for the comfort and pleasure of a few (the 1 percent)—has come back to haunt us as the power that may well be our death knell. What we thought was just another "object" in our planet—the weather—has become the greatest, most powerful "subject," whose agency we have every right to fear as greater than ourselves. Can "weather" act? Apparently, yes, and act with awesome power. So far, we are defeated in our attempts to control or even to mitigate the consequences of what we have let loose—the burning up of our planet, our one and only home.

It is not only scary—it is terrifying. No wonder that most teen literature these days is apocalyptic: young people's deepest fear is that they are losing their home (of course they cling to their helicopter parents). But all of us, deep down, fear this. It is the unacknowledged elephant in the room that many of us avoid talking about. It is not discussed in polite society, the way sex and cancer were not discussed when I was a kid. *How* could we have come to this? We, the planet's darling and most complex, glorious creation—we can, after all, imagine the universe in our heads—have come to the point where we can also imagine our planet's demise, either quickly, with a nuclear bomb, or more slowly, with climate change. We are at a fork in the road where we have never been before—capable of destroying our own home.

So, we come to our third master of suspicion—Nietzsche and his notion of *ressentiment*—a deep, pervasive fear that we are out of our depth, completely out of our depth. Nietzsche expressed it as "the death of God," that is, the end of our confidence that regardless of our sins, we are in the hands of the almighty God who would not let his children perish. We now need reasons to believe in our world, for without God, it is all up to us. Deep down, not only apocalyptic teenagers are afraid of the future, but we so-called grownups are also. We are *deathly* afraid. But if no one believes anymore, if even that cultural assumption is gone, then what stands in the way of a deep, pervasive, all-consuming despair? One might as well try to take care of one's tiny little corner of the world, since hope for the greater good, the "commons," is beyond us. This is not usually a "voiced" despair; rather, it is like a rotten stain throughout everything, a stain that cannot be erased. In fact, if asked to identify it, most of us could not. But we feel things are not right; there is something wrong at the core, but we do not know what. It used to be that sin was the problem, but sin meant something was wrong with individuals, not with the whole world, as is now the case.

But now the stain has spread throughout the world, certainly the political but also the cosmic world. It is much bigger than any of us can handle. We are overwhelmed with its horrendous dimensions. (Is this part of the reason that clowns, people like Donald Trump, gain popularity? We might as well laugh as cry.) The specters of climate change collapse and uncontrollable poverty as manifest in millions of immigrants are too terrifying to contemplate, especially if we—mere human beings without a providential, caring, powerful God—have to deal with it. The economic world (market capitalism) and the biological (climate change) are both infected and the issue seems totally beyond individual solutions, at the same time that our Western political systems are increasingly dysfunctional, especially the American system. "Things have gotten out of hand," and we despair of any solutions. Everything has gone awry and a deep melancholy has settled over us. What should we do?

We are now, perhaps, ready to delve into some of the distinctive notes from postmodern thinking that I believe open up ways to help us see how a sacrificial life for others in our world, a world characterized by extreme inequality and climate change, might be relevant. We must give up the picture of ourselves as in control, as "managing" the planet, as deserving of all the riches of the planet we can hoard for ourselves, as able to come up with the technological magic bullet for fighting climate change, as the overseers of an economic model for our planet that works from the top down, and so on. What if we really opened our minds and hearts to a very different world view that suggests a type of power that our society sees as wrong, ineffective, and maybe even foolish? What if we took the kenotic life and death of Jesus as our model and considered how contemporary science and postmodern reflection might help us live as Christians in our time?

And here we find a strange thing. Rather than the traditional story of an absolute, all-powerful God who relates to the world by controlling and demanding its allegiance, we see God as the one who relates to the world in a new and astounding way: as self-emptying love for the well-being of all creatures. We have hints of this kind of love in the saints, sometimes in mother love, and even here and there in the biological world, where give and take, reciprocity, sacrifice, and even hints of altruism emerge, but it is in the story of Jesus that Christians find both the fulfillment and the paradigmatic expression of this countercultural love.

Kenotic Theology and the Trinity

But the kenotic theological story does not stop with Jesus—it points to God in God's self. The doctrine of the Trinity—that seemingly abstract and often irrelevant notion that God is "three in one"—becomes central at this point.[1] This is the case because Christianity is not Jesus worship; it is not about him but about God, and not just about how God relates to the world but how God is in God's self. Thus, the doctrine of the Trinity—a subject that has often been used to illustrate the esoteric irrelevance of the Christian view of God (How can "one" be "three"? Do Christians believe in three gods?)—becomes the center of a profoundly immanental understanding of divine transcendence. That is to say, rather than a conundrum to baffle people about who God is, the doctrine of the Trinity clarifies and deepens our understanding of God, if it is seen as the "face" of Jesus, as we have suggested. A wide range of theologians agree. Julian of Norwich, writing in the Middle Ages, does not mince words concerning this connection: "Jesus himself, as she sees him bleeding on the cross, is the source of her understanding of the Trinity."[2] Centuries later, John Haught, an evolutionary theologian, claims: "At the center of Christian faith lies a trust that in the passion and crucifixion of Jesus we are presented with the mystery of God who pours the divine self-hood into the world in an act of unreserved self-abandonment."[3] And Jürgen Moltmann adds: "The content of the doctrine of the Trinity is the real cross of Christ himself. The form of the crucified Christ is the Trinity."[4]

This is the first and most important point to make about a kenotic theology: our understanding of who God does not come from "above," from an external or general source, from the common misunderstanding that "everyone knows who God is," which is often the opening comment of conversations about the nature of God. For instance, when scientists and theologians gather to discuss "God," an assumed generic view often prevails on the side of the scientists: God is a static, transcendent, distant, all-powerful super-being dwelling in another world. If, however, the question of who God is starts with what Jesus did in

---

1. The material on kenotic theology is taken (with revisions) from Sallie McFague, *Blessed Are the Consumers: Climate Change and the Practice of Restraint* (Minneapolis: Fortress, 2013), 191–95.
2. Grace M. Jantzen, *Julian of Norwich: Mystic and Theologian* (London: SPCK, 1987), 109.
3. John F. Haught, *God after Darwin: A Theology of Evolution* (Boulder, CO: Westview, 2000), 48.
4. Jürgen Moltmann, *The Crucified God: The Cross of Christ as the Foundation and Criticism of Christian Theology* (New York: Harper & Row, 1974), 247.

his life, teachings, and death, we have a very different view; as Grace Jantzen says of Julian's view, "since the revelation of God in Jesus is a manifestation of the totally self-giving suffering of love, this is also the most important fact about the Trinity."[5] Hence, it makes all the difference "where we start" to talk about God. Moreover, it also makes a difference what we understand the work of Jesus to be. If it is primarily a sacrificial atonement on the part of an all-powerful God, then the Trinity is likely to be seen as the mechanism for this transaction: thus, as in Anselm's view, the Son, the "second person of the Trinity," sacrifices himself for the sins of his brothers and sisters in order to save them from divine punishment by the "first person," with the Spirit, the "third person" conveying the benefits to the faithful. Here, the focus tends to be on the "persons" of the Trinity and their connecting tasks or functions. Thus, the Western understanding of the Trinity, deeply influenced by Augustine, underscores the "oneness" of God, with the three "persona" (traditionally called the Father, Son, and Holy Spirit) as functions, aspects, or modes of the divine oneness. The tendency is to see the Trinity as one substance with three natures in contrast to the Eastern view, which claims that outside of the Trinity there is no God, no divine substance. The Eastern Christian view underscores the "three-ness" of the divine and, in particular, the *relationality* of the three.[6] The result of these different emphases is that the Western understanding of God verges on an "individualism" for both God and humanity, while the Eastern view focuses on the process of giving and receiving. The first sees both God and humanity as "substances," separate beings, while the second sees them as "relationships," reciprocal processes of give and take. In other words, the Western view of the Trinity supports a paradigm of God and the world as both characterized by static, individual substances or essences, while the Eastern view assumes that life—for both God and the world—is a process in which relations are more important than entities. "Love" is not a property or characteristic of God, some attribute added on to God; "love is the supreme ontological predicate" of both God and us human beings, who are made "in the image of God."[7] In other words, we choose self-emp-

5. Jantzen, *Julian of Norwich*, 110.
6. See, for instance, the work of John D. Zizioulas and Western theologies influenced by the Eastern perspective: John D. Zizioulas, *Being as Communion: Studies in Personhood and the Church* (London: Darton, Longman & Todd, 1985); John D. Zizioulas, *Communion and Otherness: Further Studies in Personhood and the Church*, ed. Paul McPartlan (New York: T&T Clark, 2006); Patricia A. Fox, *God as Communion: John Zizioulas, Elizabeth Johnson, and the Retrieval of the Symbol of the Triune God* (Collegeville, MN: Liturgical, 2001); Haught, *God after Darwin*; Jantzen, *Julian of Norwich*; Beverley J. Lanzetta, *The Other Side of Nothingness: Toward a Theology of Radical Openness* (Albany: State University of New York Press, 2001); Karen Armstrong, *The Case for God* (New York: Knopf, 2009); Moltmann, *Crucified God*.
7. See Zizioulas, *Communion and Otherness*, 46.

tying love or nothing; we are not created beings who then choose love, just as God is not "God" who then decides to love. Rather, who God is and who we are is defined by love, by the self-emptying action of one into the other, of God into the world and of all parts of the world into each other. What it means to be a human being is simply to *choose* to be what one is: a participant in God's very own life of love. Thus, poetically, the Eastern view sees the inner life of God as an "eternal divine round dance" in which there is no inferior or superior, no first or second, but an eternal self-emptying and refilling of each by each.[8] Here, we see the glimmers of mutual reciprocity evident at all levels of evolution epitomized in the Godhead itself, now understood (for Christians who see God in the cross of Jesus of Nazareth) as the very nature of reality. The Eastern view of the Trinity is more suited to the task of conveying immanental transcendence—that is, radical, self-emptying love as the heart of the divine—than is the Western view, although many, including Augustine with his view of God as the beloved, the lover, and love itself have attempted to emphasize kenotic love.

A second implication of starting with the incarnate, self-emptying love of Jesus, epitomized in the cross, is a different view of divine power. We have touched on this subject numerous times, as it is so central to an understanding of how we human beings should act in the world. The tendency of monotheistic religions (Judaism, Christianity, and Islam) to provide support for the current radical individualism of Western culture, a view that, as we have seen, underscores human domination of nature, among other things, is aided by unqualified monotheism: as God dominates the world, so human beings, made in the image of God, should dominate the natural world. This view has supported centuries of human exploitation of nature, culminating in our current human-induced global warming from excess greenhouse gas emissions. It is impossible to overemphasize the significance of monotheism's contribution to this customary stance of human beings, as it is often the unspoken assumptions of "who we are in the scheme of things" that has more influence than any explicit statements of "who we *should* be in the scheme of things." Thus, a radically different understanding of divine power—one in which "God" epitomizes total self-emptying openness to others, all others—is not only an indictment of the common view of power as control but also a paradigm of "letting be" so profound and so inclusive that we are speechless to suggest what it means. Buddhism's *sunyata*, the "God" beyond God; the mystic's

---

8. See Elizabeth A. Johnson, *She Who Is: The Mystery of God in Feminist Theological Discourse* (New York: Crossroad, 1992), 220–21.

prayer to free us from our desire to possess God; the statement by a Christian theologian that "the Godhead is profound and utter claimlessness"; and Meister Eckhart's suggestion that there is no God beyond the distinctions of the Trinity are all attempts to address this speechlessness. In this understanding, God "gives up" all names and properties, wary of all attempts to reach to the "emptiness" of God, acknowledging the breakdown of all human attempts to say what cannot be said—that "God" is *God*. Ursula Le Guin, the science-fiction novelist, published a nice piece in *The New Yorker* magazine some years ago in which she imagined Eve deciding to "un-name" the animals, a first step toward overturning the exceptionalism of human beings in "naming" others, from the yak to God. Le Guin notes that "most of [the animals] accepted namelessness with the perfect indifference with which they had so long accepted and ignored their names." As she leaves Adam (who is wondering where his dinner is) to join the other animals, Eve notes how difficult it is to name (and thus possess others): "My words must be as slow, as new, as single, as tentative as the steps I took going down the path away from the house, between the dark branched, tall dancers motionless against the winter shining."[9] May our words, before all else, "un-name" those, including God, whom we have so glibly named and thus sought to control.

Thus, in summary, in the kenotic theological paradigm, there is continuity all the way from evolution to God and vice versa: one "reality" that is characterized at all levels by various forms and expressions of self-emptying. Hence, beginning with the incarnation of God in Jesus Christ, Christians believe that we have a paradigm of God, humanity, and the world that does not validate raw unilateral, absolute power at any stage or level of reality; rather, the inverse is the case—what appears as utopian, fantastic, and unbelievable mutual, interdependent sacrifice and self-emptying is indeed "what makes the world go 'round." Thus, one moves from this reading of the incarnation to an understanding of the creation of the world as God's gift of pulling back and giving space to others that they might live (but as the "body" of God, not as separate beings) and an understanding of human life as itself part of the divine life, but as its "image." We live by participating in God's very own life (since this is the only reality there is), but not simply as parts of God; rather, human life is learning to live into the relationality of God's own life, which is one of self-emptying love for *others*. Such a theology is not pantheistic (the identification of God and the world) but panentheism (the world as living—finding its source

---

9. Ursula Le Guin, "She Unnames Them," *The New Yorker*, January 21, 1985.

and fulfillment—*within* God's very self, the dance of self-emptying love that desires the flourishing of all life). It is a sacramental vision in which the world is a reflection of the divine in all its trillions of individual life-forms and species; thus, as G. M. Hopkins reminds us, "The world is charged with the grandeur of God" not as one shining explosion but in all its tiniest parts, even the intricate workings of a mosquito's eye.[10] The motto here is "Vive la difference." We human beings are the one life-form that does not fulfill its role as being a bit of God's grandeur simply by existing; rather, we, made in the image of God, must grow into the fullness of that reflection of God by willing to do so. And, according to the kenotic paradigm, this is what "salvation" is—not release from punishment for our sins, but a call to relate to all others (from God to homeless persons and drought-ridden trees) as God would and does.

Kenotic Theology and Postmodern Thought

Let us now return to our questions: how can religion contribute to changing people's behavior in regard to climate change, and what are some key insights from postmodern thought that can help with this project? While there are several features of postmodernity that I could mention, I want to focus on three interrelated ones: the relationship of transcendence and immanence, the human faculty of the imagination as the key instrument for understanding this relationship, and the nature of the power that unlocks this relationship—the power of kenosis (or self-emptying love).

First, the relationship of transcendence and immanence: postmodern philosopher Gilles Deleuze expresses the new relationship as "transcendental empiricism," or passive vitalism.[11] It is the movement from a focus on the transcendent to the immanent, from a focus on such questions as the existence of God to our current concern with "how might one live here on the earth?" It is the movement from an abstract, intellectual concern with the "being" or substance of something called God, to the existential and pressing issue of what discipleship to God demands of us in the twenty-first century. It is the movement from the Greek heritage of God's existence to the Hebrew issue of "what does God demand?" It is the movement from the Platonic pattern of imitating the truth that lies beyond to focusing on the Aristotelian issue of how one lives in the polis and the cosmos, in the city and in the world.

---

10. John Pick, ed., *A Hopkins Reader* (New York: Oxford University Press, 1953), 13.
11. Claire Colebrook, *Gilles Deleuze* (New York: Routledge, 2002), 69–89.

It is what some postmodern authors call "the new materialism" in contrast to seeing the transcendent dimension as "spiritual."[12] And here is one place where I think postmodernity is doing religion and particularly Christianity a real service—it is giving the Christian tradition another, contemporary way of speaking of the "incarnation."

Rather than limiting incarnation to the bodily assumption of a single human being by the divine as the primary interpretation of this central doctrine of Christianity, the new materialism is pressing Christianity to own up to its principal doctrine with a more radical interpretation than the orthodox one. In insisting that transcendence is found in immanence, that there are not two worlds—the spiritual and the bodily—but only one, theologians are called to focus their attention on the quality of this life for all rather than on the eternal life in another world for a few. While Christianity's allegiance to flesh should have resulted in an enthusiastic affirmation of this life, strangely, it has not. Rather, not only has there been widespread interpretation of salvation as a heavenly eternal life but also a rejection of the body as "good." Undoubtedly, the Black Plague of the Middle Ages with its horrendous loss of life contributed to this turn away from finding satisfaction from earthly life, but the rejection of female flesh as a temptation to male sin contributed to it as well. Whatever the causes, Protestantism particularly has suffered from this loss since, unlike Catholicism, which had two sources of revelation—Scripture and creation—the Calvinist Reformation limited knowledge of the divine to Scripture alone, thus eliminating the sacramental tradition from being a source of revelation. In other words, Calvinist Protestantism (from which much of modern evangelicalism is derived) has often suffered from a sterile over-intellectualism as well as a puritanical streak.

Another emphasis of the new materialism—its flat ontology—might also contribute to a reassessment by various theologies of the value of earthly life. The work of Timothy Morton and Jane Bennett overturning the traditional split between subject and object, between humanity and everything else, means that all aspects of nature are agents, changing themselves and their world in innumerable ways.[13] No longer can human exceptionalism lord it over others; rather, everything has some form of agency, even if it is only a plant reaching toward the sun

---

12. See, for instance, Diana Coole and Samantha Frost, eds., *New Materialisms: Ontology, Agency, and Politics* (Durham, NC: Duke University Press, 2010).

13. See, for instance, Timothy Morton, *The Ecological Thought* (Cambridge, MA: Harvard University Press, 2010); Timothy Morton, *Ecology without Nature: Rethinking Environmental Aesthetics* (Cambridge, MA: Harvard University Press, 2007); Jane Bennett, *The Enchantment of Modern Life: Attachments, Crossings, and Ethics* (Princeton: Princeton University Press, 2001); Jane Bennett, *Vibrant Matter: A Political Ecology of Things* (Durham, NC: Duke University Press, 2010).

to gain sustenance. The world is alive! One of the implications of seeing transcendence as embedded in immanence is the "honor" it gives to all forms of the nonhuman as possibilities for intimations of transcendence. Christians, especially Protestants, have been reluctant to glory in the world "charged" with God or even to suggest liminal space where the divine and the worldly might "brush" against one another. The new materialism helps religions to dare to find the divine "here and now" in the midst of both our greatest joys and most profound sufferings. I think it is difficult to overemphasize the potential of this gift from the new materialism to encourage Christianity to express a hearty, heartfelt enthusiasm for this life. Of course, doing so puts new burdens on planetary quality of life for *all*.

It is relatively easy to embrace the serendipity of earthly life if one has had a good and long one. A life well-lived is often celebrated in the obituary columns with few regrets. But surely one of the reasons that most religions have been tempted to find satisfaction in "another" world is because this one is so disappointing for many species and most individuals. And Christianity can certainly be accused of being a form of necrophilia—eating the body and blood of Jesus Christ in order to escape punishment in the next world for one's sins. Human beings have sought immortality in any way possible—from the Egyptian embalming of kings to the current practice of freezing one's body to await scientific advancement for permanent existence. In other words, the new materialism is a healthy criticism of our culture's refusal to accept death as a natural part of life—understandable, perhaps, in light of the gross unfairness of the length and quality of earthly life for so many, but nonetheless a sad detour away from embracing justice and flourishing for all.

John Caputo in his latest book, subtitled *Confessions of a Postmodern Pilgrim*, ends his book with a plaintive comment: "The world as a whole is the rose that blossoms for a while, and then disappears. We are that smile, our life is that rose, and we celebrate it. . . . At the end of life, just as in the beginning and the middle, the only thing to do is to say thanks be to life for life, for the grace of life."[14] Another example of the same perspective is Oliver Sacks's book entitled *Gratitude*, published shortly after his death. He sums up his life in the following comment: "My predominant feeling is one of gratitude. I have loved and been loved. I have been given much and I have given something in return. Above all, I have been a sentient being, a thinking animal on this beautiful

---

14. John Caputo, *Hoping Against Hope: Confessions of a Postmodern Pilgrim* (Minneapolis: Fortress, 2015), 199.

planet, and that in itself is an enormous privilege and adventure."[15] But one wonders, can the Holocaust victim or the unsuccessful Syrian refugee keep smiling at their end? This is a serious question and must be answered by all those who make the serendipity of life their creed. So, I applaud the new materialism as I also embrace a radical interpretation of the incarnation—the divine with, for, under, before, and around the Earth—but with qualifications and demurrals.

A second contribution of our postmodern authors to a revisionist Christian theology lies in the area of their reliance on the imagination as the key faculty of human reflection. It has not always been thus. While classical philosophy coming from Plato and Aristotle respected poets as the authors of good living, recent philosophy has marginalized poetry along with theology, ethics, and other "soft" forms of knowledge. Philosophy attempted to imitate as closely as possible a reductionist type of scientific thinking, eliminating the arts, ritual, and religion from serious consideration. But postmodern philosophers embrace the arts and religion; in fact, Deleuze insists that *only* imaginative discourse is worthy of being called philosophy. And it is philosophy that creates, provides, and offers the concepts that are the substance of our "worlds," the interpretations within which we live. Deleuze's main question is not how *should* one live but how *might* one life? Hence, his primary criterion is imagining "differently."

For traditional Western philosophy, it is sameness, not difference, that matters: the goal of philosophy is to reflect and imitate the truth that is outside of, and transcendent to, our world. Likewise, with traditional theology, the truth is to imitate and embody revelation as given in the Bible and/or revealed to the church. But, since the masters of suspicion (Freud, Darwin, and Nietzsche) have undermined the traditional interpretations of how to live, we are being called to think anew, to think outside the box, to think with our "wild space."[16] The notion of wild space claims that while most of our lives are lived within the contours of the dominant world view of one's times (for us, this is planetary capitalism), a part of each of us (more with some than others) questions this interpretation with the part of our experience that lies outside the dominant world view. Thus, for the disabled, homosexuals, women, the poor, and other forms of marginalization, one can look at the world through the "crack" provided by one's dissonance. As the Canadian poet and singer Leonard Cohen says, "There is a crack in everything; that's how the light gets in."[17] Wild space is a gift to

---

15. Oliver Sacks, *Gratitude* (Toronto: Knopf, 2016).
16. See my expansion of "wild space" in Sallie McFague, *Life Abundant: Rethinking Theology and Economy for a Planet in Peril* (Minneapolis: Fortress, 2001), 48–51, 188–95.

think differently, just as the kingdom of God is wild space for Christians, calling them to imagine a life from the underside, the gutter, the oppressed, the hungry, and the forgotten. The parables of Jesus are certainly forms of imaginative projection that invite the listener to assume a different standpoint, a radical one from the perspective of one's society. Very few writers have used the parable as a form of radicalization—with the notable exception of Kafka. Most people allegorize parables or "explain" them in reasonably comfortable ways, but they are meant to convert, not to comfort.

Thus, since the goal of postmodern philosophy and theology is not simply to inform but to revolutionize, "difference" again wins out over similarity. One asks two questions: who or what is left out of this interpretation, and how can one not only think differently but "feel" differently? Thus, postmodern philosopher Bruno Latour, for instance, believes it is the imagination that is most likely to spot what is left out by its "difference" (say, by its disability, poverty, "queerness," and so on).[18] Likewise, it is forms like parables that are most likely to shock people into feeling the pain of the left out, the different, since parables operate not by comfortable continuity but uncomfortable difference. Traditionally, these interpretations have been considered transcendent to society, but our authors want to insist that they are immanent. Deleuze sums up the postmodern position:

> Fiction and the imagination is part of the very production of life. We produce ideas of the self, of society and of institutions such as justice or democracy. In its legitimate form such productions are immanent; we recognize them as produced fictions for the sake of life. In its illegitimate form such productions become transcendent; we think we should obey or recognize the idea of society, justice or democracy, which supposedly governs our experience. Literature is one of the sites in which such ideas can be displayed *as fictions*.[19]

The imagination could not receive a higher commendation than this: it provides us with the very stuff of life.

Nietzsche insists that "difference," or metaphor, is the basis of all reflection, since it alone follows the continuous, changing, buzzing confusion that is "experience." It helps us move from what is to what might be, from what we know at present to what we could know in

---

17. Leonard Cohen, "Anthem," in *Leonard Cohen: Poems and Songs*, ed. Robert Flagger (New York: Random House, 2011), 188–90.

18. See for example, Latour's lovely little book *Rejoicing: Or the Torments of Religious Speech*, trans. Julie Rose (Cambridge: Polity, 2013).

19. Colebrook, *Gilles Deleuze*, 85–86.

the future. Metaphor is the faculty that allows us to see one thing in terms of another, thus to move slowly from what we know to what we are seeking to know. Hence, the metaphorical forms—parables, fiction, images, symbols, and so on—are the highest forms of language. And even such weird enterprises as Deleuze's "becoming animal" are a desperate attempt to move us out of our imprisonment within the Anthropocene, move us so we can see with eyes other than our own.[20] Notions like wild space, becoming animal, and a body without organs are necessary for creatures like us, who seem unable to lift our sight above ourselves, to stand in the shoes of others, think and feel differently, in preparation for acting differently. The goal is to change the world, not simply know or continue it as it is. Here, we see a distinctive meeting place for postmodern philosophy of transcendental empiricism and Christian theology. The reason why the imagination is so critical to changing the world is that it is the human reflective faculty that helps us think in new ways. Unfortunately, many folks consider religious and theological language to be static—to be "descriptive" rather than "metaphorical." To take a classic example, *father* is often considered to be God's "name" rather than an attempt to talk about what we do not know how to talk about, namely, who God is? We use the best language, the most meaningful language we have for this purpose, and often it is the language of intimate relationships that are important to us. But to help people face new problems, often new language is necessary. In the case of *father*, if this becomes the main or only way we talk of God in relation to climate change, then we assume that the father will take care of his children and, therefore, can take care of the consequences of climate change (or whatever is threatening the children). We need something besides infantile metaphors to face climate change with the sense of responsibility and courage that this challenge gives us. One such model is the world as God's body, which not only links up with the new materialism but is a model that invites human beings to join with God in caring for the world by helping us to focus not on a "spiritual" God who lives in another world but a this-worldly, present God whom we meet in our everyday earthly lives.

We come then, finally, to the third gift from postmodern thought for revisionist Christian theology: kenotic love. We have seen how our authors reject a metaphysical, supernatural, all-powerful God—the sovereign lord of the universe—which encourages human beings to model themselves as terrestrial sovereigns. The same image of God

---

20. See Gilles Deleuze and Félix Guattari, *A Thousand Plateaus: Capitalism and Schizophrenia*, trans. Brian Massumi (Minneapolis: University of Minnesota Press, 1987), 232–309.

that has become "unbelievable" is also being rejected as harmful to the planet; power as one-way control of the other is seen as a perversion of genuine love, whether that love is divine or human. But another possibility emerges: power as empowerment, as the self-giving of one to another in a continuous cycle of emptying and filling. We see one form of this interpretation of love in the Trinity in which God is understood not as three persons in one "substance" but as an activity of never-ending give and take. This is an understanding of God as relationship, not as a "being," with the heart of this relationship the activity of self-emptying for the other. We also have intimations of this model in evolution where new life is possible only through death, setting up a paradigm in which self-emptying is necessary for the flourishing of new and more complex life. Thus, both in postmodern science and in Trinitarian interpretation we are presented with a similar possibility for a new view of power as empowerment. John Caputo suggests this in the following comment: "Suppose that God's power over human beings is limited by love and that God takes up a place beside them in their powerlessness?"[21]

Whereas the traditional picture of God as an all-powerful lord and king among the monotheistic religions (especially Islam and Christianity) has encouraged events like the Crusades of the Middle Ages as well as the slaughter of enemies by the present-day ISIS movement, postmodernity's new materialism combined with its critique of human exceptionalism is opening the door to a very different understanding of power and possibility. The power of both God and human beings is not in the annihilation of the enemy but in empowerment through self-emptying of one for the other in a cycle of mutual flourishing. Hence, transcendence is not the being or existence of a distant, separate, all-powerful God but is an inclusive cosmic vision of flourishing life on Earth. God is "possibility," "hope," for a different kind of world in which hospitality, openness, is a key activity. Christianity is one form of this kenotic paradigm, as evident in its key doctrines: creation of the world as the body of God (or radical incarnationalism); Jesus as the "face" or image of God in his life of self-emptying love, summed up in his sacrificial death on a cross; and, as we have seen, in an interpretation of the Godhead, the Trinity, as recycling self-emptying love for the other.

As we step back and consider the gifts that postmodern philosophy might offer to a revisionist Christian theology, what stands out is a dif-

---

21. John D. Caputo, *The Weakness of God: A Theology of the Event* (Bloomington: Indiana University Press, 2006), 34.

ferent picture of the God/world relationship from the traditional one. What I have sketched above as the heart of the new picture—kenotic love—is not spelled out explicitly in postmodern philosophy. It has, however, provided the tools for a critique of the substance metaphysics of power that lies behind the traditional view. And by focusing on activity, relationship, change, openness, continuity, and embodiment, these philosophies have opened a way forward toward construction of a new world view. This world view, in which the strange, paradoxical "altruism" of reciprocal activity is evident even at the biological level, is also a window into the extraordinary, extreme example of kenotic love in God's own self, in the life and death of Jesus, and in the discipleship of some human beings, most notably in such "saints" as Dorothy Day, Jean Vanier, Nelson Mandela, and countless others less known who "love the neighbor."

6

And G*d Saw That It Was Good— *Imago Dei* and Its Challenge to Climate Justice

Wanda Deifelt

One of the heritages of our Western culture is a dualistic framework of thought. In this dualism, female is to nature as male is to culture. The stereotyped list of masculine attributes (objective, active, productive, generative, linear, dominant, and rational) is perceived as superior to feminine ones (subjective, passive, nonproductive, receptive, curvaceous, submissive, and irrational). This flawed paradigm has had detrimental effects on women and other socially disenfranchised groups, whose proximity to nature deemed them as inferior, and, similar to the entirety of creation, at the receiving end of patriarchal ideals. In theological terms, this duality has additional implications. Similar to the way nature is the "other," women have been *othered* in religious discourse and practice. Women's association with nature, reproduction, and the body has been deemed as inferior to the higher, spiritual values aspired by Christianity: denial of the body and earthly needs.

Perhaps one of the best examples of this subordination is the way in which the divine, although transcending physical barriers, is referred to primarily in androcentric language in order to linguistically exclude women. The adoption of a non-gendered, unpronounceable designation for the divine, G*d, has been a creative resource employed by an earlier generation of feminist scholars.[1] This deliberate attempt to foster inclusive and expansive liturgical language has deconstructed colonial discourses of domination and enabled inclusion (also regarding the symbolic power of naming). Although feminist theory and theology might have started with the particular experiences of women, they have broadened their scope by affirming intersectionality. In the dualistic system described above, the feminine serves to signify not only women but all those who have been made "other" throughout history: slaves, homosexuals, barbarians, heathen savages, impoverished people, and so on. The treatment received by women is comparable to these groups, since they all were denied full humanity.

Besides affirming the duality between mind and bodies—or, spiritual and material worlds—Christianity has also reinforced an escapist theology, one that projected any expectation of a life in abundance to the afterlife. In the tension between this world and the next one, Christians are supposed to focus on the afterlife instead of the present reality. We are told that because we are humans and have a soul, we have another place to call home besides this world. Conformity to Christian precepts and obedience to its teachings are described as entryways to the pearly gates of heaven. This explains the willingness to so easily abandon this world, creation itself, to seek the promises of the afterlife. It is not surprising, then, that some Christians interpret environmental degradation as a sign of the end of times, something not only to be disregarded but actually welcomed because it is seemingly a sign of the coming apocalypse.[2]

---

1. Rosemary Radford Ruether and Elizabeth Schüssler Fiorenza were among the first to employ this formulation to address the divine. It draws from the biblical tradition that enunciating the name of the deity places a hold on it and reduces its transcendence. Although anthropomorphic attributes are commonly seen in sacred texts, they nevertheless serve as metaphors pointing to an ultimate instead of an actual depiction of that ultimate reality.
2. Chris Mooney, "New Study Reaffirms the Link between Conservative Religious Faith and Climate Change Doubt," *The Washington Post*, May 29, 2015, http://tinyurl.com/l7bp4gr. The article refers to the study conducted by David Konisky and Matthew Arbuckle in which they analyze the attitude of religious communities toward climate change. Their study shows that evangelical Protestant communities, particularly those more prone to teach biblical literalism, are less likely to express concern for the well-being of the environment.

Imago Dei as a Construct

The environmental crisis is also a theological crisis. It is a reflection of the dismissal of earthly concerns in favor of the promise of otherworldly bliss. In the meantime, this theological construction leads to environmental degradation and erosion of just relationships among human beings. The hierarchy between human beings over the entirety of creation is based on a sense of species entitlement, standing on the ground that being created in the image of God, humans (and human interests) are more valuable than any other life form on the planet. This notion is obviously detrimental to the planet because it has led to rampant destruction of the environment, but it is also detrimental to humanity, corroding the way human beings act and interact among ourselves.

At the root of this is the question of what *imago Dei* entails. What is the embodiment of G*d in creation? While theologians and scholars have claimed this positively, affirming dignity and belonging, it is impossible to overlook the nefarious effects of this anthropocentric assumption: in patriarchal history and theology, the image of God was claimed to be masculine; in racist ideology, the image of God excluded anybody who did not stem from European roots; in heteronormative culture, the image of God did not include the LGBTQ+ community;[3] and in an anthropocentric world view, the image of God certainly did not expand beyond the confines of humanity.

Mary Daly aptly criticized the androcentric theological assumptions by pointing out the fallacy that if G*d is male, then male is G*d. Instead of addressing G*d as a noun, the creative divine power would be better understood as a verb.[4] Since Daly's groundbreaking work, feminist theologians have established that the reference to the divine in exclusively male pronouns is not a mere reflection of a monopoly in religious writings and interpretations. It is a projection of patriarchal and androcentric assertions unto G*d in a way that corroborates and justifies hierarchical power. This power reinforces social, cultural, political, and economic structures established to control the other, primarily women and women's bodies. To affirm that women, too, are *imago Dei* is to empower women and reestablish the status of being the embodiment of G*d.

---

3. *Queer* is used as an umbrella term for all variations of sexual orientations and gender identities that encompass the LGBTQ+ community. The sign is used to indicate that these identities are not limited to the letters represented in the acronym: lesbian, gay, bisexual, transgender, and queer.
4. Mary Daly, *Beyond God the Father: Toward a Philosophy of Women's Liberation* (Boston: Beacon, 1973), 34.

In a racist environment, the equation of the divine with whiteness has been used and abused to deny the humanity of indigenous and African American populations. The very idea that G*d could be anything but white—if one were to employ such anthropomorphic qualities—is still received with suspicion. James Cone's claim of a black Jesus continues to cause distress to many because of his fundamental and accurate attempt to debunk white supremacist theology and ideology.[5] The core question here was whether non-Europeans could claim to be made in the image of God. And although many Christians could envision this, they still would restrict it to a spiritual level, that is, that the full humanity of African Americans and indigenous populations applies only to the afterlife and not to here and now.

In the theological assertions regarding creation, it is also necessary to deconstruct the assumption that the white heterosexual male is a closer reflection of the divine image. This not only reflects the Aristotelian misconception that men represent ideal humanity (while women are depicted as botched creation). This rhetoric is carried a step further in current homophobic stances whereby those who identify as LGTBQ+ are described and treated as sinful aberrations. Because the very notion of LGTBQ+ embodiment and sexuality is proclaimed as deviant, there is a blatant denial of their *imago Dei*, that is, that those who do not conform to the normative patterns of human sexuality cannot be truly the image of God.[6]

The manipulation of the notion of *imago Dei* reveals the power in naming the divine. This power is simultaneously the extension of human projections onto G*d and the assumption of divine preference for those who can name G*d. Because G*d is described with finite language, the understanding of the divine is tainted with human (and often self-serving) expectations. Among these projections is the egocentric postulation that some in G*d's creation can more fully convey the divine image. The irony in this abuse is that humanity is no longer made in the image and likeness of G*d, but rather G*d is made in the image and likeness of humanity. This requires a closer look at the creation narratives themselves.

---

5. James Cone, *A Black Theology of Liberation* (Maryknoll, NY: Orbis, 2004).
6. On the issue of sexuality, it should be noted that Christian appropriations of creation have sublimated human sexuality in general. It continues to be widely taught that sex should be saved for heterosexual, monogamous marriage and for the primary purpose of procreation. Everything else is sinful and breaks away from ecclesial teachings. For more information about queer embodiment, see Lisa Isherwood and Elizabeth Stuart, *Introducing Body Theology* (Cleveland: Pilgrim, 1998), 95–113.

Creation in the Hebrew Tradition

The creation account that offers the foundation for the notion of humanity fashioned in the image of G*d comes from the first chapter of Genesis (Gen 1:1–2:4a) in the Hebrew Bible. Scholars tend to agree that this text, which is a liturgical poem, was composed during the Babylonian exile in the sixth century BCE. It is important to establish this setting in order to understand the text. The abstraction in its world view, the solemnity in speech, and the complexity of ideas presented infer that the creation poem in Genesis 1 was elaborated by a highly educated, liturgical group of people. Being in exile, however, they are forced to work in captivity, as cheap laborers. Those who had once been the rulers of Jerusalem (or descendants of them), as part of the elite, are uprooted and deported to Babylon, experiencing an exclusion of power.[7]

The narrative starts by affirming that, in the beginning, *Elohim* created heaven and Earth. At this time, the Earth was without form and void. Chaos prevailed. But chaos was fashioned into cosmos, so the poem closes by saying, "These are the generations of the heavens and earth when they were created" (Gen 2:4a). The account is organized in seven days, the last one being the day of rest. A total of ten things are created, but they are squeezed into seven days. The seventh day is distinctive from the others: the six preceding days open with the words "And G*d said" and each day ends with the sentence "And there was evening and there was morning." On the seventh day, however, G*d rests from all the work that was done.

On the first three days, G*d seems to prepare the setting for what is created in the last three days. It is as if a skeleton of the universe were built in order to fill it out afterward. On the first day, light is separated from darkness (Gen 1:3–5). This command is more or less repeated in Genesis 1:14–19, but in a more concrete affirmation: the greater and lesser lights are to separate day and night, work as signs, and determine the seasons and the years. On the second day (Gen 1:6–8), a firmament is created to separate the waters from beneath and from above. The deeds of the fifth day compliment this setting: aquatic and aerial animals appear (Gen 1:20–23). G*d blessed them, saying "Be fruitful and multiply and fill the waters in the seas, and let birds multiply on the earth." On the third day (Gen 1:9–13), dry land appears and the earth brings forth vegetation, plants yielding seed according to their own kinds and trees bearing fruit also according to their kind. Once

---

7. Milton Schwantes, *Projetos de Esperança: Meditações sobre Gênesis 1-11* (Petrópolis: Vozes, 1989), 30.

this environment is set, the land animals can appear and humankind be created (Gen 1:24–30). Blessing and fertility abound in a schema that uses the word *good* seven times (1:4, 10, 12, 18, 21, 25, and 31), and, on the seventh, "very good."[8]

Some deeds require a whole day to be created, while others can be created simultaneously (such as the animals and the human beings). The creations done in the first, second, and fourth day seem to demand undivided attention. On the first day, there is the separation of light and darkness. On the second day, the firmament appears, with the separation of waters from above and below. The fourth day is dedicated to the creation of the lights in the firmament—stars, sun, and moon—and they are given a particular purpose: to separate day from night. Interesting is the fact that *Elohim* had already separated the light from the darkness in Genesis 1:4. These celestial bodies, then, are not starting something new but are merely continuing a task that had already begun. Denoting their importance, three out of the seven days are dedicated to the firmament and its lights.

There is no special day for the creation of human beings, since they are created in the same day as the animals. Thus, G*d made the beasts, the cattle, and everything that creeps upon the ground. Human beings and animals share time and table: they are created in the same day and have the same diet. However, only humanity is made according to G*d's image, after G*d's likeness. Only human beings can have dominion over the fish of the sea, the birds of the heavens, the domestic animals, over all the Earth, and over every creeping thing. Human beings are also the only ones with a clear reference to gender, although a blessing and the command to be fruitful and multiply had already been given beforehand (Gen 1:22, in connection to the aquatic and aerial animals). "So G*d created human being (*ha'adam*) in G*d's image, in the image of G*d they were created; male and female G*d created them" (Gen 1:27). Humanity alone is designated as male and female. This designation is placed not solely in relation to reproduction—demonstrating that humanity comes in two genders—but also in connection to the image of G*d, who can be understood as being simultaneously male and female.

---

8. Phyllis Trible, *God and the Rhetoric of Sexuality* (Philadelphia: Fortress, 1985), 13.

Imago Dei in Text and Context:
The Babylonian Narrative of Creation

Developed during the Babylonian exile, the first chapter of Genesis addresses particular elements of the *Enûma Elish* (When Above), the Babylonian creation poem that celebrates the god Marduk (and his fifty names) as a divine champion. Based primarily on Sumerian cosmology, it is difficult to ascertain the date of the poem's composition. Scholars, however, tend to place it under the First Babylonian Dynasty (1894–1595 BCE), more specifically under King Hammurabi (1792–1750 BCE), when Marduk became the national deity. The language used in the poem points to the same period.[9] The *Enûma Elish* has become one of the main sources of Mesopotamian cosmology and is widely used among biblical scholars because of its analogies with the first chapters of Genesis.

The epic centers on the supremacy of Marduk and the creation of human beings for the service of the gods. The poem was probably recited during the Babylonian New Year, in a ritual celebrating Marduk and the power of the Babylonian city-state.[10] It starts with two deities, Apsu and Tiamat, and from them other gods are created. They make so much noise that the older deities cannot rest, so Apsu wishes to kill the young gods, but Tiamat disagrees. Aware of the threat, one of the deities, Ea, uses magic to put Apsu into a coma and kills him, thus becoming the chief god. Ea marries Damkina, and from them Marduk is born. Marduk's grandeur is vastly celebrated in the epic. He is given wind to play, and he uses it to make tornadoes and dust storms, thus disrupting the deities still residing inside Tiamat.

The gods persuade Tiamat to avenge the death of Apsu, and some of them join her, including Kingu, Tiamat's new husband. Marduk offers to save the gods if allowed to rule over them after achieving victory. When they agree, Marduk is selected as champion against Tiamat. A horrific battle ensues, and Tiamat is destroyed. Marduk tears Tiamat's body into two halves and, with them, fashions earth and the skies. He then proceeds to create the calendar, organize the planets and stars, and regulate the weather. The defeated deities are forced into labor, serving Marduk and his allies. But they complain and rebel, so Marduk has Kingu, Tiamat's former consort, slayed. With Kingu's blood, clay from the earth, and spittle from the other deities, human beings are

9. Alexander Heidel, *The Babylonian Genesis: The Story of Creation*, 2nd ed. (Chicago: University of Chicago Press, 1963), 14.
10. Rosemary Radford Ruether, *Womanguides: Readings toward a Feminist Theology* (Boston: Beacon, 1985), 38–40.

created. Their function is to do the work previously assigned to the deities: they are to maintain the canals and ditches, to irrigate the land and cultivate crops, to raise animals and fill the granaries, and to worship the gods at their regular festivals.

A Comparison between Creation Accounts

The Babylonian creation story played an important public role in that society, being recited with great solemnity each year. It served as a religious assurance to defeat "the negative forces of the universe and society and the ascendency of a political and cosmic order ruled by Babylonia."[11] The narrative presented in Genesis 1:1–2:4a uses important elements of the *Enûma Elish* and crafts an argument that undermines the power of the Babylonian deities and affirms the strength of G*d (*Elohim*). In doing so, it also presents an alternative cosmology.

For most scholars, the main point of contention between Genesis and the Babylonian creation story is the role that the heavenly bodies play. According to the *Enûma Elish*, Marduk created stations in the sky for the deities. He set up constellations to determine the year, the months, and the days. Regarding the deities, it is assumed that Genesis 1:1–2:4a is written in opposition to the world view undergirding the *Enûma Elish*. "In the capital, the main sanctuary was dedicated to the sun. As a result, the whole empire saw itself as representative of the sun. Its army, which massacred the world, did so as ambassador of celestial deities. In order to confront this military and imperial machinery, it was necessary to take away its divine authority."[12] Genesis 1:1–2:4a goes to great length to show that the heavenly bodies are not deities. They are created by G*d for a purpose: to separate day and night and to direct the seasons. Because G*d had already created light before placing the sun, the moon, and the stars on the firmament, these heavenly bodies are now reduced to celestial lanterns. In other words, they do not even generate light on their own but are channels for the light that had already been created by *Elohim* in the first place. They have no power of their own because they are created by G*d to serve a specific purpose in the whole of creation.

The line of argument employed in Genesis 1:1–2:4a, affirming the secondary role of these celestial bodies, must be understood in the context of a rhetoric-liturgical dispute with social and political consequences. The two accounts clash with each other in the understanding

---

11. Ibid., 39.
12. Schwantes, *Projetos de Esperança*, 30–31; my translation.

of the divine and the purpose of humanity. In the Babylonian story, the first generation of deities is not concerned with creating the world but with creating new beings. The nature of the divine pairs that descend from Apsu and Tiamat (Lahmu and Lahamu; Anshar and Kishar) is a matter of conjecture, since the written material available is not enough to establish their role in earlier creation stories.[13] What is clear is the fact that the original deities are presented as masculine and feminine pairs, but in the successive generation of deities there is a political predominance of masculine entities, with female deities described solely as consorts. The narrative culminates with Marduk and the destruction of the mother goddess, Tiamat. In the Genesis account, the description of the divine does not adopt a gender-specific role. The grammatically plural noun *Elohim*, as well as the use of the "royal we" in Genesis 1:26, may well place the creative deity of Israel more on a par with the second or third generations of Babylonian deities and may include the characteristics of female deities under the terminology *Elohim*. The ambiguity of the term to address the divine shows, at the same time, its generic configuration as well its translatability.[14]

The ambiguity of the plural divine creates a sharp contrast with Marduk, whose masculine attributes are highlighted as he exerts his power over the mother goddess and destroys Tiamat. The primal mother plays a key role in fertility, but, as Babylon evolves toward the ordered agricultural and urban world, her powers are a threat. Thus, Marduk becomes the champion "who defeats the primal Mother in her 'chaotic' form and 'orders' her into the separated and organized world of heaven and earth, planetary systems and settled fields, irrigation ditches and cities."[15] Using the body of Tiamat to fashion heaven and Earth as well as the blood of Kingu to fashion humanity, Marduk shapes raw material (nature) into different products (culture).

Elohim, on the other hand, creates by ordering chaos into cosmos. At no time is the Hebrew deity identified in anthropomorphic terms. In reality, God's existence is not accounted for. Unlike Marduk, for example, who has ancestors, the Hebrew tradition omits the origin of the creator. G*d is not the product of a theogony but stands outside the primal watery chaos (no longer directly identified with the characteristics of the primal mother). The cosmos is ordered through a series of verbal commands: creation happens through the power of *dabar*, through words (speech-action).[16] There is no power struggle, no con-

---

13. Maria Lamas, *Mitologia Geral: O Mundo dos Deuses e dos Heróis* (Lisboa: Estampa, 1972/3).
14. See Mark S. Smith, *God in Translation: Deities in Cross-Cultural Discourse in the Biblical World* (Grand Rapids: Eerdmans, 2010), 273.
15. Ruether, *Womanguides*, 40.

flict between younger and older generations, no dilacerating of bodies. Creation is clean and peaceful: the creator of this cosmos is simultaneously transcendent to its creation and totally in control.

Both the *Enûma Elish* and Genesis 1:1–2:4a place a great deal of importance on resting. Whereas the Hebrew story places rest as the culmination of creation, as a way to repose from all the work that was done (Gen 2:3b), the Babylonian version places rest at the beginning. It is the lack of rest that engenders the epic. The noisy gatherings of the younger gods prevent their parents and grandparents from resting. Thus, Apsu proposes to destroy them and put an end to their ways so that silence would be established and he could sleep. Rest, then, is a key point in both stories. In the Babylonian narrative, the turn of events is dreadful: Apsu is slain, Tiamat is killed, the defeated gods are imprisoned and made to work as servants, and humanity is created to take over the work of the defeated gods and feed the host of Babylonian deities. In the Hebrew story, the day of rest, *Sabbath*, is blessed and hallowed; it is created by G*d as a day to rest, to organize the people, and to assure their cultural and religious survival.[17]

While the Babylonian narrative has an array of male and female deities, the Hebrew account employs the ambiguous plural *Elohim*. The existence of female deities in the Babylonian story offers no indication that the situation of women and men is qualitatively better in that society. Rather, the *Enûma Elish* illustrates the gradual loss of power of the goddesses when society moved to a more urban and militaristic environment. Their role is reduced to that of spouses or mothers of high-ranking gods. This is the case of Damkina, mother of Marduk. Goddesses exist in a domesticated role, and their existence does not mean that the lives of the human beings, female or male, are necessarily more enjoyable.

The role of humanity is particularly divergent in these two accounts. The Babylonian account describes human beings created from a defeated deity for the purpose of servanthood. "The serfs who labor on the great plantations of the aristocracy of temple and palace are analogous to the lowly humans created to be serfs of the Gods, while the hierarchy of deities represents the hierarchy of cities in the Babylonian empire, crowned by the reigning city of Babylonia."[18] The human

---

16. Genesis 1:1–2:4a clearly draws from the prophetic tradition, where the power of the word is so fundamental. Words are, after all, the tools of the prophets. Interestingly, the same people who would not allow Amos in their midst or would imprison Jeremiah are now using the prophetic mode to articulate themselves. Those who had once downplayed the prophets are now prophets themselves. It is the word that shapes the world.

17. Carlos Mesters, *A Missão do Povo que Sofre: Os Cânticos do Servo de Deus no Livro do Profeta Isaías* (Petrópolis: Vozes, 1981).

beings created in Genesis 1:1–2:4a have a very distinctive role. They have not been created for servitude, to carry out the work the lesser gods do not wish to perform. To the contrary, humanity is to have dominion over the fish of the sea, over the birds of the air, over the cattle, over all the Earth and everything that creeps upon it (Gen 1:26). Being made in the image of G*d, human beings partake in G*d's creation with responsibility toward it.

Human beings are not created from the blood of a defeated god to live in servitude; they are made according to G*d's image and in G*d's likeness. Not only that, they come in an explicit variety of genders—and both represent the divine. The creation story in Genesis might signify an alternative for humanity: both women and men are created in the image of God. If male and female are made according to the image of G*d, then it is possible to interpret that "male and female" are also clues to identify the image of God. "To describe male and female, then, is to perceive the image of God; to perceive the image of God is to glimpse the transcendence of God."[19] The Genesis account preserves the otherness of G*d but also shows that male and female are made in G*d's image. The model of relationship is not of servanthood but of equality, with shared responsibilities.

This framework of shared responsibility and equality helps us better understand the Genesis account, in which humans are given power over creation, having dominion over the fish of the sea, the birds of the heavens, the domestic animals, over all the Earth, and over every creeping thing. The imperative makes sense in its original setting, when humanity felt vulnerable to the threats of natural disasters or overwhelmed by the tasks of daily survival. It was a way to reclaim human dignity and empower those who were disenfranchised by the Babylonian empire. But it makes less sense in an environmentally conscious age. Rather than dominion, the perils of omnicide (the ability to destroy all forms of life) warn us against the abuses that an anthropocentric world view have engendered. The very notion of *imago Dei* needs to be revisited.

Imago Dei in an Age of Global Climate Disruption

Having established the context of the creation account narrated in Genesis 1, it becomes clear why the claim that humanity is made in the image of G*d is so relevant. The Babylonian story emphasizes the

---

18. Ruether, *Womanguides*, 40.
19. Trible, *God and the Rhetoric*, 21.

power of Marduk, his victory over the Mother Goddess, and his claim to become a supreme deity. It also explains the creation of humanity for the sole purpose of serving the Babylonian deities. In this context, to affirm that humanity is made in the image of G*d is a defiance. Like a prophetic voice, to be made in the image of G*d is to restore dignity and life to those in exile. If this message was liberating in that context, how can the notion of *imago Dei* be reclaimed today to foster an environmentally conscious and just relationship with the planet in an age of anthropogenic climate distortion?

First, it is necessary to emphasize humanity's role as *creature*, and not as *creator*. While humans are placed on Earth to be caretakers and stewards of creation, they are not given absolute power over it. "Dominion" does not indicate the authority to destroy (which would ultimately be a sin). As creatures, and therefore not G*d, the distinctive role of humanity is to have free will, the power to make decisions, and to be held accountable for our actions. As creatures, humans have the capacity to err and strive to correct errors. The ability to ponder about our place in the world and the purpose of existence makes us seek for the meaning of our lives. Larry L. Rasmussen aptly articulates this through his reflection on the creatures we are, the world we have, the faith we seek, and the ethic we need.[20] In answering the questions about human existence and purpose, the Genesis account differs from the Babylonian narrative in that humans are created not for bondage and servitude but for dominion. And although "dominion" was used as an excuse for pillaging the world around us, this "dominion" should rather been interpreted as a responsibility to tend and look after creation—which ultimately belongs to God, not to us. Humanity's role is that of stewards, not proprietors.

Second, to be fashioned in the image and likeness of G*d does not make humanity G*d. Christian theology has long emphasized that the image of G*d makes humanity different from all other creatures, that is, special in the way humans relate to G*d and the entirety of creation. Nevertheless, the creation account in Genesis 1:1–2:4a indicates that everything is part of G*d's good creation and is placed under G*d's providential care. To be distinctive (in being made in the *imago Dei*) is not synonymous with superiority or self-sufficiency. The fact that humans do not even have a day for their creation—but share their day of creation with other animals—is an indication that humans are not the apex of G*d's work. As seen earlier, the creation account culmi-

---

20. Larry L. Rasmussen, *Earth-Honoring Faith: Religious Ethics in a New Key* (Oxford: Oxford University Press, 2013).

nates with rest, and it is in the capacity to rest and keep the *Sabbath* holy that humanity experiences its closeness with the divine, sharing in G*d's image. To be made in the image of G*d means not that we physically look like G*d but that humanity shares in the gift of rest afforded by G*d. This is not applicable only to humanity, since, interestingly, creation also requires rest, as the law regarding jubilee remind us (Lev 25:10).[21]

Third, human beings are human only in relationships. Although the passage of Genesis 1:27 (where humanity is created as male and female) has sometimes been misused to enforce heteronormativity (that heterosexuals reflect the *imago Dei* more closely than LGTBQ+), the novelty of the passage lies precisely in its affirmation of difference and plurality. It asserts that the image of G*d is also reflected in what is different from ourselves. Instead of ascribing dignity and value only to those who are similar to us, Genesis 1:27 is a reminder that the divine imagery is found in a variety of expressions. The fact that *Elohim* creates us as an analogy to "themselves" (plural) says as much about the divine as it says about humanity. G*d is multiple and complex.[22] Central, here, is our equality before G*d. To be able to see the divine in others is, perhaps, to understand and exercise what being made in the image of G*d means and entails: to affirm the goodness of creation (Gen 1:31: "G*d saw everything that G*d had made and indeed, it was very good"). When we recognize that those who are different from us are also a reflection of divine image, we can rehearse relationships based on mutual respect and dignity.

Fourth, as Sallie McFague has suggested, creation itself is the body of G*d, and we ought to care for the Earth as if it were G*d's body.[23] If creation is G*d's self-expression, our own embodiment needs to be acknowledged and celebrated, striving to live better on Earth and in partnership with creation. Sin is a matter of offence against other parts of the body (which, of course, includes not only humanity but the totality of creation), and salvation is a reference not simply to an eschatological reality but to the here and now. G*d is not a noun or a distant being, but being itself. The idea of G*d as a verb offers a dynamic reading on creation, one in which G*d is the source of all relationship. This "being in relation" is at the center of humanity's role vis-à-vis the entirety of creation. The over-quoted claim of human dominion needs to be paired with the realization that humanity is not the apex of divine

---

21. Jubilee is the year at the end of the seven cycles of sabbatical years. It had an impact on the ownership and management of land.
22. Catherine Keller, *On the Mystery: Discerning Divinity in Process* (Minneapolis: Fortress, 2008), 64.
23. Sallie McFague, *The Body of God: An Ecological Theology* (Minneapolis: Fortress, 1993).

creativity. Rather, human beings are part of a collective creation that G*d declares to be "very good" (Genesis 1:31). By living out the role of responsible caretakers of creation, humanity can experience that which G*d has deemed to be "very good."

Finally, we are partners in creation and need to consider what the well-being of the entire creation requires from us. "A partnership ethic is a synthesis between an ecological approach based on moral consideration for all living and nonliving things and a human-centered (or homocentric) approach based on the social good and the fulfillment of basic human needs."[24] While human beings have need for food, clothing, shelter, and energy in order to survive, nature also has needs in order to survive. To carefully balance these needs is to engage in ethical considerations, hearing not only human wants and needs but also nature's voice. When humanity takes its role of being stewards of creation seriously, it will go beyond egocentric and anthropocentric greed and strive for the well-being of both the human and the more-than-human communities.

The concept of *imago Dei* has profound consequences for environmental well-being. The notion of *imago Dei* continues to be valid, particularly in the context of disenfranchised people, whose dignity is denied, and of environmental degradation, which has contributed to global climate disruption. To be made in the image and likeness of G*d is an affirmation of worth and respect for those who historically have had their worth and respect denied. Today, this includes climate and environmental justice. It is a resounding "I am" in the midst of realities and conditions that affirm nonbeing and nothingness. The concept of *imago Dei* also needs to be revised in order to curb anthropocentric theology and practice. Human activity has been the dominant influence on climatic and environmental changes, and these actions have often been justified through religious discourse. By revisiting the creation account found in the first chapter of Genesis and interpreting the context of its assertions, we realize that the imperative to exert dominion is not one of destruction but rather one of partnership with creation. This offers an ethical framework more conducive to climate justice.

---

24. Carolyn Merchant, *Reinventing Eden: The Fate of Nature in Western Culture* (New York: Routledge, 2004), 226.

Sin and Evil

7

The Fire Alarm Is Off:
A Feminist Theological Reflection
on Sin, Climate Change, Energy,
and the Protection of Wilderness in Iceland

Arnfríður Guðmundsdóttir

Headlines about global climate change remind us that things are not as they should be. When we hear about the hazard that is threatening our Earth, "our common home," and its inhabitants, we know that something is really wrong. Our environment is in danger because of us. Theologically speaking, it means that we have not been the stewards of God's good creation we have been called to be. Believing in God, the creator of heaven and Earth, Christians cannot but have a voice in the public discussion of the current ecological situation and the challenges brought to us by global climate change. Furthermore, I believe that Christian theology provides us with useful tools and important perspectives that can help us recognize (and admit) what has gone wrong and move toward a better situation for our Earth and for us all. In this chapter, I will argue that key theological terms, such as *sin*, *repentance*, and *salvation*, can prove relevant when it comes to addressing the serious consequences of irresponsible treatment of nature and natural resources, and more particularly global climate change.

When we forget who we are as stewards of God's creation, when we forget about others and we ourselves become the center of our universe, then we bend in toward ourselves and become twisted and ingrown. To be fully bent in on ourselves is what it means to be *caught in sin*. Sin is a relational concept. It signifies a broken relationship to God, our Creator, as well as to our neighbor, nature, and ourselves. From an ecological perspective, it is crucial that we understand sin as pertaining not exclusively to the individual but also to "the social structural relationships that shape our societies and their impact on eco-systems."[1]

The Christian tradition has sometimes been accused of supporting an irresponsible attitude toward God's creation by not paying attention to the mistreatment of nature. Therefore, it is critical to make a clear distinction between "use" (*usus*) and "abuse" (*abusus*). The biblical notion of stewardship is the call to take care of God's good creation and to maintain it. If someone has transformed her call to stewardship into sheer domination and selfishness, *use has turned into abuse*. Pollution, greed, and exploitation are all consequences of a shortsighted and selfish perspective, which goes against prioritization of the benefit of human and nonhuman others. On the other hand, sustainable living and fair distribution of material goods are in accordance with good stewardship. All things considered, the notion of stewardship is a clear antithesis to any form of hubris, including the exploitation of the environment, which is inducing the severe threat of global warming.[2]

Given the contextual nature of theology, I will focus on my own context, which is Iceland, and the striking consequences of the environmental crisis and climate change. Our legal system, as well as our culture at large, is to a great extent based on a Christian heritage; the majority of people in Iceland have belonged to the Christian church for the past thousand years. Today, the Evangelical Lutheran Church of Iceland has the status of a national church, with constitutional protection. It is fair to say that Christianity, more particularly a Lutheran

---

1. Cynthia D. Moe-Lobeda, *Resisting Structural Evil: Love as Ecological-Economic Vocation* (Minneapolis: Fortress, 2013), 59.
2. *Earth 101* is an important project, and vital resource on climate science and the environmental crisis, based in Reykjavik, Iceland. See: http://earth101.is/the-project/.

version of Christianity, provides a foundation for basic values and legal codes, including the constitution. To speak theologically about major societal issues is something that has been practiced in our society for centuries. This does not mean that secularization has not shaped our society in recent decades, which it certainly has. It only means that theological discourse continues to be a part of the public discussion, even if secularization and multiculturalism are gradually changing the way we think and talk. I take it as my responsibility as a theologian to address the threat exploitation of nature and climate change is posing to the future of our island and to the Earth. Thus, in this chapter, I will reflect on the current climate disaster as a Christian feminist theologian rooted in the Lutheran tradition.

Iceland is an island just south of the Arctic Circle. In the Arctic, climate change is faster and therefore more severe than in most places, as it is warming at a rate of almost twice the global average.[3] The melting of the ice in the far North does not only affect the Arctic countries but has real and dangerous consequences for the rest of the world as well, due to for example rising of sea levels and increasing temprature.[4] This is a serious reminder to all of us that the effects of climate change in one particular part of the world are never isolated events. Indeed, more than anything else, climate change helps us understand how everything on Earth is interconnected.[5] In theological terms, belonging to the one "body of God" (to borrow Sallie McFague's metaphor), we are called to take into consideration the well-being of the whole creation, particularly those who are suffering the consequences of climate change most, namely the poor, the majority of whom are women.[6] *Planetary solidarity* helps us understand that climate change is our common responsibility, while our respective contexts determine the appropriate response.

Despite alarming information about the serious consequences of increasing greenhouse gas emissions, Icelandic politicians are planning for new heavy industrial plants to be built and are handing out per-

---

3. The reason why the Arctic is warming at this rate is because ice and snow reflect a high proportion of the sun's energy into space. While snow and ice are melting, bare rock and water absorb more and more of the sun's energy, making it ever warmer. See: "Arctic Climate Change," WWF Global, accessed May 28, 2016, http://tinyurl.com/mjkfsfo.

4. "Five Reasons Why the Speed of Arctic Sea Ice Loss Matters." https://www.carbonbrief.org/five-reasons-why-the-speed-of-arctic-sea-ice-loss-matters, accessed June 15, 2016.

5. In Sallie McFague's (*A New Climate for Theology: God, the World, and Global Warming* [Minneapolis: Fortress, 2008], 50) words: "everything is related to everything else." See also, Francis, *Laudato Sí': On Care for our Common Home* (Mahwah, NJ: Paulist, 2015), 85.

6. Mayesha Alam, Rukmani Bhatia, and Briana Mawby, *Women and Climate Change: Impact and Agency in Human Rights, Security, and Economic Development* (Washington, DC: Georgetown Institute for Women, Peace and Security, 2015), 7, PDF, http://tinyurl.com/luw5zy4.

missions to companies to drill for oil within Icelandic territories. When public authorities and citizens ignore their civic responsibilities, we all suffer, individually and communally, as injustice abounds and evil flourishes. In order to get back on track, we need to acknowledge what has gone wrong and do something about it. This is an important part of our Christian heritage: to acknowledge our responsibility toward our community (*coram hominibus*) and ultimately toward God, our Creator (*coram Deo*). Given our current ecological situation, and the challenges brought to us by global climate change, I believe theology provides us with important tools and perspectives that help us face the seriousness of our situation and turn around for the benefit of future generations.

A Sinful Situation and the Call to Turn Around

> I do not believe that sin is the enemy we often make it out to be, at least not when we recognize it and name it as such. When we see how we have turned away from God, then and only then do we have what we need to begin turning back. Sin is our only hope, the fire alarm that wakes us up to the possibility of true repentance.[7]

It is fair to say that the concept of sin does not have a good reputation. An important reason for its ill repute is that sin-talk has often been used by those in positions of domination to blame or shame other people with the intention of keeping them in their place. This has often been detrimental for women, people of color, and other marginalized groups, "whose full self and center have been denied to them."[8] A traditional understanding of sin as limited to the personal sphere also fits badly with the emphasis popular culture places on the importance of developing a positive self-image by nurturing self-esteem. Finally, sin-talk is out of fashion because it has been moralized and turned into a cliché. In her book *Speaking of Sin: The Lost Language of Salvation*, Barbara Brown Taylor maintains that pastors often avoid using the word *sin*, whether in prayers or conversations, and that some church communities have eliminated the confession of sin from their Sunday services altogether so as to make worship a more positive experience.[9] Taylor does not think this is a way to go for Christians. She writes: "Abandoning the language of sin will not make sin go away. Human beings will continue to experience alienation, deformation, damnation, and death

---

7. Barbara Brown Taylor, *Speaking of Sin: The Lost Language of Salvation* (Cambridge, MA: Cowley, 2000), 67.
8. Moe-Lobeda, *Resisting Structural Evil*, 58.
9. Taylor, *Speaking of Sin*, 4.

no matter what we call them."[10] Getting rid of sin-talk not only will leave us speechless in face of these experiences, which will increase our denial of their presence in our lives, it also weakens the language of grace, "since the full impact of forgiveness cannot be felt apart from the full impact of what has been forgiven."[11]

Interestingly, Taylor argues that secularism has replaced the language of sin and salvation with the language of medicine and law.[12] This means that "the really awful things are turned over to the courts as crimes, while the more self-destructive things are turned over to the medical establishment as mental illnesses, leaving a great deal in the middle to become strictly personal matters."[13] Taylor does not think, however, that either the language of medicine or the language of law is able to replace the language of theology, as theology makes it possible for Christians to talk about their experience of broken relationships, "with God, with one another, with the whole created order."[14] In theological language, Taylor maintains, sin is the choice to remain in broken relationships, while "the choice to enter into the process of repair is called repentance, an often bitter medicine with the undisputed power to save lives."[15] But whenever we talk about human agency and our freedom to choose what is right, it is important to keep in mind that agency and freedom to choose is not always an option. This is, for example, true for women who are caught in abusive situations. The feminist liberation theologian Ivone Gebara examines such situations in her book *Out of the Depths*. She focuses on the kind of evil "that we suffer or endure, something not chosen, the kind of evil present in institutions and social structures that accommodate it, even facilitate it." According to Gebara, "evil of this sort has no connection with conscience or choice."[16]

Sin-talk, then, allows us to describe our human situation, recognize what is wrong, and identify what needs to be done in order to make things right. Barbara Brown Taylor points out that, contrary to the medical model, "we are not entirely at the mercy of our maladies," and versus the legal model, she maintains, "sin is not simply a set of behaviors to be avoided."[17] This is why Taylor sees sin as a hopeful sign,

---

10. Ibid, 5.
11. Ibid.
12. Here Taylor is building on Karl Menninger's book *Whatever Became of Sin* from 1973.
13. Taylor, *Speaking of Sin*, 32.
14. Ibid., 57.
15. Ibid., 58.
16. Ivone Gebara, *Out of the Depths: Women's Experience of Evil and Salvation* (Minneapolis, Fortress, 2002), 1.
17. Taylor, *Speaking of Sin*, 58.

because it is only by recognizing that things are not as they should be that we have a chance to do something about it. She writes:

> Sin is our only hope, because the recognition that something is wrong is the first step toward setting it right again. There is no help for those who admit no need of help. There is no repair for those who insist that nothing is broken, and there is no hope of transformation for a world whose inhabitants accept that it is sadly but irreversibly wrecked.[18]

To face the situation and to decide to do something about it means that we are willing to accept our responsibility: our responsibility for where we are and where we are heading. This is what our Christian tradition calls repentance, "to turn around," or "to come to oneself" (Luke 15:17). The one who has lost track of her direction in life *comes to herself* and decides to do something about it. Thus, repentance starts with a decision to get back in touch with one's Creator, to acknowledge one's mission in life, and to choose a way of living that enhances the well-being of the whole creation.

I do agree with Taylor's emphasis on the importance of retrieving the theological discourse of sin and salvation for our theological understanding of our human situation and our role within creation, but I think it is critical that we do not limit our talk about sin to the personal sphere. This is why I want to stress the collective and structural manifestation of sin, in line with what Cynthia D. Moe-Lobeda does in her book *Resisting Structural Evil: Love as Ecological-Economic Vocation*, where she makes a strong argument for what she calls "the de-privatization of sin, love, morality, and spirituality."[19]

While Moe-Lobeda thinks contemporary theology has already demonstrated how sin may take structural form, she wants to take it one step further by maintaining *"that social structural sin makes monumental demands on the practice of faith and of morality, and many of those demands remain largely unacknowledged."* This is why, Moe-Lobeda argues,

> in many faith communities, response to sin is aimed at the individual's sin, rather than at social structural sin in which the individual participates simply by living as we do. *To the extent that structural sin is not taken seriously, so too, are central aspects of Christian life ignored.*[20]

If key theological terms such as sin, repentance, and salvation are

---

18. Ibid., 59.
19. Moe-Lobeda, *Resisting Structural Evil*, 19.
20. Ibid., 58 (italics in original).

going to be useful when it comes to addressing the serious conse-quences of global climate change, it is crucial that their individual as well as social-structural relevance be taken into account.

Just as the concept of sin has been hijacked by moralism, the mes-sage about salvation from sin has also had a tendency to lose its social significance. If the gospel of God's forgiving grace really means good news about the renewal of broken relationships between us and God, between us and our neighbor, and between us and the rest of the cre-ation, then the social significance of the gospel is unmistakable. Thus, the message is clear: the good news of God's forgiving grace renews our whole existence and calls us to a social responsibility and solidarity with the rest of creation.

The Controversy Regarding Intact Nature and Responsible Behavior

When reflecting on the current ecological situation, Iceland proves to be a meaningful case in point due to the very visible impact of cli-mate change, most notably, the melting of its glaciers. Iceland, with its 40,000 square miles, is the second-largest island in Europe after Great Britain. It is the least-populated country in Europe, with only 330,000 inhabitants, and close to 80 percent of the island is uninhabited. More than 11 percent of the island is covered by glaciers, one of them being Vatnajökull, the largest glacier in Europe. The weather is very mild due to the warm Gulf Stream from the south, while the East Green-land polar current affects the weather in the north and east.[21] How-ever, this may change as scientists predict that the melting of the ice fields of Greenland could hinder the Gulf Stream or stop it altogether and hence lead to a drastic cooling of the North Atlantic, which would have unforeseeable consequences for countries on the both sides of the Atlantic.[22]

Iceland is amongst the youngest landmasses on the Earth, with some of the world's most active volcanoes. There are between thirty and forty active volcanoes, which means that volcanic eruptions and earth-quakes are fairly common. This is a steady reminder of how dependent

21. The average summer temperature in Reykjavik, the capital, is 51 degrees Fahrenheit in July, while the average winter temperature in Reykjavik is about 32 degrees Fahrenheit in January. See "Cli-matological Data," Icelandic Met Office, May 29, 2012, http://tinyurl.com/mwdov9c.
22. Stefan Rahmstorf, Jason E. Box, Georg Feulner, Michael E. Mann, Alexander Robinson, Scott Rutherford, and Erik J. Schaffernicht, "Exceptional Twentieth-Century Slowdown in Atlantic Ocean Overturning Circulation," *Nature Climate Change* 5, no. 5 (2015): 475–80. See also "Atlantic Ocean Overturning Found to Slow Down Already Today," *Potsdam Institute for Climate Impact Research*, March 24, 2015, http://tinyurl.com/mxzp4ax.

we really are on nature and its behavior. At the same time, Iceland has been blessed by abundant resources, including ample wellsprings of clean water, rich reserves of boiling water underground, and last but not least, bountiful fishing grounds. Iceland's natural riches, while plentiful, are by no means unlimited. We also need to keep in mind that nature is not only powerful and potentially destructive but also extremely vulnerable when it comes to human invasion. For that reason, it is important that we remember not only *who* we are but also *where* we are and *what* is expected of us. According to our Christian heritage, we belong to God, are part of God's creation, and are called to be caretakers of everything God has created, while history tells us that it is easy to forget.

For decades, Iceland has been in the forefront when it comes to the use of renewable energy worldwide and ranks the second highest in the *Environmental Performance Index 2016*.[23] But this is only a part of the picture. While Iceland uses geothermal water to heat about 90 percent of homes and thus produces almost all of its electricity from emission free, sustainable natural resources, energy is also being used for other, not so ecologically friendly reasons. The big hydropower plants that have been built inland in order to meet the demand for more energy, especially from multinational corporations, threaten Iceland's wilderness in the uninhabited highlands in the center of the island and hence are greatly controversial. Consequently, new heavy industrial plants will increase greenhouse gas emissions, boosting the danger due to climate change.[24]

In 2003, the government started the biggest single construction project in Icelandic history, the Kárahnjúkar Hydropower Plant, by far the largest power plant in Iceland. "Kárahnjúkar dam is the tallest concrete-faced rock-fill dam in Europe and among the largest of its kind in the world."[25] The power plant is located inland, north of Vatnajökull, and harnesses two glacial rivers. When the dam was completed, a large section of pristine wilderness with rivers, waterfalls, mountains, and mossy highlands disappeared under water.[26] The plant reached full operational capacity in 2007 and provides electricity for the US multinational Alcoa's aluminum smelter, located in the east of Iceland.

The Kárahnjúkar power plant has been the focus of a heated debate, which divided the nation into two opposite factions. It is hard to

23. "Country Rankings," Environmental Performance Index, 2016, http://tinyurl.com/lz7ewa9.
24. According to the Icelandic Environment Association, "71% of all electricity in Iceland is produced for multinational aluminum corporations." http://landvernd.is/en.
25. "Kárahnjúkar Hydroelectric Power Station," Mannvit, http://tinyurl.com/lhdsqoe.
26. Arni Finnsson, "Power Driven," Iceland Nature Conservation Association, November 29, 2003, http://tinyurl.com/ks4b763.

describe what this single, gigantic venture has done to our community and our nature. Aimed at raising awareness, the documentary film *Dreamland* (2010) details the detrimental environmental and social consequences of the dam.[27] The film aims to show how a nation with an abundance of natural, nonpolluting energy choices gradually becomes caught up in a plan to turn its wilderness and beautiful nature into a massive system of hydroelectric and geothermal power plants with dams and reservoirs. Clean energy brings in polluting industry and international corporations.[28]

Without doubt, Iceland's dams and reservoirs are "the dark side of green energy."[29] The danger that something like this will happen again is real. If anything, the Kárahnjúkar power plant has taught us the importance of being proactive when it comes to protecting our precious ecosystems and the grandeur of our landscape but, first and foremost, of acting responsibly in face of the looming consequences of climate change.

Iceland's 2008 economic crisis has complicated things. After the collapse of its banking system, our country has faced the demanding task of building up a healthy economy free of corruption, mindful of the many ways the poor especially have been affected due to the pressures on the country's welfare system. The economic crisis has also put great pressures on environmental policies, but during the years following the collapse the environment was often treated as a topic that had to wait until "more serious matters" had been addressed. This attitude was evident, for example, in the voices that demanded "more aggressive fishing and the immediate harnessing of the nation's energy resources for financial gain."[30] Despite strong resistance against new dams and power plants in the highlands, the current government is in favor of new large-scale energy projects that would mean further exploitation of the pristine nature in the center of Iceland and greenhouse gas emissions escalating.

Probably the wildest idea that is being entertained today is that Iceland will serve as a provider for green energy to Great Britain through an undersea cable. Allegedly, a "UK-Iceland Energy Task Force" has been set up to examine the feasibility of the scheme.[31] Reacting to

27. *Dreamland*, directed by Þorfinnur Guðnason and Andri Snær Magnason (Reykjavík: Ground Control Productions, 2009), http://www.dreamland.is/.
28. Ibid.
29. Ibid.
30. Svandís Svavarsdóttir, foreword to "Welfare for the Future: Iceland's National Strategy for Sustainable Development; Priorities 2010–2013," 1, PDF, http://tinyurl.com/lhkzxfk.
31. Adam Withnall, "David Cameron to Announce Plan to Power UK by Harnessing Iceland's Volcanoes," *Independent*, October 29, 2015, http://tinyurl.com/kw2xrzc.

the news about the power line to Britain, Björk Guðmundsdóttir, the world-renowned Icelandic musician, together with Andri Snær Magnason, a well-known writer and one of the directors of the documentary *Dreamland*, appealed in November 2015 to the world for support "against our Government." In a press conference, they criticized the government for having plans "to pave roads, erect power lines and build power plants right through the center of Iceland, which would drastically alter the landscape and slice the highlands in half."[32]

In March 2016, a group of more than twenty Icelandic organizations signed a mission statement promoting the formation of a national park in the center of Iceland.[33] The park would comprise close to 40 percent of the country, or 40,000 km² (15,500 square miles), including the Vatnajökull Park, which is 14,000 km² (5,400 square miles). The organizations want to preserve the landscape as it is and fight any irrevocable development in the highlands. They are asking the public to sign their mission statement to protect the highlands.[34]

Constitutional Rights of Nature and the Environment

The 2008 economic crisis hit Iceland hard and led to a total crash of its financial system, due in part to the criminal financial speculation by its own banks.[35] The crash came as a huge surprise to most people. During the years leading up the crash, there had been warnings coming from financial specialists in Iceland as well as abroad, pointing toward the impending danger to the financial system as a whole. The warnings were ignored by both authorities and individuals, who decided to focus on the "booming" economy and its benefits for the entire society. The economic crisis was a real wake-up call to the Icelandic people, who had dozed off when they should have been fully alert, who had slept when they should have stayed awake. Theologically speaking, the Icelandic people failed in our stewardship. It is alarming to see the similarities between what happened prior to the collapse of Iceland's banking system and the warning signs we are now experiencing because of the changes in our climate. Too often, the headlines warning us of the looming dangers facing us are often met with utter skepticism, just like before the crash in 2008.

32. "Press Conference—Björk and Andri Snær during Airwaves, Nov. 6th," AndriMagnason.com, November 7, 2015, http://tinyurl.com/k7mj5zk.
33. "Protect the Highland," Hálendið – Iceland National Park, http://halendid.is/.
34. Björk Guðmundsdóttir, the musician, together with our former president, Vigdís Finnbogadóttir, are the leading figures behind the statement.
35. The key players within the financial system have been sentenced to prison based on their participation in the process that led to the collapse of the Icelandic banks.

The collapse of Iceland's financial system had serious consequences for the infrastructure of Icelandic society as a whole, which led to a strong demand from the people for a reevaluation and restructuring of the interior of our societal structure, including a rewriting of our constitution.[36] In the summer of 2010, Althingi, the Icelandic Parliament, passed a bill calling for the formation of a Constitutional Council with twenty-five members who were to be chosen in a general election in November 2010.[37] A National Forum was held at the beginning of November 2010 in order to propose important changes to the constitution and to collect a database for the Constitutional Council. A random sample of 950 individuals between eighteen and ninety-one years old met for one day to discuss cares and concerns relating to the governance of our country. The aim of the National Forum was to elicit principles and values the people of Iceland consider necessary for the future of our society.[38] Throughout its work, the Constitutional Council was guided by three basic principles from the National Forum —namely, distribution of power, transparency, and responsibility.[39]

The Constitutional Council assembled at the beginning of April 2011 and was given four months to write a bill for a new constitution.[40] On July 29, the council handed the bill for the proposal of a new constitution, unanimously approved by all delegates, to the Speaker of Althingi.[41] A national referendum was held on October 20, 2012, in which 67 percent of those who voted (the turn out in the referendum was a little less than 50 percent) wanted the Constitution Council's proposals to form the basis of a new constitution. Over 80 percent said they wanted natural resources that are not privately owned to be declared national property.[42] The parliament has not yet decided what will happen to the proposal, despite the clear results from the referen-

36. Our current constitution is a slightly adjusted version of the Danish constitution, given to us by the Danish king when Iceland was still a part of the Danish Kingdom. A writing of our own constitution has been in the pipelines since Iceland became an independent republic in 1944. For further information about the process of writing a new constitution, see Arnfríður Guðmundsdóttir, "Aiming for a Just Society: A Theological Response to the 2008 Economic Collapse in Iceland," *Political Theology* 14, no. 2 (2013): 188–200.

37. The members of the council came from many different backgrounds and professions, including two theologians, one of them the author of this chapter.

38. "The Main Conclusions from the National Forum 2010," November 7, 2010, http://tinyurl.com/mqy6egq.

39. *Blueberry Soup*, directed by Eileen Jerrett (Wilma's Wish Productions, 2013), is a documentary about the writing of a new Icelandic constitution following the financial crisis of 2008: http://tinyurl.com/ojy48ls.

40. During that time, the public had wide access to the council's work through the council's website, where people could write comments and offer suggestions to council members: Silvia Suteu, "Constitutional Conventions in the Digital Era: Lessons from Iceland and Ireland," *Boston College International and Comparative Law Review* 38, no. 2 (2015): 251–76, http://tinyurl.com/klw55ee.

41. Stjórnlagaráð, "A Proposal for a New Constitution for the Republic of Iceland," March 24, 2011, English translation, PDF, http://tinyurl.com/l85rq9f.

dum. The majority of the parliament, which has been in power since 2013, has been openly against the proposal, arguing against any significant changes to the constitution.

The task of the Constitutional Council was to write a new constitution that would guide the Icelandic nation toward a just society. Regarding climate change, the chapter on *Human Rights and Nature* is particularly important, in which a necessary balance between rights and responsibilities is emphasized, echoing the idea of good stewardship in the first chapters of Genesis. The fundamental Christian belief that everybody is created in the image of God is reflected in the basic principle of the equal status and equal rights of all citizens. Article 6 in the proposed bill is a rewriting of the current article on equal rights. It reads:

> We are all equal under the law and shall enjoy our human rights without discrimination, such as due to gender, age, genetic character, place of residence, economic status, disability, sexual orientation, race, colour, opinions, political affiliation, religion, language, origin, ancestry and position in other respects. Men and women shall enjoy equal rights in every respect.[43]

The inclusion of articles dealing with nature and the environment (article 33) and natural resources (article 34) in the chapter on human rights is meant to underscore the close connection between the rights of those who live off the land and the rights of the land itself. Sustainability is key. Article 33, on "nature and environment of Iceland," reads as follows:

> Iceland's nature constitutes the basis for life in the country. All shall respect and protect it.

> All shall by law be accorded the right to a healthy environment, fresh water, unpolluted air and unspoiled nature. This means that the diversity of life and land must be maintained and nature's objects of value, uninhabited areas, vegetation and soil shall enjoy protection. Earlier damages shall be repaired as possible.

> The use of natural resources shall be such that their depletion will be minimized in the long term and that the right of nature and coming generations be respected.[44]

---

42. "Advertisement of the Results of the Referendum on 20 October 2012," Ministry of the Interior, October 31, 2012, http://tinyurl.com/l75xo4z.
43. "Proposal for a New Constitution," 3.
44. Ibid., 8.

Article 34 focuses on natural resources, where the emphasis is on the ownership of the nation. This is stated in the very beginning of this article, which reads:

> Iceland's natural resources that are not private property shall be the joint and perpetual property of the nation. No one can acquire the natural resources, or rights connected thereto, as property or for permanent use and they may not be sold or pledged.[45]

Articles 33 and 34 are widely supported by the people, as they got the biggest support at the national referendum, with more than 80 percent stating that they wanted natural resources that are not privately owned to be declared national property. At the same time, they are among the most controversial of the proposed constitution and certainly one of the main reasons why the proposal has not been passed at the parliament.

Article 35, which focuses on "information on the environment and the parties concerned," is an important reminder of the shared responsibility of public authorities and individuals living in Iceland. The article stresses the common responsibility of shared stewardship entrusted to the authorities as well as the public and is a good example of the emphasis the Constitutional Council put on the equal and fair distribution of power, transparency, and responsibility, the three basic principles from the National Forum.[46]

If (or hopefully, when) the proposal is approved, the articles regarding nature and the environment, natural resources, and information on the environment will make a real difference for the future of Icelandic

---

45. Ibid. The rest of article 34 reads:

Publicly owned natural resources include resources such as marine stocks, other resources of the ocean and its bottom within Iceland's economic zone and the sources of water and water-harnessing rights, the rights to geothermal energy and mining. The public ownership of resources below a certain depth under the Earth's surface may be determined by law.

In the use of natural resources, sustainable development and public interest shall be used for guidance. The public authorities, along with those using the natural resources, shall be responsible for their protection. The public authorities may, on the basis of law, issue permits for the use of natural resources or other limited public goods, against full payment and for a modest period of time in each instance. Such permits shall be issued on an equal-opportunity basis and it shall never lead to a right of ownership or irrevocable control of the natural resources.

46. Ibid., 9. Article 35 reads:

The public authorities shall inform the public on the state of the environment and nature and the impact of construction thereon. The public authorities and others shall provide information on an imminent danger to nature, such as environmental pollution. The law shall secure the right of the public to have the opportunity to participate in the preparation of decisions that have an impact on the environment and nature as well as the possibility to seek independent verdicts thereon. In taking decisions regarding Iceland's nature and environment, the public authorities shall base their decisions on the main principles of environmental law.

society. Not only will it help the nation move toward a fair distribution of our natural resources (including the oceanic resources), but it will help us aim for a responsible use of the invaluable resources that have been entrusted to us. It would give us a chance to set long-term goals for resources such as geothermal water and "green" electricity, instead of focusing on short-term interests. Given the impending changes because of global warming, I believe the message of these articles is critical not only for everybody living on this island in the future but for all the future inhabitants of the Earth, "our common home."

Iceland: A "Classroom" Example of the Effects of Climate Change

In his speech at the COP21 Summit in Paris in November 2015, the Icelandic Prime Minister made the following remarks regarding the very visible effects of global warming in Iceland:

> Climate change is already visible in Iceland. Our glaciers are retreating. We have decided to improve the monitoring of our glaciers and to make the results—and the glaciers themselves—more accessible for visitors and the public. Iceland will become in a way a real-life classroom on the effects of climate change. With no action on emissions, the ice in Iceland could largely disappear in 100 years. Indeed, ice on land and sea is retreating in the Arctic region as a whole. Rising temperatures and acidification affect the oceans. The marine ecosystem is at risk and the only way to avert this is by cutting carbon dioxide emissions.[47]

Icelanders, including its politicians, have slowly been facing the unmistakable signs of climate change. The former minister for the environment and member of the Parliament, Svandís Svavarsdóttir, believes the Paris climate agreement has put climate issues back on the radar of Icelanders. She recalls how nobody mentioned concerns related to climate change before the 2013 parliamentary elections.[48] Now people are waking up to the facts and the possible consequences in the near and far future. An alarming case is the warming and increasing acidity of the ocean around Iceland, which is occurring faster and "more dramatic[ally] than elsewhere," according to Jón Ólafsson, oceanographer and professor emeritus at the University of Iceland. Ólafsson explains that the ocean picks up a lot of carbon dioxide when it is cold. This increases its acidity, and will result in the extinction of many species

47. Sigmundur David Gunnlaugsson, "COP21 Summit Paris 30 November 2015," Prime Minister's Office, http://tinyurl.com/mmcm5q2.
48. Vala Hafstað, "Agreement Breaks Silence on Climate," *Iceland Review*, December 15, 2015, http://tinyurl.com/kmlwdjg.

unless carbon emissions are reduced.[49] For a long-time fishing nation like Iceland, this is no light matter given the economy's high dependence on fisheries and exports of seafood.

It is the nature of glaciers to increase or decrease according to the temperature, precipitation, and other alternating factors of the climate. Glaciers, covering 11 percent of Iceland, store a total of 3,600 km^3 of ice and are retreating and thinning rapidly at present; the decrease amounts to approximately 0.3–0.5 percent every year.[50] Meteorologists are predicting that the glacial meltdown will intensify during the coming decades,[51] "leading to their almost complete disappearance in the next 150–200 years."[52] While it is often hard to identify how changes in the climate are changing our environment, in Iceland the receding of glaciers is its most visible indication. Nowhere in Europe, and in very few places worldwide, are glaciers as approachable as in Iceland. This is particularly true for Vatnajökull Glacier, the largest one in Europe, which is included in the Vatnajökull National Park, a protected wilderness area surrounding the glacier. It is in this way that Iceland becomes a real-life classroom, where people can witness the changes caused by climate change by watching the results from the monitoring system for Icelandic glaciers.[53]

As the weight of glaciers decreases, the land rises; this uplift could lead to increasing volcanic activity.[54] Since 2010, there have been three major eruptions, with serious consequences not only in Iceland but also across the Atlantic by disrupting flight throughout Europe. But while it is known that the melting glaciers effect the environment in multiple ways, "the entire chain reaction of melting ice caps, rising earth surface and volcanic activity is still not entirely understood."[55] Scientists are paying close attention to how the rising of land impacts

49. Ibid.
50. "Measuring Glaciers," Icelandic Met Office, accessed July 9, 2016, http://tinyurl.com/m5zgumu.
51. "The melting processes considered are backwasting, defined as the lateral retreat of near-vertical ice walls, or steep, ice-cored slopes, and downwasting, defined as the thinning of the ice core by melting along the top and bottom surfaces." Johannes Krüger and Kurt H. Kjær, "De-Icing Progression of Ice-Cored Moraines in a Humid, Subpolar Climate, Kötlujökull, Iceland," The Holocene 10, no. 6 (September 2000): 737.
52. Tómas Jóhannesson, Sverrir Guðmundsson, Guðfinna Aðalgeirsdóttir, Helgi Björnsson, Finnur-Pálsson, Oddur Sigurðsson, and Thorsteinn Thorsteinsson, "Response of Glaciers in Iceland to Climate Changes," Nordic Project on Climate and Energy Systems, PDF, http://tinyurl.com/o3ghqzu. See also Helgi Björnsson and Finnur Pálsson, "Icelandic Glaciers," Jökull 58 (2008): 365–86, PDF, http://tinyurl.com/ls8ncwj.
53. Ólafur Ingólfsson, "Icelandic Glaciers," Notendur.hi.is, accessed July 12, 2016, http://tinyurl.com/jvlmv6d.
54. Mari N. Jensen, "Iceland Rises as Its Glaciers Melt from Climate Change," UA News, January 29, 2015, http://tinyurl.com/mdvwdck.
55. Suzanne Goldenberg, "Climate Change Is Lifting Iceland—And It Could Mean More Volcanic Eruptions," The Guardian, January 30, 2015, http://tinyurl.com/n957j3d.

the southeast of Iceland, considering, for example, Höfn in Hornafjörður, a small town just south of Vatnajökull Glacier. Kristín Hermannsdóttir, meteorologist and head of the Nature Research Center, explains the manifold consequences for the village:

> The flow of the glacial rivers changes. The mouth of the river, where ships sail into Hornafjörður, is changing from what it was a few decades ago. Plumbing changes somewhat, sewage and water pipes, as the land rises.[56]

Attempting to resist these impending ramifications, the district has signed an agreement with the Icelandic Environment Association, "aiming at reducing greenhouse gas emission in the community by three percent a year by using environmentally friendlier cars, by sorting garbage, including organic waste, and by reducing food waste."[57] Those actions, taken by the people of Höfn in order to counteract the consequences of climate change, are in line with the projects our government has introduced to "spee[d] up the decarbonisation of transport, fisheries and agriculture."[58] However, at the same time, the very same government is planning to build more power plants to provide energy for more multinational corporations. Furhtermore, within the last three years licenses have been handed out for companies to drill for oil in Drekasvæði, a supposedly oil-rich area northeast of Iceland. It is hard to imagine how new aluminum smelters, silicon metal plants, and oil drilling can possibly comply with strategies to reduce carbon emissions, though the government has committed to a reduction target of up to 40 percent by 2030, together with the European Union and Norway.[59]

The Gender Perspective

According to the *Global Gender Gap Index 2015*, Iceland ranks number one in terms of gender equality (the seventh year in a row). Given this reputation, Iceland's representatives are expected to use every opportunity to address environmental issues from a gender perspective.[60] Not

---

56. Vala Hafstað, "Global Warming Causes Rising Concern in Höfn," *Iceland Review*, March 14, 2016, http://tinyurl.com/l5le3ey.
57. Ibid.
58. Gunnlaugsson, "COP21 Summit Paris." See also "Iceland Announces Climate Change Plan," *Iceland Monitor*, modified April 25, 2016, http://tinyurl.com/la4scs8; "Iceland Signs Paris Climate Change Deal," *Iceland Monitor*, April 25, 2016, http://tinyurl.com/my8655x.
59. "Iceland Joins 40% Emission Target," *Iceland Monitor*, modified April 14, 2016, http://tinyurl.com/kb5bv6r.
60. World Economic Forum, "Rankings," *Global Gender Gap Index 2015*, 2015, http://tinyurl.com/mfc-cbfo.

everybody does, but some do. One example is Svandís Svavarsdóttir, who served as a minister for the Environment and Natural Resources. When she attended the United Nations Conference on Sustainable Development in Rio de Janeiro, Brazil (June 2012), she passionately reminded her audience that "there is no sustainable development without gender equality and women's empowerment." She also criticized "the lack of language on gender and climate," arguing that "women and girls are the most effected, and that their access to decision making, not least on financial matters, has to be ensured."[61]

Together with Denmark, Finland, Norway, and Sweden, and along with the Faroe Islands, Greenland, and Åland, Iceland takes part in the green growth initiative "The Nordic Region—Leading in Green Growth" and the bio-economy initiative "NordBio." The aim is to launch projects in the areas of "green growth, sustainable development and bio-economy."[62] *The Green Growth* reports about those projects and other related activities.

Significant for the green growth initiatives of the Nordic Council of Ministers is the integration of the gender perspective into all the activities linked to the green growth projects. The assumption is that "green growth is also a gender issue," as women and men do not leave the same kind of ecological footprints.[63] Among other things, women and men are known to use different means of transportation and act differently as consumers. The mainstreaming of the gender dimension into the program as a whole is more specifically expressed in the implementation of the three following projects. The first project has to do with supporting extensive research on the connection between green growth and the gender dimension. The second one focuses on empowering women in decision making and business. As women tend to be more environmentally aware, the assumption is that their contribution should be more widely appreciated. Taking into account the different situation of women and men, the third project is concerned with the equal distribution of development aide. As the Nordic countries will be designating a larger proportion of their financial support to projects that allow developing nations to make the transition toward greener economies, the gender perspective will be taken into a consideration. This project of equal distribution between women and men is clearly an important commitment to planetary solidarity on behalf of

61. "Statement at the United Nations Conference on Sustainable Development, 22 June 2012, Rio de Janeiro, Brazil," Ministry for the Environment and Natural Resources, June 22, 2012, http://tinyurl.com/kysg9pc.

62. "Who Are We?" *Green Growth*, September 2016, http://tinyurl.com/k6zm256.

63. "Green Growth Is Also a Gender Issue," *Green Growth*, September 2016, http://tinyurl.com/myt-trt6.

the Nordic nations. Hopefully, it is only a beginning of something more to come.

Given their long-time emphasis on gender equality, it is critical that Nordic countries be at the forefront when it comes to integrating the gender perspective into programs and policies related to climate change. According to Charlotte Kirkegaard, the gender expert working on the Nordic Council of Ministers green growth initiative, there is much to be done in this area. She argues: "We're just at the beginning of analyzing gender inequality as a counterproductive element in the way we think about green growth." More knowledge is needed, Kirkegaard maintains, "on how the genders perform and how results from gender research could improve our ability to stimulate green growth, whether in the region itself or through development aid."[64] Kirkegaard believes it will be a question of political will and courage, the success of the gender mainstreaming, and how soon it will start to make a difference.

The Fire Alarm Is Off

Visible manifestations of climate change within the Icelandic context indicate that things are not what they should be. Faced with the severe consequences of global warming, it is important that we face the seriousness of the situation, that we recognize what has gone wrong, and accept our responsibility as caretakers of God's creation. The fire alarm is off, and it is up to us to respond. We can look the other way, pretend we have not heard (or seen) anything, and act like it is business as usual. But we can also decide it is time to recognize what is happening and call the thing "what it actually is."[65] We can see what we have done, or not done, by not taking care of God's creation and instead taking advantage of our situation, just because we could, because it was to our advantage, as individuals or as a community. We truly have a choice between treading down the same path or turning around and heading in the opposite direction.

We have had several wake-up calls within the past decade in my home country. In the beginning of the twenty-first century, Kárahnjúkar, the big dam in the middle of the island, was a loud and clear wake-up call. For those in power, it secured a quick fix to our economy and justified the damage to Iceland's pristine wilderness. The economic

---

64. Ibid.
65. To call the thing "what it actually is" is a key element in Luther's *theologia crucis*. See Arnfríður Guðmundsdóttir, *Meeting God on the Cross: Christ, the Cross, and the Feminist Critique* (Oxford: Oxford University Press, 2010), 74–78.

crisis in the fall of 2008 was another wake-up call. The people responded by demanding a change of mind, a different course, which resulted in a proposal of a new constitution, a new community covenant, aiming toward a just society. But when push came to shove, there was not enough political courage to implement the constitutional proposal. We are still waiting for the day when Parliament will have the courage it takes to put it into effect. The clear sign of global warming, the melting of our glaciers and the rising of our land, is one more call for us to rise up and respond. Most recently, a loud and clear wake-up call came from Paris. What are we going to do? Will we have the courage it takes to recognize what is happening and name it as such, and wake up "to the possibility of true repentance"? The wake-up call comes to us both as individuals and as a society. We need to do what we can, individually and collectively, if we are going to be able to turn around and start marching in the other direction. In this context, the church is called to be neither "church-as-clinic nor church-as-courtroom, but church-as-community-of-transformation, where members are expected and supported to be about the business of new life."[66] Every day we are reminded of the fact that we do not live in a perfect world. But while living in this world, we are called to live in hope for God's reign to prevail.

The ratification of the UN's Paris Agreement by Althingi, our Parliament, on September 19, 2016,[67] marks a new starting point for us as a community, and as one nation among many who have committed to a global action plan that will put the nations of the world on a track to avoid dangerous climate change by limiting global warming.[68] The action plan gives us a focus, but we as a community have to make critical decisions on how to fulfill the goal of this plan. These are decisions regarding our nature, our environment, and our natural resources. Amongst the most important tasks we are faced with in the near future is how to make use of our green energy for our cars and our fishing fleet. This is something we will only accomplish as a community working together toward a common goal. Our country has been blessed with ample resources, like our green energy, and it is our responsibility to be good stewards of God's good creation.

66. Ibid., 77.
67. "Iceland Ratifies Paris Climate Deal," Iceland Monitor, September 20, 2016, http://tinyurl.com/ktw8sec.
68. "The Paris Agreement," United Nations: Framework Convention on Climate Change, accessed June 20, 2016, http://tinyurl.com/hoz4n23.

Conclusion

Sin becomes a sign of hope when it symbolizes a new beginning through repentance toward salvation. God calls us out of our sinful state and into the new beginning: the renewal of our relationships with God, our neighbor, the whole creation, and ourselves. Such transformation takes place when we, as individuals and as communities, recognize where things have gone wrong and decide to turn around, to change the way we think and act, and open up for God's gift of salvation. Salvation means whole, safe, unharmed, or well. Our broken condition reminds us of our shortcomings. We always fall short of our goals because "the reality of a *simul iustus et peccator* still holds."[69] But at the core of our Christian faith is the hope that salvation will be ours, and we will witness the transformation of our lives together as God's creation.[70]

69. Serene Jones, "What's Wrong with Us? Human Nature and Human Sin," in *Essentials of Christian Theology*, ed. William C. Placher (Louisville: Westminster John Knox, 2003), 157.

70. I would like to extend my gratitude to the great editors of this book. I am very grateful for the exceptional editing work they have done. A warm thanks to Rachel Glasser for proofreading by article. I also would like to thank my good friend and colleague, Professor Guðni Elísson, for his constructive editorial comments. Last but not least, a big thank you to my husband, Gunnar Rúnar Matthíasson, for his insightful observations.

8

———

Trafficked Lands: Sexual Violence, Oil, and Structural Evil in the Dakotas

Hilda P. Koster

In the summer of 2016, the Standing Rock Indian Reservation in North Dakota became the frontline of the fight for climate justice.[1] At Standing Rock, hundreds of representatives of Native nations and climate activists joined the Standing Rock Sioux tribe's protest against the Dakota Access Pipeline (DAPL). This 1,134 mile-long pipeline will transport crude oil from the Bakken oil fields in western North Dakota to southern Illinois. It is projected to run under the Missouri River at the point where it has been dammed to create lake Oahe, which constitutes a serious threat to the Sioux tribe's drinking water while also violating ancient burial grounds. After months of protests, in which peaceful protesters were often brutally violated by state law enforcement, President Obama made an end to the standoff by ordering the Army

---

1. Hilda Koster lives and teaches in Fargo-Moorhead, which is on the border of Minnesota and North Dakota, on the eastern access route to Standing Rock and the Bakken oil fields in North Dakota.

Corps of Engineers to explore alternative routes for the pipeline. While the Trump administration reversed this decision, Obama's order was an important, if only temporary, victory for indigenous rights and the climate. In fact, during an election season in which none of the candidates made a priority of mitigating climate change and fighting for climate justice, the peaceful water protectors at Standing Rock became the conscience of the nation, calling on all of us to honor the Earth.

Yet, while protecting the climate and the right to clean water were the focuses of the Standing Rock protests, the protests were also about the ways the oil industry, including pipeline construction, endangers Native women and girls. The oil boom in North Dakota, made possible by horizontal hydraulic fracturing, has caused an influx of transient, often unattached male workers who live in so called "man-camps." Advocacy organizations like First Nations Women's Alliance note that these camps "are launching pads for sexual predators who endanger females."[2] Because of the camps' proximity to Native American lands and Native American women's lack of legal protection, there has been an explosion of sexual assault on Native American women and girls. The Bakken oil fields have further become a lucrative ground for sex traffickers, who often target Native American women.[3]

In this chapter I will draw out the connection between the violation of the earth by fracking and the trafficking of (Native American) women in the context of the fracking industry and present both as issues of climate justice. I will demonstrate that fracking and sex-trafficking come from the same place, namely a fundamental disrespect for physical existence and a denial of our vulnerability as embodied beings. Both attitudes fuel the predatory practices of the extraction industry. While there are many ways to reflect on this attitude theologically—indeed, arguably Christian theology itself has contributed to it in so far it has championed a dualistic and hierarchical anthropology that values mind over body and males over females—in this chapter I will use the doctrine of sin. Christian theology typically uses sin-talk to name the wrongs of the world in relation to God's intention for and with the world. Positively, the doctrine of sin serves to envision an alternative way of being in the world—a way of being that reflects

---

2. Mary Kathryn Nagle and Gloria Steinem, "Sexual Assault on the Pipeline," *Boston Globe*, September 29, 2016, http://tinyurl.com/lqolkvw. For an account of the interconnection between the extraction industry and sexual assault against Native American women, see also Winona LaDuke, *The Winona LaDuke Chronicles: Stories from the Front Lines in the Battle for Environmental Justice* (Ponsford, MN: Spotted Horse, 2016), 130–68.

3. See Amy Dalrymple and Katherine Lymn, "Trafficked," investigative series, *The Forum of Fargo-Moorhead*, January 4–11, 2015. Accessed November 7, 2016, http://www.trafficked report.com/wp-content/uploads/2015/02/TraffickedOpti.pdf.

God's desire for the flourishing of all. The discourse on sin, then, is used in this chapter as a "social diagnostic" to pinpoint at what ails us and to imagine a remedy.[4]

Yet, while using sin-talk as a social diagnostic is a powerful strategy for addressing the violation of the Earth and the pollution of the atmosphere by the extraction industry, it is a more precarious approach when it comes to sex trafficking. Not only has Christianity viewed women's sexuality as the source of sin, it also has tended to portray the prostitute as the archetypical sinner. Drawing on the doctrine of sin to address rape and sex trafficking therefore risks blaming the victim and may well reinforce the social stigmatization of trafficked women. Moreover, as feminist theologians have pointed out, Christian sin-talk has often produced feelings of guilt and self-loathing in women and other marginalized groups,[5] which is particularly devastating for the victims of sex trafficking, who, according to their own accounts, often suffer from a lack of self-worth.[6] And, finally, when used to address sex trafficking and sexual assault among Native American women and girls, Christian sin-talk could be seen as an unwitting colonial intellectual gesture. After all, Christianity represents the dominant "colonizing" culture and has been complicit in the destruction of Native American lands.[7]

This chapter treads carefully, therefore, when drawing out the potential of the doctrine of sin to renounce the violations of women's

---

4. For the use of sin-talk as social diagnostics see Ernst Conradie, *Redeeming Sin? Social Diagnostics amidst Ecological Destruction* (Lanham, MD: Lexington, 2017).

5. The locus classicus for a feminist critique of sin is Valerie Saiving, "The Human Situation: A Feminine View," *Journal of Religion* 40, no. 2 (1960): 100–112. Expanding on Saiving's analysis, the theologian Judith Plaskow offered a now classic feminist analysis of the hamartiologies of Reinhold Niebuhr and Paul Tillich. See Judith Plaskow, *Sex, Sin and Grace: Women's Experience and the Theologies of Reinhold Niebuhr and Paul Tillich* (Washington, DC: University of America Press, 1980). Saiving and Plaskow argue that the definition of sin as "concupiscence" (Augustine) or "pride" (Niebuhr) is based upon the experience of elite men and that women typically suffer not from hubris but from a lack of self-love. Since its publication Saiving's critique has been criticized for its gender essentialism and lack of attention to race, ethnicity, culture, and class by poststructuralist, womanist, and Asian woman and Latina theologians. For a helpful overview of and constructive engagement with these criticisms see Rebekah Miles, "Valerie Saiving Reconsidered," *Journal of Feminist Studies in Religion* 28, no. 1 (2012): 79–86.

6. See Dalrymple and Lymn, "Trafficked," January 8.

7. The most blatant example of this complicity is the Doctrine of Discovery, which was issued as the Papal Bull *Inter Caetera* by Pope Alexander VI in 1493 and played a central role in the Spanish conquest of the Americas. The document taught that so called "discovered lands" that were not Christianized could be colonized by Christian rulers. It also declared that "the Catholic faith and the Christian religion be exalted and be everywhere increased and spread, that the health of souls be cared for and that barbarous nations be overthrown and brought to the faith itself." Whereas the doctrine first and foremost assured Spain's exclusive rights to the lands discovered by Columbus, it became the basis of all European claims in the Americas as well as the foundation for the United States' western expansion. See The Doctrine of Discovery, accessed May 1, 2017, http://doctrineofdiscovery.org/.

bodies by sexual assault and sex trafficking in the context of the oil boom. I will take my lead from the recently issued social message on gender-based violence of the Evangelical Lutheran Church in America (ELCA),[8] one of the largest Protestant denominations in the Dakotas, as well as the 1996 landmark feminist theological study on prostitution by Rita Nakashima Brock and Susan Brooks Thistlethwaite. Both studies use sin-talk to cast sexual exploitation not as a matter of sexual purity or personal disposition, but as a matter of abuse of power. The latter, I argue, also is an important lens for understanding the violation of the earth by the extraction industry. Yet in order to adequately address the joint abuses of the earth and women's bodies, we need to attend to the structures keeping it in place, including our own complicity by way of our high-carbon life style. Thus the final part of my chapter draws on the important work on structural evil by Lutheran ethicist Cynthia Moe-Lobeda,[9] most notably her work on structural injustice. Following Moe-Lobeda, I will argue that only by developing an appropriate vision of what ails us can we develop an adequate moral imaginary: an imaginary that addresses the predatory practices of the extraction and fracking industry as structural evil.

Fractured Lands: Hydraulic Fracturing and the Violation of the Earth

We don't want to hear about fracking because we don't like how the language makes us think of, just for a moment, non-consensual sex. We don't even like to say the word, rape. We don't like talking about real rape, much less metaphorical rape. . . . the parallel is too far a stretch anyway. Hyperbolic. The land can't give consent, so it can't not give consent. and if it could give consent, it probably would. It's given us everything else we ever wanted from it.

–Stefanie Brook Trout[10]

According to climate activist Bill McKibben, hydraulic fracturing or fracking is a curse.[11] While the United States could have converted to green energy when the oil fields of Saudi Arabia and other places

---

8. See Rita Nakashima Brock and Susan Thistlethwaite, *Casting Stones: Prostitution and Liberation in Asia and the United States* (Minneapolis: Fortress, 1996); "Gender-Based Violence," Evangelical Lutheran Church in America, accessed November 8, 2016, http://tinyurl.com/mv8p9c4.

9. Susan Brooks Thistlethwaite, *Women's Bodies as Battlefield: Christian Theology and the Global War on Women* (New York: Palgrave Macmillan, 2015); Cynthia Moe-Lobeda, *Resisting Structural Evil: Love as Ecological-Economic Vocation* (Minneapolis: Fortress, 2013).

10. Stefanie Brook Trout, "Hear No Evil," in *Fracture: Essays, Poems, and Stories on Fracking in America*, ed. Taylor Brorby and Stefanie Brook Trout (North Liberty, IA: Ice Cube, 2016), 390–91.

11. Bill McKibben, "Why Not Frack," in *Fracture*, 394–403.

were dwindling and oil prices were soaring, the United States decided to use a new technique, hydraulic fracturing, to exploit heretofore inaccessible domestic reservoirs of gas and oil, such as the Bakken shale formation in North Dakota or the Marcellus Shale gas-trapping shale formation, running from western Virginia into upstate New York. Fracking, however, not only keeps the United States hooked on climate-endangering fossil fuels, it also is an extremely violent and intrusive technology: it literally rips apart the "subsurface geology" of the Earth.[12]

A Very Short Primer on Hydraulic Fracturing

Whereas the conventional extraction industry extracts oil and gas from easy accessible pools using vertical wells, oil and gas in shale formations are much harder to recover. Not only are they trapped in microscopic pores in the shale rock, shale formations often extend for many miles at the same depth below the surface of the Earth. Thus, fracking involves drilling a vertical hole, followed by a horizontal branch. After the vertical section is secured by concrete, the horizontal section of the well is forcefully perforated using explosives. The small perforations created by the blast are used to press fracking fluids, consisting of water, chemicals, and silica sands, into the rock formations. Because this is done under high pressure—more than a thousand pounds per square inch—the shale is fractured and oil or gas are released into the well. Once it rises to the surface, the fossil fuel is siphoned off at the source and piped or trucked to facilities elsewhere in the country for processing and distribution.

Fracking requires enormous quantities of water—a single fracturing treatment can consume more than five hundred thousand gallons of water—which in arid areas is a huge drain on the fresh water supply.[13] In addition, the regurgitated waste water—the water emitted from fracking wells—is highly contaminated: among other things, it contains dissolved salt, metal ions, and radioactive compounds. Because of these toxins, waste water cannot easily be reclaimed for other uses, often not even for fracking itself. Recovered waste water, therefore, is typically held in lined ponds and evaporates into the atmosphere, or is disposed of by injecting it under high pressure into rock layers deep underground. What is especially disconcerting, however, is that due

12. Ibid., 395.
13. On the environmental and social implications of fracking for freshwater resources, see Christiana Z. Peppard's excellent book *Just Water: Theology, Ethics, and the Global Water Crisis* (Maryknoll, NY: Orbis, 2014), chapter 8.

to the so-called Halliburton loophole in the Energy Policy Act of 2005, most hydraulic fracturing operations are exempt from federal regulations under the Safe Drinking Water Act (SDWA).[14] This means that the fracking industry does not have to disclose the chemicals used in the fracking solution: a serious problem in case of potential air and groundwater contamination.

Proponents of fracking are quick to point out that because hydraulic fracturing has made it possible to access domestic reservoirs of gas and oil, it has diminished the United States' dependency on foreign oil and has brought revenue and employment to areas of the country that have been economically depressed, such as North Dakota. While there is validity to these arguments, it is important to keep in mind that there is nothing subtle or innocent about fracking. It is a technique by which we violently inject tons of unknown chemicals into the ground to release oil or gas, shattering layers of rock and endangering our fresh water supplies. In addition, each fracking well requires up to 1,500 truckloads to deliver the water, sand, and well-drilling equipment to the site. Diesel trucks cause air pollution, emitting particulate matter that is linked to asthma. The construction of roads and well-drilling sites harm local ecosystems by fragmenting wildlife habitats and migration patterns.[15] Fracking wells further leak methane, which is a potent greenhouse gas (GHG). And, finally, oil wells also produce gas that cannot be economically piped to markets and, hence, much of it is burned or flared.[16]

Fracking and Climate Justice

Fracking for gas and oil not just is a serious environmental concern, but is a climate justice issue as well. Within this book, climate justice has been defined within the overall context of a Christian understanding of love and, hence, as a matter of solidarity with those, humans and non-humans, who are most gravely affected by the consequences of anthropogenic climate change. To further assess whether fracking is just, I

14. The nickname "Halliburton" refers to the contributions to this legislation by then-Vice President Dick Cheney. Cheney had personal and financial ties to the Halliburton Corporation, which performed the first commercial fracturing treatment in the United States, and greatly benefits from it. See Peppard, *Just Water*, 153–57. See also, Gretchen Goldin, Deborah Bailin, Paul Rogerson, Jessie Agatstein, Jennifer Imm, Pallavi Phartiyal, *Toward an Evidence-Based Fracking Debate: Science, Development, Democracy, and Community Right to Know in Unconventional Oil and Gas Development* (Cambridge, MA: UCS Publications, 2013), 27–28, PDF, http://tinyurl.com/mmmbeyj.

15. James Martin-Schramm, Daniel Spencer, and Laura Stivers, *Earth Ethics: A Case Method Approach*, Ecology and Justice: An Orbis Series on Integral Ecology, eds. Mary Evelyn Tucker et al. (NY: Orbis, 2015), 214–15.

16. Goldin, Bailin et al., *Toward an Evidence-Based Fracking Debate*, 12–13.

draw on the work by Lutheran environmental ethicist James Martin-Schramm, who in his 2010 book *Climate Justice: Ethics, Energy, and Public Policy* has developed four detailed climate-justice norms—sustainability, sufficiency, participation, and solidarity—which he uses to evaluate various energy sources.[17] I will briefly summarize these norms before applying them to hydraulic fracturing.

According to Martin-Schramm, sustainability is the "long-range supply of sufficient resources to meet basic human needs and the preservation of intact natural communities."[18] Sustainability assumes that the quality of life in the present should not jeopardize the quality of life of future generations and the planet as a whole. The norm of sufficiency supports this notion of sustainability in that it encourages an ethic of restraint, not waste, and, hence, stresses virtues such as frugality and generosity. Obviously, the latter applies especially to those of us in the minority world living high carbon-footprint lives: the assumption here is to use resources in such a way that basic needs are met. In addition, the norm of participation stresses "the respect and inclusion of all forms of life in human decisions that affect their well-being."[19] Participation, therefore, has to do with empowerment of marginalized human communities and the inclusion of the interest of nonhuman life forms in decision-making processes. Finally, the norm of solidarity asks that we respect the "communal nature of life" and join in common cause with those who are victims of discrimination, abuse, and oppression.[20] This definition thus resonates with the way solidarity is used in this book, namely, as a commitment to remedy the patterns that cause social, political and economic injustices.

When held up against the four climate justice norms spelled out by Martin-Schramm, fracking appears as a serious concern for climate justice. First of all, fracking allows wealthy countries to continue and even step up their consumption of fossil fuels, in spite of the fact that these countries do have the technological know-how and financial resources to convert to carbon-neutral energy sources. Since climate change especially endangers those who have contributed the least to the problem and arguably also can do the least to mitigate or adapt, fracking clearly is a matter of lack of solidarity. Second, because we simply cannot burn the gas and oil that we have access to without fur-

---

17. James B. Martin-Schramm, *Climate Justice: Ethics, Energy, and Public Policy* (Minneapolis, Fortress, 2010), 26–36. Schramm's work does not yet take into full account the explosion of the fracking industry when discussing gas and oil.
18. Ibid., 28.
19. Ibid., 33.
20. Ibid., 35.

ther endangering our climate, fracking is a matter of sustainability and sufficiency.[21] It asks that we practice an ethics of restraint.

A further significant climate-justice concern related to fracking is its consumptive use of water. Because the water used in fracking cannot be repurposed, it is basically wasted. Yet, fresh water is a limited resource that is essential for every human being, society, and ecosystem. As Christiana Peppard succinctly points out, "while we can live without fossil fuels, we cannot live without water."[22] Wasting water in large quantities for profit, therefore, is a serious violation of the climate justice norms of sustainability and solidarity: it not only jeopardizes the possibility of the flourishing of future generations in a very serious way but it also adds to the already existing water crisis in many parts of the world, a crisis that is greatly compounded by climate change. Sustainable use of water, therefore, is very much a matter of climate justice. As Pope Francis reminds us in his encyclical *Laudato Si'*: "Our world has a grave social debt towards the poor who lack access to drinking water, because *they are denied the right to a life consistent with their inalienable dignity*."[23] Allowing the industry not to disclose the chemicals used only contributes further to the lack of solidarity involved in fracking.

Trafficked Lands: Fracking and Sex Trafficking

Fracking, then, is a climate justice issue because of its contribution to climate change and its wasteful use of water, it also generates enormous social ills. As noted in the introduction, the extraction industry typically brings thousands of workers to rural areas, stretching the physical resources, social services and infrastructures of its communities to the breaking point. In western North Dakota the massive immigration of oil workers has driven up the cost of living—at the height of the oil boom apartment rents in Williston were higher than in the

21. Proponents of fracking typically argue, however, that natural gas is a far less potent greenhouse gas than coal and, hence, should be seen as a "bridge fuel" that buys the United States time to make the investments needed to transition to a truly green-energy economy, while already reducing its greenhouse gas emissions. The problem with the bridge-fuel argument is that it conveniently overlooks the fact that natural gas wells, pipelines, and transfer facilities leak relatively large percentages of methane, which is a much more potent greenhouse gas over the short term than carbon dioxide. The bridge fuel argument further assumes that while we are relying on fracking of gas and oil, substantial long-term investments are being made in the development of solar and wind. Yet, if anything, fracking has substantially slowed down, not stepped up, investments in green-energy technology. See Martin-Schramm, Spencer, and Stivers, *Earth Ethics*, 211–13; Peppard, *Just Water*, 147–50.
22. Peppard, *Just Water*, 160.
23. Francis, *Laudato Si': On Care for Our Common Home* (Huntington IN: Our Sunday Visitor, 2015), 30; italics in original.

most expensive cities and counties in the country, including New York City and Santa Clara (CA)—forcing low-income families and many others, including long-term residents, out.[24] And while the fracking industry has brought jobs and wealth to the region, this wealth has not been spread equally, nor have the social costs for that matter. One particular disturbing trend has been the explosion of sex trafficking and sexual violence. According to sociologists Thomasine Heitkamp and Elizabeth Legerski of the University of North Dakota (UND) "the male to female ratio imbalance, strenuous work and schedules in the oilfield combined with disposable income in an isolated area lacking recreation outlets have created conditions ripe for aggression and violence."[25] At the height of the North Dakota oil boom, from 2008 till 2014, dating violence increased by 72 percent and domestic violence by 47 percent, exceeding numbers that can be explained by population growth only. The housing of male oil workers in man-camps have created a ready market for sex traffickers, who, as we saw, prey on vulnerable woman and young girls, many of whom are Native American.[26]

Sex trafficking is a particularly vicious form of sexual violence: it coercively entraps women in relationships of servitude. The US Department of State defines trafficking as "the act of recruiting, harboring, transporting, providing, or obtaining a person for compelled labor or commercial sex acts through the use of force, fraud, or coercion."[27] A sex trafficker typically lures women and girls into a relationship of emotional and financial dependency, which often also includes dependency on drugs. Once hooked, these women and girls are coerced into prostitution and, in order to avoid detection by law enforcement, "trafficked" around the country by their pimp. As with most forms of pimping, women who are trafficked are threatened with violence when trying to leave the trade. They also often carry the mark of their trafficker on their bodies in the form of tattoos, indicating to other pimps

24. Katie Valentine, "This North Dakota Oil Town has the Highest Rent in the Country," ThinkProgress.org, Feb 20, 2014. Accessed January 4, 2017.
25. Melissa Krause, "Oilboom Generated 'Perfect Storm' for Sexual Violence," Williston Herald, October 21, 2016. Accessed November 7, 2016, http://www.willistonherald.com/community/oil-boom-generated-perfect-storm-for-sexual-violence/article_35800e84-9729-11e6-b03c-2feafe5fa382.html. Rita Nakashima Brock and Susan Brooks Thistlethwaite observe a close connection between sex and violence in the military that results from a culture in which (young) men are isolated from "emotionally complex social structures of their regular communities, which, in all societies, carefully circumscribe violence . . . [and are] thrust into a rigidly hierarchical, homosocial, highly stressful environment." It is common for soldiers, moreover, to seek release of their stress by visiting prostitutes. Yet, because of the military ideology, which, not unlike fracking, is "focused on conquest, power, dominance," sex often becomes a vehicle for violence. Brock and Thistlethwaite, *Casting Stones*, 76.
26. See Dalrymple and Lymn, "Trafficked," January 4–11, 2015.
27. See US Department of State, *Trafficking in Persons Report*, July 2015, 7, PDF, http://tinyurl.com/lfcb2b7.

and to the women themselves that their bodies are owned, which is yet another way these women are intimidated and dehumanized. And because of the criminalization of prostitution in most states—prostitution is a Class B misdemeanor in North Dakota—women who are trafficked usually have arrest records and other brushes with the law that further increase their dependency on their trafficker.[28] It does not come as a surprise, therefore, that trafficked women usually avoid law enforcement and service providers and, hence, often do not get help. It is indeed telling that in spite of the documented explosion of sex trafficking in the Bakken oil fields, there are no dedicated shelters for trafficked women and girls in towns in or adjacent to the Bakken oil patch.[29]

In western North Dakota, one-third of the oil wells are on the Fort Berthold Indian reservation, which is home to the three affiliated tribes of the Mandan, Hidatsa, and Arikara Nations. Whereas these tribes are profiting from the oil boom, they have experienced deep poverty and intergenerational trauma due to the inundation of their villages and lands by the 1956 construction of the Garrison Dam and the creation of Lake Sakakawea.[30] The history of trauma, combined with unemployment, poverty, and drug addiction on many reservations, including Fort Berthold, puts Native women and girls at great risk for sexual exploitation. The latter is exacerbated by the fact that, in spite of new legislation by the Obama administration, nondomestic sexual crimes committed by non-Native perpetrators on Native lands still cannot be persecuted by tribal courts.[31] As a result, Native women

---

28. In its 2015 legislative session, the North Dakota legislator passed significant anti-trafficking legislation, which contains a "safe harbor" law that decriminalizes the prostitution of minors and protects adult victims of sex trafficking by way of an affirmative defense law. This anti-trafficking legislation is part of the "Uniform Act on the Prevention of and Remedies for Human Trafficking" (chapter 12.1–41 of the Criminal Code) and includes tougher penalties for traffickers and provides for some limited funding for services to victims. See Dalrymple and Lymn, "Trafficked," January 7 and 10. Unfortunately, this new legislation still does not decriminalize prostitution, which makes for an odd distinction between victims of sex trafficking and prostitutes.

29. Sex trafficking victims usually end up in the Family Crisis Center in Williston, North Dakota, even though this center focuses primarily on domestic violence and is not equipped to handle the complicated issues of sex-trafficking victims, which may include sexually transmitted disease or dependency on drugs. More recently there has been some coordinated outreach in the oil patch to the victims of the sex trade by Windie Lazenko, herself a sex trafficking survivor. Lazenko founded 4her, an organization that works with law enforcement to provide immediate services to victims of sex trafficking. Yet, 4her depends on donations and does not have a permanent location that could serve as a safe house. The closest organization fully equipped to work with women and girls who are the victims of trafficking is Breaking Free, which is situated in Saint Paul, Minnesota. See Dalrymple and Lymn, "Trafficked," January 4–11, 2015.

30. Villages that were inundated by the Garrison Diversion Project were Elbowoods, Van Hook, and (Old) Sanish.

31. In March 2013, the Obama administration reauthorized the Violence against Women Act, which gives tribal courts the jurisdiction to prosecute domestic violence committed by non-Native men in Indian country. The provision dealing with this issue is known as Section 904 and went into

are twice as likely to experience a form of sexual assault, which only makes them more vulnerable to being exploited by the sex trade. And whereas all victims of trafficking experience prejudice, Native American women systematically experience lack of response by law enforcement when it comes to abduction or rape.[32]

Sex Trafficking, Fracking, and Women's Bodies

Like fracking, then, there is nothing subtle or innocent about sex trafficking. It is a violation of the dignity and integrity of women's humanity, commodifies women's bodies, and targets vulnerable women and girls. In her 2015 book *Women's Bodies as Battlefields*, Susan B. Thistlethwaite introduces the term "critical physicality" to talk about the violence done to women's bodies and the lens it provides on our society.[33] Thistlethwaite draws a comparison between warfare and sexual assault, both of which, she believes, come from the same place, namely, "a contempt for the body, a desire for power by dominant elite males, and hierarchical authority structures."[34] Societies typically use powerful ideology to prevent public outcry about the cost of war. In the case of warfare, the violence done to concrete human bodies and the Earth is covered up and presented as a good—for instance, the good of "keeping America safe." When it comes to the fracking and sex-trafficking industry, the violence done to women's bodies and the Earth is kept hidden by the neoliberal belief in economic growth as an unquestionable good, the promise of energy independence, and a gender ideology that views prostitutes as "fallen women" and prostitution as a victimless crime.[35] Ecofeminists, moreover, have convincingly demonstrated

effect for most of the country's 566 federally recognized Indian tribes (it does not extend to Alaskan tribes) in March 2015. See Sari Horwitz, "New Law Offers Protection to Abused Native American Women," *The Washington Post*, February 8, 2014, http://tinyurl.com/la6oymr.

32. In an article for US News, Zoe Sullivan describes an incident in which a Native woman was abducted in Minnesota, trafficked to the Bakken oil fields, yet was arrested on a minor traffic violation when she arrived at a police station after she managed to escape from her abductor. Zoe Sullivan, "Crimes against Native American Women Raise Questions about Police Response," *The Guardian*, January 19, 2016, http://tinyurl.com/kmylt5d. See also Mary Papenfuss, "Activists Fear Missing Native American Women Were Swept Up in Oil-Worker Sex-Trafficking Ring," *International Business Times*, January 20, 2016, http://tinyurl.com/l53kz66.

33. Susan Brooks Thistlethwaite, *Women's Bodies as Battlefield: Christian Theology and the Global War on Women* (New York: Palgrave Macmillan, 2015), 4.

34. Ibid, 5.

35. It may not surprise, therefore, that in the Bakken, prostitutes, not the fracking industry, are blamed for the increase in violent crime. See Dalrymple and Lymn, "Trafficked," January 9. See also Nikki Berg Burin, "Public Discourse on the Rise and Regulation of the Illicit Sex Trade during North Dakota's Economic Booms," in *The Bakken Goes Boom: Oil and the Changing Geographies of Western North Dakota*, ed. William Caraher and Kyle Conway (Grand Fork, ND: Digital Press at the University of North Dakota, 2010), 117–28. Berg Burin traces the societal prejudice toward victims of sex trafficking in the Dakotas back to a deep contempt for prostitutes that surfaced during pre-

that the violence perpetrated against women and the Earth reflects hierarchical, dualistic patterns of thought, deeply ingrained in Western societies, which put culture over nature, males over females, mind over body, and so on. These patterns of thought condition and mutually reinforce the hegemony of white, heterosexual males, which normalizes the subjugation of women, marginalized men, and the Earth.[36]

Yet, as Thistlethwaite reminds us, not all female bodies are equally available for injury: heterosexism, racism, colonialism, and classism construct women's bodies differently. The concept of critical physicality asks that we do not theorize these differences in terms of bodies in general but actually witness to "the multiple violations" of concrete bodies.[37] The latter is particularly crucial in the case of Native American women who are victims of trafficking. Here, sexism intersects with a colonial ideology that typically conceives "of the colonized races as intrinsically degenerate" and seeks "to bring [the colonized] bodies under control via segregation and/or destruction. This control is regarded as necessary for the public good."[38] Thus, Native American activists see a clear connection between the rape of the Earth by the fracking industry and the fate of Native American women. Lisa Brunner, who is the program specialist for the National Indigenous Women's Resource Center, remarks: "[Extractive industries] treat Mother Earth like they treat women. . . . They think they can own us, buy us, sell us, trade us, rent us, poison us, rape us, destroy us, use us as entertainment and kill us. I am happy to see that we are talking about the level of violence that is occurring against Mother Earth because . . . what happens to her happens to us."[39] In other words, according to Brunner, the sexual abuse of Native women reflects a broader colonial enterprise in which Native lands and communities are systematically invaded, violated, and destroyed. For Native American communities, then, sex trafficking brings to the fore the intertwined reality of exploitation, sexism, and racism within the context of a long and pervasive history of colonial violence.

vious booms. Thus, she quotes a sermon preached in 1883 at the Methodist Church of Grand Forks in which prostitutes are called "soiled doves," who bring "destruction and death to all who come their way." Ibid., 117.

36. Anne M. Clifford, *Introducing Feminist Theology* (Maryknoll, NY: Orbis, 2001), 321–22. See also Karen J. Warren, *Ecofeminist Philosophy: A Western Perspective on What It Is and Why It Matters* (Lanham, MD: Rowman & Littlefield, 2000).

37. Thistlethwaite, *Women's Bodies as Battlefield*, 5.

38. Nirmala Erevelles and Andrea Minear, "Unspeakable Offenses: Untangling Race and Disability in Discourses of Intersectionality," *Journal of Literary and Cultural Disability Studies* 4, no. 2 (2010): 133.

39. Mary Annette Pember, "Brave Heart Women Fight to Ban Man-Camps, Which Bring Rape and Abuse," *Indian Country Today*, August 28, 2013, http://tinyurl.com/lcl4ezl.

Fracking, Sex Trafficking and Sin-Talk

How may we speak *theologically* to this reality of exploitation and violence? I wager that the doctrine of sin, especially when understood as structural injustice, is a powerful tool for addressing the interconnected violation of women and the Earth by the extraction industry. In Christian theology, justice is an expression of divine love, and love is the essence of who God is. Christians confess that we are both loved by God and are called to love God by living "God's mysterious, justice making love" into the world.[40] Yet, if this indeed is the human vocation, participating in injustice, either by actively promoting it and/or by failing to recognize it, implies that we are blocking the mysterious gift of God's love. This is what Christians typically call sin.

Whereas most Christians in North Dakota would readily agree that prostitution—and, hence, sex trafficking—is a sin, they would probably balk at identifying fracking as being sinful. However, as I have argued, because fracking is a matter of climate injustice and injustice blocks the free gift of God's love, fracking clearly is sinful. The same can be said of sex trafficking, albeit that in this case the use of the language of sin is fraught with difficulty, most notably because Christianity has identified the prostitute as the quintessential sinner and female sexuality as the source of sin. As we have seen, the latter is due to the pervasive gender ideology that is part of Christianity, which unfortunately is prevalent also in much anti-trafficking work done by Christian organizations.[41]

Against this background, it is particularly important, first of all, to distinguish between sex trafficking and prostitution. Whereas the first always involves coercion, the latter can be a matter of choice.[42]

---

40. I am borrowing this beautiful phrase from Cynthia Moe-Lobeda. See Moe-Lobeda, *Resisting Structural Evil*, 57.

41. These organizations typically seek to "liberate" the victims of sex-trafficking from the "evil" or "sin" of prostitution. The implicit aim is sexual purity: survivors of the sex trade are to be re-socialized into "proper," that is, monogamous women. For instance, the evangelical theologian Glenn Harden writes that "prostitutes do not have the right to engage in sex work. This is because work that is demeaning, both to the prostitute and to the consumer, runs counter to the inherent right to respect that we share as humans loved by God." Glenn M. Harden, *The Sex Trade, Evil, and Christian Theology* (Eugene, OR: Wipf & Stock, 2016), 87. Note the not so subtle reversal of blame in this statement: the john is identified as "consumer," instead of "predator. Feminist theologian Yvonne Zimmerman argues that this account of sex trafficking and prostitution, which is prevalent especially among evangelical Christians, has informed much of the anti-trafficking legislation of the Bush administration. See Yvonne C. Zimmerman, *Other Dreams of Freedom: Religion, Sex, and Human Trafficking* (Oxford: Oxford University Press, 2013), chapter 1.

42. It is important to observe, however, that while women may choose prostitution or sex-work as a profession, more often than not prostitution involves some form of coercion. Feminist theorist Catherine MacKinnon writes therefore that "women who are prostituted in the flesh or in pornography are, in the main, not there by choice but because of lack of choices." She explains

The social message on gender-based violence issued by the Evangelical Lutheran Church of America (ELCA) therefore does not condemn prostitution per se, but instead focuses on the sin of abuse of power.[43] According to the ELCA, gender-based violence is a matter of "physical, sexual, or emotional harm directed at a person in order to create power and control."[44] Whereas gender-based violence is directly linked to gender, sex, and sexuality, it intersects with race and ethnicity in so far as sexual violence is used to reinforce the hegemony of white heterosexual males. At its root, then, gender-based violence, both as a personal act and a structural phenomenon, is the sin of creating and abusing power over others. This particular use of sin talk not only breaks with the Christian tradition's narrow connection between female sexuality and sin, but also resonates with the reality of sex trafficking as it is described in this chapter. The trafficker exercises power over women and girls by way of intimidation and violence and aims to control every part of a trafficked woman's life, even marking her body with his tattoos. In short, then, according to the definition of sin used by the ELCA's social message, sex trafficking is a sin *not* because its sells sex but because it involves the abuse of power as control that harms the fundamental personal integrity of another human being.

The social message of the ELCA echoes the important feminist theological study on prostitution by Rita Nakashima Brock and Susan B. Thistlethwaite, who, in their book *Casting Stones* (1996), are equally critical of the way Christianity has typically misconstrued prostitutes as sinners. Brock and Thistlethwaite's study relate in great detail how prostitution is a complex sociological and cultural phenomenon that cannot be understood in isolation of the structural dimensions of global capitalism, sexism, colonialism, and classism. Yet, while critical of Christianity's use of sin-talk in relation to prostitution, they too claim that when understood within the context of structural injustice, sin can be re-appropriated to condemn sex trafficking. Indeed, Brock and Thistlethwaite suggest that in the context of the sex trade, evil is "the control of others that aggravates helplessness, the use of power to

"[t]hey usually 'consent' to the acts only in the degraded and demented sense of the word . . . in which a person despairs at stopping what is happening, sees no escape, has no real alternative, was often sexually abused before as a child, may be addicted to drugs, is homeless, hopeless, is often trying to avoid being beaten or killed, is almost always economically desperate, acquiesces in being sexually abused for payment, even if, in most instances, it is payment to someone else." Catherine MacKinnon, "Pornography as Trafficking," *Michigan Journal of International Law* 26: 995.

43. See "Gender-Based Violence," ELCA.

44. Evangelical Lutheran Church in America, "Foundational Documentation for a Social Message on Gender-Based Violence," accessed November 7, 2016, 1, PDF, http://tinyurl.com/n392qhv. It is significant that the ELCA's social message deliberately speaks of gender and not just sex. Gender includes women and girls but also gender nonconforming people and non-dominant men.

inflict pain, and the willful severance of relationships of love and nurture."[45]

In addition to understanding the evil of the sex-trade as abuse of power in the context of structural injustices and oppression, Thistlethwaite and Brock follow Mary Potter Engel who has identified four non-traditional understandings of sin in relation to sexual abuse, namely, sin as distortion of feeling, sin as betrayal of trust, sin as lack of care, and sin as lack of consent to vulnerability.[46] These four understandings of sin are helpful, I believe, to further flesh out the language of sin as social diagnostic in relation to sex-trafficking in the context of the extraction industry in the Dakotas. First, the sex industry in general and sex trafficking in particular, feed on the distortion of the reality of sexual exploitation—eroticizing the selling of sex and disconnecting it emotionally from the reality of abuse—which keeps victims invisible and disempowered. In the context of the Dakotas the reality of sex trafficking is further distorted by trafficked women being cast as prostitutes seeking to profit from "honest" men who earn their money by hard work in the oilfields. This denial of the lived reality of trafficked women in turn increases their marginalization, oppression and lack of legal protection. The latter also reinforces the betrayal of trust experienced by women who are trafficked.

The third understanding of sin identified by Engel, that is, sin as lack of care, is especially relevant in the context of the fracking industry. Sex trafficking reduces women to commodities. The economic transaction censors feelings of care and silences guilt. Yet within the context of the fracking industry the sin of callousness is committed not just by the pimp and the john, but very much also by the extraction industry in so far it seeks to maximize profit by relying on a transient, male work-force. Indeed, akin to the economic transactions between pimp and john, the maximization of profit is used by the industry as justification for the social ills that come with its labor practices. This feeds into the fourth understanding of sin, namely the sin of the denial of vulnerability. Fracking requires of its workers to numb their sensitivity to our dependency as embodied beings on the soil, the water and the air. This denial hardens yet another denial, the denial of our need for meaningful relationships. In the context of the hypermasculine culture cultivated by work in the oilfields, human feelings of dependence, of neediness, of fragility become a source of weakness that is met with hostility. According to Brock and Thistlethwaite the latter often

---

45. Brock and Thistlethwaite, *Casting Stones*, 241.
46. Ibid., 243.

gets sublimated by violence, most notably violence towards women. They observe that "[s]ex then becomes a vehicle for overtly denying embodiment and vulnerability by asserting dominance over [femininity, which is portrayed as weakness, vulnerability, or 'softness']."[47]

In short, sex trafficking is sinful because it abuses power to exercise control over other human beings with the explicit purpose to increase helplessness and inflict pain. It further denies and distorts the reality of abuse and vulnerability. This reality moreover is not simply caused by pimps and johns, but is intrinsic to the predatory practices of the fracking industry. Yet, while work on retrieving sin-talk to address the exploitation that is part and parcel of sex trafficking in the context of fracking is important, indeed "saving," work, it does not yet reveal how most of us contribute to this violence simply by living our high-carbon footprint lives. The latter, I believe, is a crucial step when it comes to resisting the intertwined injustices of fracking and sex trafficking. The final part of this chapter therefore draws on Cynthia Moe-Lobeda's work on structural evil to further conceptualize the ways both fracking and sex trafficking are an evil intrinsic to our fossil fuel driven, consumer economy.

Sex Trafficking and Fracking as Structural Evil

> We don't want to hear about fracking because we don't like your alternative. If the solution could somehow be linked to consumerism, if we could do the things we love without fracking, we might be more inclined to listen. But you are asking too much. Your valuation of the future is too high.
> —Stefanie Brook Trout[48]

Like the ELCA's social message, Moe-Lobeda uses the lens of structural injustice to talk about the sins of global capitalism, sexism, colonialism, and racism. In her book *Resisting Structural Evil* (2013) she explains that structural injustice is sin that manifests itself in societal structures.[49] Whereas in many communities of faith the response to sin is directed at the individual and sin is often privatized, viewing the social character of sin allows us to see the injustices at work in "the social structural relationships that shape societies and their impact on eco-systems."[50] What this means is that groups and societies as well as individuals may be agents of sin. Moe-Lobeda explains that while these injustices

47. Ibid., 252.
48. Brook Trout, "Hear No Evil," in Fracture, 392.
49. Moe-Lobeda, *Resisting Structural Evil*, chapter 3.
50. Ibid., 59.

are often not of our making—we are not *personally* responsible for them—they are kept in place by our collective participation in them.[51]

Viewing sin as having to do with the *social* spheres of life has deep roots in biblical faith and Christian traditions. Indeed, St. Augustine, in the famous pear incident in his *Confessions*, insists that sin always has a corporate dimension.[52] Stressing the social dimension of sin does not mean, moreover, that sin does not exist in the individual sphere of life. Indeed, denying the latter would make it hard to talk about individual acts of violence perpetrated against women who are victims of sex trafficking. The point then is not to put social sin over individual sin, but to see the various ways these two spheres, the individual and the social, are interconnected. The latter has been the trajectory of various liberationist and political theologies, including feminist, womanist, and *mujerista* theologies, which use social-structural analysis for theorizing human life in social, systemic terms. Moreover, as Moe-Lobeda reminds us, because sin identifies what ails us, it also determines "what constitutes as salvation, freedom, or liberation from it, including the path toward that freedom."[53] In other words, the way we conceptualize sin shapes the cure: "a reduced understanding of sin means a truncated vision of salvation."[54]

Yet, what makes Moe-Lobeda's analysis especially instructive for our purposes is that she conceptualizes how it is that the structural character of sin makes us, the relatively privileged, readily complicit with it. To this end, Moe-Lobeda identifies several features of sin understood as structural injustice that she believes have "far-reaching implications for our moral vision,"[55] I will briefly discuss these features here. It is important to note at the outset, however, that Moe-Lobeda does not distinguish between sin and evil. She does, in other words, not reserve the term evil for the social systems of sin, such as patriarchy, and use sin for individual behavior perpetuating the evil inflicted by these systems. Instead, she uses sin and evil interchangeably to illumine the reality and dynamics of structural injustice. In addition, whereas there are many different ways theologians use the term evil, Moe-Lobeda primary concern is with "moral evil," and not with what has been labeled "natural evil" or "metaphysical evil."[56] She also does not see evil as syn-

51. Ibid., 58.
52. Augustine, *St. Augustine's Confessions*, trans. Henry Chadwick (Oxford: Oxford University Press, 2009), 2.4–10.
53. Moe-Lobeda, *Resisting Structural Evil*, 60.
54. Ibid.
55. Ibid.
56. Ibid., 64–65.

onymous with suffering. Not only is suffering not necessarily evil, suffering does not always stem from evil.

A first important feature of sin or evil as structural injustice is that it often is invisible to those who do not suffer directly from it. While we may see the symptoms of sin, for instance the victims of sex trafficking, we typically fail to probe the social structures and ecological economic relationships that produce the conditions that lead to it. Yet, as Moe-Lobeda points out, sin that we do not recognize, we cannot renounce and without recognition of what ails us, we remain captive or complicit to sin. It is the odd paradox of privilege, however, that even when we recognize structural sin and repent, we often cannot divest ourselves from its structures by way of our individual actions.[57] For instance, while we may renounce the violence and injustice perpetrated by the oil industry, our lives, especially the lives of the economically privileged, are interwoven with an economic system dependent on fossil fuels. This does not mean, however, that individual acts do not matter. On the contrary, Moe-Lobeda stresses that the fact that "individual actions are relatively powerless in the face of structural sin does not mean that personal efforts to counter it are immaterial, ineffectual, or unnecessary."[58] Indeed, while individual actions in and of themselves cannot change structural injustices, structural injustices cannot be changed without them either.

We are caught up then in structures of injustice that we often fail to acknowledge and renounce and that cannot easily be changed by individual acts. We further do not actively choose to be part of social structures that are unjust: we are socialized into a society built on social injustice and ecological violence. Thus, the third feature of structural injustice insists that unjust structures are inherited; and, hence, they "seem normal and natural to us, and at times even divinely ordained."[59] The latter is true especially for gender and race relations but applies also to colonial relationships. Structural injustice moreover exponentially expands with the expansion of power. Concentrated power and wealth usually serve the relentless pursuit of self-interest regardless of the harm done to others. Thus, the expansion of power of transnational oil companies enables the pursuit of (domestic) fossil fuels, out of greed and interest in economic power, in spite of the damage to the climate,

57. Ibid., 61.
58. Ibid., 62.
59. Ibid., 63. Interestingly, Moe-Lobeda sees herein some use for the concept of original sin: "original sin may signify the socially transmitted state of being entangled in structural injustice from birth by virtue of participation in a society built on social injustice and ecological violence. That entanglement deepens as one serves as a conduit for transmitting uncritically accepted injustice to future generations, simply by living the life prescribed by society."

the water, and indigenous communities. Ordinary citizens are typically made complicit in this pursuit of relentless self-interest either by sharing directly in the profit—for instance, by selling drilling rights to oil companies—or, indirectly, as a consumer.

The features of structural injustice spelled out above provide, I believe, a helpful description of the way structural evil operates within the context of fracking, blocking our moral vision. Moe-Lobeda expands on this analysis by culling from Dietrich Bonhoeffer the insight that structural sin or evil often appears as good and, hence, hides from the consciousness of its perpetrators. Thus, the damages done by our relentless pursuit of fossil fuels are covered up by a perceived "moral good," such as "the good" of energy independence and economic growth. The wicked nature of evil, according to Bonhoeffer, is precisely its ability to hide or "appear disguised" as "light, charity, historical necessity, or social justice."[60] It is for this reason, then, that Moe-Lobeda prefers not to distinguish between sin and evil: "seeing structural injustice as structural evil illumines how it is woven into our daily lives and how it hides under the guise of good, inevitability, divine mandate, or social necessity."[61]

In her analysis of the moral oblivion that results from the hiddenness of structural evil, Moe-Lobeda further draws on structural violence theory. Here she relies on Johan Galtung's well-known work on peace and conflict resolution. Following Galtung, she explains that, on one level, structural violence is "the physical, psychological, and spiritual harm that certain groups of people are experiencing as a result of the unequal distribution of power and privilege."[62] It is pervasive and often deadly for those with very little access to power and privilege, as is the case with Native American women. Yet, according to Moe-Lobeda, structural violence also points to "the complicity or silent acquiescence of those who fail to take responsibility for it."[63] Thus whereas structural violence does express itself by way of direct, person to person violence it typically does not have one perpetrator but is built into the structures of society. Sexism, racism, and colonialism are all forms of structural violence therefore. Structural violence is especially difficult to address, however, because it consists of "interlocking forms of oppression" by which those who benefit from one form, may be victimized by another.[64] It is relatively easy to see this played out

---

60. Dietrich Bonhoeffer, *Letter and Papers from Prison*, ed. Eberhard Bethge (London: SCM, 1967), quoted in Moe-Lobeda, *Resisting Structural Evil*, 66.
61. Moe-Lobeda, *Resisting Structural Evil*, 78.
62. Ibid., 72.
63. Ibid.
64. Ibid., 77.

in the sex-trafficking epidemic in the context of the Bakken oil boom. Whereas Native women victimized by sex-trafficking are not getting legal help and protection due to the structural violence of racism, colonialism and sexism, the communities perpetrating this violence are themselves being colonized by the corporate economic interests of oil-companies, even though they are also economically benefiting from it. The latter is not meant as an excuse but as a reminder of the complexities of structural violence. Failing to acknowledge the interlocking forms of oppressions may result in failure to empower people to address structural violence. Finally, as Moe-Lobeda demonstrates also, structural violence is being nourished by cultural violence, that is, the "ideologies, institutional policies and practices embedded in society that appear natural, normal, inevitable, or divinely mandated."[65] We have identified aspects of such violence, such as the pervasive gender ideology involved in stereotyping victims of sex trafficking as criminals or the commodification of women and the Earth, throughout this chapter.

In short, then, combining Moe-Lobeda's analysis of structural injustice with structural violence theory not only allows us to see how we are all implemented in structural evil, but also helps us to address our moral passivity in face of it. For the antidote or remedy to structural evil is the development of a structural moral vision. Obviously, because structural evil is hard to recognize and most of us are somehow complicit in it, this is not an easy task. Indeed, one may say that it is a matter of divine grace. Yet, Moe-Lobeda stresses time and again, and I concur, that because moral evil is the result of social and historical processes, and, hence, is fueled by human agency, it can be changed.[66] The task of the theologian, then, is to expose structural evil, including the role religion plays in perpetuating this evil, so as to open up pathways for a critical vision, breaking the cycle of moral oblivion and passivity. Yet, as Moe-Lobeda reminds us as well, in order for this vision to translate into action it needs to be accompanied by seeing alternatives, that is, a vision of "what could be."[67] This vision does not come from a future eschatological ideal, but rather emerges when we listen deeply to, and stand in solidarity with, indigenous peoples and other climate activists, who call us back to our rootedness in the soil, our dependency on clean water and unpolluted air, and our kinship with other animals and the Earth.

---

65. Ibid.
66. In her contribution to this volume Cynthia Moe-Lobeda draws on the power of the Spirit to conceptualize how we may move from moral oblivion and inertia to meaningful action.
67. Ibid., 112.

Conclusion

In this chapter, I have used sin-talk as social diagnostic to expose fracking and sex-trafficking as structural evil. The first part of my chapter
drew on the four climate justice norms developed by James Martin-
Schramm—namely, sustainability, sufficiency, participation, and solidarity—and argued that fracking is a serious concern for climate justice. I then turned to the concept of "critical physicality" introduced
by Susan Brooks Thistlethwaite to demonstrate that the violations of
women's bodies by sex trafficking in the Bakken oil fields are intrinsic
to the predatory practices of the extraction industry and raise profound questions about our solidarity with vulnerable communities and
the earth. After drawing out the entanglement of fracking with sex
trafficking, I turned to sin-talk in order to expose the violations of ecosystems and women's bodies by the fracking industry as structural evil.
I argued that for Christians this move is important in order to recognize the many ways in which the injustices committed are part of the
very structures of our society. Yet while the structural character of
evil makes it hard to turn away from sin, structural evil is the product of human communities and, hence, change is possible. Or so is our
hope: that we may be given the vision and courage to live God's justice-making, mysterious, and marvelous love into the world, in solidarity with the victims of the structural injustices committed by fracking:
trafficked women and girls, indigenous communities, the climate, and
the Earth.

Incarnation

9

"Ukugqiba inkaba"—Burying the Umbilical Cord: An African Indigenous Ecofeminist Perspective on Incarnation

Fulata Lusungu Moyo

In isiZulu, closest to my lost and forgotten mother tongue, *Ukugqiba inkaba* means "burying the umbilical cord." To ask, "Where are you from?" one would say, *"Ikuphi inkaba yakho?"* which literally means "Where is your umbilical cord (buried)?" Among the Ngoni people of northern Malawi,[1] my ethnic group, the ritual of burying the umbilical cord signifies one's connection to Mother Earth, the place of one's roots and belonging. For them, just as the umbilical cord connects the baby to the mother for the baby's sustenance and survival while in the mother's womb, so burying the umbilical cord from the born baby connects the baby to Mother Earth for belonging and sustenance for life.[2]

---

1. The Ngoni have their roots in the *mfecane* peoples, which gave rise to the Zulu Kingdom, which scattered all other Ngoni ethnic groups over southern Africa between 1815 and 1840.

Using an indigenous African ecofeminist ethics, this chapter affirms the role of incarnation the*logy as the basis for ecological justice—an intersection of ecological and social justice that includes gender and racial justice. A the*logy of incarnation rooted in African ecofeminist ethics calls us to live the Christian gospel in such a way that it becomes an important part of healing the wounds caused by ecological and gender injustice. As African American theologian Eboni Marshall Turman has pointed out, because we are "*homoousious* with Christ,"[3] we are Christ bearers. This means that while more is demanded of us, more is also available to us. Acknowledging Turman's point that bodies, especially those that defy normativity, are a the*logical problem, this essay elaborates an incarnational ecofeminist the*logy by looking specifically at the body of Mary, the mother of Jesus, and the body of Mother Earth. The upshot of our revisionist incarnational the*logy is to truncate the patri-kyriarchal manipulation of incarnational doctrine.[4]

My the*-ethical methodology is also based on the importance of storytelling, which reflects my culture's indigenous ways of knowing and being. Storytelling thus situates my the*logy as an African womanist theologian. Storytelling further turns the culturally invisible, embodied experience into audible words so as to "hear into speech" an important ritual that otherwise is remembered only privately by the mother. Similarly, in the story of Mary, as Luke 2:19 affirms: "Mary treasured up all these words and pondered them in her heart." Storytelling is like a gentle but steady incense that burns the essence of Mary's treasure so that its healing aroma can empower women and Mother Earth toward healing and liberation. It is appropriated as a method of the*logical and moral discernment of the mysteries of the doctrine of incarnation.

2. Similarly, Elizabeth Amoah, writing about Mercy Amba Oduyoye's life as a Ghanaian, unveils the Akan people's belief that the yield of the seed planted with the placenta and umbilical cord of a newly born baby foretells the future influence of the baby. See Elisabeth Amoah, preface to *African Women, Religion, and Health: Essays in Honor of Mercy Amba Oduyoye*, ed. Isabel Apawo Phiri and Nada Sarojini (Maryknoll, NY: Orbis, 2006), xviii.

3. *Homoousious* is a Greek term that is used in the Nicene creed (325 CE) to define the being of Christ as God-human-being of the same (*homo*) essence (*ousia*) with God. Eboni Marshall Turman uses the term to express our relationship with Christ as Christian women, to be of the same essence. Eboni Marshall Turman, "Black and Blue: Uncovering the Ecclesial Cover-Up of Black Women's Bodies through Womanist Reimagining of the Doctrine of the Incarnation," in *Reimagining with Christian Doctrines: Responding to Global Injustices*, ed. Grace Ji-Sun Kim and Jenny Daggers (New York: Palgrave Macmillan, 2014), 74.

4. *Kyriarchy* was coined by Elisabeth Schüssler Fiorenza in 1992 to define her theoretical concept of systemic, unequal gender power relations as part of interconnected, interacting, and self-extending systems of domination and submission. As an intersectional extension beyond patriarchal gender, *patri-kyriarchal* includes many other isms, not least anthropocentricism, classism, colonialism, racism, and militarism, and also homophobia and other expressions of dominating hierarchies, by which the subjugation of individuals or groups of people is internalized as well as institutionalized as normality. Elisabeth Schüssler Fiorenza, "Glossary," in *Wisdom Ways: Introducing Feminist Biblical Interpretation* (Maryknoll, NY: Orbis, 2001), 211.

Storytelling accomplishes three things. First, it has the power to create subversive memory, which arouses and mobilizes collective energies for creating justice in a patri-kyriarchal context, where women's experiences are often made invisible. Second, storytelling resurrects the often-buried experiences of motherhood, puts them into words, and weaves women's narratives into a tapestry of personal theologies of new life, hope, and healing. Third, storytelling also weaves this sacralized burying of the umbilical cord into a sacramental life and liturgy, thus integrating women's bodies, minds, souls, and spirits in the mystery of a deep connection and interdependence with Mother Earth and her web of life.

Dialoguing with Priscilla Eppinger's and Eboni Marshall Turman's incarnational theologies, this chapter unfolds in four sections, starting with the telling of the story of Mary's motherhood as the bridge or interconnection between God and humanity. It intends to make visible and defy what patriarchal incarnational discourse has, by implication, made invisible:[5] the role of Mary's biological motherhood. I argue that diminishment of this biological fact has been a deliberately calculated patri-kyriarchal conspiracy to trivialize and domesticate women's role and power in the origin of life. This conspiracy serves to uphold ethical relational principles that sustain hierarchy and disembodiment in order to privilege males and maintain emotional distance.

Second, I tell the story of my birth and the burying of my umbilical cord by my mother. This common Malawian indigenous ritual embodies the basis of the interconnectedness and interdependence between humanity and Mother Earth. I then use my own narrative as a stepping stone into ethnographic research of two matrilineal societies in Southern Malawi, the aYao and aMang'anja, where this practice not only remains the basis of women's co-mothering with the Earth but traditionally (prior to the colonial missionary imposition of the patri-kyriarchal model of church leadership) was also the justification of women's religious leadership. Acknowledging my context as a Christian African womanist, the narrative of the burying of my umbilical cord illuminates aYao and aMang'anja women as God's intermediaries and guardians of Mother Earth.

In the third section, I analyze the role of women as God's intermediary in the movement of ecological justice among the indigenous communities of the aYao and aMang'anja in southern Malawi. In these communities, women's religious leadership roles are rooted in their

---

5. Within the Christian perspectives, I note that the figure of Mary is more centrally located in Roman Catholicism's popular piety than in Protestant piety.

given experience of womanhood, specifically as life givers and procreators with the divine. As co-mothers with Mother Earth, their shared insights posit an example of good practice as well as a challenge to the global ecological justice movement with regard to women's leadership roles. Conversely, I also articulate how patri-kyriarchy has manipulated traditional accounts of motherhood in order to disempower women by associating women's fertility in the indigenous conception of ritual potency with impurity taboos. The latter, however, only presses the urgency of connecting ecological justice with gender justice in the quest for holistic justice, where intersectionality becomes imperative. This connection becomes even more urgent and relevant in this historical moment of climate injustice, whose impact affects especially those at the margins of societies—the majority being women and children.

Fourth and finally, by focusing on the story of Mary's embodied motherhood, this chapter connects the the*logy of the incarnation to the discourse and praxis of ecological and gender justice in an important way. Imagining the burying of the umbilical cord as a ritual Mary participated in after giving birth to Jesus articulates the critical importance of the physicality of Mary's motherhood for incarnation the*logy. It allows us to root salvation in the emotionally interconnected and interdependent relationship of a mother and her child and to see this relationship as a blueprint for our own relationship with Mother Earth. In other words, by connecting the role of Mary's body in the incarnation with both my personal narrative and the practices of aYao and aMang'anja women, I connect Mary's motherhood to the motherhood of the Earth. I believe that in doing so, we render the mystery of life and death as part of a the*logy of incarnation in new and unexpected ways.

"In the Beginning Was the Word": Embodying Incarnation through Jesus's Buried Umbilical Cord

In the beginning was the Word, and the Word was with God, and the Word was God. He was in the beginning with God. All things came into being through him, and without him not one thing came into being. What has come into being in him was life, and the life was the light of all people. The light shines in the darkness, and the darkness did not overcome it. (John 1:1–5)

Mary must have been a young girl when the angel appeared to her and called her to a fully ordained ministry of motherhood. "Do not be afraid, Mary, for you have found favour with God. And now you will conceive in your womb and bear a son and you will name him Jesus" (Luke 1:30–31).[6] Before Mary's pregnancy became visible, she had to journey to visit her much older cousin Elizabeth, wife of Zachariah: "Mary set out and went with haste to a Judean town in the hill country, where she entered the house of Zechariah and greeted Elizabeth" (Luke 1:39–40). This journey was a sisterhood solidarity imperative, providing Mary sanctuary from the risk of condemnation and even death by stoning for "adultery." After all, Mary was betrothed to Joseph, and she was not under Joseph's roof when she was impregnated. Despite Elizabeth's lack of practical experience, her sanctuary provided mentorship in the mysteries of motherhood for God's child bride and teenage mother. On the one hand, Elizabeth's own navigation of an unusual conception paved a shared journey into the mutual vulnerability of an "illegitimate" pregnancy and first-time motherhood. On the other hand, as an older woman Elizabeth must have had experience accompanying younger women in her community through the trials and cultural expectations of being a mother. Through sisterhood solidarity, she shared the richness of her knowledge with the young and likely frightened Mary.

The Roman imperial call for census meant that Mary was destined to give birth in the shepherds' caves in the village of Bethlehem, far away from Nazareth, her home. It further meant that Mary's identity and belonging were subsumed by those of Joseph's, Jesus's "surrogate" father.[7] In a manger, through Mary's womb and birth canal, the word came into the world and Mary's placenta became one with Mother Earth. Given that it usually takes about one to two weeks for a child's umbilical cord stump to fall off after being severed from the placenta, we can reasonably assume that Jesus's cord was buried in Nazareth after the holy family returned.[8] The grotto at the heart of the Church of

6. All scripture references are from the NRSV.
7. A surrogate is a woman implanted with an embryo created by in vitro fertilization (IVF), using the intended father's sperm and a donor egg where the donor is not the surrogate. The resulting child is genetically related to the father but genetically unrelated to the surrogate. Biologically, men do not have a womb for an embryo to be created using IVF. However, in the God-human drama of the holy family, theologically Joseph's relationship to Jesus makes more epistemological sense if surrogacy is appropriated to his fatherhood. Unlike the surrogate mother, whose connection to the child is severed upon birth due to her lack of genetic connection to the child, Joseph's "surrogate" fatherhood theologically becomes the official connection: Jesus's genealogy is even traced through him rather than through Mary.
8. Rabbi Jeremy Lawrence, asserts that while Judaism does not attach special significance to the placenta, it and the umbilical cord are the property of women. Some religious literature refers to their burial. The placenta has normally been disposed of by the doctor or midwife, yet it is likely that first-century Jewish women would have buried the umbilical cord. If the latter can be verified, then Mary must have buried Jesus's umbilical cord. Refer to the section "Jewish Perspective by Rabbi Jeremy Lawrence," in Christopher F. C. Jordens, Michelle A. C. O'Connor, Ian H.

the Annunciation bears the Latin inscription *hic Verbatum caro factum est* (Here the Word was made flesh). In the absence of bodily details about Mary's birthing process of Jesus, one can imagine Jesus's umbilical cord buried several archeological years beneath this grotto, put there by his mother, Mary, to connect her motherhood of Jesus to the Earth. Otherwise what other aspect of incarnation could have taken place in Nazareth after the birthing experience in Bethlehem that would qualify it as a place where Word became flesh?

This silent and private ritual carried out by Jesus's mother is often ignored, yet it is a crucial part of how "the word became flesh and lived among us" (John 1:14). For together with all our buried umbilical cords, Jesus became part of Mother Earth's womb. In this way, we all are interconnected and interdependent children of the same mother, with Jesus as our older brother. In this chapter, I therefore argue that an incarnational the*logy of ecojustice should take as its departure this ritual—indigenous to African cultures—as an important process of transferring the connection from womb-mothering to ecosystem-mothering. How can an ecofeminist incarnation the*logy, in its process of doctrinal reimagination,[9] appropriate such an indigenous ritual? Such an epistemological reimagining would help decode incarnation's patri-kyriarchal imposition, thus allowing us to retell such doctrinal mysteries through the embodied experiences of birthing life by way of the exploited bodies of Mother Earth and women.

Under the Mvunguti Tree (*kigelia pinnata*): Fulata, a Healer and Reconciler

When I was conceived, my mother hoped I would be a boy. Four girls and only one boy were too few boys for my Ngoni father, who needed help in carrying out "masculine duties" such as shepherding cattle—it is no wonder I was encouraged to grow up like a tomboy to help out my

---

Kerridge, Cameron Stewart, Andrew Cameron, Damien Keown, Rabbi Jeremy Lawrence, Andrew McGarrity, Abdulaziz Sachedina, and Bernadette Tobin, "Religious Perspectives on Umbilical Cord Blood Banking," *Journal of Law and Medicine* 19, no. 3 (2012): 504–6.

9. In their jointly edited book *Reimagining with Christian Doctrine*, Grace Ji-Sun Kim and Jenny Daggers introduce "reimagining" Christian doctrine as part of the subfield within feminist theology that continues to engage with doctrine. Addressing the question of how effectively such imagining can respond to gender injustice, the book works from the conviction that Christian theology, including doctrine, is an ongoing pilgrimage. They argue that reimagining doctrine unlocks the power of Christianity's rootedness in God's call to thirst and work for justice and righteousness. While acknowledging the twentieth-century feminist theologians' criticism of Christian doctrine as shaped by patriarchal power relations through the centuries, they reclaim it as part of Christian theology and embrace it in the continuing process of dialogue, reimagining, and understanding. Kim and Daggers, *Reimagining with Christian Doctrine*, xi–xii.

father. Born prematurely as a result of "domestic" violence, I was too tiny to put my mother's life at risk with my insistence on coming out feetfirst. The traditional birth attendant predicted that I would not live beyond two weeks.[10] I defied her prediction, and two weeks after my birth, my umbilical cord stump fell off and was ritualistically handed over to Mother Earth.

While I was in my mother's womb, my umbilical cord ritually connected me to her, allowing her blood and all life-giving nutrients to flow and be shared according to the needs of my growing body. After the internal connection was severed, my buried umbilical cord connected me to Mother Earth, an emblem of my total dependence on her for all life-giving nutrients for my body for as long as I live. She became my ever-present mother; she is carrying my umbilical cord within her earthly womb. As her daughter, I am accountable to her. Out of love for, reverence for, and my intrinsic symbiotic relationship with her, I will always care for her—because caring for her is caring for myself. I am not on a higher level than her, nor is my relationship of care for her dependent on my good will, as implied by the Christian stewardship model. She is part and parcel of me; I am connected to her, belong to her, emotionally as well as relationally.

Since I did not ask which particular tree I was born under, I adopted a mvunguti tree, the site where my father is buried, as the place both of my birth and of the burial of my umbilical cord. The mvunguti tree is a common indigenous African tree traditionally connected to fertility and healing, popularly known as a "sausage" tree due to the shape of its fruits, which grow about a hundred centimeters (about three feet) long and up to eighteen centimeters (about seven inches) wide, and weighing as much as ten kilograms (twenty-two pounds). My adoption of the mvunguti tree, which has now grown into old age close to my father's grave, makes me wonder, however, what could have happened if maize, cassava, or sweet potato seeds had been planted with my placenta and umbilical cord. As a member of the Circle of Concerned African Women Theologians,[11] I learned from our founding mother,

10. Having defied the birth attendant's prediction by living beyond two weeks, I qualify as someone who is endowed with divine gifts of wisdom, knowledge, and healing rooted in deep compassion for creation. My father and mother told me this when I was growing up. Every morning, my mother would inquire about what I "saw" in the night, checking on what I dreamed because she believed that through dreams, I could see the supernatural as someone who has capacity to live in the in-between spaces within the physical and spiritual realms. Over the years, I have learned the importance of recording my dreams, however insignificant they seem.

11. The Circle of Concerned African Women Theologians was founded by Mercy Amba Oduyoye and others in 1989 with the mission to carry out research, write, and publish on religion and culture from African women's perspectives so as to make sure that African theology included the experiences and perspectives of women. Motherhood experiences (like the burying of the umbil-

Mercy Amba Oduyoye, how among her ethnic group, the Akan people of Ghana, the buried placenta and umbilical cord are marked by planting seeds of a food crop like yam: "A bumper yield of yams . . . followed the planting of seed together with [Oduyoye's] placenta and umbilical cord."[12] The adopted mvunguti tree of my birth has known many years of bumper yields of its medicinal fruits, which people in the surrounding communities have harvested and used to heal different ailments. It symbolizes what my Ngoni community believes about my life as one born feetfirst and having survived beyond the predicted two weeks, namely that I am a healer and reconciler.[13]

As a young girl, I was told of a time when my father carried me to the top of a hill to stop the rain that was destroying the crops because it had come at the wrong time. I was told to point my hand to all the four corners of Mother Earth; I was guided to thank the divine for the gift of rain on behalf of the community. I was also taught how to beseech for mercy to stop the rain in order to spare the crops. I do not remember whether the rain stopped, but it probably did.

Despite the intrinsic powers given to me at my birth, I was unable to follow my vocation as a spirit medium because of the missionary-based condemnation of African indigenous spirituality as pagan and evil. Moreover, this missionary prejudice was combined with the patrilinealism of the Ngoni community—as a woman it would have been difficult to be accepted as a religious leader. I have often admired the aYao and aMang'anja women: in these communities, women who display intrinsic "anointedness" take on religious leadership roles, as God's intermediaries and guardians of Mother Earth. Yet, the needs of our planet have presented a moment of *kairos* for me, in which I may reclaim my womb-born power and create an African ecofeminist/womanist movement for ecological and gender justice—a protection and healing movement that deals with injustice in all its intersectionality.

ical cord), myths, and folk tales that help socialize young women are at the heart of women's aspects and encounters with religion, theology, and culture. See Mercy Amba Oduyoye, *Daughters of Anowa: African Women and Patriarchy* (Maryknoll, NY: Orbis, 2005).

12. Amoah, preface to *African Women*, xviii.

13. The Ngoni ethnic groups, as an offshoot from the Zulu Kingdom in South Africa, are patrilineal, not matrilineal like the aYao and aMang'anja. While in some Ngoni contexts, leadership can be either male or female, in the matrilineal societies of Malawi, religious leadership was mainly female. This was based on the given reality of the women's motherhood and therefore their interconnectedness to Mother Earth as agriculturalists. See K. M. Phiri, O. J. M. Kalinga, and H. H. K. Bhila, "The Northern Zambezi—Lake Malawi Region," in *General History of Africa*, vol. 5, *Africa from the Sixteenth to the Eighteenth Century*, ed. B. A. Ogot (Berkeley: University of California Press, 1992), 608–39; James Amanze, *African Traditional Religion in Malawi: The Case of the Bimbi Cult* (Blantyre: Christian Literature Association in Malawi, 2002), 125.

Women as Intermediaries and Guardians:
The M'bona, Chisumphi, and Bimbi Rainmaking Cults in Malawi

The matrilineal aMang'anja (Anyanja/Chewa) and aYao peoples are agriculturalists whose subsistence depends entirely on the rainy season. As a result, their religiocultural life has focused on ensuring that rains are regular and good. According to James Amanze, "religious beliefs exercise great power over a people living under an agricultural subsistence economy left to the mercy of ecological forces."[14] The aMang'anja and aYao people believe in a Chauta (the Big Bow for Rainbow) God, the Supreme Being conceived as Rain-giver, who is accessible through mediating ancestral spirits.[15] According to Isabel Phiri, the aMang'anja were known for their well-organized rain cults from the fourteenth to the sixteenth centuries. She quotes J. M. Schoffeleers, who argues that up to the twentieth century, in Lower Shire (Southern Malawi), "territorial mediumships were almost exclusively female."[16] According to Schoffeleers, the shrine of the M'bona Cult was believed to be visited by a spirit of the High God in the form of a great snake. He was provided with a human "wife," known as M'bona, who acted as an intermediary for God, prophesying God's commands to the aMang'anja people. The title M'bona for this spirit "wife" was taken from the aMang'anja (chiChewa) word *wona* (to see). M'bona was thus a seer, indicating her mediumistic powers.

Among the two aMang'anja clans in central Malawi, labor was divided between the Phiri and the Banda: "The Phiri, to whom the traditional chiefs belonged, retained political power and the Banda maintained a close relationship with the land and were credited with the power of making rain."[17] In Southern Malawi, women intermediaries (mostly known as M'bona) practiced at several rainmaking shrines.

---

14. Amanze, *African Traditional Religion*, 10.
15. Ibid., 125; Martin Ott, *African Theology in Images* (Blantyre: Christian Literature Association in Malawi, 2000), 277; J. W. M. van Breugel, *Chewa Traditional Religion* (Blantyre: Christian Literature Association in Malawi, 2001), 50.
16. Both M'bona and Mangadzi (or Makewana) were sometimes referred to as "wives" of the High God who was in charge of rain. Isabel Phiri argues that the idea of a "wife" of God (a God believed to be androgynous) must have meant something different from our idea of a wife as a sexual partner. Rather, a "wife" could be seen as a female intermediary, exalted and so intimate with God as to even speak on God's behalf. It could also be a patriarchal conspiracy to equate women to the status of a "wife" and, therefore, a lower status than husbands—thus equating God to the masculine element in human husbands. See, I. A. Phiri, *Women, Presbyterianism and Patriarchy* (Blantyre: Christian Literature Association in Malawi, 1997), 26; J. M. Schoffeleers, "The Interaction of the M'bona Cult and Christianity, 1859–1963," in *Themes in Christian History of Central Africa*, ed. T. O. Ranger and John Weller (London: Heinemann, 1975), 14–15; J. M. Schoffeleers, "The Chisumphi and M'bona Cult in Malawi: A Comparative History," in *Guardians of the Land*, ed. J. M. Schoffeleers (Gweru: Mambo, 1999), 176.
17. Amanze, *African Traditional Religion*, 152.

This territorial mediumship was originally exclusively in the hands of women, a fact intrinsically rooted in the life-giving power of women, which placed them in direct kinship with Mother Earth. In the Chisumphi (God as Giver of Rain) Cult, where the priestess Makewana, or Mangadzi,[18] was the keeper of the rain shrine, it was believed that she controlled the rain. According to Isabel Phiri, Makewana "was responsible for ceremonies to bring rain, as well as to utter prophecies and make divination. It is said that Makewana would disappear into the sacred pool of Malawi for three days at a time in order to call down the rain."[19] Makewana was able to survive because she was at one with Mother Earth, whose presence was embodied by the pool. Phiri asserts that although the Chewa people believed in only one High God (Chisumphi), Makewana was given the title of God (Chisumphi) because she was his important representative, who, when possessed, spoke in his voice.

In his *African Theology in Images*, Martin Ott attempts "an anthropological and theological evaluation and analysis" of the visual inculturation of Mua Mission,[20] a Roman Catholic mission center that houses the KuNgoni Arts Centre.[21] In analyzing the image of Makewana as a high priest and rainmaker, Ott suggests that she appears to be a powerful woman, one who would measure up to a goddess. Isabel Phiri, acknowledging Makewana's great influence, also argues that in Makewana's connection to the High God, the aChewa recognize the feminine nature of God as nurturer. Like Mother Earth, Makewana (literally "mother of children") contains nurturing concepts of God that are expressed within the chiChewa concept of God as Leza. Josephus C. Chakanza contends that "*Leza*, from the verb *kulera* in Chewa and Tonga means one who rules or rears. *Leza*, then, refers to God as the one who nurtures rears or rules creation. . . . Makewana means mother of all children and by implication, mother of all people. A mother has characteristics of nurturing and rearing children."[22]

The Makewana, Mangadzi, and Bimbi peoples trace descent through

18. Mangadzi and Makewana were not the same person as far as Chewa expert historian Kings M. Phiri is concerned. While Mangadzi was from the Banda clan, Makewana was from the Phiri clan. Kings Phiri argues that Makewana established her own power at Bunda-Msinja at the expense of Mangadzi. See Phiri, *Women, Presbyterianism and Patriarchy*, 29.

19. Ibid., 30.

20. Ott, *African Christianity in Images*, 1.

21. KuNgoni Centre of Culture and Art at Mua Mission in Malawi is a Catholic mission center headed by Claude Boucher of the Missionaries of Africa, or White Fathers. His Malawian name is Fr Chisale. It is a center that contextualizes theology using the arts in sculpture, painting, music, and dance done by Malawians. See "KUNGONI Online," accessed May 13, 2016, http://www.kungoni.org/.

22. J. C. Chakanza, "Some Chewa Concepts of God," *Religion in Malawi* 1 (December 1987): 7.

the maternal line because of women's role in nurturing and rearing children. Within such matrilineal systems, women's power is rooted in their motherhood roles. Contrary to James Amanze's claim that the aMang'anja world is a man's world, Isabel Phiri alleges that, before the coming of Scottish missionaries, the Chewa world was more of a woman's world than a man's world. Women had significant influence in decision-making in their communities, where progeny were not only traced through the mother but also connected to Mother Earth by way of the buried placenta and umbilical cord. If Mary had given birth to Jesus among these matrilineal matriarchs, not only would it have been natural to trace Jesus's descent through his mother, but any patriarchal connection of his divine ancestry would have seemed blasphemous since women, not men, were God's intermediaries. The embodying of incarnation the*logy through the experience of mother-hood would thus have been inherently enhanced.

Anthropologists John and Jean Comaroff connect the ritual potency of human agency to a community's state of moral rectitude[23]—its state of "coolness." In the rainmaking shrines that existed amongst the aMang'anja and aYao people, only women who, through old age, had reached a state of "coolness" regarding sexual activity and menstruation could enter the shrine and carry out rainmaking rituals on behalf of their communities. The chief of the community as well had to observe sexual abstinence during this period. The state of what can be called "sexual equilibrium" was a necessary prerequisite to appease the Supreme Being through the mediation of ancestors in assuring that rain would come. While the aMang'anja and aYao people interviewed could not explain the connection between the state of moral rectitude and the ritual potency of human agency, we can glean insight from the Comaroffs' research on the Tswana—similar to the aMang'anja and aYao people—for understanding ritual cleanliness known as *mdulo* taboos.[24] The *mdulo* complex is the contextual conception of the state of moral rectitude (or lack thereof) within the Malawian communities.

23. The Comaroffs define the ritual potency of the rainmaker, for example, as the combination of knowing how to release the necessary essence to activate the clouds and the necessary and conducive state of moral rectitude existing in the community concerned. This definition is not specific to the Tswana people, whose experiences the Comaroffs are articulating; it is an accurate reflection of the aMang'anja and aYao people as well. Jean and John Comaroff, *Of Revelation and Revolution: Christianity, Colonialism and Consciousness in South Africa* (Chicago: University of Chicago Press, 1991), 209–10.

24. For a detailed discussion on ritual cleanliness among the aYao or aMang'anja communities, read Fulata L. Moyo, "The Red Beads and White Beads: Malawian Women's Sexual Empowerment in the HIV/AIDS Era," *Journal of Constructive Theology* 11, no. 1 (2005): 53–66; Breugel, *Chewa Traditional Religion*; Joseph DeGabriele, "When Pills Don't Work—African Illnesses, Misfortune and *Mdulo*," *Religion in Malawi* 9 (1999): 9–23.

This connection of women's fertility in the indigenous conception of ritual potency with impurity taboos highlights the urgent need to connect ecological activism for justice with that of gender justice in the quest for holistic justice.

Mary Birthing Jesus: Embodying Incarnation The*logy for Ecological Justice

In exploring Christian ecofeminism as *kenotic* ecology, Priscilla Eppinger argues that incarnation theology, rather than creation theology, provides a better model for an appropriate anthropological/ecological relationship between humanity and the environment. The questions that guide her discussion include: What constitutes authentic humanity? Where do we humans fit in our cosmology? What meaning do we make of our place? Eppinger justifies drawing on Christianity on the grounds of its wide global influence. She is critical, though, of Christianity's fostering of a global (political) economy that overconsumes natural resources. Seeing Christianity's entanglement with global capitalism, Eppinger critiques Christianity's embrace of the stewardship model, in which God relates to creation as an owner in a hierarchical, top-down manner. As stewards, human beings derive their mandate to care for the eco-community from God's hierarchical-patriarchal ownership. In this view, nonhuman nature is merely the recipient of care; it is not a community to which humans belong and with which the sacred is entangled. To be a steward is to be a manager. While you can be a good or a bad manager, stewards by definition retain power and authority over the resources entrusted to them.[25] This model, together with the creation theology in which it is rooted, has not been an effective model for ecological justice and is in dire need of change. As Eppinger states,

> In engaging a praxis-oriented ecological theology, then, one would examine the ecological implications of any particular belief, assess those outcomes in relation to the overall values underlying the theological system, and determine whether the theology as constructed coheres to its internal value system. If not, more constructive theological work is in order.[26]

In the doctrine of incarnation, Jesus Christ is understood to be fully human and fully God. So, Christ becomes the preeminent model.

---

25. Priscilla E. Eppinger, "Christian Ecofeminism as Kenotic Ecology: Transforming Relationships away from Environmental Stewardship," *Journal for the Study of Religion* 24, no. 2 (2011): 47.
26. Ibid., 48–49.

Within the kenotic incarnational model for ecology, which embraces relationships of interconnectedness and valuing of all members of the Earth community, we find an ethic of ecojustice. Eppinger argues that while humans seem on the surface to be more powerful members of the eco-community, a closer look reveals that we are totally dependent on the environment for our well-being. We therefore should take more responsibility for the care of those the anthropocentric world has deemed less powerful. Eppinger's kenotic incarnational theology underscores her call for more human responsibility, as exemplified by the self-emptying God who humbly became human so as to build a life-giving, just communion with creation.

Eppinger does not examine Mary's role in this kenotic incarnation theology, focusing rather on Jesus's self-emptying, or kenosis. Eppinger's incarnation theology thus downplays Mary's powerful experience of God coordinating with her to make Word become flesh. Within the embodied incarnation the*logy I put forward, however, Mary's mothering of Jesus and her burying of the placenta and his umbilical cord are important rituals. They root our interconnectedness in a shared motherhood, Mother Earth, as creation, as well as with the God-human. In this common motherhood, Jesus becomes our brother who leads us into holistic salvation, especially through ecojustice, by his self-giving love. So, at the heart of the collective burying of our umbilical cords in the womb of Mother Earth, our interconnectedness and interdependence becomes an emotional loving bond of mother-children. With the latter, our call to work for ecological justice becomes a matter of life and death. Mother Earth has become part of our own flesh and blood, since part of us exists within her body. We also exist interdependently with her, for our survival.

Womanist theologian Eboni Marshall Turman highlights elements of Mary's embodied role in incarnation theology. She also succinctly captures how churches play down certain bodies; for our argument, it is the female body of Mary.[27] Turman endorses the Chalcedon definition of faith as revealing the deep significance of the incarnation as the only way our transformation can be fulfilled, in the fullness of Jesus as fully human, fully God; the one who walks *with* us in a world of suffering but is also *in* us.

Addressing the invisibility of Mary's role in giving birth, Turman challenges the black churches that hold the Chalcedon definition of faith dearly and yet still practice sexism, designating women clergy solely to the role of deacon. By obscuring Mary's motherhood role,

---

27. Turman, "Black and Blue," 72.

Christianity treats Mary like the black church treats female clergy—pushed to the periphery. Even when these women have been ordained like their male counterparts, they end up serving in voluntary roles like Paul's *doulos* (bond-servants devoted to serve another), whereas the men become leaders in the church. The black churches use lesser roles to assert and normalize these women's invisibility.

In addition, the Christian belief that Mary remained a virgin even after giving birth has made her an idealized image rather than an authentic human being. As a real woman who had menses, was pregnant, and bled in giving birth, Mary most certainly would have had sexual intercourse with her husband, Joseph, and borne children through natural processes. The uplifting of virginity as a purer state of moral rectitude articulates patri-kyriarchal Christianity's fear of sexuality and expresses the pervasive and long-lasting attempt to control women's bodies and flourishing as sexual beings. This fear and control is at the heart of the disembodied incarnation theology, a theology that supposedly has deep understanding of the logos but refuses to articulate in full what being human means.

Conclusion

While I agree that incarnation the*logy and not creation the*logy should be the basis for ecological justice, the former needs to be further embodied within the ritual that connects Mary's motherhood of Jesus with that of Mother Earth by way of giving attention to the burial of Jesus's umbilical cord. This customary ritual within my own culture might have been a practice of Jewish women at the time of Jesus's birth. It brings out a truly embodied the*logy of incarnation that takes seriously the actuality of the word becoming flesh in a very concrete way. Incorporating such a ritual into incarnation the*logy, the basis of ecological justice-making, not only will it base our ecojustice making in the reality of our solidarity as interconnected and interdependent with Mother Earth but it will transform us into healers of relationships, reconciling the human community with Mother Earth, as our life-committed passion.

10

Motherhood and Christ in an African Ecofeminist Theology for Climate Justice

Isabel Mukonyora

Climate change is a global problem, although experienced differently depending on the specific ecological destruction of a given area. Among the Shona in Zimbabwe, political conflicts over the possession of land have been made worse by climate change related droughts, mass poverty, and the spread of diseases such as HIV/AIDS. Not only are droughts more frequent in Zimbabwe,[1] there are reports of social upheavals caused by drought in other parts of the continent as well. And, all over Africa, it is the rural poor whose lives are most dramatically affected by climate change and environmental destruction. In Zimbabwe, climate change related droughts have exacerbated a process of internal migration among the rural populations from their

---

1. Historians usually refer to Rhodesia, the name used to describe the illegal white supremacist regime in power from 1964 until 1979 when the British government supervised the first democratic elections held in the country. Robert Mugabe has been the president of Zimbabwe since 1980.

ancestral lands to local cities and across the border to different cities in South, Central, and East Africa.[2] Yet, because cities have neither the infrastructure nor the resources to accommodate newcomers, migrants often end up in one of the many slums on their outskirts.[3]

This chapter seeks to construct an African Christology for climate justice from the lived understanding of Christ at the margins of Zimbabwe's capital city, Harare, most notably the pieces of *masowe*, or urban wilderness, that can be found just outside of its many suburbs.

Harare is Zimbabwe's leading commercial, communication, and industrial center. Besides the manufacturing industries of goods such as textiles, steel, chemicals, and beer, the building industry is responsible for the growth of northern suburbs such as Borrowdale, Mount Pleasant, Avondale, and Marlborough. At the margins of these affluent neighborhoods are meadows or pieces of urban wilderness. Those meadows reflect the human suffering of the people who use them the most. Not only are they completely barren in some parts and almost swampy in other parts, the meadows also show signs of ecological destruction caused by toxic waste. Builders and factory workers dump concrete and metal cans filled with industrial waste, such as broken bricks, glass, and other materials, threatening not just the vegetation and animal life but also the well-being of the poor who use these meadows to grow and sell food, wash clothes, recreate, and worship.

The ideas shared in this essay result from close observation of a few small communities of African Christians, the so called Masowe Apostles, worshipping in the meadows of northern Harare, on the outskirts of Mount Pleasant. Going out to pray in the wilderness makes sense for the Masowe Apostles because it is better than spending the weekend in undesirable living quarters, often tucked away in the backyards of the homes of rich and powerful employers. The Masowe Apostles are a so-called African-initiated church, popular among the Shona people, that originated with a wandering prophet, Johane Masowe (1914–78).[4] Elsewhere, I have demonstrated that the Masowe Apostles are an example of an oral indigenous Christianity;[5] here, I will argue that the Masowe, who have a large number of female followers, are preaching a Christology that has strong potential for an African ecofeminist theology

---

2. Isabelle Mukonyora, "Masowe Migration: A Question for Liberation in the African Diaspora," *Religion Compass* 2, no. 2 (March 2008): 84–95.

3. Timothy Burke, *Lifebuoy Men, Lux Women: The Commodification, Consumption, and Cleanliness in Modern Zimbabwe* (London: Leicester University Press, 1996).

4. The term *African-initiated church* describes congregations whose founder figures are African prophets, distinguished from churches established by European missionaries.

5. Isabel Mukonyora, "The Complementarity of Male and Female Imagery in Theological Language: A Study of the Valentinian and Masowe Theological Systems" (PhD diss., University of Oxford, 1999).

of Earth healing due to its strong emphasis on African motherhood, indigenous female images for the High God, Mwari, and the holistic healing qualities identified with Mwari and Christ by way of these indigenous deities or images.

Historical Roots for an African Eco-Christology

Since the founder of the Masowe Apostles, Johane Masowe, laid the foundation for the African interpretation of the doctrine of Christ, it is important to outline his influence and preaching. A Shona-speaking prophet, Masowe moved away from his ancestral home when he was in his early twenties due to the social upheavals caused by colonial conquest, urbanization, the 1930s' economic depression, and severe drought, which caused much suffering and death among the Shona people.[6] Masowe sought a better life for himself, while also intending to find an alternative way of spreading the gospel. He attracted followers who shared his quest for belonging. Interestingly, the majority of these followers were women whose motherly connection with the land was so distorted by Westernization that they saw themselves as people wandering in the wilderness. The women were interested in finding ways of coping with life in a society that was making it difficult for them to live in rural areas after having been left behind by husbands looking for jobs in the city. Women who migrated to the city in the hope of finding jobs were not welcome during the thirties, forties, fifties, and sixties. Because of the lack of options society left them, Shona women eked out a living on the fringes of cityscapes by growing crops and learning to weave baskets to sell on the streets. Anyone preaching to those suffering on account of unemployment, diseases, and other misfortunes can count on devotees. By way of his identification with John the Baptist and preaching to the marginalized on the outskirts of urban centers, Masowe transformed the urban wilderness by making it possible for people to turn their feelings of marginality into a ritual of "wandering in the wilderness" while worshipping the High God, Mwari, during a time of colonial oppression.

To this day, the members of wilderness churches are most known for walking around selling handmade goods to make a living. The ritual behavior of the Masowe Apostles makes them very popular, moreover.

6. The term *Shona* refers to eight or nine dialects of the same Bantu language spoken by the majority of people in Zimbabwe today. Johane Masowe's dialect is common in eastern Zimbabwe. The women in Harare spoke a fairly standard Shona, allowing people to mix dialects as long as they could understand each other. This linguistic fact is important to recognize because African Christians who use the word "masowe" to either describe themselves or the sacred wilderness to which they go to prayer have a long history of migrating in sub-Saharan Africa.

Nowadays, it is possible for anyone who travels to cities such as Harare, Gweru, and Bulawayo in Zimbabwe, and further to Gaborone in Botswana; Johannesburg, Durban, and Cape Town in South Africa; Lusaka and Ndola in Zambia; and, Nairobi and other cities in sub-Saharan Africa, to meet men, women, and children going outdoors to pray in white robes. These robes seem to be the result of reading Revelation, where several references are made to the children of God who dress in white robes and glorify God (Rev 6:11; 7:9-17)

According to his early followers, Masowe was rather like Jesus, born of a virgin, namely a Shona woman who received news about giving birth to the infant Johane while her husband was in prison and she was coping with his absence.[7] While stories about virgin births are rare in Shona culture, there is a tradition of recognizing messengers of God by the symbolic language used to dramatize their spiritual knowledge. In the case of Masowe, the biblical-theological tradition of proclaiming the significance of a prophet by drawing attention to a virgin birth is being co-opted by the Shona to play up the significance of their own leader. Yet, according to Dillon-Malone, the relationship between Masowe and the women who surrounded him in the wilderness is best understood in terms of the role that led him to adopt the feminine title of *Izwi raMwari*, a "voice" or messenger of God. *Izwi* is she who unveils God's meaning and purpose through women, also called virgins who act as agents of knowledge. The *Gospel of God*, a set of texts filled with stories about Masowe and his teaching, instruct Masowe Apostles that "the sisters have a role to fulfill as the messengers of God among the people."[8] The same texts associate the devotees with the church and their voices with divine wisdom. Hence, there is a link between Christ as God incarnate and his Virgin Mother: both represent the Logos or divine wisdom revealed on Earth.[9]

By the time Masowe died of cardiovascular disease, he had not only made it easy for women to follow his teaching because they nursed him and prayed for and with him more than men, especially as he was often sick, he had also developed an interesting pattern of God-talk with women symbolizing divine wisdom reflective of their important role as child bearers, farmers, and traditional stewards of the

---

7. Clive Dillon-Malone, "The Conception, Birth and Youth of Johane Masowe," in *The Korsten Basketmakers: A Study of the Masowe Apostles, An Indigenous African Religious Movement* (Manchester: Manchester University Press, 1978), 142–43.

8. Clive Dillon-Malone, *Gospel of God: VaPositori VaJohane Masowe* (Lusaka: Teresianum, 1987), 145–54. Although it is impossible to ascertain, Dillon-Malone claims that the group of women who lived with Masowe were unmarried and honored their virginity as "wives of God." Cf. Isabelle Mukonyora, "Johane Masowe's Life and Death Dramatizations," *Swedish Missiological Themes* 88, no. 3 (2000): 409–30.

9. Mukonyora, *Complementarity of Male and Female*, chapter 8.

Earth. I believe, therefore, that Masowe is taking us beyond questions about a liberation theology for the poor to a more radical position where he elevates women in a predominantly patriarchal society. As Elizabeth Schmidt has observed, Shona women suffered because they became "beholden to two patriarchies," limiting them to the rural margins of a colonial society where farming on barren soil made the relationship with nature far less about celebrating the divine gift of Mother Earth and more a form of slavery in a culture where missionary teachings about gender roles reinforced their subordination to men.[10] Against this background, Masowe's use of women as the *imago Dei* created something of an African feminist liberation theology for survivors of colonial conquest, urbanization, and the rise of a capitalist economy. Besides drawing the attention of women who needed to feel at home as followers of Christ, Masowe invokes the idea of Mary, God bearer, and, hence, elevated motherhood as a key to interpret the significance of Christ. Connecting the concept of motherhood among the Shona with early Christian doctrine, Masowe Apostles' interpretation of the doctrine of the mother of Christ becomes an important resource for addressing climate justice insofar as it connects salvation with both justice for the poor and the healing of the Earth.

Motherhood among the Shona

As a first step to flesh out an African ecofeminist Christology of Earth healing, I, therefore, want to look at the ideas of motherhood found in the predominantly patriarchal Shona culture, which is the background of the Masowe Apostles. According to both Daneel and Schoffeleers, the Shona High God, Mwari, is a territorial deity who protects lineages of kings, yet is often worshipped using social values best represented by African mothers.[11] Thus, it is useful to revisit the Shona past in order to help readers realize the importance of motherhood to the indigenous religion and culture.

As highlighted in the story of the founder of the Masowe Apostles, the experiences of reality that are African and Christian make it possible to utilize these theological ideas for an age of climate injustice. Before the industrialization and spread of Christianity in Zimbabwe,

---

10. Elizabeth Schmidt, *Peasants, Traders, and Wives: Shona Women in the History of Zimbabwe, 1870–1939*, Social History of Africa (Portsmouth, NH: Heinemann, 1992), 14–42. Cf. Jock McCulloch, *Black Peril, White Virtue: Sexual Crime in Southern Rhodesia, 1902–1935* (Bloomington: Indiana University Press, 2000), 36–54.

11. M. L. Daneel, *The God of the Matopo Hills: An Essay on the Mwari Cult in Rhodesia* (The Hague: Mouton, 1970), 22–25. Matthew Schoffeleers, introduction to *Guardians of the Land: Essays on Central African Territorial Cults* (Gweru: Mambo, 1999), 1–41.

Shona women combined the role of mother with farming food crops, gathering firewood, and fetching drinking water. Women thus made a big difference in the lives of men and children, who were viewed as members of the lineage of the husband. Giving birth is not the only experience to take into account in the development of motherhood, however. Children, especially firstborn sons who later become ancestors, turned to their mothers for answers to life problems, as well as for lessons on how to reason and discern the truth.

Given the importance of motherhood in traditional Shona society, it does not come as a surprise that the traditional High God could be worshipped by way of maternal images, such as *Mai Vedu* (Our Mother) or *Dzivaguru* (The Great Pool). Because motherhood is connected with fertility, traditional knowledge, wisdom about ecosystems, and the continuation of the tribe, the association between the divine wisdom and women's *izwi* (voice) is worth noting, especially in a society increasingly plagued by droughts. Thus, Daneel has pointed to the significance of the fact that the guardian of *Matonjeni*, the most well-known shrine used to worship Mwari, was usually an elder woman.[12] Worshipping at the shrine, which has a large pool of water at its center, addresses problems of infertility and drought.[13]

Among the Shona, Mwari is the creator of the sun, moon, stars, and, as far as humans are concerned, the source of life. African Christians who started praying to God in the wilderness a hundred years ago found a way of dramatizing their belief in God's intervening power through prayers for the sustenance and healing of earthly life.[14] Not only had the god Mwari in the wilderness always been connected with fertility and Earth healing, the creator and redeemer God of the Bible was interpreted this way as well.[15] Interestingly, therefore, African theology does not have the crippling problem of Aristotelian binary thoughts about the superior male and inferior female natures, which ecofeminist theologians seek to dismantle.[16] As the African Catholic theologian Mari-Anna Pöntinen puts it, "embracing both qualities (of the male and female) in the image of God is characteristic of African traditional concepts of the Supreme Being,"[17] and "Divine Motherhood is complementary to the Divine Fatherhood."[18] At the same time, how-

---

12. Daneel, *God of the Matopo Hills*, 25.
13. Isabel Mukonyora, "Women and Ecology in Shona Religion," *Word & World* 19, no. 3 (Summer 1999): 276–84.
14. Herbert Aschwanden, *Karanga Mythology: An Analysis of the Consciousness of the Karanga in Zimbabwe* (Gweru: Mambo, 1989), 11–42.
15. Ibid.
16. Rosemary Radford Reuther, *Sexism and God-Talk* (Boston: Beacon, 1983), chapter 1.
17. Mari-Anna Pöntinen, *African Theology as Liberating Wisdom: Celebrating Life and Harmony in the Evangelical Lutheran Church in Botswana* (Leiden: Brill, 2013), 257–58.

ever, the poor treatment of women in Zimbabwean society, who are often treated as the possessions of men, must be mentioned. Clearly, the symbolic realm is not directly reflected within social reality. Nonetheless, it is important to state that, traditionally, motherhood allowed women to exercise meaning-shaping power, if not always concrete influence and autonomy. Indeed, by way of an African Christology highlighting both the mother and the son as agents of knowledge, we find that the worship of Mwari continues to reflect the struggle for survival in the day-to-day lives of poor women, as well as the hope for salvation expressed by the concrete acts of healing the sick, loving one's neighbor, and acting as stewards of the Earth.[19]

Motherhood and Christ in Early Church Doctrine

The idea of African women as "mothers" connects with the concept of Mary as the God bearer found in the doctrinal statement of Chalcedon in 451 CE. As it happens, firstborn sons were considered so special that their mothers enjoyed more respect than other women. So, learning about Mary as the God bearer did not really create a conflict of understanding for the Shona people.[20] In order to capitalize on the connection between Mary, the Mother of Christ, and the veneration of motherhood among the Shona people, I want to revisit the statement of the Council of Chalcedon and the world of ideas behind the suggestion that the Virgin Mary was, in fact, Theotokos (Womb of God).[21] The Council of Chalcedon in 451 CE reads,

> In all things like unto us, without sin; begotten before all ages of the Father according to the Godhead, and in these latter days, for us and for our salvation, born *of the Virgin Mary, the Mother of God,* according to the Manhood; one and the same Christ, Son, Lord, only begotten, to be acknowledged in two natures, unconfusedly, unchangeably, indivisibly, inseparably; the distinction of natures being by no means taken away by the union, but rather the property of each nature being preserved, and concurring in one Person and one Subsistence, not parted or divided into two persons, but one and the same Son, and only begotten, God the Word,

---

18. Mukonyora, *Complementarity of Male and Female*, 136–64.
19. Mukonyora, "Johane Masowe's," 409–30.
20. We are talking about a Shona religion and culture where women were also exploited and abused by men who treated women as possessions and viewed Mwari as a territorial spirit in whose name people fought for control of both the land and women. Terrence O. Ranger, *Revolt in Southern Rhodesia, 1896–7: A Study in African Resistance* (London: Heinemann, 1967), 19–24.
21. Nowadays, theology should be taught from a global perspective, especially these matters of doctrine that are expected to unite believers from different cultures in the past and, arguably, the present.

the Lord Jesus Christ; as the prophets from the beginning [have declared] concerning Him, and the Lord Jesus Christ Himself has taught us, and the Creed of the holy Fathers has handed down to us.[22]

This doctrinal statement explains the theological significance of Christ as the "begotten before all ages of the Father." The story of Christ as God having a mother is not that strange to anyone accustomed to ancient myths of creation, which typically combine male and female imagery in accounts of the origins of life.[23] In this context, the formulation of a doctrine inspired by the Hellenistic world of many gods and goddesses concerned with fertility and the continuation of life, Christ, as the "only begotten" son of God, sounds more complete with a mother in the picture than without. I will briefly look at two popular goddesses of the Greco-Roman empire, Isis and Athena respectively, for whom motherhood meant sustaining life through ideas about ethics.

Isis of Egypt was a popular virgin goddess-mother whose son was king. There was a high regard for virgins as well as certain virtues of womanhood, starting with that of motherhood, at shrines dedicated to Isis. Isis was not just venerated as the king's mother, however, she was also worshipped as follows:

> I am nature, the parent of all the gods, mistress of all the elements, the beginning of all ages, sovereign of the gods, queen of the *manes* [spirits of the dead], and first of the heavenly being.... My divinity, uniform in itself, is honored under numerous forms, various rites, and different names ... but the sun-illuminated Ethiopians, and the Egyptians renowned for ancient lore, worship me with due ceremonies, and call me by my real name, "Queen Isis."[24]

The way Isis is portrayed here is important insofar as the language points to a deity "of all the elements." As the Theotokos, she is the bearer of all the elements, nature itself. Looking back at Chalcedon from this historical and cultural perspective is interesting: it reveals the Son of the Virgin Mary as the means by which we may comprehend God as the master of all the elements. Against this background, it makes sense, then, to examine ideas about women and motherhood in Shona religion and culture as the background for interpreting Christ. Indeed, there is a striking correspondence between the image of "the

22. Hugh Kerr, ed., *Readings in Christian Thought* (Nashville: Abingdon, 1990), 76; my italics.
23. Aschwanden, *Karanga Mythology*, 11–48.
24. Shelagh Ranger, *The Word of Wisdom and the Creation of Animals in Africa* (Cambridge: James Clarke, 2007), 87.

Virgin Mary, the Womb of God," and Christ as the Savior of the world on one hand, and female imagery used to create a metaphorical language about Mwari as a mother, great womb, the *fons et origo* of all of life, on the other hand.

Another important cultural influence when it comes to the account of motherhood in the early church is the Greek goddess Athena. Known as the goddess of the city, Athena was the embodiment of wisdom, reason, intelligent activity, arts, and literature. The fact that she was worshipped as the patron of Athene, the city famous for inventing the bridle, the trumpet, the flute, the pot, the rake, the plow, the yoke, the ship, and the chariot, is important to note, since it means that among her many devotees must have been women who depended on tilling the soil for survival in a patriarchal world.

Because Athena is also often portrayed as the goddess of war, she may seem at odds with the idea of motherhood best associated with interpretations of the Virgin Mary as the Mother of the Savior of planetary life. Nevertheless, Athena complements Isis when it comes to the conceptualization of the Mother of Jesus in the early church. The fact that her patronage of the city led many citizens of the Greco-Roman Empire to worship Athena as the goddess blessing people whose livelihoods depended on farming is interesting to remember at this time when Western technologies have fragmented our connections with the elements of nature. Athena "permitted" humans to live off "the elements of nature."[25] She therefore complements Isis, mistress of all the elements. Indeed, together Isis and Athena strike the right balance between the cosmic scope of motherhood and the particular shape of maternal care through which life is being sustained.

Because it is important to relate doctrinal language to the wider culture in which the early church and its doctrines originated, the Virgin Mary and Mother of God referred to at Chalcedon should be looked at against the background of Hellenistic culture. The syncretism one finds is, in fact, not so very different from the type of syncretism in the African Christianity of the Shona people.

An African Ecofeminist Christology for Climate Justice

This chapter has argued that motherhood is part and parcel of an African eco-Christology in which the proof of the full humanity of Jesus lies in his empathy with women. The powerful effects of love and

---

25. Jesse Harasta, *Athena: The Origins and History of the Greek Goddess* (Cambridge, MA: Charles River Editors, 2013), chapter 2.

divine wisdom as something shared in the urban wilderness become an important vehicle for articulating the significance of Christ for a continent riddled by droughts, famine, and social upheaval.

In Harare, the urban wilderness on the city's outskirts attracts small communities of white-robed African Christian women. After a year of ignoring the small communities and individual women who eke out a living by planting food crops in the same wilderness, in case of good rains, I realized the need to construct an African Christology for climate justice from their lived spirituality.[26] Just as Jesus is portrayed in the Scriptures as a prophetic figure driven by the need to address victims of oppression, and the poor and sick as people who belonged to the margins of the city of Jerusalem, African Christians in "the margins" of large cities draw attention to the suffering and death out of which is born the hope for salvation. While in many ways a place of destitution, the masowe is "sacred wilderness" for the small groups of women and children who gather here to pray two or three times a week. Indeed, it is not the droughts, poverty, and sickness alone that attract lots of mothers to go to the wilderness, but hope for the healing of Earth, humans, and all the living.

When it comes to the Shona religious language used to pray in the wilderness, something striking happens insofar as language about God combines male and female imagery in stories of creation, as it does in ways of accounting for the revelation of an ecological deity. For example, Daneel describes Mwari as a patriarchal God with a female dimension. He goes further to say that Shona language about God has been so deeply physical that God was said to have eyes (Maziso), ears (Nzewe), and a mouth (Muromo). In short, sentient beings are a reflection of the glory of God, the Creator. His voice or Izwi was said to come from the womb of God, symbolized by the body of a woman.[27] Hence, there is a special focus on women's fertility, not to mention skills and words of wisdom associated with services rendered to society through nurture of the Earth.[28] God's presence is thus felt when women give birth, the rains fall, and the sun shines upon Earth.

While it has not been the intention of this chapter to show that African Christians from the lower ranks of Zimbabwean society already know what we mean by a "doctrine of climate justice," it is important to be reminded that Mwari was traditionally known as an ecological

26. Isabel Mukonyora, *Wandering a Gendered Wilderness: Suffering and Healing in an African Initiated Church* (New York: Peter Lang, 2007). The preface describes how I arrived at the conclusion to spend time doing theology with the experiences of my marginalized neighbors practicing Christianity outdoors.
27. Daneel, *God of the Matopo Hills*, 24–26.
28. Ibid.

deity. In addition, by using the image of Mary as the "Womb of God" and/or "Source of the Life of Christ" to revisit Christology, I have sought to highlight that women fulfill key roles as mothers and stewards of the Earth in Shona culture. Finally, it is important to be reminded that Masowe Apostles are not interested in proving they can read biblical texts at prayer as do Western-oriented African Christians.[29] Instead, they address existential questions about God's existence in a society experiencing oppression and environmental devastation. In the end, therefore, an African doctrine of motherhood and Christ for climate justice that takes its point of departure in the religious experiences of female Masowe Apostles points to a world in which salvation means healing of relationships among all the living and nonliving beings struggling for survival in a world of economic and social injustice and environmental destruction.

29. Matthew Eric Engelke, *A Problem of Presence: Beyond Scripture in an African Church* (Berkeley: University of California Press, 2007).

Cross and Salvation

11

Seeds, Cross, and a Paradox of Life from Death: A Postcolonial Eco-Christology

Jea Sophia Oh

Very truly I tell you, unless a kernel of wheat falls to the ground and dies, it remains only a single seed. But if it dies, it will produce a lot of grain.

—John 12:24

In order to live, one must die. This is the paradox of life from death, which is the principle of life. Jesus compared his death on the cross to a seed that falls to the ground and dies. A seed has the potential to bear fruit because there is life in a seed. All living organisms have fecundity that is not limited to a few species of (female) mammals only. The secret of life is in its hybrid process of disintegration and proliferation, as numerous grains come after a kernel of wheat falls to the ground and dies. Nonetheless, if it remains only a single seed, it eventually loses its life.

This process of life out of death can be found in all living organisms. Death is not the opposite to life but an inevitable process of life that was not even avoidable to Jesus on the cross. The philosopher John D. Caputo calls the crucifixion "the weakness of God."[1] Caputo writes that the genuine divinity of Jesus is revealed in his helplessness, his cry of abandonment, and in the words of forgiveness he utters. Paradoxically, Caputo sees the weakness and helplessness of the cross as the power that reveals Jesus's divinity. What Caputo calls "the weak force of God" is indeed the power of life, which cannot be knocked out by the colonial sovereign power. This intertwined power of weakness and the processes of life from death are given to all the living organisms, including Jesus as being truly human (*vere homo*).

Human beings have changed the climate on this planet, and that has changed everything, especially how we grow food. Some believe GMOs help fight climate change. GMOs are a solution to the increase of food shortages due to climate change. Moreover, and in the short run, GMOs can reduce fuel consumption on farms due to a reduced need to spray crops and fertilize. Nonetheless, the undeniable relevance of GMOs should be rethought from a life-centered perspective. The secret of life in a seed is now genetically modified by human colonization over nature. The colonial superpower of GMOs has created superseeds and superweeds that will eventually destroy our ecosystem and biodiversity by extorting fecundity from seeds. However, power also comes from the bottom of the structure that has been deemed the subaltern.

Understanding the Foucauldian heterogeneity of power as sovereign power and bio-power,[2] this essay suggests bio-power as an alternative power, "the power of vulnerability." In *The History of Sexuality Vol. I*, Foucault talks about heterogeneity of power, power from above and below. While sovereign power is legitimate and repressive, bio-power is productive and immanent. Foucault views sovereign power as negating, legislative, prohibitive, censoring, and homogenous while he recognizes bio-power as always productive, immanent, exercised, capillary, and resisted. We can find bio-power from seeds and the cross that resists the colonial power and brings forth the multiplicity of life.

The Colonizer: Power of Sovereignty

Then the soldiers of the governor took Jesus into the governor's headquarters, and they gathered the whole cohort around him. They stripped him and put a scarlet robe on him, and after twisting some thorns into a

1. John D. Caputo, *The Weakness of God: A Theology of the Event* (Bloomington: Indiana University Press, 2006), 43.
2. Michel Foucault, *The History of Sexuality Vol. I: An Introduction*, trans. Robert Hurley (New York: Vintage, 1978), 94–95.

crown, they put it on his head. They put a reed in his right hand and knelt before him and mocked him, saying, "Hail, King of the Jews!" They spat on him, and took the reed and struck him on the head. After mocking him, they stripped him of the robe and put his own clothes on him. Then they led him away to crucify him. (Matt 27:27–31)

While the assumptions of omnipotence have dominated Christian imaginations of God, the path Jesus walked to his crucifixion (the *Via Dolorosa*) does not portray divine power this way. Assumptions of divine omnipotence seem to be disproved by the legitimate, worldly power when Jesus was mocked, stripped, and crucified. Jesus was literally killed. As the Gospel story tells it, the crucifixion then utterly demonstrates the monopoly of sovereign or almighty power exercised by the Roman authorities. The crucified Jesus is a sign of the violence done by the colonizer.

When humans understand power as sovereign power that comes from above not below, they often also assume an all-powerful God who rules the world from on high in a unilateral and controlling manner. Humans tend to justify their dominance over the powerless by mimicking this divine omnipotence. According to theologian Catherine Keller's way of problematizing the divine omnipotence, if power means power-over, then God is either weak or nonexistent by the standards of dominance. She writes, "The more the powers of dominance succeed, the more God fails, the more the powers of dominance fill the vacuum. The dominative model of divine power prepares the way for modern secularist uses and knowledge of power, mechanizing its operations and rendering one set of beings powerful and all other sets proportionately powerless."[3] Keller especially rejects the portrayal of the relationship between God and the world as an all-powerful divine parent to a powerless child-victim, recognizing such figures as complimentary poles in the historical cycle of abuse.

The universal repetitions of the abuse of power can be seen at every level of our social orders. Sovereign power retains a monopoly on violence that seems to be invincible by democratic process. People who are marginalized by way of a dominant power structure are called the subalterns. A subaltern is someone who has a lower rank in the reigning socioeconomic, political hierarchy. Thus, a subaltern indicates someone who has been marginalized or oppressed by way of the sovereign power because of her lower rank. On the cross, Jesus became a subaltern at the hands of the sovereign power of his day.

---

3. Catherine Keller, "Power Lines," in *Power, Powerlessness, and the Divine*, ed. Cynthia Rigby (Atlanta: Scholars Press, 1997), 59.

Indeed, Jesus died as a subaltern who could not save himself from colonial violence. Gayatri Chakravorty Spivak points out that the subaltern is denied access to both mimetic and political forms of representation.[4] An example of mimetic forms of representation is the media's portrayal of human beings. Subaltern groups are usually underrepresented or presented in inferior ways in the media. Jesus was crucified as a mimetic and political subaltern, that is, as a member of a group without adequate cultural and political representation. His words, *Eli, Eli, lema sabachthani?* (My God, my God, why have you forsaken me?) were scattered into the air as a mute signal of the very concrete powerlessness of the subaltern. Jesus as a subaltern was entirely muted.

When I see the crucified Jesus as a postcolonial subject, I find resonances between Jesus's powerlessness and the subjugation of nature by human colonization. Spivak suggests a marginalized woman as a gendered subaltern in patriarchal systems. Spivak's notion of the subaltern makes me recognize nature as an ecological subaltern in this anthropocentric world. Similar to the human subaltern as the "othered subject," nature is the "othered subject" insofar as it is subjugated by discursive management and control. The worldly sovereign power of the colonizer exercises destructive activities, such as killing, marginalization, oppression, exploitation, coercion, contamination of the environment, and the destruction of the ecosystem. The latter is expressed by way of the Korean word *jugim* (killing). *Jugim* is not death, because death is a part of life and always exists as a necessary aspect of the process of life. Rather, *jugim* means all the activities of an anti-life, a package of social pathology. In contrast, the Korean term *salim* means making things alive, restoring, and enlivening. Is the cross only a sign of *jugim*? Or can the cross become a sign of *salim*?

The Cross: Power of Vulnerability

Nothing is less sure, of course, than a god without sovereignty, nothing is less sure than his coming, of course.[5]

Caputo develops the theological implications of Derrida and imagines a thinking of God that is weak and non-sovereign. He asserts that God is not the Father Almighty but the power of powerlessness. Caputo dif-

4. Gayatri Chakravorty Spivak, "Can the Subaltern Speak?," in *Marxism and the Interpretation of Culture*, ed. Cary Nelson and Lawrence Grossberg (Urbana: University of Illinois Press, 1988), 278.
5. Jacques Derrida, *Voyous: deux essais sur la raison* (Paris: Galilée, 2003), 161; translated into English by Pascale-Anne Brault and Michael Naas as *Rogues: Two Essays on Reason* (Stanford: Stanford University Press, 2005), 114.

210

ferentiates his weak theology from the traditional ontological theology by calling it strong theology. He argues that God is not an omnipotent onto-theo-cosmo-logical power source of the universe but the unconditional demand for beneficence that shocks the world with a promise that is not kept, as the heart of a heartless world. In other words, God's transcendence is not onto-theo-logically towering over finite beings, nor is it to be taken politically as a sovereign master who supplies the paradigm for the human mastery over nature. For Caputo, God is the call from below that summons us to rise beyond being, and beyond ourselves.[6] Caputo recognizes the weak force of God in the broken body on the cross and distinguishes the weak force from the sovereign power of the Roman Empire. Caputo identifies the helpless body of Jesus crucified on a Roman cross as the greatest symbol of the weakness of God. He writes,

> The perverse core of Christianity lies in being a weak force. The weak force of God is embodied in the broken body on the cross, which has thereby been broken loose from being and broken out upon the open plane of the powerlessness of God. The power of God is not pagan violence, brute power, or vulgar magic; it is the power of powerlessness, the power of the call, the power of protest that rises up from innocent suffering and calls out against it, the power that says no to unjust suffering, and finally, the power to suffer-with (*sym-pathos*) innocent suffering, which is perhaps the central Christian symbol.[7]

Thus, Caputo's God is not a fully sovereign God but an indeterminate weak force; the power of powerlessness that nonetheless lays an unconditional claim on our planetary living.

Jesus on the cross was utterly abandoned by God: "He saved others; he cannot save himself. He is the King of Israel; let him come down from the cross now, and we will believe in him. He trusts in God; let God deliver him now, if he wants to; for he said, I am God's Son" (Matt 27:42–43). Caputo's God without sovereignty is the suffering God who co-suffers with creation. This weak force is the power of vulnerability rather than the power of sovereignty. The crucified Jesus signals the power of vulnerability, the weakness of God. The power of vulnerability is not merely powerlessness but a different kind of power. Caputo sees the weakness of God as the power of salvation. Therefore, the weak force functions beyond the alternative power.

Caputo's notion of power of the powerless is similar to Foucault's

6. Caputo, *Weakness of God*, 39.
7. Ibid., 43.

bio-power. Bio-power is not one from above but below. Foucault viewed sovereign power as representing itself as negating, legislating, prohibiting, censoring, and homogenous while he recognizes bio-power as always productive, immanent, exercised, capillary, and resisted.[8] Applying Foucault's analysis, power cannot be the possession of the colonizer only because where there is sovereign power there is resistance. Bio-power is the power of survival. Foucault claims that life is more than the struggle for survival but has the power to pursue happiness and satisfaction, which is, indeed, more powerful than sovereignty. As such, Foucauldian bio-power resonates with both Caputo's power of the powerless and the Korean idea of *salim* (enlivening), since *salim* indicates a quality beyond survival and hence is a life-enhancing movement.

Korean American theologian Wonhee Anne Joh writes that the suffering on the cross is not utterly about self-abnegation but also comprised of powerful elements of *jeong*. *Jeong* is a Korean word that means right relationship. The suffering of the cross is not limited to notions of compassion, affection, solidarity, relationality, vulnerability, and forgiveness. Instead, Joh argues that the event of the cross discloses both the horror of abjection (*han*) and the power of love (*jeong*).[9] Joh calls the cross "the powerful love ethic." To her, the cross signifies inclusive relatedness, which must be sustained by living with, in, and through the power of *jeong*.[10] The ethic of the cross, then, is an ethic of vulnerability expressed in and through compassion for the most vulnerable, those that we deem to be subaltern, powerless, and marginalized. This is not limited to humanity. Soil, air, water, trees, and seeds have suffered the most from climate change, which is a result of humanity's destruction of the Earth.

Jesus's ethic is an ethic of vulnerability and compassion. Jesus commands us to care for those who are sick, hungry, or thirsty, the strangers and the prisoners, because "just as you did it to one of the least of these, you did it to me" (Matt 25:40). Although climate change is not mentioned in the Bible, climate change is above all a justice issue in the twenty-first century. Jesus commands us to care for the "least of them," and currently nature is the new ecological subaltern. The apostle Paul writes in Romans 8:22, "We know that the whole creation has been groaning as in the pains of childbirth right up to the present time." Seeds, land, air, water, trees, birds, fishes, rabbits, and human

8. Foucault, *History of Sexuality*, 94–95.
9. Wonhee Anne Joh, *Heart of the Cross: A Postcolonial Christology* (Louisville: Westminster John Knox, 2006), 73.
10. Ibid., 74.

212

beings are all vulnerable to climate change. Human beings have colonized other planetary beings and the planet herself to the extent that life itself is now under threat. Nature has become the subaltern.

Jesus's ethics teaches us to love our neighbor. Who is our neighbor? In the context of climate change, to love God is to love God's creation. Pope Francis's encyclical *Laudato Si'* has made many aware of the connection between faith, spirituality, and environmental concern. The analysis of environmental problems cannot be separated from the "analysis of human, family, work-related and urban contexts, nor from how individuals relate to themselves, which leads in turn to how they relate to others and to the environment."[11] We are interconnected and interdependent with our fellow creatures. We are not entities separated from nature. We human beings live and die with our fellow creatures. Following Keller's notion of *creation ex profundis* (creation out of the deep), Caputo imagines creation as a fluid organism in which "nothing is perfect":

> They are made of *humus*, of *tohu wa-bohu* and *tehom*, so there is an element in them which is not precisely God's image but in which God is trying to fashion his image, a certain irreducible alterity that God wants to cultivate, fertilize, plant, order, and bring around to the divine way of doing things but whose irreducibility and resistance the Lord God is just going to have to learn to live with and hope for the best.[12]

Thus, we human beings live and die with our fellow creatures on this planet. Climate change has brought many ecological changes. Climate change and GMOs are interrelated processes because climate change is projected to have significant impacts on agricultural conditions, food security, and food supply. GMOs have been developed to solve the problem of food supply by using biotechnology. GMO seeds are a product of biotechnology that genetically manipulates microorganisms. Caputo criticizes genetic modifications as a "Methuselah Project":[13] "We are attempting to escape biology altogether, to relieve life of its dependence upon its fragile biological base and, in principle, of its dependence upon the balmy climes of planet Earth."[14] Indeed, technoscience is stepping in where only theology dared to tread. This is an

---

11. Francis, *Laudato Si': On Care for Our Common Home* (Huntington, IN: Our Sunday Visitor, 2015), par. 141.
12. Caputo, *Weakness of God*, 72.
13. Methuselah (Hebrew: מְתוּשֶׁלַח) is the man reported to have lived the longest, 969 years, in the Hebrew Bible. Caputo created this term to explain human's intervention in nature by using biotechnology. For example, the Methuselah Foundation is an organization of professional and nonprofessional volunteers who are dedicated to raising the awareness of the potential for near-term science-based aging interventions using modern technologies.

act of playing God. Caputo asks, "Isn't this exactly what Yahweh feared, which led him to guard the way to the tree of life?"[15] However, before guarding the tree of life with a blazing sword due to humankind's destruction of the covenant, there was a conditional allowance: "See, I have given you every plant yielding seed that is upon the face of all the earth, and every tree with seed in its fruit; you shall have them for food" (Gen 1:29); "You may freely eat of every tree of the garden; but of the tree of the knowledge of good and evil you shall not eat, for in the day that you eat of it you shall die" (Gen 2:16–17). Hence, reminiscent of Marjorie Suchocki's constructive reiteration of the original sin as a "rebellion against creation,"[16] Caputo's critique against GMOs unmasks human audacity, which overpowers and ruins the beauty of life.

The Indian scientist and environmental activist Vandana Shiva writes, "Terminator technology to produce sterile and suicide seed violates the freedom of seeds to reproduce."[17] GMO seeds are suicide seeds that are modified by causing second-generation seeds to be sterile. It is, indeed, self-*sabotaging*. Eliminating fecundity of life means extinction of species. It is a rape of the sacred nature through the use of technology. When seeds become manufactured by biotechnology, seeds are no longer living organisms but products with price tags. We have been stealing life from nature by producing GMOs. GMOs are the human colonization of nature. As Shiva describes, biopiracy is "the ultimate colonization of life itself," within the interior spaces of the bodies of women, plants, and animals.[18] Due to bioaccumulation, entire organisms of this planet suffer from the lethal consequences of GMOs. The freedom of people to grow their own food is threatened. Millions of years of natural evolution and diversity of seeds are being wiped out in a generation. Among the myriad subalterns, seeds are also the subalterns that need to be decolonized.

Seeds have a right to reproduce on their own. Indeed, God sanctions the Earth in Genesis: "Be fruitful and multiply!" The text continues: "Let the earth put forth vegetation; plants yielding seed, and fruit trees of every kind on earth that bear fruit with the seed in it. And it was so. The earth brought forth vegetation: plants yielding seed of every kind, and trees of every kind bearing fruit with the seed in it. And God saw

14. John D. Caputo, *Hoping against Hope: Confessions of a Postmodern Pilgrim* (Minneapolis: Fortress, 2015), 138.

15. Ibid., 139.

16. Marjorie Suchocki, *The Fall to Violence: Original Sin in Relational Theology* (New York: Continuum, 1994), 60.

17. Vandana Shiva, *Manifestos on the Future of Food and Seed* (Cambridge, MA: South End, 2007), 97.

18. Vandana Shiva, *Biopiracy: The Plunder of Nature and Knowledge* (Boston: South End, 2009), 5. See also "Monsanto Indian Farmer Suicide," YouTube video, 4:51, posted by "HuggLinton," June 26, 2007, http://tinyurl.com/qhvmpls.

that it was good" (Gen 1:11–13). God allows humans to eat from every tree with seed in its fruit except the tree of knowledge. Indeed, the forbidden tree and the tree of life are the same tree. Every tree at the same time is a tree of life and a tree of forbidden fruits. Nature, including human nature, is vulnerable when it is exposed to violence (*jugim*). The core message of this event is God's ethic of "do not harm, *Bal Tashchit!*"

> They will not hurt or destroy on all my holy mountain; for the earth will be full of the knowledge of the Lord. (Isa 11:9)

Seeds: Power of Hybridity

In John 12:24, Jesus compares his death on the cross to a seed that falls to the ground and dies. This verse contains the secret of life, which is beyond the conventional meaning of death as the opposite to life. A seed, though containing in itself the source of life, remains alone and not really alive unless it falls to the earth. Its death, then, is life, for it releases the power of life (*salim*) that the husk held captive before, and this power multiplying itself in successive grains would cover the whole field with a harvest of fruits.

Death is not the opposite of life; it is a part of life and always already exists as a necessary aspect of the circle of life. Life reflects the full cycle of birth, growth, death, and transformation into different forms.[19] Through death, the mysterious cycle of life is recurring again and again as infinite repetitions. This is how creation is being fruitful and multiplies. The German philosopher Friedrich Nietzsche recognized life as the eternal return, "This life as you now live it and have lived it you will have to live once again and innumerable times again. . . . The eternal hourglass of existence is turned over again and again."[20] For Nietzsche, a moment is related to eternity in this wheel of life. Thus, life returns back to life as the eternal recurrence in which nothing is useless but everything is a part of the eternity. This paradoxical process of hybridity is the power of life.

Like a seed contains our past and future, the cross is the most hybrid space through which all living beings are entangled via the power of love (*jeong*). The meaning of *jeong* is basically (accumulated) love between the self and the other as time goes by. Thus, Koreans say that "*jeong* has been accumulated." Therefore, Koreans also say that "*jeong* is difficult to detach." Joh writes, "Out of the interconnectedness of heart, *jeong* emerges in a transformation becoming within the intersti-

---

19. Jea Sophia Oh, *A Postcolonial Theology of Life: Planetarity East and West* (Upland, CA: Sopher, 2011), 20.
20. Friedrich Nietzsche, *The Gay Science*, trans. Thomas Common (Mineola, NY: Dover, 2006), 194.

tial space between the self and the other."[21] The cross has commonly been deployed to revictimize the vulnerable. However, the final repetition may unfold otherwise. Keller quotes Bruno Latour's Edinburgh lecture: "All the hatred we have expressed toward one another cannot destroy the profound mutual love and solidarity that flow deeply between us—a love that empowered blacks to open their arms to receive the many whites who were also empowered by the same love to risk their lives in the black struggle for freedom."[22] Keller goes on to say, "Wave folding into particle, breath into body, hand into hand, melody into ear, seed into dirt. Earth into human, violence into trauma, carbon into atmosphere, climate into climatology. Word into world, world into word. Outside in, inside out, the edge turns to layer, to tissue, complication, pleating. . . . But the cut is never clean. It only exposes more folds. All the way down and out. And the vertical axis is itself twisting, bending into spirals diffracted by everything they transverse."[23] In this complex, interconnected planet, everything is related to every other thing.

Life is from death and vice versa. The opposite of life, killing (*jugim*), is not death. Violence is broadly customized in our daily life and systematically pursued. *Jugim* refers not only to the destruction of living organisms but also to all the attitudes that are contrary to the natural process of becoming.[24] Nonetheless, the cross symbolizes *salim* (enlivening) in the midst of *jugim* (violence). The power of life transcends *jugim* in spite of the structures of sufferings. Even though biotechnology has produced ugly monster seeds, we can still hope for the flowers due to this reversal power of nature. Eternal recurrence is a hopeful message for a seed. A seed is an involution of its parent plant. A seed is the transition between life and life, the bridge over death, and the connection of generations. A seed is the collected wisdom of millions of years of evolution. At long intervals, the universe enters into a seed state, a profound state of involution of simplicity, out of which, once again, the infinitely diverse universe springs forth.

Life is interconnected. This entangled planetary body as a whole is the incarnation of Christ that Keller calls "intercarnation." Intercarnation is that we still repeatedly crucify. Keller boldly argues that the becoming of any creature reverberates in a universe readable as God's body.[25] By ruining seeds and the Earth, we crucify God's body.

21. Joh, *Heart of the Cross*, 75.
22. Catherine Keller, *Cloud of the Impossible, Negative Theology and Planetary Entanglement* (New York: Columbia University Press, 2014), 302.
23. Ibid., 169.
24. Oh, *Postcolonial Theology of Life*, 22.
25. Keller, *Cloud of the Impossible*, 308.

Our planet is a macrocosmic body of delicate sense organs and, hence, is sacred nature. Nature's return is the power of hybridity, which is becoming together. Thus, the vulnerable nature cannot be utterly ruined by any destructive powers (*jugim*). If there is original sin, the violence of rebellion against creation, as Suchocki reiterated, must be original salvation that is *salim* (all diverse activities that make this planet alive), restoration, reconciliation, rehabilitation, recycling, reversal, reunion, and resurrection as Jesus rose again from the dead. Life always returns through the dead.

After two days of East Coast Storm Jonas in January 2016, it's hard to imagine with all the deep snow on the ground that spring will ever come again. Nonetheless, I found a dandelion popping up through the snow while walking on a path. And so be it, Amen!

> Every seed contains the potential to save the world. Each seed can keep millions of people from starvation. Each seed is a mirror and guardian of the world's future.[26]

---

26. His All Holiness Bartholomew, *Sacred Seed* (Point Reyes, CA: The Golden Sufi Center, 2014), 9.

12

———

Salvation for All! Cosmic Salvation
for an Age of Climate Injustice:
A Korean Perspective

Meehyun Chung

When Christianity was introduced to Asia, it brought not only the message of the Bible but also certain aspects of Western culture, norms, and images. For instance, one of the most popular paintings of Jesus is the image of Jesus at the age of thirty as a handsome Caucasian man with long blond hair and blue eyes. Although this painting does not reflect the historical Jesus of Palestine, it has greatly impacted Korean Christianity, most notably its Christology.[1] The image of Jesus with

---

1. The Korean Church is proud that their first Christian church was founded by a Korean, who himself received the gospel in China. Long before organized Western missionary activity in Korea, Koreans already experienced both Catholic and Protestant-like gatherings and movements. It is a common misunderstanding, therefore, that Christianity was spread mainly through North American missionaries. American missionaries did bring Koreans the painting of a white Jesus, however, which was widely distributed in Christian homes, schools, hospitals, and churches.

Anglo-Saxon features often serves as a substitute for the first-century Jewish man and also underlies notions about the divine within the conventional beliefs of many Christians. It has become a symbol of Christianity as well as a visual metaphor for Orientalism, permeating the Christian Korean self-understanding at both a conscious and unconscious level.

As described by Edward Said, Orientalism is the expression of the popular ideas that Western people hold about Eastern culture.[2] According to Orientalism, Occidentals are academic, scientific, and rational, while Orientals are emotional, nonacademic, and superstitious. Orientalism dominates how the West views the East, a view that, in turn, is internalized by the East. Within Korean Christianity, the Euro-American Western image of Jesus symbolizes wealth and power. Since Christianity was brought in part by Western missionaries, it was identified with the monetary wealth of Western society. This made it hard to distinguish between the religious content of the Bible and Western culture itself. Western norms became *the* norm for everything in the East. Western norms obtained cultural dominance at the expense of local indigenous wisdom and cultures.

Protestant and Catholic missionary work in Asia began approximately three centuries ago, and from the start has considered traditional knowledge and narrative wisdom as pagan, heretical, and barbarian. The aim was to replace the thought systems and traditional values of the people in the so-called mission field with a Western understanding of the world. This type of binary categorization between East and West continues to dominate, even in today's postcolonial era.

Yet, while Western technology and science have brought rapid development to many aspects of Korean society, they have also brought environmental destruction and pollution.[3] And, because Western science and technology are closely related to Christianity, it is important to carefully look at Christianity's teaching about nonhuman nature, in particular within the context of Christology and soteriology and the way these teachings impact Korean society on account of its missionary past. My intention is not to reestablish Occidentalism, nor do I intend to return to a pre-Christian past. Instead I seek to propose a postcolonial Christian soteriology that builds on Christianity's lost nature spirituality in a constructive way and within the context of contemporary Korean Christianity, culture, and society.[4]

With this purpose in mind, my chapter seeks to find answers to the

---

2. Edward W. Said, *Orientalism* (New York: Vintage, 1979), 1–4.
3. One example is the production of silver mercury. While it allows for an easier production of silver compared to other traditional methods, it also causes the very serious problem of land pollution.

following questions: In what way has Christian mission contributed to gender oppression and ecological destruction in Korea? Has Christianity's role been only negative while traditional religions, such as Buddhism and Donghak, have been eco-friendly?[5] Ultimately, however, this chapter asks how we may rethink Christology and salvation in an era of anthropogenic climate change. At its heart, salvation means restoring the broken relationship between God, humanity, and nature. Salvation is about the comprehensive healing of all of creation's relationship with God. In an era of rising sea levels, desertification, and increased social tensions due to scarcity of resources, this implies a shift in perspective from a human-centered to an Earth-centered soteriology by way of a cosmic Christology.

Christian Missions and Women's Liberation

When it comes to Korean Christianity, the role and position of women need to be understood in the context of its missionary history.[6] This is not a popular point of view. Due to the colonial past, mission is either actively rejected or simply ignored by Korean Christians. However, in order to understand Korean Christianity—and to practice an indigenous ecofeminist theology—reflection on its missionary past is paramount. For one thing, it is important to understand the collaboration between imperial colonialism and mission, specifically because from the start, the church's missionary zeal has gone hand in hand with colonial power. Within this context, the hierarchical relationships between ethnicity, nation, gender, and nature were not only strongly interconnected but also often reinforced, even where transformed.

Traditional mission work quite often involved and exemplified gender discrimination and segregation. While "inner" mission activities—diaconal works and nursing—were considered mainly female responsibilities during the nineteenth and twentieth centuries, "outer" missional work and *oikumene* were considered male responsibilities. Everything related to what was classified as "inner" was considered passive, female, and mundane, in stark contrast to everything related to "outer," which was considered active, male, and prestigious. In fact, and in accordance with established Christian tradition, missions were seen as tasks for men. It was considered self-evident that mission was

4. The term *postcolonial view* refers to a non-dualistic way and method. It means recognizing different values without being judgmental according to a one-dimensional spectrum.
5. Hyun-shik Jun, "Tonghak Ecofeminist Reinterpretation of Sin, Evil and Spirituality in Relation to the Ecological Crisis" (PhD diss., Northwestern University, 2001).
6. This part is based on the following article: Mee-hyun Chung, "Mission Possible! Toward a New Perception of Mission," *Madang* 13 (2010): 52–58.

a male responsibility, while necessary and related "minor" labors were women's responsibilities.[7] Inspector Joseph Friedrich Josenhans of the Basel Mission even stated that "women are but an impediment to mission."[8]

Although women were either seen as a hindrance to men's calling to missionary work or were thought to be fit for support roles only, they often did assume great responsibility and performed demanding jobs, such as running schools for girls or overseeing orphanages. Starting in the late nineteenth century and the early twentieth century, single Western women were sent out into the so-called mission fields with distinct autonomous responsibilities. These women no longer only travelled as wedded companions ("mission brides"),[9] and they attained positions they would not have achieved in Western society at that time. Traditional missionary work, however, supported obedient and diligent women rather than a feminist movement. Karl Hartenstein (1894–1952), director of the Basel Mission, emphasized this aspect, "In any case, female mission work may not be connected with the emancipation movement of the woman. The independence and development of the gifts of the woman must be established in the welfare and social work, but not in the woman movement, which has an anti-religious root."[10]

The introduction of Christianity into Korea did lead, at least in part, to forms of emancipation or liberation for women from types of bondage in traditional Korean society, such as cultural roles influenced by Confucianism. However, Christianity was unable to be a truly liberating force due to its own patriarchal teachings and ideas, which, when combined with local patriarchal culture, at times only reinforced gender hierarchy.[11] While male missionaries did on occasion promote the emancipation of women, they still brought male-dominant ideas in their biblical and theological teachings. After the end of colonial power, gender often became a tool of control in the former mission fields and colonial countries. For example, because white men felt that Western society had already achieved gender equality while people of color were yet to develop this in their own context, Euro-American

---

7. See Christine Keim, "Mission und Menschenbild-eine weibliche Perspektive," *Zeitschrift für Mission* 1–2 (2006): 51–53.

8. Waltraud Ch. Haas, *Erlitten und Erstritten. Der Befreiungsweg von Frauen in der Basler Mission 1816–1966* (Basel: Basileia, 1994), 31.

9. See Dagmar Konrad, *Missionsbräute. Pietistinnen des 19. Jahrhunderts in der Basler Mission* (Münster: Waxmann, 2001).

10. Christine Keim, *Frauenmission und Frauenemanzipation: eine Diskussion in der Basler Mission im Kontext der frühen ökumenischen Bewegung 1901–1928* (Münster: Lit, 2005), 97.

11. Patriarchy does not merely mean biological male dominance but includes, more generally, the ideology of rule and attitudes of dominance.

males (and females) continued to exercise paternalism toward people of color, which did very little for the liberation of Asian women.[12]

Another important issue is that of race and class, which played out between female missionaries, including wives of missionaries, and indigenous women. While some Western women working within the mission field gained independent agency still denied to women in their own countries, this was not the case for women of color. The ethnocentricity of Western Christian missions created an environment where white missionary women, as representatives of a superior Christian culture, were symbols of emancipation, while indigenous women of color, along with their respective cultures, were devalued and demeaned. Moreover, because emancipation through mission was often most effective within the middle class or the elite, the pressing problems of the common people were neglected. Thus, the small elitist groups of native women actively supported by women missionaries were usually incapable of practicing solidarity with the yet more marginalized.

The discussion of gender in missions should therefore not be limited to a discussion of gender equality; a broader, more formative discussion is required, correlating gender to all aspects of social, economic, cultural, and political life. Conceptual categories such as ethnicity, class, sexual orientation, physical ability, age, and religion, along with gender, have inclusive as well as exclusive functions, and an effective analysis of any of them can only be undertaken within a thorough and encompassing critique of power structures. The desired approach to gender and feminism is based on context and includes a reflection on color and race, as well as class; it can no longer simply be a white ideology exported from the Global North to the Global South and the East. To strengthen such an awareness means to promote self-esteem, critical thinking, and self-determination.

Salvation from an Ecological Point of View

Before Christianity was introduced in the Global South, most traditional cultures and indigenous religions were connected with pantheism. Within these religions, there was a simultaneous respect for and a fear of nature. Prior to the Christian missions in Korea, pantheism was popularized through Asian religions like Shamanism, Taoism, and Buddhism.[13] Yet, in spite of the embrace of the sacredness of nature, there

---

12. In terms of financial support from the Global North, gender is one of most important indicators of project management.
13. Traditional Asian religions (e.g., Buddhism and Taoism) are more eco-friendly compared to West-

was a certain fear of nature as well. The latter was often reinforced by the experience of seemingly incurable diseases and natural disasters. Prior to the introduction of Western medicine around the end of the nineteenth century, many people suffered from malaria and other epidemic diseases. Oriental medicine and traditional methods of healing—both of which relied more extensively on nature—were not effective when it came to curing these diseases. Medical missionaries, on the other hand, successfully applied Western medicine to treat these previously incurable epidemics and tropical diseases. Modern Western technology like electricity was also introduced. Western ways of thinking became gradually dominant in ordinary daily life. As a result, people's attitude toward nature changed. Western science, technology, and medicine took away the fear of nature. Unfortunately, it also fundamentally altered the attitude of veneration and respect for nature that had been part of indigenous Korean spirituality.

The latter was exacerbated by the fact that Western missionaries failed to understand Asian spiritual cosmology. They had difficulties with the spiritual approach of indigenous religions to the natural world and, hence, missed their deep spiritual relationship with nature. They did not reflect on it theologically because in their eyes it looked demonic, pagan, or superstitious.[14] Lynn White points to the role of Christian missionaries in the destruction of nature within indigenous cultures, which was carried out as a kind of exorcism: "For nearly two millennia, Christian missionaries have been chopping down sacred groves, which are idolatrous because they assume spirit in nature."[15] This kind of attitude has also been transplanted to Korea and remains an important cultural force even after the missionaries have long departed. Whole indigenous cultures were viewed with Orientalist eyes—that is, as inferior and ripe for conversion to the "proper" Western way of life, belief, and practice. For instance, herbal medicine, which is an eco-friendly traditional healing method, was ignored while Western medicine spread as standard practice. As a result, the healing power of nature has been forgotten and neglected, and traditional customs and practices have been displaced.

Because missionaries were cautious not to create confusion between (indigenous) spirits and the Holy Spirit, they avoided talking about God's sustaining presence in nature as Spirit. Instead Christian mis-

ern religious thought and practice. For instance, Lao Su's "Taodokyung" is full of life-centered images especially focused on water and life.
14. See Allan Anderson, *Moya: The Holy Spirit in an African Context* (Pretoria: University of South Africa Press, 1991).
15. Lynn White, "The Historical Roots of Our Ecological Crisis," *Science* 155 (March 1967): 1204.

sionaries exclusively preached God's work in Christ and, hence, made salvation their focal concern. And because Korean Christianity has been much affected by the North American fundamentalism of the nineteenth century,[16] it has preached a human centered, otherworldly salvation. The latter has caused several problems when it comes to understanding salvation. First, it has led to a one-dimensional understanding of salvation favoring individual salvation over social salvation and, hence, a soteriology that disregards issues of social and economic justice. Second, its emphasis on eternal life in the afterworld has come at the expense of preaching the salvation of this world. And, finally, its anthropocentrism has led to neglect of God's sustaining and salvific presence in and to the rest of creation.

Yet, while most mainstream Korean soteriology is problematic, I believe that because it is the core message of Korean Christianity, a Korean ecotheology should begin with soteriology. Such a soteriology would need to overcome the above-mentioned shortsighted, one-dimensional approach and retrieve a view of nature as sacred. Instead of fear of nature, Korean theology should work out of and engender a respect for nature. To this end, Korean theology needs to move beyond the binary ideology of Orientalism and Occidentalism and find a constructive third way for our postcolonial period. For this reason, this essay argues that instead of returning to the pantheism of a precolonial, pre-missionary past, we should embrace a sacramental understanding of nature that is panentheistic. Within such a panentheistic understanding of God and world, salvation may be visualized as inclusive of all that is. Indeed, I will argue in favor of a notion of salvation not as liberation from this world but as healing of the binaries of this world: the binaries between human beings and nonhuman nature, men and women, poor and rich, East and West.[17]

It is important at this point to acknowledge the contribution of

16. North American Christian fundamentalism was a response to European liberalism in the nineteenth century. American missionaries who were sent to Korea in this time period were very much influenced by the ideology of fundamentalism.
17. Generally speaking, Christian liturgy, including communion, is focused on human-centric salvation. The center point is the blood of Jesus and, hence, can be called a "red" salvation. This focus often comes at the exclusion or neglect of creation-centered ideas. A red salvation tends to be individualistic and oriented toward the afterworld. It is anthropocentric in that it views the natural world as a stage or background for human salvation only. Ultimately, only human beings are going to heaven. Red salvation, then, has nothing much to do with the other-than-human world: it promotes soteriological exclusivism and otherworldliness, which in turn reinscribes social segregation and discrimination, and the devaluation of nature. However, through communion, people not only participate in the body and blood of Jesus and affirm belonging to the Christian community, they also experience the beauty and value of nature. In our time of ecological crisis, it is important, therefore, to restore the sensitivity to the *cosmic* dimension of Christology, which allows for a proper relationship with nature.

Korean *Minjung* theology to rethinking salvation. *Minjung* theology can be seen as the Korean form of liberation theology. It employs a biblical and theological hermeneutics from the point of view of the poor and marginalized. Salvation is, thus, intrinsically related to socioeconomic structures in this world. And, whereas *Minjung* theology initially was mainly concerned with economic justice, lately it has also included reflection on gender and ecology.[18]

Attention to ecology in Korean theology can be traced back to the beginning of the 1990s when awareness of the ecological crisis erupted at the same time that democratic reform movements in Korea also emerged. Within the context of the economic crises of the 70s and under dictatorship, there was no space to think about wider environmental issues.[19] Economic exploitation was the major problem of the time. Eventually, however, feminist groups, as well as parachurches and civil rights movements, began highlighting the relationship of the oppression of women and nature. As a result, awareness of ecojustice has gradually increased, in spite of the fact that we are still a long way behind on this issue at the macro and micro levels.

Rediscovering the Inclusive Meaning of Salvation for Abundant Life

In order to address the interconnected oppression of both women and nature, we need to restore the "I-thou" relationship at every level. In the words of North American ecofeminist theologian Sallie McFague, we should be looking at nonhuman nature and human others with "a loving eye" instead of having "an arrogant eye."[20] Both gender and ecological justice "cannot be separated from salvation, and salvation cannot come without a new humility that respects the needs of all life forms on earth."[21]

As mentioned above, the perception of salvation in Korean theology

18. There have been many attempts to use *Minjung* theology to reflect on social movements and even the arts. These reflections have not yet been published much in academic, peer-reviewed journals. Female *Minjung* theologians, especially, are using *Minjung* theology to reflect on the contemporary social and ecological situation, such as the plight of migrant workers or the ongoing militarization of the Korean peninsula. The artist Yongnim Kim is an example of a visual artist expressing the *Minjung* movement by way of her drawings. See "110429," YouTube video, 6:41, posted by Peter Choi, May 9, 2011, http://tinyurl.com/l73q5ju.

19. During the first Republic of Korea, which was founded in 1948, Korea was ruled by an authoritarian, anti-communist regime, which was overturned by the democratic movements of the 1960s only to be replaced by a militaristic dictatorship. The latter came to an end with the introduction of a civil government in 1987. It took until 1993, however, before Korea got a democratically elected president.

20. See Sallie McFague, *Super, Natural Christians: How We Should Love Nature* (Minneapolis: Fortress, 1997), 32–36.

changed under the influence of liberation theology. Interestingly, the latter came to Korean churches through the Commission on World Mission and Evangelism (CWME). The International Missionary Conference, which was held in 1952, introduced the concept of *"Missio Dei,"* which related salvation to social concerns. The world mission conference of the CWME of 1973 followed suit and emphasized the significance of "social salvation." This was reinforced in 2013 when, at the tenth General Assembly of the World Council of Churches, cosmic salvation was the focal emphasis. At this assembly, which was held in Korea, the CWME document "Together towards Life: Mission and Evangelism in Changing Landscapes" was approved. This important document reflects several key changes to the understanding of salvation. In what follows, I will highlight these changes in three points.

Balance between Individual Salvation and Social Salvation

The first important change introduced by these developments is the creation of balance between individual and social salvation. To correct a one-dimensional perception of salvation, it is important to reconceptualize and reprioritize the relationship between the individual and society. "God did not send the Son for the salvation of humanity alone or give us a partial salvation. Rather the gospel is the good news for every part of creation and every aspect of our life and society. It is therefore vital to recognize God's mission in a cosmic sense and to affirm all life, the whole *oikoumene*, as being interconnected in God's web of life."[22] With these words, the document attempts to correct the exclusivistic mind-set of the past and to recall and highlight God's salvific relation to all of creation. Salvation, as well, is not just social but holistic. Inclusive salvation refers to the restoration of the whole person—body, soul, and mind. God's mission is not only defined as deliverance of the soul. "We do not believe that the earth is to be discarded and only souls saved; both the earth and our bodies have to be transformed through the Spirit's grace."[23] Salvation refers to the integrated healing of both mind and body that has always been part of the perception of reality within Korean traditional medicine. It is comprehensive, not dualistic. Salvation through Jesus is related to healing in diverse situations (Matt 9:22; Mark 10:52; Luke 17:19). Jesus's ministry aims at the restoration of both individual healing and collective heal-

21. Jooseop Keum, ed., *Together towards Life: Mission and Evangelism in Changing Landscapes* (Geneva: World Council of Churches, 2013), 11.
22. Ibid., 5.
23. Ibid., 10.

ing. The Christ event of cross and resurrection is aimed at the restoration of the universe as a whole for abundant life (John 10:10). It is a healing process in a dualistic world.

God expects the holistic restoration of the *oikos*, which includes all creatures. Salvation means healing to restore the entire wounded world. Hence, the event of cross and resurrection brings about a healing process of the binary opposition between word and flesh, holy and secular, heaven and Earth, God's being and human being, Word and flesh. Salvation understood as healing is the restoration of relationship at the level of the body, the individual, society, and the cosmos. The object of salvation, furthermore, should be enlarged to include the whole creature; as the document explains, "Humanity cannot be saved alone while the rest of the created world perishes. Eco-justice cannot be separated from salvation, and salvation cannot come without a new humility that respects the needs of all life on earth."[24]

God's salvific purpose for the world started with the act of creation itself; thus, from the beginning, its scope is significantly wider than individuals or even just human creatures and societies. God's mission continues to preserve and sustain the life of *all* creatures. The love of the triune God is directed not only to human beings but also to the whole of the created world. Jesus Christ did not become flesh to bring partial salvation but came to Earth to offer full salvation. In other words, salvation through Jesus Christ embraces all of creation, including human beings and nature. It reaches not only the sentient being but also the insentient being.

> God's mission begins with the act of creation. Creation's life and God's life are entwined. The mission of God's Spirit encompasses us all in an ever-giving act of grace. We are therefore called to move beyond a narrowly human-centered approach and embrace forms of mission which express our reconciled relationship with all created life. We hear the cry of the earth as we listen to the cries of the poor, and we know that from its beginning the earth has cried out to God over humanity's injustice (Gen 4:10).[25]

Salvation can never be separated from the broader context of creation.

However, salvation of the world as restoration and healing is an enormous process and a project that demands hard scrutiny and attention to painful truths and realities. Healing of this kind intrinsically involves healing the wounds inflicted by the oppression of and vio-

24. Ibid., 11.
25. Ibid., 9.

lence against women and nature; to do such requires us to make the structures of oppression visible. This can only be done when we identify with the poor and marginalized. Indeed, what is needed is a mission in reverse, from the margin to the center. For only when we start from the margin can we both truly "see" our structural brokenness and "know" of God's healing spirit at work in the world.

Mission from the margins counteracts injustices in life, church, and mission. It seeks to be an alternative mission movement against the perception that mission can only be done by the powerful to the powerless, by the rich to the poor, or by the privileged to the marginalized. The latter perceptions contribute to oppression and marginalization. Mission from the margins recognizes that being in the center means having access to systems that lead to one's rights, freedom, and individuality being affirmed and respected; living on the margins means exclusion from justice and dignity. Living on the margins, however, can provide its own lessons. People on the margins have agency and can often see what, from the center, is out of view.[26]

Balance between the Afterworld and This World

We need to participate actively in our earthly life. It is not just the afterlife that is important, but also this life on Earth. Heaven without Earth is empty, and Earth without heaven is blind. If we have a foundation of ultimate hope in heaven, we cannot look away from our life and ignore the urgent issues of our world. The tension between the afterlife—what we are promised and what we hope for—and this world is always present and can be productive insofar as it helps us see more clearly the injustices and pain of our present situation. Yet, when we focus only on the afterlife, we forget our transformative responsibilities toward this world. Vice versa, when we focus only on this world, we forget the world's ultimate salvation, which may lead to despair. For this reason, it is important to maintain a balance between the afterworld and this world. We live in the hope of the fulfillment of God's reign, which already exists among us on this Earth but has not yet been completed.

The life of this world is valuable because Jesus reordered the world of death toward life—a particular kind of life that is centered in sharing and renunciation of greed that threatens to consume our neighbors and fellow creatures. "We affirm that the economy of God is based on values of love and justice for all and that transformative mission resists

26. Ibid., 15.

idolatry in the free-market economy. . . . Mission, then, is to denounce the economy of greed and to participate in and practice the divine economy of love, sharing, and justice."[27]

It is important to recover both the dialectical tension and balance between this world and the afterworld. Salvation shouldn't be limited only to heaven, this will neglect a much needed focus on the healing of this earth.[28] "Mission spirituality motivates us to serve God's economy of life, not mammon, to share life at God's table rather than satisfy individual greed, to pursue change toward a better world while challenging the self-interest of the powerful who desire to maintain the status quo."[29]

Eco-centered salvation is related to the event of liberation because it breaks the chain of oppression in spiritual and physical form. It also symbolizes liberation from oppressive bondages of all types in this world. It is dramatically envisioned in the biblical pictures of the Sabbath, sabbatical year, and Jubilee for justice (Exodus 20; Deuteronomy 5; Leviticus 25). All of these have images contain economic, political, social, individual, and ecological dimensions to notions of liberation, salvation, and freedom. Ecofeminist notions of salvation especially invest the exodus, as well, with gratitude and joy—as the event of permanent release from bondage in slavery; the exodus, like the Sabbath and Jubilee, expresses the multidimensional reality of salvation. The notion of salvation thus can be adapted to promote the breaking of the chains of human rule over other creatures, including nature. It reminds us of the goodness of creation and of the covenant between God and creation. To speak using the famous phrase of Karl Barth, "Creation is the external basis of the covenant. The covenant is the internal basis of creation."[30]

God's ultimate goal is to preserve and restore God's creation. "Mission that begins with creation invites us to celebrate life in all its dimensions as God's gift."[31] Those who are liberated and healed are called to take responsibility for the oppressed other, including nonhuman others. The covenant of love between God and human beings orients us toward the whole of creation; liberation through Christ calls us to restore and heal the broken relationship between humans and nature, and men and women. Those who believe in the salvation of the

---

27. Ibid., 39.
28. Jan Milic Lochman, "Die soziale Bedeutung der Eschatologie," in *Dogmatik im Dialog 1. Die Kirche und die Letzten Dinge*, ed. Fritz Buri, Jan Milic Lochman, and Heinrich Ott (Gütersloh: Gütersloher Verlagshaus, 1973), 140.
29. Keum, *Together towards Life*, 13.
30. Ibid., 38.
31. Ibid.

whole of creation not only should not be involved with the oppression of other creatures, it is their gospel duty to advocate for the liberation of all oppressed creatures as true equals.

Ecofeminist salvation does not mean a simple redistribution of power, however. Rather, ecofeminism seeks to redefine the very perception of power. It replaces power over others with an understanding of power as the *empowerment* of others. Moreover, the resurrected Jesus shows a new perception of power as the power of weakness that overcomes death. The power of resurrection is the power of the executed peasant over imperial power—the divine rejection and overthrowing of empire through the raising of the criminal body tortured by imperial authority. The cross and resurrection, therefore, encourage us to stand up against violent death due to abuse of power, which centrally includes the destruction of marginalized bodies and ecosystems.

Transformation from Human-Centered Salvation to Life-Centered Salvation

The focal subject of *Missio Dei* as articulated by the conference bodies—and as an operative influence on our reflections here—is the God who is Creator, Savior, and Sustainer. This God, in contradistinction to the God of hierarchies and anthropocentrism, is the God who actively makes God's life available to all creation and whose presence in history and creation is at the center of our acts of witness, resistance, and advocacy on behalf of others. Our activity, then, is a participation in God's liberative activity and history in creation. And it is to this that we give voice in witnessing to and working for others, but especially the poor, the oppressed, the marginalized, and nonhuman fellow creatures. As *Together towards Life* states: "Witness (*martyria*) takes concrete form in evangelism—the communication of the whole gospel to the whole of humanity in the whole world. Its goal is the salvation of the world and the glory of the triune God. Evangelism is mission activity which makes explicit and unambiguous the centrality of the incarnation, suffering, and resurrection of Jesus Christ without setting limits to the saving grace of God."[32] Along with an extended and revised interpretation of salvation, the perception of mission itself thus has also shifted and now includes the whole of creation. "God's love does not proclaim a human salvation separate from the renewal of the whole creation. We are called to participate in God's mission beyond our human-centered goals. God's mission is to all life and we have to both

32. Ibid., 29.

acknowledge it and serve it in new ways of mission. We pray for repentance and forgiveness, but we also call for action now. Mission has creation at its heart."[33]

Our witness to and advocacy on behalf of the renewal of the whole creation, however, takes places within the immediate context of human destruction of nature in every manner. Against this horizon, the Christian faith must actively reveal the structures that reinforce and contribute to the oppression of nature, and must reassert the formative theological patterns that restore a proper mutual relationship of human beings to nature in which humans have to learn from nature instead of dominating over it. "We need a new conversion (*metanoia*) in our mission which invites a new humility in regard to the mission of God's Spirit. . . . In many ways creation is in mission to humanity; for instance, the natural world has a power that can heal the human heart and body."[34] At this point, the work of the Holy Spirit is crucial. It is part of our mission to detect God's Spirit at work in the world and understand God's methods of liberation and, even more, God's self-revelation in God's creation. Mission happens through the mutual activity of human beings and God's Spirit. "The mission of the church is to prepare the banquet and to invite all people to the feast of life. . . . It is a sign of the liberation and reconciliation of the whole creation which is the goal of mission."[35]

Life-centered salvation is related to opening our horizon toward the whole of life. Here, the theology of Karl Barth is especially helpful in illuminating the universal horizon of God's revelatory and liberative work, which ultimately turns on God's freedom in self-giving to creation. The crucial point for Barth is, according to Ben Myers, that God's grace is free grace: it is nothing other than God himself acting in freedom. And if God acts in freedom, then we can neither deny nor affirm the possibility of universal salvation.[36] Anthropocentric views of salvation actually impose categorical segregation between human beings and other creatures; life-centered salvation, on the other hand, attempts to overcome this kind of limitation: God creates and sustains our universe, and human beings are not the rulers of this universe but a part of this universe. And as God is not only creator of the universe—hence, the author and architect of *all* salvation—but also a God who goes out to his creation himself in self-donation, our ethical

33. Ibid., 38.
34. Ibid., 10.
35. Ibid., 37.
36. Ben Myers, "Why I Am Not a Universalist," *Faith and Theology* (blog), June 23, 2006, http://tinyurl.com/jwrmcjc; Karl Barth, *The Doctrine of Reconciliation*, Church Dogmatics IV/3, trans. G. T. Thomson (Edinburgh: T&T Clark, 1983), 477–78.

response, grounded in this recast vision of divinely oriented liberative and life-giving salvation, then is unlimited in scope and boundary.

This vision, as well, ought to change completely our understanding of the theological relationship of human beings to nature itself. It is inappropriate, for example, to categorize human beings' role vis-à-vis the rest of creation in terms of stewardship (Gen 1:28). For the fact of the matter is that nature does not need us. Because we can only maintain our lives at the expense of nature, nature is better off without us. Indeed, while nature will flourish without humans, human beings cannot live without nature. Not only do we depend on nature for our sustenance, but nature also has healing power over the human heart and body. Yet, we cannot restore ourselves when we have a distorted relationship with nature. Correcting this requires a perception of nature as an independent yet equal subject, which ought to engender respect and love for nature.

It is further necessary to restore the biblical perspective of the cosmic Christ. The incarnate Christ is an expression of God's love (Col 1:13–20). Jesus Christ is himself the incarnate love of God. *In Christ, the transcendent triune God becomes immanent—closer to us than we are to ourselves.* In Jesus's humanity, God and world are distinguished but not separated. Moreover, in the hypostatic relationship of Jesus's humanity and divinity, the created is brought into ineluctable relation with the uncreated; through that unbroken union, we are made ineluctably to participate in God and God's love. From the Eastern tradition, we see, even more, that the incarnate, broken, and resurrected body of Christ transfigures God's relationship to the entire creation. The resurrection of Christ is the event of the breaking of the sway of death, destruction, and exploitation over all creation, and the restoration of the broken relationship among God, human beings, and nature. God's love in Christ overcomes the forces that work against the web of life and heals the wounds afflicted by dualism and separation. The cosmic Christ thus restores the "original blessing" of the interrelated web of life and expands the target of salvation to all of creation.

The cosmic Christ and a cosmic soteriology, hence, pursue not only a "red salvation," which is related to the individual soul by way of the blood of Jesus Christ, but also a "green salvation," which is related to the social and ecological dimension of life.

Suggestions for an Ecofeminist Understanding of Salvation in the Korean Peninsula as Closing Remarks

Due to the seriousness of our current ecological crisis, we can no longer escape the many ways our lives are embedded in the universal web of life. With regard to global challenges, it is urgent to enact dramatic changes and engender a conversion (*metanoia*) on the well-being of Earth's ecosystems. Therefore, the perception of salvation and mission should also be changed to elicit a new, mutual, and symmetrical attitude toward human and nonhuman others. We need to attune ourselves to God's Spirit in nature and to practice a different type of power. Indeed, we need to find a new humility regarding the mission of God's Spirit. Humans can participate in communion with all of creation in celebrating the work of the Creator Spirit, who is also the Spirit of redemption.

"Evangelism leads to repentance, faith, and baptism. Hearing the truth in the face of sin and evil demands a response—positive or negative (John 4:28–29; see also Mark 10:22). It provokes conversion, involving a change of attitudes, priorities, and goals. It results in salvation of the lost, healing of the sick, and the liberation of the oppressed and the whole creation."[37] Due to gratitude for salvation, which is given to us as a gift of grace through the crucifixion and resurrection of Jesus Christ, we are invited to seek a theological paradigm shift in the face of the ecological crisis of the contemporary world.

A Korean ecofeminist theology has much in common with Western ecofeminist understandings. However, it also has special concerns and issues, mainly due to the division of the Korean peninsula and the ever-present threat of militaristic danger. Korean ecofeminist attempts should start, therefore, with a promotion of *metanoia*. We are all implicated in the promotion of hostility and resentment between South and North Korea. There has been ideological blindness on both sides. No one is innocent in this sense.

Because ecofeminist theology seeks to overcome dualism and binary distinctions, it can be a catalyst in Korean Christianity for reconciliation. To transform hatefulness is the most important matter. Our broken relationships with others, including nonhuman others, is caused by one-dimensional domination, uncritical authority, impossibility of communication, and greed for power domination. An ecofeminist soteriology for the Korean peninsula should be understood in a multi-relational and intersectional way. It means ecofeminist reflection should

---

37. Keum, *Together towards Life*, 30.

234

seek to correct dominance, oppression, exclusivism, and injustice. It thus is related to advocacy not only for marginalized people but also for nature. It should overcome both Western mechanical dualism and Korean opposition between enemy and friend due to the long division of Korea, which has so very much affected people's minds and attitudes. Within this context, it is necessary to underline that the final word of judgment belongs not to humanity but to God. It is God's free gift of love and forgiveness that calls us to exercise more tolerance toward each other and to seek for commonality instead of distinction.

Transforming the understanding of salvation opens up the possibility of a life-centered spirituality that allows us to overcome systemic evil not only in Korea but also globally. When salvation is understood in a more inclusive way—that is, inclusive of the individual, the social, and the ecological dimensions of life—and as being radically non-androcentric and this-worldly, it orientates us toward life. Such a spiritual orientation will break the oppression of marginalized people and nature. Separation between God and human beings, men and women, and humans and nature will be changed. Dualism, like faith and action, soul and flesh, should be tackled.

In summary, an ecofeminist soteriology is characterized first of all by a creation-centered inclusive idea of salvation beyond human-centered and androcentric ideas. It further promotes a liberation-oriented salvation that leads us beyond fear and domination toward embracing the human and nonhuman other in a relationship of both love and respect. Third, ecofeminism promotes a comprehensive, healing-oriented salvation. These characteristics of salvation could be adjusted to the Korean context and society where dualistic binary and hostility dominate everywhere. Soteriology from an ecofeminist perspective could further contribute to the eradication of predominant anthropocentric and androcentric tendencies in Christian theology and promote an understanding of Christian mission and action toward economic, ecological, and gender justice. Breaking the bondage of all fear is possible through the power of this gospel until we meet God, who will release us from fear, face to face.

Spirit

13

Ecowomanist Wisdom: Encountering Earth and Spirit

Melanie L. Harris

Spiritual ecology is a discourse that focuses on the spiritual foundation and study of the ecological movement. Framed by themes such as spirit, the sacredness of earth and interconnectedness, this term suggests a different approach to interdisciplinary conversations engaging religion, gender, and ecology. It argues that religious studies makes a significant contribution to conversations about climate change, earth justice, and ecology because it recognizes that the earth is sacred by its very nature. That is, while it is often viewed as a discipline of intense self-reflection and critique, deconstruction, and confession, religious studies enters interdisciplinary dialogue with environmental studies from a more constructive and affirming approach. This approach is reflective of womanist methodology that honors both deconstructive and constructive sides of analysis.

At its core, womanist ethics focuses on uncovering the voices of women of color and especially women of African descent who experience, survive, and even thrive in spite of multilayered oppressions. Womanist ethics can also be defined as an approach to social religious ethics that centers the religious, theological, and theo-ethical reflections of women of color and their strategies of resistance to racial, gender, sexual, economic, and environmental injustice. Instead of rendering black and African women's voices and perspectives invisible, womanist religious thought honors these perspectives as valid sources for theological and ethical inquiry. Womanist epistemology, then, includes a variety of sources of literary, oral, and aural her-stories, as well as songs, poetry, hymns, and wisdom sayings that emerge from black women's culture. Womanist analysis reflects a commitment to uncovering these women's theological, ethical, and religious reflections by focusing on multiple elements of a woman's complex subjectivity.[1]

Emerging from traditional race-class-gender analysis, womanist ethical analysis more deeply examines theological and religious constructions that negate the "wholeness" or full existence of black women who deal with the realities of social injustice and multilayered oppressions. In an attempt to undo the complicated ways that the intersecting oppressions, including, racism, classism, sexism, heterosexism, and ecological injustice can function in the lives of women of African descent, womanist analysis is deconstructive and multilayered. It uses race, class, gender, heterosexist, economic, and ecological analysis to deconstruct hierarchal systems of power and patriarchy. It carefully examines normative ethical codes based on the logic of domination and white supremacy. This kind of womanist analysis helps to debunk untrue myths and false theories regarding the lives, theories, and experiences of women of African descent.[2] Womanist analysis is also constructive in that it seeks to glean wisdom, values, and ethical mores from the stories, lives, writings, and theo-ethical reflections of women of African descent in order to inform new epistemologies. This work helps develop strategies of resistance and survival for the whole of humanity and all of creation.

The development of womanist epistemology, then, incorporates the stories, sermons, writings, and grandmother sayings familiar to women

---

1. The reference to Southern culture in the womanist definition coined by Alice Walker is important in that it signals the importance of community and wholeness characteristic of the all-black community in which Walker was raised and the deeply important ties of kinship and relationship to nature and Earth, as well as the crucial bonds between black people who were all confronting, surviving, and thriving in spite of multiple forms of racial, cultural, and social oppression. Walker's reference to the Southern culture and the meaning of womanist is explained more deeply in Alice Walker, *Anything We Love Can Be Saved: A Writer's Activism* (New York: Random House, 1997), 79–82.
2. Emilie M. Townes, *Womanist Ethics and the Cultural Production of Evil* (New York: Palgrave McMillian, 2006).

of African descent. In addition, womanist epistemology includes and critiques western theories of justice, and theo-ethical responses espoused by Augustine, Calvin, and the methodologies of Reinhold Niebuhr and Martin Luther King Jr. To be sure, womanist approaches are varied but generally incorporate deconstructive and constructive approaches. These approaches also emphasize the importance of both theory and praxis. However diverse the methods and approaches, womanist ethics validates the experience of women of color and women of African descent as important sources for theological ethics and religious studies.

Ecowomanism

From a womanist perspective, spiritual ecology acknowledges African, Native American, and indigenous cosmological perspectives that consider the earth as sacred and nature as a reflection of the divine.[3] The words of poet and activist Alice Walker accurately describe this perspective when she writes that she believes in, "Earth as God—representing everything—and Nature as its spirit."[4] More commonly known as ecowomanism, a womanist spiritual ecological perspective can be described as an approach to environmental ethics that centers the perspectives, theo-ethical analysis, and life experiences of woman of color and specifically women of African descent. These voices contribute new attitudes, theories, and ideas about how to face ecological crises. The approach applies womanist intersectional analysis to issues of environmental concern in order to engage the complex ways racism, classism, sexism, and heterosexism operate in situations of environmental injustice, including numerous cases of environmental racism. In addition to investigating cases wherein landfills and other potentially hazardous facilities are deliberately placed in racially identified and lower-income neighborhoods, ecowomanism embodies a religious perspective that highlights the sacred ties women of color have with the earth and how this relationship informs moral action.

As such, ecowomanism addresses religious and theoretical links between women and the earth, and the shared identity that women and the earth have as creators (that is, women as creators of human

3. It is important to note that there is a spectrum of theistic, pantheist, and panentheistic perspectives that coexist in ecowomanism. This will be discussed later in the essay, but for the sake of clarity, *panentheistic* understands that God is a part of the universe and also transcends it. *Pantheist* understands God is everything and everything is God. A traditional theistic view understands God to be creator of Earth and nature. Again, the spectrum of these beliefs (and more) is acknowledged in ecowomanism.
4. Walker, *Anything We Love*, 9.

beings, home spaces, social movements, books, and life, and Earth as creator of all life). This analysis leads to careful scrutiny of western theories that feminize the earth and Christian Platonist dualisms that bifurcate the earth and the heavens, thus negating the sacred power associated with the earth. It also explores the similar ways women of color across the globe have been oppressed by societal, dualistic, and patriarchal norms in comparison to how the earth has been devalued.

More specifically, ecowomanism helps to uncover patterns and parallels between acts of violence against the earth and systemic patterns of violence faced by women of color. From a religious perspective, this reveals the need for a fresh sense of theological justice, examination of inter-relationality, and a rearticulation of the idea of womanist wholeness that forms a base for an ecowomanist ethic.[5] Some of the ethical principles embedded in this ethic regarding human-to-human and human-to-earth relationships include "genuine love, responsibility, understanding, honesty, trust, compassion and forgiveness."[6] Other earth-affirming values included in this ethic are equality, economic-justice, earth-justice, and sustainable community.

Logic of Domination

Highly critical of ecological perspectives that have been adopted by historic environmental organizations but hold little connection to an environmental justice paradigm, an ecowomanist perspective highlights the significance of race-class-gender analysis in environmental justice work. It also examines how the logic of domination is woven into colonial ecological frames. Both terms are described here. The logic of domination is a concept based on Platonist value dualisms that attribute an opposing value relationship between two entities. It is described by ecofeminist Karen J. Warren in her book *Ecofeminist Philosophy* as being connected to mechanistic views of nature that were developed by natural philosophers of the seventeenth century.[7] These

---

5. See Alice Walker, "Beyond the Peacock: The Reconstruction of Flannery O'Connor," in *In Search of Our Mothers' Gardens: Womanist Prose* (New York: Harcourt Brace Jovanovich, 1983), 42–59. See also interpretations of the theme of wholeness written by womanist scholars including Melanie L. Harris, *Gifts of Virtue, Alice Walker, and Womanist Ethics* (New York: Palgrave Macmillan, 2010).

6. This list is compiled by Karla Simcikova's analysis of Alice Walker's ecowomanist identity and summarizes Walker's promotion of "coexistence on the planet, based on the recognition of our connectedness to one another through our common humanity." In addition to the values cited, Simcikova includes unity in diversity, equality, reciprocity, harmony, and peace in the world as other significant values gleaned from Walker's work. See Karla Simcikova, *To Live Fully, Here and Now: The Healing Vision in the Works of Alice Walker* (Lanham, MD: Lexington, 2007), 5.

7. Karen J. Warren, *Ecofeminist Philosophy: A Western Perspective on What It Is and Why It Matters* (Lanham, MD: Rowman & Littlefield, 2000).

philosophers were greatly influenced by the western mathematical tradition that has served as a base for dualistic thinking, hierarchal patterns,[8] value-hierarchal thinking, and conceptions of power that negatively view nonhuman parts of creation.

According to anthropological studies concerning the environment, the logic of domination presents an oppositional relationship between humanity and nature and provides a value dualistic framework placing humanity over nature.[9] Evidence of how this concept shaped theology can be found in the writings of the Calvinist reformation, wherein the perspective of the "fallen world" was readily accepted over and above sacramental views of nature.[10] Ecowomanism presupposes a holistic perspective of all creation and adopt the "idea of cyclical processes, of the interconnectedness of all things, and the assumption that nature is active and alive."[11] Far from the disjointed view of nature, this perspective emphasizes the relationality between parts of nature. Thus,

> no element of an interlocking cycle can be removed without collapse of the cycle. The parts themselves thus take their meaning from the whole. Each particular part is defined by and dependent on the total context. . . . Ecology necessarily must consider the complexities and the totality. It cannot isolate the parts into simplified systems that can be studied in a laboratory, because such isolation distorts the whole.[12]

Whereas theories of mathematical formalism influenced this view of nature that "divided [it] into parts and [argued] that the parts can be rearranged to create other species of being," spiritual ecological perspectives such as ecowomanism are based on the web-of-life concept and interconnectedness.

African Cosmology and Interconnectedness

The meaning of interconnectedness is described well in the first principle of the 1991 National People of Color Environmental Leadership Summit.[13] It states, "Environmental Justice affirms the sacredness of

8. Carolyn Merchant, "Epilogue," in *Readings in Ecology and Feminist Theology*, ed. Mary Heather MacKinnon and Moni McIntyre (Kansas City: Sheed & Ward, 1995), 82–86.
9. Ibid.
10. Rosemary Radford Ruether, "Ecofeminism: Symbolic and Social Connections of the Oppression of Women and the Domination of Nature," in *Ecofeminism and the Sacred*, ed. Carol J. Adams (New York: Continuum, 1993). The scientific revolution in the sixteenth and seventeenth centuries in England also supported the dualistic perspective in science that alienated the human realms from the natural realm.
11. See Merchant, "Epilogue," 82–86.
12. Ibid., 84.

Mother Earth, ecological unity and the interdependence of all species, and the right to be free from ecological destruction."[14] This concept of the web of life and interconnectedness is also reflected in many African religious cosmologies and as such serves as an important base for ecowomanist thought. While it is imperative to be mindful of how ecological colonial assumptions, such as the equation of Africanness to nature must be examined, African cosmology generally presents a holistic perspective. That is, it regards the realms of nature, humanity, divinity, and spirit as interconnected. Black religious ethicist Peter J. Paris describes the relationality expressed in the cosmology by naming each of the realms "ontologically united and hence interdependent."[15] Paris argues that African cosmology embodies a common moral discourse or ethical world view about relationality shared among African diasporic peoples across the globe. This ethical world view helps to shape black religious ethical perspectives on environmental care and earth-justice. Thus, any black religious perspective that adheres to an African cosmological perspective and engages the environment necessitates reflection on the interrelatedness between the realms of earth, humanity, divinity, and spirits.

The work of African theologian John S. Mbiti also offers clear insights on how the interrelatedness of the realms in African cosmology functions. In his book *Introduction to African Religions*, Mbiti writes that many African societies view the Earth as a "living being."[16] While is it unwise to make colonial assumptions that categorize all African rituals into western religious categories it can be said that in many African societies, natural elements are considered to embody the spirit of a divine entity or spirit(s). Therefore, by honoring nature, one is also honoring the essence of a spirit or divinity. Like, Paris, Mbiti also writes about the important moral aspect of an African cosmological perspective. According to him, an African cosmology embodies a belief in a natural and moral order that exists in the universe to maintain harmony. It undergirds a moral order and obligation for black peoples to take care of the earth, as well as themselves. This moral order is established by the universe and functions to guide human interaction and ultimate respect of the earth.

Black religious perspectives that adhere to a belief in the interconnectedness of the realms in African cosmology present this ethical

13. D. E. Taylor, "The Rise of the Environmental Justice Paradigm," *American Behavioral Scientist* 43, no. 4 (2000): 508–80.
14. Ibid., 566–67.
15. Peter J. Paris, *The Spirituality of African Peoples: In Search for a Common Moral Discourse* (Minneapolis: Fortress, 1995).
16. John S. Mbiti, *Introduction to African Religion* (London: Heinemann Publishers Limited, 1991), 43.

imperative for harmony between all realms in the universe as a sacred aspect of everyday ethical life.

Ecowomanist Modes of Resistance

Building upon Emilie M. Townes's concept of *countermemory* as a mode of resistance, I also argue that the web-of-life concept and interconnectedness in many African religious cosmologies serve as a mode of resistance to systems of domination inherent in empire.

The web-of-life concept embedded in many African religious cosmologies offers a counter perspective to the logic of domination and Platonist dualistic views depicting the earth and nature as separate and apart from the human realm. The web of life serves as a countermemory and mode of resistance that allows us to reshape an ethical imperative and sense of care of the earth. Townes clearly explicates the concept of countermemory in her book *Womanist Ethics and the Cultural Production of Evil*,[17] arguing that it can be used as a tool of resistance to reshape, alter, and reconstruct the meta-narrative of history in order to honor the voices of those left out of history. She writes that countermemory is not the "rejection, but rather the reconstitution of history. . . . Countermemory is the patient and persistent work of mining the motherlode of African American religious life. It is a methodological strategy that helps combat the hollow legacy of this kind of gross iconization of Black identity. Countermemory helps to disrupt ignorance and invisibility."[18]

There are at least two ways in which an ecowomanist perspective uncovers two modes of resistance to the logic of domination and negates colonial ecological frameworks. The first is noting the earth as sacred and the importance of constructing methods that uncover the sacred and powerful connections between women and the earth. Often deemed heretical, pagan, and sacrilegious, the powerful connections that can be observed between human life-givers (mothers/creators) and creation as Mother Earth are treated as primary resources for ecowomanist spiritualities. Theo-ethical reflection that uncovers these kinds of connections that honor the earth as an intimate part of God in creation, as well as articulate a womanist commitment to justice can be found in the work of Ecowomanist theologian Karen Baker-Fletcher.

In several of her writings the ethical imperative for earth-care is

17. See Townes, *Womanist Ethics*.
18. Ibid., 46.

made evident in her discussions on the distinctions between pantheistic and panentheistic perspectives. In her essay "A Womanist Journey,"[19] she lifts up the work of Alice Walker's *The Color Purple* and
provides theological analysis of the conversation between two primary
characters in the novel, Celie and Shug.[20] Using this theological conversation about the nature of God shared between two African American
women as a foundation, Baker-Fletcher concludes that the model of
God that can be interpreted from Shug's—and perhaps Walker's—theological imagination is a *panentheistic* model of God. Articulated best
in Sallie McFague's *The Body of God*,[21] this panentheistic perspective
understands that "everything that is is *in* God and God is in all things
and yet God is not identical with the universe, for the universe is
dependent on God in a way that God is not dependent on the universe."[22] Baker Fletcher agrees with this model and explains that
Walker's illustration of God as "Trees. Then air. Then birds. Then other
people,"[23] suggests an intimate relationality between the earth and
humanity consistent with a panentheistic perspective.

A second mode of resistance to the logic of domination that comes
from an ecowomanist perspective is the interconnectedness between
humans and the earth expressed in many African indigenous religious
cosmologies. Uncovering and celebrating the interrelatedness between
humans and the earth is seen not only as radical but also as a part of the
agenda for liberation theologies. As I have written in my earlier work,
the theme of interconnectedness "not only serves as a model of relationality but also strengthens the ethical imperative for earth justice
alive at the core of Black Liberation Theology."[24]

In addition, studies of how African indigenous religious traditions
have survived imperial and colonial rule are helpful in uncovering how
ecowomanism and spiritual ecological discourses resist colonialization
and empire. According to empire scholar Pashington Obeng, resistance
can be witnessed in the role and veneration of the ancestor in many
African and African Indian religious traditions. In his article "Religion
and Empire: Belief and Identity among African Indians of Karnataka
South India," published in 2003, Obeng builds on a paper presented at
the American Academy of Religion investigating the same subject.[25] In

19. Karen Baker-Fletcher, "A Womanist Journey," in *Deeper Shades of Purple: Womanism in Religion and Society*, ed. Stacey M. Floyd-Thomas (New York: New York University Press, 2006), 158–75.
20. Alice Walker, *The Color Purple* (New York: Harcourt Brace Jovanovich, 1982).
21. Sallie McFague, *The Body of God: An Ecological Theology* (Minneapolis: Fortress, 1993).
22. Ibid., 149.
23. Walker, *Anything We Loved*, 8.
24. Melanie L. Harris, "African American Religion and the Environment," in *African American Religious Cultures*, ed. Anthony B. Pinn (Santa Barbara, CA: CLIO-ABC, 2009), 491–98.
25. For published reflections, see Pashington Obeng, "Religion and Empire: Belief and Identity among

the paper, he points out that the power dynamics established in certain imperial contexts reveal how some African Indian religious traditions tried to absorb dimensions of other religions coming into their regions and how the histories of certain marginalized religious groups survived by subversively existing alongside the dominant power. This move of resistance echoes an ecowomanist perspective.

Contrary to modes of over-consumerism and a strange interweaving of capitalist and Christian virtues of abundance, ecowomanism argues for a decentering of theological epistemologies that energize a fossil fuel economy. An ecowomanist approach examines popular value sayings such as "He who dies with the most toys wins," and questions whether the individualistic theoretical premise allows for experiencing earth as community. An ecowomanist approach also asks questions like, who are those with climate privilege, and who are those with climate debt? Does race, class, gender, and heterosexist privilege influence decision making regarding who has access to healthy climate (clean water, clear air, and so on) and who does not?

As with most womanist work, ecowomanism unashamedly acknowledges the Spirit. It builds upon Alice Walker's acknowledgement of the same in her definition of womanist in which she articulates a devotion and honoring of the spiritual reality that embraces and empowers black women's lives. She writes that a womanist "loves the Spirit" and suggests that there is a mystical reality that speaks prophetically into the reality of the times of environmental crisis that we are living in.

Perhaps most important about an ecowomanist acknowledgement of Spirit is that as an approach emerging from third wave womanism, the reference to Spirit honors religious pluralism, the variety of religious faiths, and interfaith dialogue among women of African descent.[26] That is, contrary to a focus on a solely Christian-oriented understanding of the Holy Spirit, Sophia, or even Gaia, ecowomanist responses insist that the Spirit that speaks to women of African descent can take shape in a myriad of ways and through many different religious traditions. This interfaith reality of ecowomanism leans more into a constructive theological approach than a classical one, and at the same time honors the voices, lives, and spiritual paths of women. In this sense, the ecowomanist insistence to incorporate Spirit, across and beyond religious categories, allows ecowomanists of many different traditions to explain what and how the Spirit moves in them and their own traditions.

African Indians of Karnataka, South India," *Journal of the American Academy of Religion* 71, no. 1 (2003): 99–120.

26. See Harris, *Gifts of Virtue*, 130–38.

Conclusion

Ecowomanist analysis of structures of oppression and its commitment to Earth justice places climate justice at the heart of theological inquiry about climate change while also offering important methodological tools for addressing it. Ecowomanism is committed to dismantling systems of oppression and deconstructing the logic of domination. It offers a fresh path toward establishing earth justice and constructing a way of living into peace in and with the earth.

Ecowomanism is deeply committed to justice. As such, it addresses the important link between social justice and environmental justice. As analytical as the approach may be, ecowomanism weaves into its structure, analysis, and conceptual frame an element that sometimes cannot be explained or articulated: the presence of the prophetic Spirit, which gives voice to the speaker, reader, student, and scholar of ecowomanism in a time crying out for climate justice.

14

The Spirit as Moral-Spiritual Power for Earth-Honoring, Justice-Seeking Ways of Shaping Our Life in Common

Cynthia Moe-Lobeda

The Spirit of the Lord is upon me because he has anointed me to . . . set at liberty those who are oppressed. . . .

The movement of the Spirit of God in the hearts of men and women often calls them to act against the spirit of their times or causes them to anticipate a spirit which is yet in the making. . . . They are given wisdom and courage to dare a deed that challenges and to kindle a hope that inspires.

—Howard Thurman, *Footprints of a Dream*

Climate crisis, the crucible of existence for high-consuming people today, renders haunting contradictions. God creates a world and declares it "*tov*." The Hebrew *tov*, commonly translated as "good," actually means more than "good." It implies a goodness that is life furthering, a life-generating capacity. While human creatures are called to serve God's purposes in the world, we do the opposite; through climate change, we are undoing that very *tov*, Earth's life-furthering capacities.

The searing contradictions run yet deeper. God calls the human creature to love neighbor as self (Matt 22:39) and to love as God loves (John 13:34; 15:12). To the contrary, we are causing death and destruction for "climate vulnerable" people the world over.[1] Hundreds of millions will be displaced or killed by climate change.[2]

Wherein lies the moral-spiritual power to reverse this trajectory of horror? Scripture and theology teach that the Holy Spirit empowers human beings to participate in God's healing and liberating engagement with the world. This chapter probes that claim as it relates to the climate catastrophe in which we are so complicit. "We" here refers to the high-consuming portion of Earth's people, including me and many readers of this volume. I begin by noting the depth of contradiction between our calling to serve God's creating, saving purposes and our participation in climate sin.

The moral crisis inherent in climate change is manifold. Consider three layers.[3] First, the people who "suffer most acutely [from climate change] are also those who are least responsible for the crisis to date."[4] To fully acknowledge this is to be tormented by it; others are dying from how we live. Second, "climate privileged" societies and sectors may respond to climate change with policies and practices that protect us to some degree from the ravages of climate change while deserting others—the most "climate vulnerable"—to death or devastation.[5] And finally, measures to reduce carbon emissions designed by privileged sectors may further endanger climate vulnerable sectors. A team of Indian scholars points out that "poor and marginalized communities in the developing countries often suffer more from . . . climate mitigation schemes than from the impacts of actual physical changes in the cli-

---

1. "Climate vulnerable" refers to nations and sectors that are particularly vulnerable to the impacts of climate change. As defined by the IPCC, "vulnerability" refers to "the degree to which a system is susceptible to, or unable to cope with, adverse effects of climate change." IPCC Working Group 2, 2001, *Third Assessment Report, Annex B: Glossary of Terms*.
2. See http://ipcc.ch/; see also "Series: Turn Down the Heat," The World Bank, 2012–14, http://tinyurl.com/ly8vfel. "Loss of land" due to "flooding caused by climate change . . . could lead to as many as 20 million climate refugees from Bangladesh" alone. Melissa McDaniel, Erin Sprout, Diane Boudreau, and Andrew Turgeon, "Climate Refugee," *National Geographic*, June 17, 2011, http://tinyurl.com/khhv5ky.
3. This and the following two paragraphs draw heavily on: C. D. Moe-Lobeda, "Climate Change as Climate Debt: Forging a Just Future," *Journal of the Society of Christian Ethics* 36, no. 1 (Spring/Summer 2016): 27–49.
4. Maxine Burkett, "Climate Reparations," *Melbourne Journal of International Law* 10, no. 2 (2009): 509–42.
5. I use "climate privilege" to indicate nations and sectors most able to adapt to or prevent the negative impacts of climate change.

mate."[6] For example, biofuel plantations may use land that could grow food for hungry people, and large dam projects aimed at reducing fossil-fuel use may displace large numbers of people into urban poverty.

The situation screams white privilege, class privilege, and environmental racism. Caused overwhelmingly by descendants of Europe, climate change is wreaking destruction first and foremost on impoverished people, who also are disproportionately people of color. The island nations and costal peoples of Bangladesh, China, parts of Africa, and elsewhere who will be forced to flee their flooded lands; subsistence farmers whose crops are undermined by climate change; and impoverished people unable to compete in the "free market" economy when food prices are driven up by decreased yields of rice, wheat, and corn due to climate change are not the people largely responsible for greenhouse gas emissions. Nor are they, for the most part, white.

Many voices of the Global South recognize this as climate debt or climate colonialism and situate it as a continuation of the colonialism that enabled the Global North to enrich itself for five centuries at the expense of Africa, Latin America, indigenous North America, and parts of Asia.[7] "Climate violence" seems to me an accurate descriptor. It is wed to economic violence.[8]

Within the United States, too, economically marginalized people—who are also disproportionately people of color—will remain most vulnerable to ongoing suffering from the extreme storms, respiratory illness, food insecurity, and disease brought on by climate change.[9] This is suggesting not that some people are exempt from climate-change impacts but rather that some are vastly more vulnerable than others.[10]

6. Soumya Dutta, Soumitra Ghosh, Shankar Gopalakrishnan, C. R. Bijoy, and Hadida Yasmin, *Climate Change and India: Analysis of Political Economy and Impact* (New Delhi: Daanish, 2013), 12.
7. The National Council of Churches of India declares: "Climate change and global warming are caused by the colonization of the atmospheric commons. The subaltern communities are denied of their right to atmospheric commons and the powerful nations and the powerful within the developing nations continue to extract from the atmospheric common disproportionately. In that process they have emitted and continue to emit greenhouse gases beyond the capacity of the planet to withstand. However the subaltern communities with almost zero footprint are forced to bear the brunt of the consequences of global warming." Rev. Christopher Rajkumari, executive secretary, Commission on Justice, Peace and Creation, National Council of Churches in India, personal conversation with the author, November 20, 2010, Nagpur, India.
8. The economic practices and policies that transfer(red) riches of Africa and Latin America to Europe and North America (and more recently to Asia) result(ed) in exploitation of people and in climate change.
9. A report by J. Andrew Hoerner and Nia Robinson (*A Climate of Change: African Americans, Global Warming, and a Just Climate Policy for the U.S.* [Oakland: Environmental Justice and Climate Change Initiative, 2008], PDF, http://tinyurl.com/mrsoj2l) shows that "global warming amplifies nearly all existing inequalities" (ibid., 1), "African Americans are disproportionately affected by climate change" (ibid., 2), and some approaches to reducing greenhouse gas emissions have disproportionately adverse impacts on African Americans.

This gut-wrenching contradiction—creatures called to love their neighbor and to serve and preserve garden Earth (Gen 2:15) doing the opposite—and its horrific consequences shatters my world.[11] It also feeds hope. Hope poured forth for me when I learned that Jesus's "commandment" to "love neighbor as self" (Matt 22:39) is not in the first place a commandment. It is a promise. The verb form is not the imperative; it is the future indicative. Indeed, Jesus is saying that you *will* indeed love. This is the case also in the parallel gospel texts, in the Pauline literature, and in the Leviticus text (19:18) that Jesus cites. Where on Earth will we find the moral-spiritual power to live into this promise?

Christians have long claimed that the power for serving God by loving their neighbor comes from God through God's Spirit. The language and imagery used for millennia to describe that power is *ruach, pneuma, espiritu,* Holy Spirit, Spirit. The Spirit is the face of God who carries the love of God to us and enables us to love God, self, and others in return. She is the breath of God given to people (and other created things) enabling them to serve God's work toward abundant life for all.

That unclaimed power is the focus of this inquiry: how can today's North American church receive and embody moral/spiritual power through the Holy Spirit to reverse our suicidal dash into climate catastrophe and the climate injustice embedded in it? To pursue this question, we pose three others and explore the first two of them. My hope is that this exploration lays groundwork for the reader and others to grapple with the third question, addressing it in particular contexts. I offer a few hunches for directions that probing the third question might take.

At issue here is the relationship between divine power in the Holy Spirit and human power for doing God's work on Earth. We seek insight

10. As early as 2001, the Third Annual Report of the IPCC alerts that "the impacts of climate change will fall disproportionately upon developing countries and the poor persons within all countries, and thereby exacerbate inequities in health status and access to adequate food, clean water, and other resources." "Question 3," *Climate Change 2001: Synthesis Report,* IPCC, 2001, http://tiny url.com/l7zhvhw.

11. Theologically, the problems of climate sin extend even beyond these betrayals of the call to love one's neighbor. See Cynthia Moe-Lobeda, *Resisting Structural Evil: Love as Ecological-Economic Vocation* (Minneapolis: Fortress, 2013), chapter 3 for discussion of the following: A second aspect of climate sin concerns the ancient faith claim that God dwells within Earth's creatures and elements. If so, then the Earth now being "crucified" in climate change is, in some sense, also the body of Christ. Are those of us most responsible for global warming and the extinction of tens of thousands of species per year crucifying Christ? A third problem concerns revelation. Christian traditions hold that God reveals Godself in creation. God's self-revelation is necessary for the life of faith. Nevertheless, we are endangering the first "book" of revelation. Finally, Christians claim that human beings are created "in the image of God." Yet, if global warming continues unchecked, we may be an endangered species; we are endangering the existence of the creatures crafted "in the image of God."

that will enable us faithfully to accept the power of the Spirit for challenging the world views, power structures, public policies, and life practices that suck us into climate horror. The challenge is particularly vexing given the enormously powerful economic and ideological structures established to maintain a fossil-fuel based global economy that is dedicated to maximizing growth, consumption, profit, and concentration of wealth.[12] Moral-spiritual power to curtail the climate crisis means also moral-spiritual power to confront these power structures and the ideologies that justify them.

Two caveats are in order. First, ambiguity, possibility, absurdity, challenge, and self-deception accompany efforts to understand more fully the power of God's Spirit in human life. Vast diversity—even incompatibility—characterizes attestations to the Spirit from the biblical witness through the centuries to the contemporary world. Thus, paradox pervades the quest: We can claim only provisional understanding rather than absolute knowledge. Yet, we are called to stake our lives on that provisional understanding. Second, what can be found in one short chapter is but a glimpse of what the quest calls us to uncover.

Question One: According to biblical witness, what does the Spirit's morally empowering role look like? What forms does it take? What does the Holy Spirit do in relationship to human moral agency?[13]

We consider the morally empowering role of the Spirit first as suggested in the Hebrew Scriptures and secondly as indicated in the Second Testament.

Hebrew Scriptures[14]

"Spirit," where it refers to the Spirit of Yahweh, translates the Hebrew *ruach*.[15] According to the Hebrew Scriptures, the ancient Hebrews

---

12. Among those structures are the fossil fuel industry, the industrial agriculture industry, and the speculative investment industry.

13. This section draws heavily on and excerpts parts of Moe-Lobeda, *Resisting Structural Evil*, chapter 6.

14. In addition to works cited, this section draws upon Michael Welker, *God the Spirit*, trans. John F. Hoffmeyer (Minneapolis: Fortress, 1994); Mark Wallace, *Fragments of the Spirit* (New York: Continuum, 1996); Jürgen Moltmann, *God in Creation: A New Theology of Creation and the Spirit of God*, trans. Margaret Kohl (San Francisco: Harper & Row, 1985).

15. *Ruach* is used 378 times in the Hebrew Bible (Yves Congar, *I Believe in the Holy Spirit: The Complete Three Volume Work in One Volume* [New York: Crossroad, 1997], 3–4), 264 of which are translated in

experienced a power of the One they called YHWH reaching into their lives and into the entire created world, making things happen according to the will of that One. They called this power *ruach*.

Ruach (like *pneuma*, *espiritu*, and spirit, its most frequent renditions in Greek, Latin, and English, respectively) has multiple denotations and connotations in the biblical texts. Its meanings shift over the centuries of the Old Testament and among different cultures. Those meanings range from a forceful movement of air to the fundamental energy of God.

The word's root significance "probably had to do with the movement of air"[16] or, more specifically, with a "gale,"[17] but over time took on varied meanings. At times, *ruach* is a tempestuous or raging wind coming forth from God or sent by God to move things dramatically, materially, and with life and death consequences (that is, the wind that separated the Red Sea in Exod 14:21 and 15:10). Elsewhere it is a breath, an impersonal supernatural force, or a temporary or roving mood or disposition sent by God to occupy a person and influence their behavior (*tharis*, the "spirit of jealousy" in Num 5:14, and the evil *ruach* from the Lord sent to torment Saul in 1 Sam 16:14).

Ruach may be the breath or animating life-force of all living things usually but not always given and withdrawn by God (Gen 7:22; Ps 104:29–30). The essential vivifying force or energy of a human being is *ruach*. ("Into your hand I commit my *ruach*" in Ps 31:5.) Most significant to us here, *ruach* may refer to the essential energy of God.[18] When giving God's *ruach*, God puts it "within" the individual (Ps 51:10; Ezek 36:24–38), the people (Isa 63:11),[19] or "all flesh."[20]

As a force that vivifies the human, *ruach* is the deepest self, the essential energies of the person, the source of feeling, thinking,

the Septuagint as *pneuma* (Veli-Matti Kärkkäinen, *Pneumatology: The Holy Spirit in Ecumenical, International and Contextual Perspective* [Grand Rapids: Baker Academic, 2002], 25). *Neshamah* also is rendered "spirit" or "breath" in English. However, where the spirit is that of Yahweh, it is *ruach*.

16. Alasdair I. C. Heron, *The Holy Spirit* (Philadelphia: Westminster, 1983), 3–4.

17. Helen Schungel-Straumann, "Ruah (Geist-, Lebenskraft) im Alten Testament," in *Feministische Theologie. Perspektiven zur Orientierung*, ed. Maria Kassel, 2nd ed. (Stuttgart: Kreuz, 1988), 59–73, esp. 61, cited in Moltmann, *God in Creation*, 318n4.

18. The porous nature of boundaries among these is clear in the varied translations of a single text. Genesis 1:2 is translated variously as "a wind from God swept over the waters," the "spirit of God," or "a mighty wind." Psalm 51:12 is translated "uphold me [with thy] free spirit" in *Young's Analytical Concordance* and as "sustain in me a willing spirit" in NRSV. The *ruach* of God, of humans, and as an elemental force is not always clearly distinguishable.

19. In Isaiah, the people attest that God's "*ruach* is poured upon us from on high" (32:15), and God pledges, "I will pour my *ruach* upon your descendants" (44:3).

20. "I will pour out my *Ruach* upon all flesh" declares God according to Joel 2:28. "All flesh" in the Hebrew Bible at times refers to human beings, at others to all flying creatures and creatures of the land including humans, and sometimes times to all living beings. Often the referent is unclear, and scholars debate it.

responding. (The *ruach* of Pharaoh was troubled in Gen 41:8.)[21] In this sense, *ruach* of a human and *ruach* of God are inseparably linked, sometimes in fact indistinguishable to the extent that the text is unclear whether the *ruach* of the person is given by God or is God within the person.

When and where God's *ruach* is withdrawn, the human *ruach* too perishes, and along with it, life. God's *ruach* gives life and is necessary for life to remain. "The *ruach* of God has made me" (Job 33:4). If he should take back his *ruach* to himself, "all flesh would perish together, and man would return to dust" (Job 34:14–15). The *ruach* as force of true life in the human being is utterly dependent upon the life-force of God extended to the human.

But, when poured out on people or put within them, what does God's *ruach* do that might enable people to live according to the ways of God?

In short, according to the Hebrew Scriptures, the Spirit of God is the force of God emanating from God that enables people to act or that acts in people. It is that dimension of God that reaches into the depths of the person or the people and awakens agency—or is agency—for being and doing what is pleasing to God. The *ruach* of God is "used to speak of God present and active in the world and in particular among human beings. . . . The *ruach* of Yahweh . . . is his living impact here and now. . . . The *ruach* of God in the Hebrew Scriptures does not as a rule describe God's inner personality . . . [but rather] God's activity in relationship to the world."[22] This Spirit usually refers to God's presence and activity in specific times and places rather than to God's general ubiquitous presence.[23] Yves Congar summarizes the role of God's Spirit in the Hebrew Scriptures as "first and foremost what causes [humans] to act so that God's plan in history may be fulfilled. It always refers to a life energy."[24] In fact, as Moltmann notes, by the postexilic Israel, "God's historical activity in the world is attributed to the *ruach* of Yahweh.

Second Testament

The Second Testament describes a presence and power of God reaching into Jesus's life, speaking to him, leading or driving him, filling him, and empowering him. The writers of these texts called that power *pneuma* or *pneuma* of God. Where the Spirit comes upon, fills, speaks to, bids, drives, leads, or anoints Jesus, the result is tremendous power for

---

21. The power of life in a more impersonal sense as in lifeblood is more often denoted by *nephesh*.
22. Heron, *Holy Spirit*, 8.
23. An example of an exception is in Psalm 139:7: "Where can I go from your spirit [*ruach*]?"
24. Congar, *Holy Spirit*, 3.

remaining faithful to God in the face of temptation, for proclaiming the reign of God and the Jubilee message, for knowing the truth, and for liberating, healing, and giving sight.

While meeting with the disciples for the last time, as described in John 14–16, Jesus says that God will send the "Advocate, to be with you forever" (14:16). "This is the Spirit of truth" (14:17) who "abides with you" and "in you" (14:17). This Spirit, Jesus declares, "will teach you everything, and remind you of all that I have said to you" (14:26). This parallels the Spirit's role in the lives of the prophets.

After Jesus's ascension, the apostles and people who repented and were baptized received this Holy Spirit (Acts 2:38). Many of them experienced or witnessed a power of God reaching into their own or other people's lives, making things happen according to the ways of God. This power touched both individuals and communities. These earliest believers apparently understood themselves, as individuals and as a body, to be filled with (Rom 8:9) and led by the Holy Spirit and to be empowered by and receive gifts from that Spirit for doing the will of God. God's will, in their estimation, seemed to be that all would hear the "good news" and would fashion ways of life oriented around "all that [Jesus] has commanded," including the commandment to love neighbor as self. This power—like that which reached into Jesus's life—was called *Pneuma* and was understood to be the *pneuma* of Jesus himself, the risen Christ. Latin translations rendered this *pneuma* as *espiritu*, which in turn became "Spirit" for English speakers.

The Spirit according to the Second Testament reveals Christ, sanctifies and justifies, gives life, sets people free from the law of sin and death, leads, prays on behalf of, renders people children of God, bears witness through the human spirit, intercedes within the children of God when they know not how to pray as they ought, enables people to live according to or in the Spirit rather than the flesh (*sarx*), and allots or activates particular fruits or gifts. These gifts include strength, courage to proclaim Jesus as Lord in the face of other gods, prophecy, speaking in tongues, discernment, intercessory prayer, generosity, faith, love, and healing. Many of these gifts are useful for neighbor-love. Indeed, Paul admonishes that these gifts are given "for the common good" (1 Cor 12:7), not for the elevation of the individual.

The Spirit was understood to live within the people. In the words of theologian Veli-Matti Kärkkäinen, the coming of the Spirit is the coming of God's power and presence to "dwell in and among the people."[25] This is variously expressed as "being in Christ," God's love being

---

25. Kärkkäinen, *Pneumatology*, 34.

"poured into our hearts through the Holy Spirit" (Rom 5:5), "Christ dwelling within," and "the Spirit of God dwell[ing] in you" (Rom 8:9).

In heeding the direction of the Spirit and using the gifts of the Spirit, people in the first-century Jesus movement manifest a paradox. They tend to gain and use power for doing whatever the Spirit bids them to do. Yet, they do so with mistakes, misjudgments, and other manifestations of their human fallibility. Clearly, the Spirit does not enable perfection in living according to God's bidding.

In the Second Testament, as in the Hebrew Scriptures, the Holy Spirit is the face of God that leads people to walk according to the ways of life set out by God through the Torah, the Hebrew Prophets, and Jesus of Nazareth. In both Testaments, these ways of life are centered in God's command to love God and to love one's neighbor with a love that extends beyond the boundaries of interpersonal relationships.

At times, heeding the Spirit is dangerous. This bears repeating. At times, heeding the Spirit is dangerous.

Much is *not* clear. The implications of these findings for how contemporary people are to live and respond to the economic and ecological violence inherent in our lives are up for interpretation. It depends, of course, upon how one understands "ways of life set out by God" and what it means to love one's neighbor.

Nevertheless, a few things pertaining to moral agency for the work of neighbor-love in the face of climate violence and economic violence may be said with some surety. The texts of the First and Second Testaments, held together, testify that:

- The power and presence of God—in some way that we cannot comprehend—is immanent, dwelling within human communities, as well as transcendent.

- The Holy Spirit that is "poured into" communities and individuals is the same divine power and presence that animated Jesus (Rom 8:11).

- This Spirit dwelling within communities and individuals brings moral power for neighbor-love.

- That love will be lived out, and will be lived out with many mistakes, shortcomings, and other realities of human fallibility and finitude.

- The presence of this Spirit has a transformative impact.

- Following the Spirit's bidding may bring danger and frequently brings vast changes in relationships, both interpersonal and with society as a whole.

These biblical claims overturn all tacit assumptions that the people of God may sit back and continue to live in ways that destroy the Earth's *tov* (life-furthering goodness) and neighbors whom we are called to love.

Question Two: Given this biblical witness, what hinders or impedes our capacity to receive, trust, and heed the Holy Spirit as moral-spiritual power for countering ways of life that breed climate injustice and for building more just and regenerative alternatives?

First Factor: Killing the Spirit's Abode

Throughout the ages, theologians have claimed the presence of God's Spirit dwelling within the created world. The Holy Spirit, said Irenaeus of Lyons, "is diffused throughout all the earth."[26] Martin Luther insisted that "nothing can be more truly present and within all creatures than God himself with his power."[27] For Catholic theologian Elizabeth Johnson, the "Spirit is the living God at her closest to the world, pervading the whole and each creature to awaken life and mutual kinship."[28] The Spirit, writes ecotheologian Mark Wallace, is the "life-force . . . living within all life-forms."[29] These voices and countless others testify that God as the Spirit is "flowing and pouring into all things."[30]

What then happens when this original and ongoing dwelling place of God's life-creating and life-saving work—Earth's life systems—is being destroyed? What happens when its capacity to regenerate life is being undone? As we continue to destroy the conditions for life on Earth, what happens to the Spirit embodied in that very life? People's capacity to hear, trust, and heed the Spirit may well be compromised by the reality that we are killing the Spirit's abode.

---

26. Irenaeus of Lyons, *Against Heresies* (Whitefish, MT: Kessinger, 2007).
27. Martin Luther, "That These Words of Christ, 'This is My Body,' etc., Still Stand Firm against the Fanatics," in *Luther's Works*, vol. 47, *The Christian in Society*, ed. Franklin Sherman and Helmut T. Lehmann (Minneapolis: Fortress, 1971), 58.
28. Elizabeth A. Johnson, *She Who Is: The Mystery of God in Feminist Theological Discourse* (New York: Crossroad, 1992), 147.
29. Mark Wallace, *Finding God in the Singing River: Christianity, Spirit, Nature* (Minneapolis: Fortress, 2005).
30. Martin Luther, *Luther's Works*, vol. 26, *Lectures on Galatians, 1535, Chapters 1–4* (St. Louis: Concordia, 1963), as cited by Larry Rasmussen, "Luther and a Gospel of Earth," *Union Seminary Quarterly Review* 51, no. 1–2 (1997), 22.

Second Factor: Domestication of the Spirit in Western Theology

Western theology has tended toward weak pneumatology. Often linked with the Latin/Orthodox split that culminated in the eleventh century, a tendency to diminish and tame constructions of the Spirit actually began long before that time. Has this progressive "domestication" of the Spirit throughout the last two millennia deadened the Euro-Western church's capacity to perceive, heed, and receive the power and presence of God's Spirit?

"Domestication" here includes: interiorizing and spiritualizing the Spirit, subordinating the Spirit to the other two persons of the Trinity, privatizing the Spirit, collapsing the Spirit into the church, and minimizing aspects of the Spirit's work that might cause upheaval or challenge power or privilege.

Spiritualization and Interiorization of the Spirit

The church's move into cultures more shaped by Greek thought than Hebrew began to diminish the "principle of action" central to the Spirit in the Hebrew Scripture. As Yves Congar explains,

> Spirit has different connotations when translated from Hebrew into Greek. . . . The Greeks thought in categories of substance, but the Jews were concerned with force, energy and the principle of action. The spirit-breath was for them what acts and causes to act and, in the case of the Breath of God, what animates and causes to act in order to realize God's plan.[31]

Nevertheless, some Greek patristic writers continued to articulate the Spirit's active power seen in Hebrew Scripture.[32] Their writings indicate a Spirit understood to indwell the church, sanctify and animate it, inspire the prophets and apostles, work intimately with the Word in the work of salvation and creation, provide courage and fortitude to the martyrs, and enable humans to choose what is good and consistent with God's ways. Irenaeus of Lyons, leader of an early second-century community persecuted by imperial Rome, developed the most sophisticated pneumatology of the church by his time. He saw the Spirit as a life-giving force, powerfully active in both creation and its restoration

---

31. Congar, *Holy Spirit*, 3.
32. See John Anthony McGuckin, *The Westminster Handbook to Patristic Theology* (Louisville: Westminster John Knox, 2004), 167.

(salvation).[33] This latter role is vitally important for our considerations here.

The Spirit, according to Irenaeus, is a subjective power activating people to "mature" or grow into who we really are in the likeness of God.[34] This includes "renewing [humans] from the old habits into the newness of Christ."[35] The Holy Spirit rested on Jesus in order to "accustom" humanity to communion with God and accustom God to dwelling in humankind. The Spirit teaches and shapes us to love what is good and to choose it over evil; when we err or choose wrong, the Spirit continues to teach and lead us. Thus, it is the Spirit who leads "the just in the path of justice."[36] This all begins in baptism, and this instruction by the Spirit takes place in the church. Irenaeus's focus is not primarily the individual; it is humankind as a whole and the entire cosmos. Not surprisingly, Irenaeus's pneumatology "adopted and adapted Jewish traditions."[37]

Later, through Athanasius and the Great Cappadocians, a rich doctrine of the Spirit as powerfully present and active in the events of life blossomed in Eastern Christianity.

In contrast, groundwork for Western Christianity's pneumatology was laid by Augustine, for whom the Spirit was more exclusively interiorized.[38] For Augustine, the Spirit is *vinculum caritatis* (bond of love between the "Father" and the Son), "the inner love of the Trinity, the inner animating principle of the church, the source of the inner life of the soul."[39] This drive toward interiorization, especially as expressed in his *De Trinitite*,[40] "guided [Augustine's] Western successors for a thousand years or more."[41]

The shift is dramatic and contradicts the Spirit's power in guiding and enabling action in the world, as seen in the biblical witness. This redirection continues to inform common assumptions about spirituality in Western Christianity. Often spirituality is compartmentalized

33. Perhaps in part due to Irenaeus's commitment to refute the tendency of Marcion and others labeled as "gnostic" to separate the God of creation from the God of salvation and their accompanying tendency to reject the Hebrew Scripture as part of the Christian Bible.
34. Irenaeus of Lyons, *Proof of the Apostolic Preaching*, trans. Joseph P. Smith (Westminster, MD: Newman, 1953), proof 5.
35. Irenaeus, *Against Heresies*, 3.17.1.
36. Irenaeus, *Proof*, proof 6.
37. Anthony Briggman, *Irenaeus of Lyons and the Theology of the Holy Spirit* (Oxford: Oxford University Press, 2012), 205.
38. Eastern emphasis—as evident especially in Basil of Caesarea—included this interior role of the Spirit as the love that binds the Trinity into an eternal "dance" of communion, but far less exclusively so. The Spirit's agency in the world is not displaced.
39. Heron, *Holy Spirit*, 88; see also ibid., 90–91.
40. See especially Augustine, *De Trinitate*, 6.7.
41. Heron, *Holy Spirit*, 88.

into the arenas of prayer, contemplation, Bible study, worship, confession, inner self-awareness, and so on, and is not associated with active efforts to render social change, to follow the "path of justice." Spiritual formation groups might pray together and share reflections on the inner life but are less likely to dissect the workings of institutional racism and climate colonialism in order to work toward dismantling them as spiritual practice.[42]

Subordination of the Spirit to the Other Two Persons of the Trinity

The developing Eastern tradition, in contrast to the West, tended toward a more cosmic and all-encompassing sense of the Spirit's power and role. With rare exception, it held that all three "persons" of God are involved in creating, saving, and sustaining the world.[43] Irenaeus writes repeatedly of "two hands of God" as main characters in the great drama of redemption. These two hands are Son and Spirit, or Word and Wisdom.[44] This affirmation of the Spirit's activity in creating and saving is seen in multiple figures, perhaps most poetically in the Great Cappadocians, especially Saint Basil, and later in John of Damascus, who writes:

> We likewise believe in the Holy Ghost, the Lord and Giver of life . . . who is participated in by all creation; who through himself creates and gives substance to all things. . . . Accordingly, all things whatsoever the Son has from the Father, the Spirit also has.[45]

The Orthodox position, in no uncertain terms, affirms the Spirit as equal with the Son, proceeding directly and only from the Father (in distinction from the West's confession of the Spirit as *filioque*—that is, the Spirit proceeds from both Father and Son) in order to create, save, give life, and bring all of creation to participate in the movement of the triune God.[46] This Spirit is "uncreated, complete, almighty, all-working,

---

42. Exceptions are exciting. A "spiritual formation" group at Pacific Lutheran Theological Seminary is called "anti-racism work as spiritual practice."

43. Briggman (*Irenaeus of Lyons*, 205) argues that some theologians of the third and early fourth centuries "no longer identified the Holy Spirit as Wisdom, as one of the Hands of God, or as the Creator," as did their predecessor, Irenaeus. In this, they devalued the Spirit relative to the Word, identifying only the Word as wisdom, as a hand of God, and as having a role in creation. The only Greek theologian among these figures identified by Briggman is Origen. This trend reversed itself in the Greek church (but not in the Latin church) by the later fourth century when the Spirit once was seen in Greek theology as creating and saving along with the other two persons of the Trinity.

44. Son and Spirit "raise man to the life of God." Irenaeus, *Against Heresies*, 5.1. The role of the Spirit in salvation is evident throughout *Against Heresies* and also in his *Proof of the Apostolic Preaching*.

45. John of Damascus, *Exposition of the Orthodox Faith* (Oxford: J. Parker, 1899), 1:viii.

46. Heron, *Holy Spirit*, 85.

all-powerful, infinite in power."[47] She is *"transformer of creation by whose energy the cosmos is transfigured."*[48] Indeed, this Spirit, as expressed by Irenaeus, John of Damascus, and the Great Cappadocians, is not subordinate to, less important than, or less present and active in the material world than is Jesus Christ. What moral-spiritual power for change in how we live is lost when we downplay that person of God who works within human beings to move us into ways of living that cohere with God—a God who is restoring Earth's *tov*, not endangering it with climate change?

Privatization of the Spirit—Peace of Mind

In the biblical texts, the work of the Holy Spirit is rarely a private affair between an individual and God. "Protestant theology and piety," in contrast, have "traditionally privatized the range of the Spirit's activity, focusing on the sanctifying work of the Spirit in the life of the individual believer, and emphasizing the Spirit's gift of personal certitude" and inner peace.[49] The Spirit may become primarily a refuge from turmoil, a salve for pain.

Orthodox sacramental theologian Alexander Schmemann expresses the subtle dangers of this move.

> Lost and confused in the noise, the rush and the frustrations of life, [the human] easily accepts the invitation to enter into the inner sanctuary of his [or her] soul and to discover there another life, to enjoy a "spiritual banquet" amply supplied with spiritual food. This spiritual food will help him [or her] . . . to restore peace of mind . . . to lead a more wholesome and dedicated life, to "keep smiling" in a deep religious way.[50]

Will this private inner peace and "religious smiling" nourish resistance to the economic, political, military, and ideological power structures that undergird climate change, especially where resistance is fraught with complexity, danger, and moral ambiguity?

---

47. Ibid.
48. Ibid., 84 (my italics).
49. Johnson, *She Who Is*, 129. See also Lora M. Gross, "Spirit and Resistance: A Theological Perspective on Lillian Hellman," in *Resistance and Theological Ethics*, ed. Robert H. Stone and Robert L. Stivers (Lanham, MD: Rowman & Littlefield, 2004), 286.
50. Alexander Schmemann, *For the Life of the World: Sacraments and Orthodoxy* (Crestwood, NY: St. Vladimir's Seminary Press, 1973), 12.

Collapsing the Spirit into Ecclesiastical Structure and Ministry

Yves Congar argues that "the Holy Spirit has sometimes been forgotten," or overshadowed, by teachings and liturgical practices that assimilate its functions into those of the church and, in the case of the Roman Catholic Church, the functions of the pope and the Virgin Mary.[51] Congar is not alone in arguing that, to a significant extent, the Spirit has been eclipsed by the church. Elizabeth Johnson notes:

> Post-Tridentine Catholic theology . . . [tended] toward institutionalizing the Spirit, tying the Spirit's activity very tightly to ecclesiastical office and ordained ministry. . . . The cumulative effect of this rather meager Western pneumatological tradition has been that the full range of the reality and activity of God the Spirit has been virtually lost from much of [Western] Christian theological consciousness.[52]

This trajectory has ancient roots. In the second and third centuries, the charismatic Montanist movement made claims to authority, based on the Spirit, that threatened ecclesial authorities, who ultimately condemned the Montanists. Subsequently, official church teaching linked the Holy Spirit to ecclesial authority. Papal pronouncements took on the status of Spirit inspired. Obscured was the Spirit's activity in lay believers' lives, unchastened by mandates of the institutional church.

Minimizing the Spirit's Work That Might Cause Upheaval or Challenge Structures of Power and Privilege

Could it be that ecclesial "fear" of the Spirit's power has limited our capacity to realize that power? Finnish theologian Veli-Matti Kärkkäinen argues:

> The church's ambiguous experience with charismatic and prophetic movements has often led the leadership of the church to try to control the work of the Spirit out of fear of chaos and lack of order. Some theologians wonder, for example, whether the church catholic in its rejection of the second- and third-century charismatic-prophetic movement, Montanism, lost an opportunity to integrate charismatic pneumatological spirituality more fully into its life.[53]

---

51. Congar, *Holy Spirit*, 159–66. Congar offers numerous illustrations.
52. Johnson, *She Who Is*, 130.
53. Kärkkäinen, *Pneumatology*, 18n9.

Centuries later, the reform movements that paved the way for the Reformation saw a dramatic increase in attention to the Spirit as a power not mediated by the church. Those movements and their successors, the Anabaptist wing of the Reformation, were denounced and repressed (first by the pre-Reformation Catholic church and then by the magisterial Reformation) in part for their teachings about and experience of the Spirit unmediated by the church.

Perhaps in our day another threat that the Spirit presents to structures of power and privilege is the insistence by Paul that the gifts of the Spirit are meant to be used for the common good, not for the private good.[54] The mandates and norms of advanced global capitalism promote using one's gifts to serve one's own interests (the private good); one should maximize profit, wealth concentration, and fossil-fuel extraction for profit to the extent allowed by the law, regardless of the costs to the common good—costs such as climate change and exploitation of humans and Earth. The finance-driven economy does not count the social and ecological costs of private good. To "serve first the common good" would call a screeching halt to that norm. If the Spirit bids us to serve the common good, then she is indeed a danger to finance-and-corporate-driven global capitalism.

This is not surprising. The power of the Spirit, as acclaimed in Scripture and the church's first centuries, surpasses all human power structures. It draws people into allegiance to God over all other authorities. It "accustoms" humans to life as God would have it and gives courage for that life, despite the contrary demands of imperial forces.[55] Such power would cast fear into the hearts of entrenched power and privilege.

Domestication of the Spirit: In Sum

The Spirit of Yahweh, revealed in biblical texts, is an undeniably active moral force in the material world. God's *ruach* acts within human beings, shaping their attitudes, behaviors, and corporate life. She acts on/in other living creatures and Earth's elements, propelling them to heed God's will. The bidding of the Spirit has life and death consequences. She confronts powers of deception and domination. Almost never is the Spirit of the Holy One interiorized, privatized, eclipsed by human authority structures, or withdrawn from confronting powers that counter God's will.

---

54. I owe this insight to Ron Moe-Lobeda in conversation.
55. Irenaeus describes the Spirit as "accustoming" humankind to union and communion with God and "accustoming" God to dwelling within humans.

In contrast, as articulated by Wolfhart Pannenberg, in Western theology [the doctrine of the Holy Spirit] seems curiously "watered down" from its biblical fullness.[56] The cumulative effect of movements to domesticate or "water down" the Holy Spirit has been to obscure the socially transformative effects of being recipients and bearers of it. If the Spirit is "first and foremost what causes [humans] to act so that God's plan in history may be fulfilled,"[57] then this loss is a travesty almost beyond comprehension in its magnitude.

The issue here is the impact of this trajectory of domestication on the moral-spiritual agency of contemporary Christian persons and communities as they seek to be faithful in the context of climate catastrophe. How does this domestication keep the Spirit from working within us to save this good creation from climate sin? What is the enormous loss of moral-spiritual power wrought by "watering down" the "person" of the Trinity who enables us to act according to the life-giving, life-saving love of God?

While the loss is overwhelming, equally tremendous are the gifts to be received in reversing that domestication. To those gifts we turn shortly. But first, consider a third factor hindering our capacity to receive and heed the Spirit.

Third Factor: Moral Oblivion

If God's Spirit works through human agency, then factors blocking human agency also block the Spirit. In previous work, I have probed factors blocking human agency for resisting systemic domination, including ways of life that generate climate change.[58] One of those factors is moral oblivion. That is, failure to recognize (1) the magnitude of devastation to Earth's life systems and to vulnerable people wrought by the global economic framework that enables our over-consumption and brings climate catastrophe, and (2) viable alternatives. Human agency for countering climate injustice and the policies, principles, and life practices undergirding it depends upon seeing both the enormity of climate disaster and the reality of more just and sustainable alternatives.

Such moral vision is crucial for both theological and practical reasons. Theologically, freedom from sin begins with confession and

---

56. Wolfhart Pannenberg, *The Apostles Creed in the Light of Today's Questions*, trans. Margaret Kohl (Philadelphia: Westminster, 1972), 130.

57. Congar, *Holy Spirit*, 3.

58. Moe-Lobeda, *Resisting Structural Evil*, chapter 4; and Cynthia D. Moe-Lobeda, *Healing a Broken World: Globalization and God* (Minneapolis: Fortress, 2002), chapters 2 and 3.

repentance; moving away from climate sin requires seeing it so that we may confess and repent. In practical terms, motivation to live differently requires daring to see the actual consequences of how we now live (both the environmental harm and harm to people) and the vibrant alternatives that are in the making all over the world. To illustrate, we will be more likely to challenge the fossil fuel orgy if we recognize, among other things:

- The ubiquitous presence of petroleum in the products and activities of daily life.
- That using the reserves of oil, gas, and coal now slated for extraction will doom Earth's web of life.
- The brutal human costs to the people in many lands where oil is drilled and processed.[59]
- The alternatives.[60]

Inviting the Spirit to work through us toward climate justice may entail a commitment to moral vision that dares to see more clearly both "what is going on" and "what could be." Sophisticated forces work against such vision.[61] Daring to see opens a door to the Spirit's life-giving power. We take this up in question three.

Question Three: What do these findings suggest to Christian communities of the Global North about how we might receive and embody more fully the Spirit of God for the sake of countering climate injustice and building more ecologically sound and socially equitable ways of living?

I do not have answers to this question, and I pose it partly to invite readers' ardent engagement with it. Below are my initial hunches regarding paths of inquiry.

De-domesticating the Spirit may be a crucial calling for the church entangled in climate colonialism. Imagine a faith community dedicating a year to discerning what it means to open itself to God's Spirit hungering to work within and among them toward climate justice. Imagine

---

59. For instance, Ogani people of the Niger Delta; indigenous peoples of Ecuador; First Nations peoples of Alberta, Canada; people of the Mississippi River Chemical Corridor; and countless more.
60. By this, I mean alternatives at all levels of social organization—household, business, institutions of civil society, public policy/governance, and world view/consciousness.
61. For an account of some of those forces, see Moe-Lobeda, *Resisting Structural Evil*, 81–109.

this entails also a commitment to counter moral oblivion with moral vision and to treat the Earth as the abode of God (thus addressing all three factors noted above). This community, let us say, will dare to learn from the ancient Hebrews' engagement with *ruach*, from Jesus and his followers' lives in the *pneuma* of God, and from Irenaeus and others in the earliest church communities.

Decompartmentalized Spirituality

A beginning point would be decompartmentalizing "spirituality" from other dimensions of life, expanding notions of what constitutes "spiritual practices" and "spirituality." To illustrate: Efforts to join in the Spirit's work of liberating and healing from climate injustice would be seen as spiritual exercises. If the Spirit reveals the truth and "will teach you everything," then efforts to understand truth that enables movement toward climate justice would be a practice of spirituality. This would include, for example, learning to see the climate impacts of eating beef, the role that unconscious white supremacy plays in our failure to take seriously the current climate horrors being experienced by many people around the world already, or how to replace fossil fuels with renewables.

Spirit as Equal to the Word and Spirit as Activating Change

I am deeply struck by the weighty moral implications of Western Christianity subordinating the Spirit to Jesus Christ and interiorizing or deactivating the Spirit's role. Many streams of contemporary Christianity take with utmost seriousness the saving work of Christ, accomplished long ago. "Jesus died to save us from our sins" is, for many, the central Christian belief. However, the person of God who is present *now* to work in and on us—the Spirit—is taken less seriously.

What if, taking a clue from Irenaeus, our imagined community decided to reclaim the Spirit and Christ as two hands of God of equal import in human life. And, taking a clue from the ancient Hebrews and from Irenaeus, what if they recognized the Spirit as highly active in all arenas of life, changing them toward choosing the good, leading them in paths of justice, and thereby molding them and humankind into fuller communion with God? What would help the community receive this change of consciousness and life habits accomplished by the Spirit? How would the people reshape worship in order more openly to receive this gracious gift? How would they learn to listen for this Spirit? If the Spirit's work was as vital to us as that of Christ and we accepted the Spirit as transforming our living, how might Christians respond to the climate crisis as a result of the Spirit's bidding in all aspects of life—economic, political, lifestyle, and more? How would we live differently?

Moral Vision

Moral oblivion—failure to see the truth of what is going on and the truth that viable alternatives exist—may be the most virulent ingredient of inertia for climate-privileged people in the face of a climate disaster that is devastating climate-vulnerable people. As we have said, this moral oblivion, by thwarting human agency, is thwarting the Spirit's work in and through that agency.

Vítor Westhelle demonstrates that "truth"—in the New Testament—means "negation of oblivion," or "revealing the concealed."[62] And the Spirit "is the Spirit of truth" (John 14:17) who "will teach you everything" (John 14:26). Westhelle notes two forms of this truth-telling by the Spirit.

- Revealing social realities that had been concealed by lies. For our intents here, this includes revealing what is concealed by positions of climate privilege.

- Revealing or recognizing "Christ where Christ was not seen, especially where Christ was least expected, or where Christ had been hidden by Christian piety." In our situation, this might mean Christ present within Earth's creatures and elements.[63]

Our imagined community might be led by God's "Spirit of truth" to negate moral oblivion by cultivating moral vision as a spiritual practice. I have long taught that moral vision entails seeing three things at once. The first is seeing "what is going on." This includes recognizing the causal links between our lives on the one hand, and Earth's demise and profound human suffering on the other. Doing so is an act of moral courage and can be devastating unless accompanied by a second and a third form of vision.

The second is seeing "what could and should be"—that is, more just

---

62. In *alētheia*, the Greek word for truth in the New Testament, the prefix *a-* denotes a negation of *lēthē*, which means oblivion or concealment. Vítor Westhelle, "Freeing the Captives: Speaking the Truth" (paper delivered at Multicultural Theologians Seminar, sponsored by the ELCA, July 29–August 1, 2008).

63. Christ's presence within the elements of Earth is an ancient faith-claim and has been present throughout two millennia in some Christian traditions.

and ecologically sound ways of living—practices, policies, and world views. The third mode of vision sees that we human creatures are not alone in the quest for more just and sustainable ways of living. The sacred life-giving, life-saving Source of the cosmos—the Spirit—is with and within Earth's elements and creatures, luring creation toward God's intent that all may have life and have it abundantly (John 10:10). This Spirit is enabling life and love ultimately to reign over death and destruction.

Moral power for living toward climate justice may grow from the soil of these three held in one lens. Vision of this sort is subversive because it reveals a future in the making and breeds hope for moving into it. Cultivating this vision may well be allowing "the Spirit of truth" to "negate oblivion" and "teach" us how to live faithfully in these times.

Moral Vision: A Fourth Lens

Recently, my understanding of moral vision has changed to include a fourth lens. It is the lens that always sees the goodness, beauty, and infinite meaning in every moment and every place. This lens recognizes, as Rita Nakashima Brock and Rebecca Ann Parker so convincingly argue, that this Earth is meant as a paradise for its creatures (humans included) to relish wildly with all of our senses. A paradise in which all experience meaning, joy, deep and fulfilling relationships, sensuous pleasure, self-respect, love, and the meeting of basic needs.[64]

I have a hunch that this form of vision, wed to the other three, will entice and empower us to receive and embody the Spirit's life-giving power. This is the power to recognize and resist world views, power arrangements, policies, and practices that perpetuate our current mad orgy of consumption and the corporate-and-finance-driven global economy that requires and enables it. And this is the power to forge more just, sustainable, and life-supporting alternatives. This power is the Spirit of the living God, shaping us to love neighbor as self and to serve and preserve garden Earth.

Sacramental Practice

De-domesticating our understanding of and relationship to the Spirit of God may have profound implications for the practice of Eucharist and baptism. Christians claim that the Spirit enters the people in bap-

---

64. Rita Nakashima Brock and Rebecca Ann Parker, *Saving Paradise: How Christianity Traded Love of This World for Crucifixion and Empire* (Boston: Beacon Press, 2009).

tism and the Eucharist. Is it possible that domesticating the Spirit has to do with how we practice the Eucharist and baptism? Since at least the time of Irenaeus of Lyons, the Eucharist has been known by some as a school for seeing and a fountain of power for faithful living.[65] For many communities in the first two centuries, baptism was understood as entry into a life of Spirit-led allegiance to Jesus, rather than to imperial Rome. That allegiance was costly; for many, it meant risking death by torture. Do our sacramental practices, in contrast, render an interior and private sense of the Spirit, a Spirit who does not lead us to challenge the powers of domination and empire, a safe, non-risky sense of the Spirit?

How will the people of God in the Global North practice the sacraments anew in ways that undo the truncation of the Spirit's power in our lives? Perhaps we would baptize in lakes and rivers that the community has been restoring from ecological disaster, or during demonstrations against the building of mines or coal-export plants on indigenous people's land. Imagine celebrating Eucharist as the centerpiece of anti-racism training while planting trees,[66] or while advocating for renewable energy laws, fair trade, or just wages.

How would we enact Eucharist and baptism if the former is a "school for seeing" and the latter a ritual in which the community declares risky allegiance to Christ over allegiance to whatever lures us away from embodying justice-seeking neighbor-love? Might such rethinking of sacramental practices open doors for "de-domesticating" the Spirit?

Perhaps the confirmation class and adult forum would join forces to research the ecological and social justice impacts of every item used in the sacraments—the wine, bread, water, chalice, plates, cloths, cross, hymnals, and more. Revealed would be the economic systems by which we exploit both Earth and others without knowing it. Most North American congregations would find a huge carbon footprint of producing and transporting items used in the sacraments. From oil field to font, the synthetic fibers in paraments might travel in gas-fueled vehicles from an oil rig in Alaska through processing as fabric in China to *maquiladoras* in Northern Mexico. From wheat to bread, the communion loaf might traverse the continent. Minerals in the cross may have been extracted from indigenous lands in South America in processes that plundered and toxified the land, exploited the people, and released huge quantities of greenhouse gasses. Next, the community might commit itself to approximating sacramental practice that

65. T. J. Gorringe, *The Education of Desire: Towards a Theology of the Senses* (Harrisburg, PA: Trinity Press International, 2002), 104.
66. In the Association of African Earth-Keeping Churches, the Eucharist includes planting trees.

had zero carbon impact, benefitted the workers involved, and did not negatively impact people through extractive industries. In this, the confirmation class might link with the World Council of Churches and its work for indigenous rights. The "Spirit of truth" who "will teach you everything" would be at work, opening unforeseen doors to growth in justice-seeking love.

Communal Embodiment

Western understandings of moral agency are shaped by modernity's elevation of the individual as the primary unit of human being. Where Spirit is seen as a transformative power within human beings, it is articulated largely as an individual phenomenon. Yet, as we have noted, the biblical witness shows the Spirit's work in and on communities. When the Spirit comes at Pentecost, for example, she comes to a body of people. The Spirit is calling into being a reality that the disciples do not yet perceive; they do not know it exists. Nor do we—except in glimpses. It is a communal reality, a body of Christ far bigger than the individual—in the words of the ancients, a union and communion.

Lament likewise is often assumed to be an individual matter. However, the biblical witness speaks also of communal lament. Emilie Townes, in a powerful sermon on Joel, suggests that communal lament opens the door for the Spirit's transformative work. Communal lament, as Townes explains it, is the assembly crying out in distress to the God in whom it trusts. It is a cry of sorrow by the people gathered, a cry of grief and repentance, and a plea for help in the midst of social affliction. Deep and sincere "communal lament . . . names problems, seeks justice, and hopes for God's deliverance." Lament as seen in Joel, she says, drawing upon Walter Brueggemann, forms people; it requires them to give name and words to suffering. "When Israel used lament as rite and worship on a regular basis, it kept the question of justice visible and legitimate."[67]

Perhaps for us too, communal lament is integral to communal embodiment of the Spirit and integral to socioecological restoration. Could it be that worship enabling the community to hear the Spirit and empowering them for social and ecological healing will include profound communal lament—lament for the ways in which our lives endanger Earth's life systems and vulnerable neighbors far and near? Imagine churches offering space for public lament and repentance.

It may well be that "What does it mean for 'me' to live as if the

---

67. Emilie M. Townes, *Breaking the Fine Rain of Death* (New York: Continuum, 1998), 24.

liberating Spirit of God has made her home in 'me'?" is not the right question. We will know more fully the Spirit's living, active, liberating presence as we learn to reclaim it within us collectively and as we reexperience the moral self not first and foremost as an "I" but as a "we." We are, I sense, called to repent of and resist climate colonialism and rebuild more just ways of living in a mode of being that is vastly foreign to contemporary US Christians formed by the individualism of modernity, the privatization of life under neoliberalism, and the privatization of God's Spirit. It is a communal mode of being, being as "we"—a cloud of witnesses spanning ages and continents, seeking more just and sustainable ways of living within Earth's web of life.

In Spirit-imbued communities of resistance and rebuilding, the Spirit may be calling forth the God-given communion that already exists but that we only glimpse dimly. To follow that bidding, we will need to counter the magnetic pull of "the way things are." It is the tendency to put new wine in old wine skins, to think that little tweaks in life are adequate. We are in good company; our faith forebears in ancient Israel and in the Jesus movement too were vulnerable to that seductive lure.

Interfaith, Extrafaith, and Beyond the Human

If we hunger for the Spirit to work within us toward climate justice and abundant life for all, we will live with eyes open for the Spirit at work throughout the Earth community so that we may align ourselves with that liberating healing work. While religious fundamentalism is on the rise, another marker of our day is deep interreligious respect and engagement among many people. If humankind is to meet the unprecedented moral challenge of survival with equity and dignity in the face of climate change, then all of Earth's great wisdom traditions—both religious and scientific—must plumb their depths for resources to share and bring these resources into conversation with each other. The Spirit may be one unifying dynamic within religious traditions.

Communal embodiment extends beyond the boundaries of the church as we know it. De-domesticating our experience of the Spirit will include recognizing and being fed by the Spirit alive and at work in other religious traditions beyond Christianity, Judaism, and Islam, and in people and communities not identifying with religious traditions. Moreover, the Hebrew Bible is clear that God's Spirit is at work also in other-than-human aspects of this good creation—especially in the winds, waters, and mountains.

Closing

A fundamental promise of Christian faith is resurrection; the reign of God's love triumphs over all forces of death and destruction. The horror of climate disaster is not the end of the story. The end of the story is life raised up out of death and devastation, abundant life for the Earth community. The Spirit is God's power at work in the world toward that end. We have noted that, according to the Hebrew Scriptures, "after times of devastation . . . that has befallen as a result of unfaithfulness or departure from life as God would have it, God's Spirit . . . brings life, flourishing, and righteousness [right relationships] out of social chaos, at times delivering people from collective self-destruction or folly." That hope speaks to the heart of our reality. How, we have asked, can today's North American church receive and embody moral/spiritual power through the Holy Spirit to reverse our suicidal dash into climate catastrophe and the climate injustice embedded in it? To pursue this question, we explored three others. May this brief inquiry help us to hear and heed that gracious Spirit so that we may join ever more fully with her life-savoring, healing, and liberating work.

Mary and the Church

15

Virgins: Resources for an Ecotheological Praxis

Theresa A. Yugar

Latin American Marian imagery is a fusion of (at least) three different religious world views.[1] The first is a Spanish Catholic European epistemology that emphasizes God as singular, male, and omnipotent. The second is a Mesoamerican cosmovision where God is plural, male and female, and cosmic.[2] The third world view is the South American ecocentric relationship with Pachamama.

Whereas Mary's intercessory role in Catholic Europe is anthropocentric, solely between humans and the Son of God, in the Americas, Mary's intercessory role broadens to include the Earth and the cosmos. In Cemanahuac and in the Tahuantinsuyo, the European Mary has

---

1. I want to acknowledge my colleagues Juan A. Tavárez and Alan A. Barrera at California State University, Dominguez Hills for collaborating with me on this chapter. Both of them are members of the *Asociación Hispanounidense*.
2. Davíd Carrasco, *Religions of Mesoamerica: Cosmovision and Ceremonial Centers* (San Francisco: HarperSanFrancisco, 1990), 166. Carrasco defines a cosmovision as: "A worldview that integrates the structure of space and the rhythms of time into a unified whole."

absorbed important ecological qualities of indigenous goddesses such as Tonantzin and Pachamama, both of whom were understood in the Mesoamerican-Inca world view as Mother Earth. The thesis is that Marian imagery centered in the Americas reflects elements of an ecological theology. Moreover, humanity can appreciate and adapt Mary's indigenous Latin American qualities as an ecological intercessor with global appeal who can inspire an eco-justice theology for an "ecological conversion," which would bring harmony between all living entities, human and nonhuman.[3]

Marian Devotions in the Old World

The early Christian tradition adopted a formal ecclesiastical appreciation of Mary's role as the Theotokos, Greek for "God-bearer," during the Council of Ephesus dating from the fourth century. Starting in the fifth century, Mary's role expands from Theotokos to Mediatrix, intercessor between humanity and Christ.[4] In the fifteenth century, upon her appearance in Mexico, Mary is dressed as a potent cosmic symbol of universal equilibrium.[5] In our twenty-first century, Mary transitions from Mediatrix to an ecological intercessor between Earth and God. And to acknowledge her new earthly constitution, Pope Francis elevates her to "Queen of All Creation."[6] Therefore, throughout the centuries, one can trace Mary's ever-evolving path from Theotokos, to Mediatrix, to cosmic icon, to Queen of All Creation.

Marian Devotions in Latin America

Before having been given the preeminent title of Queen of All Creation by a Latin American pope, Mary underwent a powerful transformation when she encountered the native female deities of the Americas. In Catholic Europe, Mary is a minor protagonist in the salvation of humanity. She is an incomplete agent who is denied her agency as

3. The ideas for this chapter, including select syncretistic names used for Mary, have their origin in Verónica Cordero, Graciela Pujol, Mary Judith Ress, and Coca Trillini, *Vírgenes y diosas en América Latina: La resignificación de lo sagrado* (Montevideo: Colectivo Con-spirando Chic, 2004). In Latin America, this collective of women seeks new visions in the fields of spirituality, ethics, feminist theology, and ecofeminism. In a personal conversation, Ress, founding member of the collective, asserted that "we are called to reflect on policy, the universe, body, culture and everyday life." This paper is a humble attempt to do precisely that.
4. Margaret R. Miles, *The Word Made Flesh: A History of Christian Thought* (Malden, MA: Blackwell, 2005), 109, 150.
5. Juan A. Tavárez.
6. Pope Francis, *Laudato Si': On Care for Our Common Home* (Vatican City: Libreria Editrice Vaticana, 2015), 146–47.

co–redemptrix with the male triune God. By contrast, Mary in Latin America becomes whole and is a central character with cosmic dimensions.

In 1531, when Mary appeared in Mexico as Our Lady of Guadalupe, she was layered with the cosmic symbolism prevalent among the Nahua people. Her appearance was a response to the cosmic distress that the native population endured by the destructive actions of Spanish invaders who desacralized their sacred Earth, resulting in an Eurocentric eco-racism toward the New World. The conquest/invasion was a religious-cosmic holocaust. The Nahua living deities were systemically murdered and smashed into rubble. Mexican anthropologist and historian Miguel León-Portilla cites the Tlamatini who describe the encounter as "the violent clash of thinking and faith of the Europeans with the spiritual world of the ancient Mexicans."[7] As a result of a postapocalyptic New World, the Mesoamerican natives had a cosmic revelation, which coincided with the Judeo-Christian revelation of the New Testament: "a woman clothed with the sun, with the moon under her feet, and on her head a crown of twelve stars" (Rev 12:1). This apocalyptic woman with cosmic elements thus came to be known as Our Lady of Guadalupe.

Mexico, Tonantzin, and Our Lady of Guadalupe

Our Lady of Guadalupe is a creative force and a focal center of energy in the Latin American struggle for liberation and ecological justice. She energized the independent movement of Mexico and the Mexican Revolution. Today, her creative power manifests in her capacity to regenerate the spirit of millions of individuals. On December 12, millions of her universal children are drawn to her light, to feast on her sunrays that can only be explained as a spiritual photosynthesis.[8] Once nourished by her transformative powers, her children convert their daily struggles into spiritual light. Therefore, her spiritual children become the "light of the world." Drawing on Matthew 5:13–14, one could say that they are not only the light of the Earth but also the Earth's salt. As salt of the Earth, Guadalupe's children are called to protect and safeguard the natural resources of the Earth.[9]

---

7. Miguel León-Portilla, *Aztec Thought and Culture: A Study of the Ancient Nahuatl Mind*, trans. Jack Emory Davis (Norman: University of Oklahoma Press, 1990), 69.
8. Juan A Tavárez.
9. Ibid.

Our Lady of Guadalupe, "Queen of All Creation"

In spite of Pope Francis's use of European theological epistemology, he does seem to understand Mary's role in creation and even crowns her "Queen of All Creation." As Queen of All Creation Mary intercedes on behalf of the Earth and the poor and relates an ecological message of stewardship, which stands in contrast to the misinterpretation of the Genesis account that humans are called to dominate the Earth. Pope Francis states:

> We are not God. The earth was here before us and it has been given to us. This allows us to respond to the charge that Judaeo-Christian thinking, on the basis of the Genesis account which grants man "dominion" over the earth (cf. *Gen* 1:28), has encouraged the unbridled exploitation of nature by painting him as domineering and destructive by nature. This is not a correct interpretation of the Bible as understood by the Church.[10]

Interestingly, the correct interpretation of Genesis 1:28 has always been part of the Mesoamerican world view. Thus, Tonantzin-Guadalupe has a cosmic appeal because she embodies the sacredness of all creation: "She is the Woman, clothed in the sun, with the moon under her feet, and on her head a crown of twelve stars" (Rev 12:1).[11] This indeed can be seen as revelation's reference to Our Lady of Guadalupe.

As Theotokos, Mediatrix, and cosmic icon, Our Lady of Guadalupe thus can be seen as embodying Pope Francis's argument that Mary is the Mother and Queen of All Creation. For he states: "In her glorified body, together with the Risen Christ, part of creation has reached the fullness of its beauty."[12] The beauty of the fullness of Mary is when she became whole in Latin America. Her wholeness is the result of bringing together her identification with Mother Earth, prevalent in the Mesoamerican world view, with her role as the Mother of All Creation, which was always part of the Latin American Catholic world view.

Ecotheology of Tonantzin-Guadalupe

Tonantzin-Guadalupe embodies the spiritual and religious practices of the Cemanahuac nations in the Americas. Like the female deity Tonantzin, Our Lady of Guadalupe too is a cosmic lunar portal whose

---

10. Pope Francis, *Laudato Si'*, 42.
11. Ibid., 146.
12. Ibid., 147.

body is metaphorically the universe or the cosmos at large. Yet, unlike the Judeo-Christian God who reflects a male hierarchy of power based on domination and exploitation, Tonantzin-Guadalupe is a miraculous figure whose model of divine power reflects an organic view of the world that is rooted in an epistemology of relationships in which all life systems are interrelated. The power she embodies is an egalitarian one that holds the Earth in her protective care.

As an earthly portal, Tonantzin-Guadalupe drills deep into the inner core of the Earth. From the Earth's inner core she is energized, and the sunrays behind her can now be understood as a volcanic explosion coming from the Tepeyac hill. Metaphorically speaking, the Tepeyac hill becomes part of the volcanic mountain ranges around Mexico City, such as El Popocatepetl, but El Tepeyac hill is a religious volcanic mountain, and Tonantzin-Guadalupe is its eruption. And her volcanic eruptions have caused social seismic waves that have caused historical earthquakes, such as Mexico's independence movement and the Mexican Revolution. In the twenty-first century, Tonantzin-Guadalupe is about to erupt again to bring an ecological earthquake to replenish the land from five hundred years of ecological exploitation. Most notably, she will dislodge the manipulative and aggressive capitalist promoters of genetically modified crops, who are the ones that threaten Mexico's symbolic and most important national crop: corn. By threatening this sacred crop, multinational corporations with their genetically modified organisms negatively impact the DNA of the Mexican people. One has to be reminded that Latinx are the "Children of the Corn." According to the Mesoamerican cosmovision, the great preconquest gods formed the first Americans from corn dough. Thus, any assault to this sacred crop is a direct attack on the biodiversity of the people of the Americas. Tonantzin-Guadalupe, the Empress of Corn, will inspire her children to rise against GMO corporations across Latin America.

Mary in South America

In the Southern Hemisphere, Tonantzin was equivalent to the Inca female deity Pachamama. Mary's associations with Tonantzin derived from Pachamama, but Pachamama was not personified. Pachamama was solely represented as sacred soil without any true embodiment except for the mountains.[13] In the postconquest Inca cosmovision, Pachamama retained her divine status as the Spanish attempted to merge her with Mary by incorporating some of the aesthetics of

13. Alan A. Barrera.

Pachamama. As a result, in the religious iconography from the Cuzco School, Mary is depicted as a mountain-shaped image, closely resembling the Andean people's abstract image of Pachamama. A well-known example of this new aesthetic is *La Virgen del Cerro de Potosí.*

The Cuzco School of the viceroyalty of Peru produced great artistic imagery of Mary closely resembling Pachamama. As a result, *La Virgen del Cerro de Potosí* became part of the Spanish colonial enterprise. Thus, *La Virgen del Cerro de Potosí* played a pivotal role in the Spanish assertion of their divine right to claim the silver riches of the hill. The Spanish artistic expression of the Andean Mary through an imperialistic lens justified the exploitation of the land. This point proves what Pope Francis laments that Christians have misinterpreted the Holy Scriptures. The challenge in the twenty-first century is to revisit these holy images of the Andean Mary and reinterpret them as ecological symbols of ecological restoration, reflective of Pope Francis's understanding of Mary as Queen of All Creation.

Peru: *La Virgen de la Candelaria de Puno*

Prior to the conquest, the region of Lake Titicaca, which is shared by Peru and Bolivia, was sacred ground. It dates back to the period of the Tiahuanaco civilization, 1,600 years ago.[14] From this sacred lake, the Inca created its symbolic narrative, which is the foundation of its empire. In the Inca pantheon, one of their main goddesses was Pachamama.

Pachamama is a living being. The mountains, the rocks, the oceans, the rivers, the trees, and the flowers are all living manifestations of Pachamama. For the Andean people, Pachamama is sacred for she provides the harvest; the fruits of the earth come from her maternal womb.[15]

In Peru, the Spanish counterbalanced the Andean veneration of Pachamama with *La Virgen de la Candelaria de Puno*. They built her shrine near the shores of Lake Titicaca. *La Virgen de la Candelaria de Puno* appeared to the common populace, who were miners and weavers.[16] When the Spaniards sought to demolish the native homes and appropriate the nearby mines, *La Virgen de la Candelaria de Puno* intervened on behalf of the indigenous people. Inhabitants invoked her for protection. She appeared in an apparition where she was surrounded by flames fighting against the demon, understood as being the Spaniards.

14. Cordero et al., *Vírgenes y diosas en América Latina*, 82.
15. Alan A. Barrera.
16. Cordero et al., *Vírgenes y diosas en América Latina*, 113.

La Virgen de la Candelaria de Puno was both the Miraculous Virgin and Weaver Goddess, who helped the women in the field.[17] She protected both the miners and the richness of the mines that was their livelihood. In the postconquest world, *La Virgen de la Candelaria de Puno* also appeared surrounded by flames to the common people, who she cared for and protected.

Bolivia: *La Virgen de Copacabana*

In Bolivia, the Spanish combined the veneration of Pachamama and Mary through *La Virgen de Copacabana*. This Andean Mary was depicted in Spanish iconography as a representation of Pachamama. Mary's triangular gown symbolized the Andean mountains. Her crown resembled the clouds that lingered above the Andean mountain ranges.[18] *La Virgen de Copacabana* is still associated with Pachamama. The devotion of *La Virgen de Copacabana* has ecological nuances relating to the Andes. The devotees of *La Virgen de Copacabana* make pilgrimages for a good harvest. They also ask her for favors for "their family, work, health, businesses, trips, and problems with sadness."[19] In this way, Mary shares qualities with Pachamama as the people pray to her and give thanks for her blessings. Most importantly, Mary, like Pachamama, is also Mother of the Poor to the native population of the region.[20]

Ecuador: *La Virgen de la Peña*

La Virgen de la Peña was associated with Pachamama and the Virgins of the Sun, a select group of women who historically served the Inca empire in sacrificial rituals and as warriors. In Inca history, the Virgins of the Sun were protagonists and valued for their dual roles as virgins and warriors.[21] Like Mary, The Virgins of the Sun were personified as young, beautiful, and virgin.[22] *La Virgen de la Peña* was also personified with qualities associated with Pachamama because she provided refuge for the native population in the crevices of caves in mountains. Thus, Mary, like Pachamama, was a motherly figure who both embraced her children and protected and consoled the native population. Along with providing refuge for the native population, the Spanish *La Virgen de la*

17. Ibid., 111, 113.
18. Alan A. Barrera.
19. Cordero et al., *Vírgenes y diosas en América Latina*, 95.
20. Ibid., 96.
21. Ibid., 159.
22. Ibid., 158.

Peña was venerated for miracles in situations where it did not seem like hope could exist. In response, altars were made of wood to thank her for such miracles. Moreover, the indigenous celebrated Mary by placing images of her on rocks. The indigenous people believed that if they followed the priest in search of the church that they would find refuge. She provided refuge for her children and people in the caves and mountains. She promised to liberate them from a plague if they searched for the priest of the region and converted to the Catholic religion.[23]

Chile: *La Virgen de la Piedra de Quilacoya*

In Chile, the cosmological world view of the Mapuche people does not include a sacred female deity or any personalized images of the divine. As part of the colonization project, the Spaniards introduced *La Virgen de la Piedra de Quilacoya*, thus refashioning the European Mary into a sacred rock. Her legend was that a young native person encountered a beautiful rock in the form of Mary. Immediately, he went to show his owner the rock. He believed that Mother Nature had given the rock to him and to the community. His owner valued the rock, and thus it was cleaned and a niche was found where it could remain and individuals could offer prayers to Mary. During this time, the land flourished.[24] Time passed and a new owner oversaw the rock, but he treated it as property. He did not believe in the sacredness of the rock, and the Mapuche people were saddened. Simultaneously, the animals of the region were sick and dying. Moreover, the harvests were not producing seeds. Time passed and the owner had a change of heart. He recognized the error of his ways with respect to Mary's rock and vowed to care for it always. Soon after, the people and animals of the region began to flourish again.[25] This legend is part of the Spanish effort to synthesize Mary with the Mapuche's understanding of their ecology.

La Virgen de la Piedra de Quilacoya was decorated with the flora of the Mapuche ecosystem.[26] Mary becomes the sacred rock as Pachamama becomes one with nature. Modern Mapuche religiosity still centers on a cosmic universe where *la naturaleza* (nature) constitutes their experience of the sacred. Subsequently, in a Mapuche world view, Mary is not just associated with flowers, trees, and rocks; Mary *becomes* the sacred

---

23. Cordero et al., *Vírgenes y diosas en América Latina*, 161.
24. Ibid., 235.
25. Ibid.
26. Ibid., 229–30.

rock and the flowers of the Andes, which to them is a living animated being.[27]

Each year on the eighth of December, *La Virgen de la Piedra de Quilacoya* is venerated on the Feast of the Immaculate Conception, when the Catholic Church celebrates the conception of Mary free from the burden of original sin. Therefore, *La Virgen de la Piedra de Quilacoya* represents the purity of Mother Earth. So, whenever humanity contaminates Mother Earth through oil spills, fracking, carbon dioxide, then humanity commits a sin against the Immaculate Conception of Mother Earth, that is, Mary.

Conclusion

In Latin America, Marian imagery and devotion emerged in a sixteenth-century, postconquest world, which was catastrophic not just for its indigenous peoples but also for the eco-region at large. Indeed, the Latin American region experienced nothing less than a holocaust, an intentional genocidal enterprise by the Spaniards motivated by an imperial, capitalistic agenda that resulted in the destruction of highly developed civilizations whose religious sensibilities deeply valued all sentient and insentient entities in the entire cosmos. In the name of the male, triune God of Christianity, life in Latin America was literally and metaphorically at stake as Spaniards sought to undermine the agency of the people in the region through the deliberate displacement of their deities.

In Latin America, Mary was received by the native people as one of many female deities within the Mesoamerican and Andean pantheon of gods and goddesses that were worshipped prior to the sixteenth-century conquest. In the devotion of Mary, therefore, clear points of contact exist between the old and new worlds. Marian imagery in Europe and Latin America includes her role as intercessor and maternal figure who protects and provides for the daily needs of her children. Still, in Europe and the Americas, Mary's intercessory role reflects two different value systems and world views. In Catholic Europe, Mary's primary intercessory role was predominantly anthropocentric between humans and the Son of God. By contrast, in Latin America, Mary's intercessory role is more geocentric as it centered on the Earth. As distinct from Marian icons in Europe, the native goddesses Tonantzin and Pachamama are inextricably interrelated with the entire cosmos. Like Pachamama, Mary is personified as present and alive in sacred

27. Cordero et al., *Vírgenes y diosas en América Latina*, 229–30.

places and entities, including rocks, caves, the moon, and stars. Unlike Mary in the European Church, Tonantzin and Pachamama maintain harmony, equilibrium, and balance between all living entities, human and divine.

Thus, the Catholic Mary of Europe in her many manifestations throughout Latin America brought equilibrium back into the collective lives and cosmic universe of all life entities, peoples and Earth included. In contrast to the Western, European God, who was male and modeled an exploitative sensibility, the many faces of Mary, including Our Lady of Guadalupe, *La Virgen de la Candelaria de Puno, La Virgen de Copacabana, La Virgen de la Peña*, and *La Virgen de la Piedra de Quilacoya*, were born out of Mesoamerican and Andean cosmovisions and created new models of a divine God who was female and just.

In the twenty-first century, the issue for Christians and non-Christians alike on a global level is that, consciously or unconsciously, they are still working with ideological frameworks that reflect that of the Spanish *conquistadores* who colonized Latin America. Thus, the challenge for us today is to change the capitalistic ideological mindset and value systems that were inherent in a sixteenth-century Spanish European epistemology that continues to exploit and oppress individuals, communities, and Earth on a global level.

16

___

Environmental Activism in the Philippines: A Practical Theological Perspective

Joyce Ann Mercer

On a mountaintop near Baguio City in the Philippines, a group of indigenous women successfully oppose the plunder of their ancestral lands by foreign mining companies. They choose a distinctly embodied form of action for their protest: standing in the way of heavy machinery, the women bare their breasts in a move intended to shame the mining company into retreat.[1] The company soon abandons their mining operations and vacates the area. Elsewhere in the Cordillera mountains, however, mining companies profiting from large-scale mineral extraction have left behind waste toxic enough to cause the biological death of several rivers, including the Abra River in Benguet Province, formerly home to some of the most significant plant diversity in the

---

1. I have described this action in greater detail elsewhere. See Joyce Ann Mercer, "A Practical Theological Approach to Ecofeminism: Story of Women, Faith, and Earth Advocacy," in *Body Memories: Goddesses of Nusantara, Rings of Fire, and Narratives of Myth*, ed. Dewi Candraningrum (Jakarta, IDN: Yayasan Jurnal Perempuan, 2014), 93–106.

region. Indigenous peoples such as the Kankanaey and the Ibaloi have been dislocated from their ancestral lands and livelihoods by these mining operations.[2]

Farther south, in the capital city of Manila, a young woman leads a campaign to protect Freedom Island, a fragile wetland habitat for migratory birds where the livelihood of an urban poor community dependent on fishing for their survival is also at risk. In 2013, activists scored a small victory there when the Ramsur Convention on Wetlands listed Freedom Island as a wetland area of international significance. That victory was short-lived, though, as in 2016 the government went back on its earlier declaration to protect this area with plans to build a new international airport on reclaimed land. Activists continue their work to save the bay in spite of harassment and even death threats.

Such situations reveal the shape of ecojustice work in the Philippines today: the two examples of successful interventions are situated within a much larger, ongoing story of struggle, in which threats to the ecological integrity of the Philippines are many and difficult to overcome. This chapter addresses issues of ecological justice in the Philippines from a practical theological perspective, through the lens of women's environmental activism. I write from my location as a Euro-American woman with significant commitments to the Philippines through my previous work in theological education there, and through ongoing relationships and in solidarity with a circle of Filipino church workers and activists courageously working for fullness of life amid struggle. I also write as a Christian feminist practical theologian, committed to a way of "doing theology" that is participatory and locally engaged, focused on lived experience as a place where God may be known, holding the well-being of women (in all our diversity) in the foreground of thinking and acting, and taking small steps toward transformation of situations of suffering, injustice, and oppression.

Why Women?

Why does it matter to look at Filipino ecological concerns through the perspectives of women activists? After decades of ignoring the experiences and voices of women in international conversations about peace building, economic development, environmentalism, and global health issues, the 1990s saw a shift in which women's perspectives at last

2. Cordillera Peoples Alliance, "Case Study on the Impacts of Mining and Dams on the Environment and Indigenous Peoples in Benguet, Cordillera, Philippines" (report, International Expert Group Meeting on Indigenous People and Protection of the Environment, Khabarovsk, Russian Federation, August 27–29, 2007), Word doc., http://tinyurl.com/kce8r2s.

became audible as gender became a legitimated category of analysis in these discourses. It matters to see the environmental issues of the Philippines through the stories of women activists, first because these women live and work in close connection to the everyday impact of ecological destruction and to the hopes for change, and therefore may have important insights and knowledge only available through their relationship to the issues.

Second, some researchers suggest that women's positions in many societies, particularly those in the so-called "developing" countries like the Philippines, make them more vulnerable to the negative effects of climate change and environmental destruction, because of their roles as caregivers, providers of food and water, and as those whose social roles give them a greater responsibility for the building and maintaining of community, which is threatened by community displacement, loss of land, and other consequences of ecological destruction.[3]

It may be that attending to the differential impact of ecological decline on women will add to our awareness of what is needed for all people to thrive. At the same time, however, other thinkers critique such assertions as problematically essentialist, locking women into fixed role definitions based on traditional divisions of labor and assumed vulnerabilities related to their childbearing capacities.[4] For instance, Leach critiques assumptions about women's environmentally related survival activities as if they necessarily comprise "repositories of spiritual and cultural value" alongside "a priori notions of women's special relationship with the environment." She suggests that the activity of a woman in a developing nation gathering food in the forest may indicate less about her special relationship with nature and more about her social position and a lack of access to other resources that would provide income.[5]

With these critiques in mind, I chose to interview several women environmental activists (and research news reports of the work of those I could not interview) as one way to provide space for learning from the experiences of women as agents of environmental change. Although some of these women activists articulated a notion of women's special connection with the environment, my choice to

3. Katy Jenkins, "Women, Mining, and Development: An Emerging Research Agenda," *The Extractive Industries and Society* 1, no. 2 (2014): 329–39. Gerlie T. Tatlonghari and Thelma R. Paris, "Gendered Adaptations to Climate Change: A Case Study from the Philippines," in *Research, Action and Policy: Addressing the Gendered Impacts of Climate Change*, ed. Margaret Alston and Kerri Whittenbury (Dordrecht: Springer, 2013), 237–50, doi 10.1007/978-94-007-5518-5 17.
4. Melissa Leach, "Earth Mother Myths and Other Ecofeminist Fables: How a Strategic Notion Rose and Fell," *Development and Change* 38, no. 1 (2007): 67–85. See also Rebecca Elmhirst, "Gender and Sustainability: Lessons from Asia and Latin America," *Gender & Development* 21, no. 2 (2013): 413–15.
5. Leach, "Earth Mother Myths," 73.

attend to them comes not from any assumed essential relationship of these women to the Earth but rather from my interest in foregrounding women's often less visible contributions to the larger whole of eco-justice work and in better understanding their perspectives on gender and ecology.

Practical Theology and Ecotheology

Ecotheology and practical theology share in common an approach that places concrete realities in the foreground of theological construction. It is useful, therefore, to sketch out what a practical theological approach to environmental justice in the Philippines looks like. Practical theology works at the intersections of the lived experiences of people (and communities) and theological-meaning making, toward transformation that supports the flourishing of God's creation. As such, it comprises one approach among various other theological methods for understanding and empowering action around environmental issues theologically. Practical theology generally begins in a description of a particular context or situation, in this case the ecological degradation taking place in the Philippines. Seeking to make sense of the situation at a deeper level, practical theologians engage in interdisciplinary inquiry, using an array of disciplines alongside indigenous or local wisdom about the situation, in an effort to come to a more adequate understanding of the particular lived reality—the coexistence and thriving of humans and the rest of creation—with which we are concerned.

To better understand the Filipino ecological context in which tailings spills from large-scale mining bring about the biological death of rivers,[6] for example, one must draw upon global economics, postcolonial theory, sociology, the cultural and religious practices of particular indigenous peoples, some basic knowledge of the chemistry of mining, and understandings of biodiversity. In addition, the local wisdom of those whose lives are intertwined with the rivers and with mining provides further perspectives taken into account by practical theologians. In other words, a practical theological approach to ecojustice necessar-

---

6. One of the most toxic effects from large-scale mining occurs when rocks surfaced during mining activity that contain metals are exposed to oxygen. The exposure creates sulfuric acid. Continued release of acid can "mobilize" heavy metals such as lead and mercury. The most common way to contain this problem is to keep the rocks completely under water in a "tailings dam." Rupture of a tailings dam puts a catastrophic amount of toxic waste into the larger body of water, as was the case in the Bicol area tailings spill that destroyed the life of the Abra River, or the 1996 Marcopper Mines tailings spill contaminating the Boac River. See William N. Holden, "Mining Amid Typhoons: Large-Scale Mining and Typhoon Vulnerability in the Philippines," *The Extractive Industries and Society* 2, no. 3 (2015): 450.

ily involves an interdisciplinary conversation in which various forms of knowledge beyond theology become resources that can help to explain the Filipino ecological situation.

Practical theologians are not content merely to describe and explain a given situation, however. As theologians, we also ask what resources may be found in Christian tradition, in the lived experience of faith communities, and in Scripture for making *theological* sense—constructing theological meanings—of the situation of ecojustice in the Philippines. Exploring the biological death of a river due to mining waste, practical theologians wonder about the gap between this tragic situation and the "dream of God"[7] for the flourishing of creation. What theological notions of God's love and justice critique the river's death in which both aquatic life and human communities are sacrificed for monetary gain of the already wealthy in some faraway place? What stories from Scripture speak to the possibilities of reconciliation between those who denigrate the gift of water, those most deeply affected by such ecological destruction, and the river itself?

Practical theologians frequently engage in "internal critique" of Christian tradition, reading theological interpretations that have supported ecological abuses, for example, through norms that foreground God's desire for the flourishing of the whole creation, norms found within theology, Scripture, and experience. Many inadequate interpretations of the tradition take place because lived experience—human and otherwise—sometimes has not been considered normative in the construction of theology, allowing abstract doctrinal claims to assert a logic detached from the concrete reality of actual existence. Among practical theologians, lived experience operates as both a source and a norm for theological meaning making, which frequently leads to internal critique of traditional theological claims. This process of "reading the tradition against itself" with ecological well-being as normative thereby critiques the inadequacy of theological notions of human personhood, church, and society that some Christians have utilized to sanctify ecological suffering. Such critical work parallels a similar process among feminist theologians who read various theological claims in the light of norms such as freedom and justice for women. Thus, among feminist practical theologians, an additional guiding question asks what theological interpretations of the given situation—in this case environmental degradation in the Philippines—may also speak to the freedom and well-being of women.

---

7. This phrase comes from Episcopal theologian Verna Dozier, used here as an eschatological reference to the imagination of God's desire and hope for what God has created. Verna J. Dozier, *The Dream of God: A Call to Return* (Cambridge, MA: Cowley, 1991).

Finally, for practical theologians, the methodological elements I name above—description, analysis, and theological interpretation—provide guidance for strategic action oriented toward transformation of situations where injustice, suffering, or oppression obscure the dream of God for the flourishing of creation. Practical theology is not only a way of thinking but also a "way of doing." That is, it also works to support and engage in faithful action in the world. It is easy to see the convergences between practical theology and feminist ecotheology with their shared concerns for the intersections between justice for women and for the Earth that include an agenda for action.

In practice, the various elements of this method are far less discreet or linear than they appear in the above description. Consequently, in what follows, I intermingle description and interdisciplinary analysis, theological reflection and gestures toward strategic action, as I explore ecological issues in the Philippines by seeking out the perspectives of a few women activists who are close to environmental struggles in their everyday lives. For this chapter, I highlight the work of activists Glacy Macabale, Sister Mary John Mananzan, and Sister Stella Matutina.[8] Listening to them describe what is most urgent among environmental issues in their contexts and to their discussions of their work as advocates for ecojustice, a picture emerges of the close relationship between ecological degradation, human rights issues, and economic neocolonialism in the Philippines. At the same time, however, the narratives of these and other women involved in environmental justice work in the Philippines point to a hopeful, restorative image of the church as a community of witness and empowerment for an ailing ecosphere and of women as leaders called to ministries of care in which human flourishing is bound to that of the Earth. I now will turn to two contexts of women's environmental activism in the Philippines, the Manila Bay reclamation project and large-scale foreign mining operations.

Manila Bay and the Solar City Reclamation Project

Manila, the Philippines' capital city, is one of the most densely populated urban areas in the world. Yet, just beyond Manila's shoreline, two islands provide habitat for more than eighty species of migratory birds, eleven varieties of mangroves, and a variety of other marine life. The

8. Quotations come from interviews with Glacy Macabale and Sister Mary John Mananzan conducted during June 2016 by Skype. The activism of Sister Stella Matutina and of SAMIN (Sisters' Association in Mindanao) is widely reported in international news and information sources of human rights and ecojustice groups, from which I draw for this account.

Las Piñas-Parañaque Critical Habitat and Eco-Tourism Area includes Freedom Island and Long Island, with around 175 hectares (approximately 423 acres) of fragile wetlands. In addition to the habitat they provide for such richly diverse nonhuman lives, the waters around these islands also provide homes and livelihood to a large number of Manila's coastal fisherfolk and urban poor communities. But since 2011, this critical habitat has been the focus of efforts by foreign investors and development-hungry politicians to "reclaim" Manila Bay, intent on filling in an expanse of the bay to create land for shopping malls, international tourist hotels, and construction of a new international airport.

Glacy Macabale, campaign director for the Save Freedom Island Movement, initially became active in opposing the Manila Bay reclamation project out of her previous history of involvement with an urban poor alliance in the coastal area. Initially, her concern was over the displacement of fisherfolk who were repeatedly made to leave their coastal homes for inland government resettlement areas where they had no livelihood.

> They are driven from their houses. The government even blames them for the problems, saying that these urban poor are responsible for the garbage and pollution in the bay; that their houses cause the continual flooding in Manila; and even that they are the ones responsible for ecological destruction. . . . I had an "exposure" in that community, living among them, getting to know their families and their stories. I came to realize that they are the ones taking care of the environment in that place.

Glacy Macabale acknowledges that there are some in the community who do not fit this description. "Not everyone is the same—of course there are some who throw garbage into the water or who do not take care of the place. But of the people I know, they depend on the water and want to take care of it."

Against the claims of some critics that environmentalism is the concern of affluent people from the Global North and not of poor people in the "Two-Thirds" world,[9] who are necessarily too focused on survival

9. The tendency to categorize so-called Third World environmentalism exclusively in terms of survival concerns at the level of biological sustainability and a focus on equitable distribution of resources, while characterizing the environmentalism of First World affluent groups in terms of aesthetics or more "transcendent" concerns, such as the preservation of species diversity and consciousness of global ecological degradation, in effect participates in the polarization between development and environmental justice, according to Jyotirmaya Tripathy. As the activists in this chapter indicate, though, matters of local survival and global consciousness are closely connected. Tripathy's critique suggests the need for a more nuanced perspective on the relationship between economic development needs and environmentalism in economically struggling con-

to be concerned about environmental issues, Macabale maintains that the urban poor people of Manila have a strong stake in the health of the environment, in part because their survival depends on it. "The concerns of the earth and the concerns of the poor are linked." This, she points out, is especially true among fisherfolk, a situation made particularly clear in the aftermath of an earlier reclamation project in the bay to build a coastal highway and then later for the building of a massive shopping and entertainment center, the Mall of Asia:

> Before, when there were no reclamation projects around Manila Bay, these fisherfolk could make their living from fishing. Now, each of these fisherfolk only catch between three and five kilos per day. It is not enough to make a living, and it reflects the destruction of marine life taking place since the first reclamation [of Manila Bay, dating back to the Marcos government]. One grandfather I met told me that before, even if they had no money, the family could still eat from their catch of fish. Being fisherfolk is the only life they know, the only way they can make their living. So the demolition of their houses deprives them of their only livelihood.

At the same time that Macabale focuses on the destruction of the coastal urban poor communities occasioned by real estate development of Manila Bay, she is deeply concerned as well about the effects of habitat destruction on migratory birds and sea creatures, including several endangered species unique to the Philippines. "At the Save Freedom Island Movement we hold activities such as bay cleanups that get people to come together in nature, to take responsibility for it. When I was younger, I could take a walk and see the birds, the butterflies. Now children and teenagers do not have that experience." Also high on her list of concerns is the area's aquatic forest of mangroves, which will be destroyed in the reclamation. The mangroves provide important protection of the coast from storm effects, in addition to producing key nutrients that make these stands of mangroves a critical habitat for migratory birds.

Glacy Macabale's advocacy for the human and nonhuman inhabitants of Manila Bay sometimes locates her in opposition to powerful business and political interests, and she has experienced harassment and even death threats in the course of her environmental activism: "Around April 2011, one of our conveners received a text saying . . . that they know where we stay in community and they can 'take us out,'

---

texts such the Philippines. Jyotirmaya Tripathy, "Indian Environmentalism, and Its Fragments," in *Ecoambiguity, Community, and Development: Toward a Politicized Ecocriticism*, ed. Scott Slovic, Swarnalatha Rangarajan and Vidya Sarveswaran (Lanham, MD: Lexington, 2014), 71–84.

and we will be an example to other people who are resisting about the project." There have been other instances of harassment and threats as well, including efforts by one politician to recruit her into providing information about the work of Manila Bay anti-reclamation activism in exchange for money. "We know that activists for the environment face danger. We are all aware of the killings, the disappearances. But we cannot be halted by fear of what might happen, when we know what *will* happen to Freedom Island and to the people if we fail to act." Journalistic accounts name the Philippines as one of the "most dangerous countries for environmental activists," citing the deaths of some thirty-three activists in 2015 alone.[10]

What gives Glacy Macabale the energy to keep doing this difficult work? She describes her spirituality as a combination of "nature-love" and "relationship to the people, especially the urban poor people," that underlies her commitments to this environmental activism. She believes, first, that the educational work of the Save Freedom Island Movement helps to raise awareness about the importance of Freedom Island in the Filipino ecosphere. Second, the organizing and relational activities of coming to know fisherfolk who live in the "floating community" on the waters near Freedom Island, and advocacy for the urban poor whose housing and livelihoods are threatened by the bay reclamation project, also keep her energized to continue working for ecojustice. "If we did not do this work, maybe no one would know about the harm to migratory birds and the mangrove area, or the unjust displacement of the most vulnerable people in Manila. Maybe we will not be able to get everything we hope for, but we must be a witness to what is going on here."

Large-Scale Mining, Militarization, and Displacement

In both the north and south of the Philippines beyond Manila, the central focus of many activists turns to mining. Because the Philippines is a land rich in mineral resources, it has long been a target of foreign businesses interested in extracting those resources for profit. Successive political administrations in the Philippines have seen foreign mining operations as a much-needed source of employment and economic development. Most have therefore encouraged foreign mining compa-

10. "At least 33 environmental activists were murdered in the Philippines last year, making it one of the deadliest countries for land and environmental defenders in 2015, a report by Global Witness revealed Monday," according to a June 20, 2016 story on ABS-CBN News (an international news service focused on the Philippines). "33 Environmental Activists Killed in PH in 2015: Report," ABS-CBN News, June 20, 2016, http://tinyurl.com/mpd9k4z.

nies to set up operations in the country, albeit with certain restrictions designed to protect Filipino interests and land, such as legal requirements that foreign companies not own more than 40 percent of a particular mining operation. Under the influence of a neoliberalist economic climate backed by the World Bank,[11] however, laws regulating foreign mining underwent liberalization favoring the interests of the mining industry. Many question whether the Filipino people actually experience benefits of the economic development touted as the rationale for laws encouraging mining often at the expense of the land, water, and people.

The law known as the Mining Act of 1995 loosened previous executive orders regarding mining activity by foreign companies in the Philippines by changing the required percentage of ownership maintained by Filipino mining investors from its previous 60 percent level to only 40 percent, meaning that foreign companies with majority ownership in these Filipino mineral extraction sites can now have a controlling interest in the decisions and activities of these mines. In addition, the 1995 act included corollary statutes allowing for 100 percent foreign ownership of mining property. This liberalization of policy to encourage foreign investment led to a rapid influx of Australian, European, and US-based companies interested in extracting mineral wealth from the Philippines. The Roman Catholic Church in the Philippines, often through its bishops, has a long history of campaigning to stop large-scale, foreign owned mining activity because of its dual effects on people and the natural environment. Since 1995, the Catholic Church has worked for the repeal of the Mining Act of 1995, as have Protestant churches, in partnership with NGOs. In the meantime, however, mining "accidents" leading to environmental devastation are plentiful.

In 2007, waste from an Australian mining operation poured into the Albay Gulf in Bicol when heavy rainfall caused the tailings dam to break, releasing acids and cyanide waste from the Rapu-Rapu mining project into the water. This is only one example, albeit a particularly heinous one, of the destructive impact of mining.

Such devastating environmental impacts of large-scale mining are what cause Sister Mary John Mananzan to state unequivocally, "I consider mining and logging as the most urgent environmental issues in the Philippines today." As is the case with Glacy Macabale's concern for the Manila Bay, Mananzan's concern about mining involves both its

---

11. See Steven J. Klees, "World Bank and Education: Ideological Premises and Ideological Conclusions," in *The World Bank and Education: Critiques and Alternatives*, ed. Steven J. Klees, Joel Samoff, and Neely P. Stromquist (Rotterdam, NLD: Sense Publishers, 2012), 49–65.

destructive effects on the nonhuman environment and also its potentially devastating impacts on vulnerable people.

Mananzan sees strong links between economic neocolonialism and the environmental issues in large-scale mining:

> This [neocolonialist attitude] is seen especially in the mining industry. Mining companies are very careful about ecological protection in their own countries but wantonly destroy the environment in their mining activities in the Philippines, cutting down trees, causing pollution in rivers and seas, etc. and depriving indigenous peoples of their land and even threatening their lives. We fight this by lobbying in congress for the abrogation of the Mining Act of 1995, by peoples' protest at mining sites, and by supporting the indigenous peoples' fight for their ancestral lands.

Sister Mary John Mananzan's current forms of activism defy stereotypes of protest marches and political rallies alone. They include the use of social media and television to provide a widespread public platform for the stories of Lumad (indigenous people) whose lives are affected by mining. Mananzan hosts a TV talk show, *Nun Sense Makes Sense*. "We have partnered with schools of Indigenous peoples (Lumad) in Mindanao. Because of militarization [of mining areas] and the killing of Lumad leaders, we have arranged for Lumads to spread their message in other parts of the Philippines. Specifically I have invited them as guests in my TV talk show." In this way she tries to draw attention to their plight.[12]

Mananzan situates her activism for the environment within a religious vocation that holds together concern for the Earth and for the well-being of people. For Mananzan, environmental activism emerges directly out of her theological commitments:

> Way back in 1978, I joined EATWOT—Ecumenical Association of Third World Theologians. In 1981 we formed a Women's Commission, which developed a feminist theology of liberation from the perspective of Third World women. From the very start we included in the corollaries of our hermeneutic principle the care of the environment. This is what inspired me to develop modules on Eco-feminism in the Institute of Women's Studies. I also have written theological essays, for example on a Feminist Interpretation of Genesis 2, Ecological Advocacy in the Philippines.

A former chairperson of GABRIELA (the network of feminists and feminist organizations in the Philippines), Mananzan, now almost eighty

---

12. See also Germelina Lacorte, "Nun Seeks International Attention for Lumad," Inquirer.net, December 20, 2015, http://tinyurl.com/kbzu27n.

years old, continues to participate in a wide range of political actions around issues affecting women, indigenous peoples, and the environment.

Earlier in her ministry, Mananzan carried both concerns for the well-being of women and for the environment into her academic work at St. Scholastica's College in Manila, where she founded the Institute of Women's Studies in 1988.

> In 1997 we decided to combine the feminist cause with the environmental struggle seeing a close connection between the two. We developed courses on Ecofeminism, and Creation Centered Spirituality. To give this a fitting venue we bought a 1.4-hectare farm in Mendez, Cavite which we called the Women and Ecology Wholeness Center. We put up a bio gas digester, a windmill, a solar frame and ventured into organic farming.

The farm, besides being the venue for gender studies courses, is "also a showcase for ecological good practices like organic farming, solar lighting, bio gas digester. Participants of our gender courses are women and men from all sectors—grass roots, professionals, religious. . . . We show in our modules 'Towards Ecological Healing' and 'Creation Centered Spirituality' the close relationship between how patriarchy treats both women and nature."

Advocacy for Indigenous Peoples as Environmental Activism

Mananzan earlier made reference to the killing of Lumad leaders, a recent set of events on the Southern Filipino island of Mindanao in which large numbers of Lumad have experienced displacement from their ancestral lands and their farms as a result of overseas mining operations. The Lumad, along with environmental activists from churches and various climate-justice organizations, have faced violence from the military and paramilitary forces sent to quell the protests against the mining industry. Religious activists have expressed concern that the government uses the potential presence of militarized opposition groups as an excuse to squelch anti-mining activists' protests of foreign mining activities.

Particularly in Mindanao, clashes between the military and anti-mining and other human rights activists supporting the land rights of the Lumad have accelerated. In December 2015, Sister Stella Matutina received a German human rights award for her "years of working with the marginalized of Mindanao, particularly the Lumad, against the encroachment of large-scale mining and other extractive industries in the ancestral domains of indigenous people and the atrocities committed by state security forces and military-backed militias." Matutina is part of an organization called SAMIN, or Sisters Organization of Mindanao, an organization of three hundred nuns working for environmental justice and human rights in Mindanao. In her acceptance speech she said,

> There is a bloodbath in Mindanao. Here I weep daily for indigenous leaders and environmental activists who have been assassinated by the Philippines military. Out of the 72 leaders of indigenous peoples who have been extrajudicially killed under the present Aquino government in the Philippines, 56 of these are indigenous *lumad* of Mindanao. . . . In 2009 . . . I was illegally arrested and detained by the Philippine Army together with 3 of my lay companions, as we were conducting community awareness on mining and its effects in the remote villages of Cateel township in Davao Oriental province. . . . Yet this did not deter me and other environmental and human rights activists to wield our proverbial swords even as the corporate dragons continued to spew fire and venom through military harassment, false legal charges, surveillances, and an unending spate of extrajudicial killings of leaders and activists. We were able to oust the Philippine Youband Corporation. . . . Our small Benedictine Community is working for an indigenous community school of the Manobo people . . . an armed group gathered all the community people including women and children, 300 of them in all. The school's director, Emerito Samarca . . . was gunned down and slit in the throat. The community's leaders, Dionel Campos and Aurelio Sinzo, were singled out from the crowd. The assassins demanded everyone to look as they shot the two in the head.[13]

The Filipino military denies any role in the killing or harassment of anti-mining activists. The local wisdom of people such as Matutina who were present during these occurrences suggests otherwise, however.[14]

13. Sister Stella Matutina, "Reflection: 'I Am Sister Stella Matutina . . . A Prophet in My Own Land,'" *InterAksyon*, December 11, 2015, http://tinyurl.com/m44waw7.
14. In 2015, Dionel Campos—the chair of the Lumad organization that has been successful in keeping large-scale mining out of the mineral-rich Andab valley—was assassinated along with two other activists. In addition to the deaths of indigenous leaders, other anti-mining activists, including church workers, have also been targeted in disappearances and extrajudicial killings. In 2011, an Italian missionary priest, Father Fausto Tentorio, known to be very active in defending the rights of indigenous people and protection of the environment from the entry of large-scale mining in their area, was shot and killed. Clemente Bautista, the national coordinator of Kalikasan People's Network for the Environment, stated in a press release at the time, "Fr. Fausto is the sixth anti-mining advocate killed this year. Like Palawan environmentalist Dr. Gerry Ortega and small-scale miners' leader Santos Manrique, all of them have opposed large-scale mining projects in their areas." Kalikasan People's Network for the Environment, "Killing of Anti-Mining Italian Priest Condemned by Environmental Activists," *Philippine Indigenous Peoples Links*, October 17, 2011, http://tinyurl.com/lgpb6t3.

The Economics of Environmental (In)Justice in the Philippines

From the standpoint of a practical theological approach to the environmental issues facing Filipinos, it is important to search out additional perspectives that can help explain the situation described by Glacy Macabale, Sister Mary John Mananzan, and Sister Stella Matutina as they talked about their environmental activism. For that, I turn to the work of geographer David Harvey, whose approach to the "human geography" of postmodern living draws on a particular view of economics and power relations.

David Harvey's phrase "accumulation by dispossession" is an apt description of the (neoliberal) economic dynamics underlying the ecological issues named by the three activist women.[15] Accumulation by dispossession refers to the ability of markets to continue growth even in the absence of the reproduction of capital, through privatization of assets and redistribution of its benefits from public to private sectors, accomplished through "dispossession." The transfer of public assets (such as natural resources, geographical spaces considered to be public or held by a benevolent state for the public use, and so on) into private ownership dispossesses the public of a given asset (for example, ancestral lands) and commodifies it, while also resulting in the concentration of capital in the hands of private owners, in this case, the land developers behind the Manila Bay reclamation project and the privately owned mining companies engaged in large-scale mining.

Filipino liturgical theologian Ferdinand Anno describes a form of this process that took place in the history of the indigenous Igarot people of the Cordilleras, when colonial authorities demanded that people possess land deeds. Such notions of individual personal property possession were and are culturally antithetical to Igarot notions of the people as belonging to the land collectively, Anno contends. But under this colonial policy, any "undocumented" land not secured by a deed or title became classified as "public lands" under the jurisdiction of the government, who could determine their appropriate usage, in an act of dispossession. The colonial administration was then free to dispense the land to private holders or other parties in its favor.[16]

In the discourse surrounding accumulation by dispossession, privatization may even be accompanied by rhetoric suggesting that it

15. David Harvey, "The 'New' Imperialism: Accumulation by Dispossession," in *The New Imperial Challenge: Socialist Register 2004*, ed. Leo Panitch and Colin Leys (London: Merlin, 2004), 63–87.
16. Ferdinand Anno, "Indigenous Theology: Sources and Resources Perspectives from the Philippines," *The Ecumenical Review* 62, no. 4 (December 2010): 371–78, doi 10.1111/j.1758-6623.2010.00077.x.

ultimately benefits the people through economic development of the nation. This happens, for example, when foreign mining and real estate developers' operations find legitimation as a means of providing jobs and other benefits to the local community in spite of the effects of those operations on the environment in which that community is situated. However, in the process of "accumulation by dispossession," there often is little visible benefit to the people. Rather, private financial interests experience a protected status, often through militarization of mining areas, for instance, or the forced relocation of poor communities, which actually brings about a considerable amount of harm to the "public." Harms such as population displacement, habitat destruction, and land and water pollution by those who have no stake in the place other than as a site for resource extraction or land development toward capital accumulation happen with impunity, as the value of market growth and continuing accumulation of assets trumps other factors such as preserving the dignity of people and the life of nonhuman species. As theologian Lee Hong Jung summarizes this reality:

> The global free market has become the complex venue where all living beings in the web of life have been turned into commodities. . . . Under globalization, the myth that development naturally leads to unlimited growth is definitely exposed in terms of the ever-growing number of people living below the poverty line, in spite of substantial economic growth. The so-called development projects ensure big profits for big business but bring massive displacement for indigenous and aboriginal peoples, and ecological destruction of their lands.[17]

While this scenario is a contemporary economic reality, it has roots in the Philippines' long colonial history. A nation made up of some 7,100 islands, the Philippines is a resource-rich natural environment, particularly with regard to minerals and sea life, a feature on which early Spanish colonizers sought to capitalize in the sixteenth and seventeenth centuries. When American colonizers later took their place, they too laid claim to the natural assets of the Philippines for their own profits. Throughout the colonial period, churches both Protestant and Roman Catholic were co-opted by their governments to aid and abet the political and commercial interests of foreign colonizers. It is beyond the scope of this chapter to offer a nuanced discussion of the

---

17. Lee Hong Jung, "Eco-Justice and Global Climate Change as an Issue in Asian Ecumenism," in *Asian Handbook for Theological Education and Ecumenism*, ed. Hope Antone, Wati Longchar, Hyunju Bae, Huang Po Ho, and Dietrich Werner (Eugene, OR: Wipf & Stock, 2013), 304.

colonial history of the Philippines. Suffice it to say that today, practices of privatization and state redistribution of wealth through polities encouraging privatization are in part a colonialist legacy, set in motion by colonial land grants and the Spanish hacienda system,[18] as well as by historical patterns of American favoritism toward those in the Filipino government, business, religious, and military sectors willing to use their influence and power to support American military and commercial interests in the Philippines. As Yves Boquet describes the relationship between the Philippines' colonial past and present day economic colonialism, "in the context of a relatively weak government undermined by corruption at all levels, a good part of urban planning is in fact led by private developers who control large tracts of land inherited from the Spanish style of colonization."[19]

The struggle against this contemporary form of colonialism is made even more difficult when blanket rhetoric of economic growth as "good for the nation" is allowed to obscure the harmful consequences to the environment. Glacy Macabale commented, for example, that with local and national political interests in economic development in the foreground, the Department of the Environment issued a "Document of Environmental Compliance" to the developers of the Manila Bay reclamation project, essentially authorizing the project as one that meets the standards for environmental protection set by law, in spite of clear evidence to the contrary. But the result of liberalized pro-privatization policies is that both rural and urban areas of the Philippines have become contested spaces in which the interests of economic development are pitted against those of both the natural environment and the people. Theologian Lee Hong Jung offers a succinct assessment of results of this contest when he says, "Globalization is simply incompatible with ecological environmental sustainability."[20]

18. The hacienda system originated in the Spanish colonial period. The Spanish crown made land grants to Spanish colonizers (*hacenderos*) who then extracted unpaid labor of indigenous people to work on the estate. Profits went to the land holders. The Catholic Church was a major landholder in the hacienda system. Over time, this same system expanded to include land grants to elite Filipinos, generally the *mestizo*, who were of mixed Filipino-Spanish heritage (and who therefore had fairer skin). They exploited local landless Filipinos for their agricultural or mining labor on the haciendas. These elite landowners also engaged in "land grabbing," buying up the land of small farmers around the plantation to amass vast estates. The result is that large quantities of land are held by a very small, elite minority of families in the Philippines. The system continued well beyond the period of Filipino independence (1947) and even today forms the basis for the vast disparity between a wealthy, elite landholding class and the majority of Filipinos, who are not land owners. Filipino analysts often refer to the system as a modern form of feudalism, in which an aristocratic patron-landholder provides employment, medical care, educational resources, and so on for local peasants, who work in often oppressive conditions for substandard wages.
19. Yves Boquet, "Metro Manila's Challenges: Flooding, Housing and Mobility," in *Urban Development Challenges, Risks and Resilience in Asian Mega Cities*, ed. R. B. Singh (Tokyo: Springer, 2015), 449.
20. Jung, "Eco-Justice," 305.

A Theo-Logic of Environmental Activism

What theological sense might one make out of the ecological situations of the Manila Bay and of large-scale privatized mining? How might theology be a resource toward transformative action? First, to state the obvious, the ecological conditions described by Glacy Macabale, Sister Mary John Mananzan, and Sister Stella Matutina depict strong connections between the well-being of humans and that of the nonhuman environment. This interconnection has not always been well-regarded within the Christian tradition, which generally has favored a view of humanity as standing over the rest of the creation. By now, critiques of patriarchal interpretations of the Genesis creation stories that sacralize the domination of the nonhuman created order by humans are well known. Such interpretations rely on a theological anthropology of humans as "God's most special creations" above others, a view that then justifies the establishment of a hierarchy of authority among creatures, with human beings at the top.

It is not difficult to see how such an anthropology transfers to support a colonial mentality in which colonizers are "God's most special creations," standing in dominion over other humans deemed implicitly or explicitly to be a different kind of creature altogether (subhuman) and, therefore, appropriately, the object of imperialist constructions of their subjectivity.[21] As ecofeminist theologians point out, religious discourse is not neutral. It is implicated in Earth-destroying practices. As American theologian Sallie McFague, for example, puts it, "This [patriarchal] language is not only idolatrous and irrelevant—besides being oppressive to many who do not identify with it—but it may also work against the continuation of life on our planet."[22]

In contrast to such problematic notions of a hegemonic order of creation, the experience of interrelatedness between mangrove aquaforests, migratory birds, and urban fisherfolk as described by women environmental activists points to a different arrangement in which connections exist amid differences and interreliance characterizes relationships among diverse species/creatures, while each have their particular vulnerabilities and capacities. In this perspective, interrelatedness and interreliance are understood not as deficits but as "nec-

---

21. See, for example, Ivone Gebara's explanation of "God, an ecological problem," in which she stresses that since we have never seen God in God's fullness, we attribute imagery and characteristics to God, many of which are problematic for the Earth: "Our image of God becomes an accomplice to the destruction we perpetuate in the world." Ivone Gebara, "A Reform That Includes Eco-Justice," *Dialog* 55, no. 2 (2016): 119.
22. Sallie McFague, *Models of God: Theology for an Ecological, Nuclear Age* (Philadelphia: Fortress, 1987), ix.

essary conditions" for life in its fullness. As Brazilian ecofeminist theologian Ivone Gebara writes, "the survival of one group depends on another, and . . . on them depends the survival of the earth and of all living beings."[23]

If we read this experience of interrelatedness and interreliance as possessing a normative dimension alongside the voices of Scripture and Christian tradition for making theological claims about personhood, these elements (lived experience, Scripture, Christian tradition) stand in a critical yet productive relationship with one another. The experience of women activists provides a critical corrective to colonialist theological and scriptural interpretations, interrupting their hegemonic logic of domination.[24] Indeed, engaging the lived reality of these women activists, fisherfolk, and indigenous Filipinos as a material source for theology that has normative consequences presses forward an internal critique of the tradition, in which those parts of the tradition and scripture focused on the reign of God and the flourishing of all are allowed to critique and relativize interpretations that support the dehumanization of people and the destruction of the ecosystem. Ecofeminist theologians have a long history of critiquing this logic, which has significant implications for theological understandings of human personhood.[25] Seen through the lens of such a hermeneutic of all creations' flourishing, the resulting anthropology is one in which humanity is constituted at least in part through its creative and empathic engagement with the other members of the ecosphere.

Such a theological anthropology suggests practices of attention to the whole interrelated environment—rather than to its separate fragments—in policy decisions about land and resource use. People whose lives are intertwined with sea creatures cannot be arbitrarily relocated to inland arid spaces without losing something key to their humanity. I think what I am approaching here is the notion that among Manila's

23. Ivone Gebara, *Longing for Running Water: Ecofeminism and Liberation* (Minneapolis: Fortress, 1999), 9.
24. Among those advocating for the place of lived experience as itself theological, Filipina indigenous activist and ecofeminist Victoria Tauli-Corpuz, "Reclaiming Earth-based Spirituality, Indigenous Women in the Cordillera," in Rosemary Radford Ruether, ed., *Women Healing Earth: Third World Women on Ecology, Feminism, and Religion* (Maryknoll, NY: Orbis, 1996), 106, asserts that the everyday struggles of Igarot women defending their ancestral lands is an expression of Earth spirituality.
25. Feminist ecotheologians from both the Global South and North continue this critique. See especially Aruna Gnanadason, *Listen to the Women! Listen to the Earth!* (Geneva: World Council of Churches, 2005); Rosemary Radford Ruether, *Gaia and God: An Ecofeminist Theology of Earth Healing* (New York: HarperOne, 1994); Rosemary Radford Ruether, *Women Healing Earth: Third World Women on Ecology, Feminism and Religion* (Maryknoll, NY: Orbis, 1996); McFague, *Models of God*; Sallie McFague, *The Body of God: An Ecological Theology* (Minneapolis: Fortress, 1993); Heather Eaton, *Introducing Ecofeminist Theologies* (London: T&T Clark, 2005); Mary C. Grey, *Sacred Longings: The Ecological Spirit and Global Culture* (Minneapolis: Fortress, 2004).

fisherfolk, the fish have a constitutive role in making the people fully human. I assert this even within the recognition that people's roles and sources of livelihood, such as fishing, are constructed out of the available context and are not rigidly imputed as fixed identities. Even with the assumption of the fluidity of roles and identities, it remains the case that within the particular circumstances of life for these urban coastal dwellers in Manila, fish become "necessary" in some constitutive way. It would be useful to explore in the future the possible reciprocal implications of this idea for the "creaturehood" of fish and mangroves in relation to human beings.

Such a view of persons as in some way constituted by relation to the nonhuman creation suggests, furthermore, that human beings are not really "private" entities, if *private* means the ability to compartmentalize and separate one's actions as they affect the self from the consequences of one's actions as they affect others, both human and nonhuman. We are, instead, deeply contingent beings. *Contingency* refers to that which is dependent on something else. It references the possible rather than the certain. An acknowledgement of contingency need not issue in romanticized notions of perfect harmony and the erasure of distinctions between beings. In fact, there is not much romance about contingency. Contingency is hard. The recognition that my being depends on—is contingent upon—other beings brings demands, struggles, and limits to freedom. It does not wipe out agency, and yet it does circumscribe personal agency in some ways. At the same time, being that is situated around its individual, collective, and species contingency also brings possibilities of a different kind of relationship between persons and the larger environment.

One such possibility is a relationship between the human and nonhuman creation characterized by human empathy for the reality and experience of the "creaturely other." We may not be able to know whether plants or land "experience empathy," and to posit this as a mutual phenomenon between humans and other creatures is probably anthropomorphic hubris. But humans can be empathic. Perhaps an acknowledgement of human contingency in relation to the nonhuman environment can invite persons to "feel with and for" plants, rivers, land, birds, mangroves, and animals whose existence and well-being is often at risk and also obviously contingent—often upon human decision-making and concern for what is clearly "other." A theological anthropology that makes the cultivation of empathy a primary characteristic of contingent human existence has vast implications for everything from how Christians nurture the young to the ways we observe and honor with gratitude other creatures' contributions to our living.

These understandings of interrelatedness, interreliance, and contingency resonate well with biblical themes concerning mutual support among Christians and with practices of mutual aid between the churches found in the New Testament (particularly in the Pauline corpus, but elsewhere as well: see for instance Acts 2:32–47). If such a vision of mutual connection and aid is part of the "dream of God" for God's creation dwelling together on the Earth, then surely this vision critiques the present reality in which one creature gains at the expense of another and relations of mutual concern are not often evident in the arrangements between people and environment. The dream of God is an eschatological construct that receives its content from what and whom we know God to be through Scripture and as revealed in the life, person, work, and resurrection of Jesus. Even as it critiques our current social and power arrangements in which humans plunder the created environment, it also constitutes an image of hope as God continues to work for the fulfilling of that dream in our midst.

In a similar way, the fact that activists like Glacy Macabale, Mary John Mananzan, and Sister Stella Matutina can give witness to the suffering produced by environmental degradation points toward what is at least an implicit hope for change. The point of witnessing (*martyria*, in Greek) is both accompaniment and acknowledgement, both of which can produce the possibility of change. This image of witnessing as a primary calling of human beings in relation to the environment is not passive. Rather, it holds out the possibility that when human beings accompany the "creaturely others" and the Earth itself in its state of ecological despair, when human beings acknowledge the suffering residing there and thus give witness to the gap between the dream of God and the lived reality of human-ecological relations, faithful action empowered by such a witness can render transformation.

This is an eco-ecclesiology in which to be an empowered and empowering witness can become an act of repentance and redemption, facilitating reconciliation where harm has broken connections. Situations of ecological harm make evident the complexity and unlikelihood of "right relations" between humans and the rest of the creation as something we can accomplish by sheer virtue of our will to do so. As is the case in other situations that Christian traditions understand as *sin*, this impossibility of "making one's *self* right" threatens to freeze persons into their positions as perpetrators of harm. In an ecclesiology of empowering witness, church is not only a place of human action but also of divine encounter. The God who is gracious enough to give us, in all our contingencies, the possibility of life-affirming relationships with the nonhuman environment surely can and will act to redeem and sanctify what needs new life.

The work of the Filipino women activists described above is a partial contribution to the much larger struggle to transform destructive practices that harm people, land, and other creatures in that country's diverse ecology. Their commitments—personal, political, and theological—point toward a changing theological notion of what it means to be human and what it means to be church that can hold together the painful realities of destructive ecological practices with moments of hope, working for change, and promises of renewal born out in their work.

Hope and Eschatology

17

¡Somos Criaturas de Dios!—Seeing and Beholding the Garden of God

Nancy Pineda-Madrid

In contemporary theological writings, there is no dearth of works exploring what it means for human beings to be *children* of God. However, now more than ever we need to grasp and relish who we are as *creatures* of God. Our theological anthropology is doomed to distortion if considered in isolation from a healthy biology, ecology, and cosmology. Our world's current environmental crisis emerges, in part, from a deeply flawed theological anthropology. We far too often regard human beings as set apart from the rest of the natural world to such a degree that the significance and value of other creatures is rendered negligible by comparison.[1]

In many Latino/a communities, the often-heard Spanish expression *somos criaturas de Dios* (we are creatures of God) calls forth an appre-

---

1. I am grateful to Francine Cardman who read this essay in draft form and made many helpful suggestions.

ciation of our creatureliness. We are creatures of God! Alejandro García-Rivera once wrote, "The ultimate mystery of being human is not so much reason but that the human is a creature of God. What is human cannot be known without reference to God, and that reference lies not with the distinctiveness of the human but with the connectedness of creation."[2] This understanding of the human person encourages greater care for our common home, the Earth (a vital concern if life is to continue to flourish on the Earth in the centuries and millennia to come), and relatedly, greater care for the community of creatures with whom we share planet Earth. The time for conversion is now. To that end, this essay argues that a robust theological appreciation for, and interpretation of, "human beings as creatures of God," furthers eschatological hope by foregrounding human beings' common fellowship with all other creatures of God.

Now is the time to rethink, at a fundamental level, the God-human relation. What kind of new imaginative framework might transform how people of faith understand the place of human beings in the world? What kind of renaming would expand human beings' reverence for the natural world? Is this necessary? If the interconnectedness of all human beings and all nonhuman creatures takes center stage, then might such a focus give rise to an understanding that promotes greater ecological justice? What I am suggesting here is an anthropology of creatureliness.[3] The first part of this essay explores the need for this fresh imaginative framework and argues that without the wider scope that this new framework conveys through its focus on creatureliness, the possibility of our knowing and loving God is lessened. Indeed, this first section presumes that the purpose of thinking is "to produce habits of action" informed by our best account of truth.[4] So, calling for, and participating in, the forging of a new imaginative framework is for the purpose of reorienting how we act in the world through reimagining ourselves in relation to God and the cosmos. Ideally, such thinking encourages a truer way of living in the natural world and a truer way of relating to God. These two, humans' relationship to the natural world and to God, are utterly integral to one another, thus inseparable.

The second part of this essay develops further an anthropology of creatureliness by proposing that support for a *Criaturas de Dios* frame-

2. Alex García-Rivera, *St. Martín de Porras: The "Little Stories" and the Semiotics of Culture* (Maryknoll, NY: Orbis, 1995), 94.
3. I am taking the idea of an "anthropology of creatureliness" from Alejandro García-Rivera's *St. Martín de Porras.*
4. C. S. Peirce, "How to Make Our Ideas Clear (1878)," in *The Essential Peirce: Volume 1 (1867–1893)*, ed. Nathan Houser and Christian Kloesel (Bloomington: Indiana University Press, 1992), 132. See also in the same volume, "The Fixation of Belief (1877)," 111–12.

work certainly requires reasoned argument, but this alone is insufficient. A reasoned argument may fail to ask, what moves the human heart? What kind of imaginative thinking awakens people of faith to the idea that we are *Criaturas de Dios*? If we assume this way of understanding ourselves, then what might this mean for how we live?

Embracing this new way of thinking and acting in the world positions eschatological hope at the forefront. Eschatological hope is the hope made visible through the committed efforts of those who advance, above all else, the coming of the reign of God in history. The bleak contingencies of history—be they environmental destruction, violence, brutal tragedies, crushing poverty, and the like, often beyond our control—render hope fragile and vulnerable. Hope may seem weaker, particularly in the midst of grim times, when evil and the anti-kingdom feel increasingly more palpable. Yet, it is precisely in such times that eschatological hope matters most. The third part of this essay considers the ways in which a *Criaturas de Dios* framework furthers this kind of hope.

¡Somos Criaturas de Dios!

Scientists now see a shift that began in the eighteenth century—namely, the magnitude of human beings' impact on the Earth's climate and ecological systems. So pronounced was the change that chemist Paul Crutzen developed a name for the new geological period that we are now in: the Anthropocene.[5] Today, there exists a vast scientific consensus that our global climate system is warming the planet and that the cause of this warming is the release of greenhouse gases brought about by human habits of consumption and waste. Consequently, the biodiversity of our planet has suffered dramatically and the Earth's fresh water and oceans are in peril, all to the detriment of the flourishing, and future, of human life on planet Earth.[6]

In our time, we may observe two competing narratives, one being the narrative of the market: everything is viewed as a commodity and everything is defined within a fully commodified world that overwhelmingly views human beings themselves as, ultimately, commodities. The second narrative is based on values informed by the gospel. In this second narrative, all commodities and economics must be sit-

---

5. *Collins English Dictionary—Complete & Unabridged 2012 Digital Edition*, s.v. "Anthropocene," accessed June 25, 2016, http://tinyurl.com/k3uawuz. Here, *Anthropocene* is defined as "a proposed term for the present geological epoch (from the time of the Industrial Revolution onwards), during which humanity has begun to have a significant impact on the environment."
6. Francis, *Laudato Si': On Care for Our Common Home* (Huntington, IN: Our Sunday Visitor, 2015). Hereafter cited parenthetically in the text as *LS*; all numbers refer to paragraphs.

uated within a much broader expanse and context of value. Theology must continue its work on a robust and compelling vision of this second narrative. Indeed, since the publication of *Rerum Novarum* in 1891, Catholic social teaching has challenged conceptions of human beings as objects and as disposable—that is, as market commodities whose value is determined by the laws of supply and demand alone and without regard for what human beings contribute through their work and what they need for their flourishing.

The best research today on climate injustice should move us both ethically and spiritually. Our concern for climate injustice must be considered in light of the poor and outcasts, as Pope Francis urges us to do. In his words: "We are faced not with two separate crises, one environmental and the other social, but rather with one complex crisis which is both social and environmental" (*LS*, 139). Those who are most vulnerable in our world, the economically poor, often suffer the effects of the degradation of the environment. In other words, the quest for a more just world has geographical implications. People with economic resources, often those living in the wealthiest countries, use their money to cushion themselves against the environmental degradation that their lifestyle has inflicted upon the Earth. They do not suffer the impact of ecological damage, only the economically poor suffer this. The "new tyranny" of unfettered capitalism contributes mightily to planet Earth's degradation.[7] In play is a presumptive market ideology that drives out all other forms of valuing humanity, the natural world, and the cosmos.

We live within a paradox. While modernity's influence has led to a sharp increase in human understanding of the forces shaping the natural world, at the same time, human cultures, especially urban cultures in wealthy industrialized countries, have, by and large, grown more alienated from the natural world. This paradox raises unavoidable questions, "What sort of knowledge is it that enriches our understanding but leads us to self-destruction?" García-Rivera observes that "it is the sort of knowledge that enriches our understanding of the cosmos but not of the place of the human in the cosmos."[8] Recently, Pope Francis expressed a similar insight:

It cannot be emphasized enough how everything is interconnected. Time and space are not independent of one another, and not even atoms or subatomic particles can be considered in isolation. Just as the different

7. Francis and Sean McDonagh, *On Care for Our Common Home "Laudato Si'": The Encyclical of Pope Francis on the Environment* (Maryknoll, NY: Orbis, 2016), 17.
8. Alejandro García-Rivera, *The Garden of God: A Theological Cosmology* (Minneapolis: Fortress, 2009), 3.

aspects of the planet—physical, chemical and biological—are interrelated, so too living species are part of a network which we will never fully explore and understand. . . . It follows that the fragmentation of knowledge and the isolation of bits of information can actually become a form of ignorance, unless they are integrated into a broader vision of reality. (LS, 138)

The fragmentation of knowledge is precisely that from which we suffer. It has led to a self-understanding that does not serve us well. John Muir named this aptly decades ago, "Most people are on the world, not in it—have no conscious sympathy or relationship to anything about them—undiffused, separate, and rigidly alone like marbles of polished stone, touching but separate."[9] Theologically, when we recognize the value of every animal, every plant, and the ecosystems that support them, that each of these has its own unique relationship to God, then this recognition encourages in humans not only a transformed ethical behavior but also a transformed sense of human identity. Humans come to see themselves anew as neighbors to all creatures who also live on planet Earth.[10]

To reframe how we understand ourselves, and thus encourage a more interconnected sensibility, necessitates foregrounding how human beings are interrelated with nonhuman creatures as well as with God. Indeed, it is to recognize that love of God requires no less of us. The example of Saint Martín de Porras (1579–1639) may hint at a way forward for a new imaginative framework. After all, he was known as the Saint Francis of the Americas. Recall that Saint Martín was a mulatto, his father being a white Spaniard of noble birth and his mother a freed black slave. Both of his parents guided his study of the art of healing and medicine. His work in healing benefited many who lived at the margins of society: widows, orphans, prostitutes, indigenous, blacks, mestizos, and mulattos as well as animals. A new way of thinking about human beings and other creatures comes into view with an account of Saint Martín offered by Fray Fernando Aragones:

One of the Dominican friars in St. Martín's convent walked into a room near the kitchen to find a strange sight. At the feet of St. Martín were a dog and a cat eating peacefully from the same bowl of soup. The friar was about to call the rest of the monks in to witness this marvelous sight when a little mouse stuck his head out from a little hole in the wall. St. Martín without hesitation addressed the mouse as if he were an old friend. "Don't

9. John Muir, *John of the Mountains: The Unpublished Journals of John Muir* (Madison: University of Wisconsin Press, 1966), 320.
10. Elizabeth A. Johnson, *Ask the Beasts: Darwin and the God of Love* (London: Bloomsbury, 2014), xvii.

be afraid little one. If you're hungry come and eat with the others." The little mouse hesitated but then scampered to the bowl of soup from which the dog and the cat were eating. The friar who was watching all this take place tried to speak but no words came out of his mouth. Here before his eyes, at the feet of the mulatto St. Martín, a dog, a cat, and a mouse were eating from the same bowl of soup, natural enemies eating peacefully side by side![11]

Differences among various animals, among human beings, and, truly, among all species created by God do not necessarily lead to our becoming antagonistic to one another. For all species share a deeper bond. "We are bound in common fellowship. Each of us is, after all, a *criatura de Dios*, a creature of God. Our creatureliness becomes the basis for sharing our resources. We all can drink from the same bowl of soup, for we are creatures not of some universal humanity but of one Creator."[12] By drawing forward the notion of *criatura de Dios*, García-Rivera invites us to think more deliberately about the ways this idea may suggest a reframing of humanity's relationship to nonhuman creatures and to the Creator. What if being a creature of God was the fundamental self-understanding of human beings? Would this not affirm the deeper bond that human beings share with nonhuman creatures? Might this give us a way of understanding our place within the natural world and not apart from it?

Nonhuman creatures, animals, possess a dignity and bearing that is to be respected because God holds the lives of animals in God's hands, just as God holds the lives of humans. Once, when a fellow friar questioned Saint Martín on his regard for animals, asking "are they people?" Saint Martín replied, "they are *criaturas de Dios*."[13] Implicit here is that human beings and animals both find their meaning in the world in that all these species are creatures of God. The value and dignity of all species is found in that God created them. Animals, in other words, should be fed, cared for, and treated respectfully precisely because they share, along with humans, in the condition of creaturehood.

Theologically, what is being suggested here is the preeminence of an anthropology of creatureliness. For the fundamental mystery of the human is found in the reality that we are creatures of God. Without in any way diminishing that humans possess singular gifts and abilities (that is, reason, imagination, self-consciousness, freedom, and so on), the condition of our creaturehood must nonetheless take on a preem-

---

11. García-Rivera, *St. Martín de Porras*, 4.
12. Ibid., 4–5.
13. Ibid., 91.

inent, singular significance. This is typified in Saint Martín bringing a single bowl of soup and instructing a dog, a cat, and a mouse to each eat from the same bowl at the same time in peace with one another. The image of these three eating together at the foot of Saint Martín signals an anthropology of creatureliness that necessarily recognizes a hierarchy of being, one that without a doubt includes human beings.[14] This hierarchy of being calls for a more sophisticated appreciation of all creatures—sophisticated in that we cannot have absolute regard for one creature at the expense of all others. With regard to asymmetrical relationships between humans and other creatures, this difference must not be used to create a dualism whereby humans are seen as holding absolute value in a way that renders the value of animals and/or plants as simply expendable. Again, the value of each is not symmetrical; nonetheless, an absolute dualism is not viable. It is beyond the bounds of this essay to delve into this challenge further. Suffice it to say that there is a need for a much more carefully considered, and critically developed, anthropology of creatureliness.

While an "anthropology of creatureliness" may sound awkward in the English language, in Spanish this phrase has a more organic quality owing to the use of the word *criatura*, a common word for child, primarily used in the vernacular, often by women. *Criatura* is typically translated simply as "creature," yet in the quotidian usage, it carries various meanings in Spanish. It is used to refer to both humans and animals; typically the user intends to express an affection and/or a compassion with the use of this word. Moreover, a "related word, *criado*, means 'servant' as well as 'created.' The word *crear* is etymologically related to 'criar.' Where the former means create, the other means to give birth as well as to nurse or take care of. Even more interesting, the words *Creador* and *Criador* are sometimes used interchangeably to refer to God."[15] In brief, *criatura* carries a rich sensibility ready-made for what is being suggested herein.[16]

In his own context, Saint Martín expanded the meaning of *criatura de Dios*, giving it a broad scope such that it is used to assert a fundamental connectedness among the most unlikely of human beings as well as among human beings and all other creatures—animals, plants, and so on.[17] *Criatura de Dios*, as Saint Martín used it, resonates with some passages of Scripture that call attention to the creaturely state of human

14. Ibid., 94–95.
15. Ibid., 85.
16. I am grateful to Pedro Rubalcava for clarifying the meanings of *criar* and *crear*, as well as for his musical composition that informed my work. See *Toda la Creación Verá* (All Creation Will See), score, 2015, private collection.
17. García-Rivera, *St. Martín de Porras*, 85–105.

beings alongside nonhuman creatures (for example, Job 12:7–10; Isa 11:6; Rom 8) as well as with works from the tradition, most notably in Augustine's *Confessions* (10.6.9) when he, in examining his love of God, asks the creatures of the Earth, who is this God?

Conversion: Cultivating an Anagogical Imagination

While Christian theology has long rightly assumed the task of developing reasoned, intelligent, public arguments for the claims being advanced. Reason alone has never been sufficient, which is particularly the case in this essay. Theologizing must encourage a longing and desire for God. A cogent interpretation of an anthropology of creatureliness by itself, therefore, may not sufficiently compel a transformation of human thinking, feeling, and habits of lifestyle. Transformation on all these levels requires a new-found appreciation, an experience that moves the heart, much like falling in love. How can human beings recover a sense of affection for and familiarity with creation and the cosmos? For far too long, theology has not addressed humanity's stunning loss of intimacy with the cosmos, even though "the roots of Christian doctrine reach deep into the soil of cosmic awareness,"[18] a point recognized by a growing number of theologians today.[19]

An anthropology of creatureliness is intended neither to undermine the uniqueness of each human person nor to minimize the rational self-consciousness of the human being but rather to hold in view that, in the call to know and love God, humans have for too long focused far more attention on knowing God than on loving God. In the quest to love God, the question of fellowship with nonhuman creatures as well as humans must command greater attention. And fellowship must include, as Saint Martín's example demonstrates, developing fellowship with the great variety of nonhuman creatures. To love God, in other words, human beings, as conscious as humans are of themselves, need to cross the boundaries between humans and nonhuman creatures. This must be a human initiative since nonhuman creatures do

18. Ibid., 2–3.
19. See for example: Johnson, *Ask the Beasts*; Sallie McFague, *The Body of God: An Ecological Theology* (Minneapolis: Fortress, 1993); Rosemary Radford Ruether, *Gaia and God: An Ecofeminist Theology of Earth Healing* (New York: HarperOne, 1994); Gloria Schaab, *Trinity in Relation: Creation, Incarnation, and Grace in an Evolving Cosmos* (Winona, MN: Anselm Academic, 2012); Robert J. Russell, William R. Stoeger, and George V. Coyne, eds., *Physics, Philosophy, and Theology* (Vatican City: Vatican Observatory, 1988); Ivone Gebara, *Longing for Running Water: Ecofeminism and Liberation* (Minneapolis: Fortress, 1999); Celia Deane-Drummond, *Christ and Evolution: Wonder and Wisdom* (Minneapolis: Fortress, 2009); Denis Edwards, *How God Acts: Creation, Redemption, and Special Divine Action* (Minneapolis: Fortress, 2010); J. Wentzel van Huyssteen, *Alone in the World? Human Uniqueness in Science and Theology* (Grand Rapids: Eerdmans, 2006).

not possess a self-consciousness that would allow them to freely and knowingly take this kind of initiative.[20]

When we read the signs of the times today, Pope Francis has made clear, they urge a conversion, a personal and social transformation toward a committed "ecological citizenship" expressed in habits of the mind, affect, and practice (LS, 202, 211, 213–16). To a great degree, conversion comes about by attending to what moves the human heart. The experience of something truly beautiful moves our hearts, lifts us up, and accordingly, carries a religious dimension.[21] As imago Dei, humans bear a theopoetic imagination, an imagination that is fundamentally open to the indwelling of the Holy Spirit. If human reason becomes severed from theopoetic imagination, then human reason becomes dry, arid—lacking spirit and ultimately "deprived of truth."[22] As Hans Urs von Balthasar has so eloquently expressed it:

> In a world without beauty—even if people cannot dispense with the word and constantly have it on the tip of their tongues in order to abuse it—in a world which is perhaps not wholly without beauty, but which can no longer see it or reckon with it: In such a world the good also loses its attractiveness, the self-evidence of why it must be carried out. [A human being] stands before the good and asks [themselves] why it must be done and not rather its alternative, evil. For this, too, is a possibility, and even the more exciting one: Why not investigate Satan's depths? In a world that no longer has enough confidence in itself to affirm the beautiful, the proofs of the truth have lost their cogency. In other words, syllogism may still dutifully clatter away like rotary presses or computers which infallibly spew out an exact number of answers by the minute. But the logic of these answers is itself a mechanism which no longer captivates anyone.[23]

In order to draw the human heart toward the good, and foster a human heart desirous of the good, to lift up the lowly requires an anagogical imagination.

An anagogical imagination refers to that which draws our souls to God, stirs our awareness of the transcendent in our lives, and heightens our consciousness of God's presence in the experience of the beautiful. An anagogical imagination foregrounds the experience of divine beauty,

20. García-Rivera, St. Martín de Porras, 99–105.
21. Alejandro García-Rivera, The Community of the Beautiful: A Theological Aesthetics (Collegeville, MN: Liturgical, 1999), 158.
22. Roberto S. Goizueta, "U.S. Hispanic Popular Catholicism as Theopoetics," in Hispanic/Latino Theology: Challenge and Promise, ed. Ada María Isasi-Díaz and Fernando F. Segovia (Minneapolis: Fortress, 1996), 263.
23. Hans Urs von Balthasar, The Glory of the Lord: A Theological Aesthetics, vol. 1, Seeing the Form (San Francisco: Ignatius, 1982), 19.

yet never for its own sake but rather as a means of deepening our relationship with God. The experience of the truly beautiful evokes a movement of the heart, and "this movement of the heart is the 'spark,' the 'lighting of the fuse,' that inspires and sets in motion the interpretation of the Good and the True."[24] An anagogical imagination necessitates a distinction between philosophical aesthetics and theological aesthetics: the former is concerned with the nature of beauty in itself, while the latter is acutely focused on how we come to know God in the experience of beauty. The seductiveness of beauty makes this all-important distinction fraught with difficulty. The truly beautiful presents the challenge of human perception and intentionality. Human beings so easily slip into being so captivated by the object of beauty that the source of genuine beauty, namely God, recedes from human consciousness.

The soul's ascent to God, at the heart of an anagogical imagination, does not refer to an experience separate from fleshiness. It takes inspiration from Mary's song of praise in the Gospel of Luke: "My soul magnifies the Lord, and my spirit rejoices in God my Savior" (Luke 1:46–47). As this Marian praise suggests, and in the tradition of Augustine, anagoge concerns a movement within Creation and not outside of it. Even though Augustine was strongly influenced by Platonic forms, Augustine's understanding of anagoge stands in contrast to a Platonic form. "[What Augustine sought was] to find rest for his restless soul not in the rarified atmosphere of the Manicheans but in the Creation-grounded beauty of God."[25] A line of Muir's captures well how humans can be stirred by the beauty of nature, which points to God. "No synonym for God is so perfect as Beauty. Whether as seen carving the lines of the mountains with glaciers, or gathering matter into stars, or planning the movements of water, or gardening—still all is Beauty!"[26]

An anagogical imagination invites human beings into a participation with and a beholding of all creatures, human and nonhuman, as part of the garden of God. Such beholding does not follow from detached observation or descriptions of creatures that rest content in their thoroughness. Beholding rests in the recognition of a "dissimilar similarity" in the relationship between every creature and the Creator. According to Pseudo-Dionysius, this means that each creature is a symbol representing God. As creatures, human beings in particular possess the capacity to know and love God. Human beings can behold the grandeur and majesty of God evident in the extraordinary and varied

24. García-Rivera, *Community of the Beautiful*, 185.
25. Ibid., 31.
26. Muir, *John of the Mountains*, 208.

creatures that proclaim their Creator. For a human being to behold is to present oneself as disposed to being uplifted not through one's own efforts but through the grace of a lavishly generous God. Moreover, according to García-Rivera:

> Pseudo-Dionysius makes plain the explanatory power of emphasizing the difference between the Creator and creatures. The difference makes possible an "uplifting," an "anagogy," which consists of a participation of the creature in the Creator made possible precisely because of its distance from the Creator. Thus, "dissimilar similarity" is, at once a participation and a distancing. As such, Pseudo-Dionysius sets up a "dynamic" analogy, an anagogy.[27]

Eschatological Hope

Beholding encourages human beings to see God's presence in all things and, by extension, to see the future that God intends for all things. Beholding directs our attention to eschatological hope. "Christian eschatological hope is marked by the demand that we remain open to the transcendent future of God."[28] Nowhere and at no time is this more difficult than when humans confront the tragedies and horrific vicissitudes of life, and choose to affirm eschatological hope by seeking reconciliation with those who are known enemies and those who have caused grave harm. When humans remain firm in their attempts to blunt the effects of evil in the world, then eschatological hope comes more sharply into view. It flows directly from the mystery of Christ's incarnation, ministry, crucifixion, and resurrection and remains ever open to the end that God intends for all creatures and all the natural world.

We affirm eschatological hope through expanding our capacity and ability to see God's presence in all things, to see the inner meaning of all things. This ability for humans is never merely a question of ever more acute observation; it is invariably a question of our participation, of recognizing our God-given place within the universe. "Our ability to see a cosmos is our ability to experience God's presence in all things."[29] In the example of Saint Martín, we find that

> the dog, the cat, and the mouse story reveals the creatureliness of the human, an identity found through the capacity for cosmic fellowship

27. García-Rivera, *Community of the Beautiful*, 81. See also García-Rivera, *Garden of God*, 93–104.
28. Margaret Campbell, "Resurrection," in *Dictionary of Feminist Theologies*, ed. Letty Mandeville Russell and Jeanette Shannon Clarkson (Louisville: Westminster John Knox, 1996), 242.
29. García-Rivera, *Garden of God*, 22.

given the human creature by the Creator. By participating in the creatureliness of each other and of the cosmos, the human creature discovers
who he or she is, because the Creator of the human creature is also the
One who created the cosmos. . . . The dog, cat, and mouse story may be an
eschatological image, an image of the end times, but it is also an image of
what the journey to the end time will look like. The road to heaven will be
found through the charitable search for human identity.[30]

What is key here, then, is that the search for human identity, the end
for which humans are intended by God, and the journey toward this
end are all intimately interrelated to one another in the human experience of creatureliness.

Thus, an anthropology of creatureliness holds forth the possibility
of proclaiming eschatological hope by its offer of a provisional vision
of the end time and a recognition of the journey to the end time. First,
when human beings primarily understand themselves as *criaturas de
Dios*, as members of the community of creation, then the kinship that
all creatures share emerges at the center. García-Rivera calls this vision
"the cosmic eucharistic-like fellowship" and a "fellowship of sacramental grace."[31] Elizabeth A. Johnson describes this as a framework
that highlights connection, relationship, and solidarity among God's
creatures, noting that "this model's different imaginative framework
unleashes aesthetic, emotional, and ethical responses that express ecological sensibility at a fundamental level."[32] The differences between
species are not glossed over but rather take on meaning in the context
of a wider whole; the human species finds its place and meaning within
the cosmos, interrelated with all God's creatures, instead of set apart
from the natural world.

To call for an anthropology of creatureliness is not to obfuscate the
unique gifts of human beings in relation to the Creator. Humans, of
course, have the capacity to know who we are in relation to the Creator and have the capacity "to bridge the ultimate asymmetry between
themselves and their Creator,"[33] while nonhuman creatures are incapable of either of these forms of self-knowledge. Humans have created
many categories for naming themselves, and with imagination and
drive, a human being may discover which of these categories apply,
or not, to them specifically. This potential process of self-discovery
is indicative of human freedom, the capacity to express oneself and,

30. García-Rivera, *St. Martín de Porras*, 102. See also Anthony Kelly, *Eschatology and Hope* (Maryknoll,
NY: Orbis, 2006).
31. García-Rivera, *St. Martín de Porras*, 94.
32. Johnson, *Ask the Beasts*, 268–69.
33. García-Rivera, *St. Martín de Porras*, 100.

in so doing, to take possession of oneself, as Karl Rahner has noted.[34] This most prized characteristic, freedom, is unique to human beings and, accordingly, a characteristic not found in nonhuman creatures. The capacity allows human beings to consciously enter into relationship with other humans, with God, with animals, and so on. Note that human beings can enter into asymmetrical relationships—in other words, not only with other human beings but with, for example, animals—and into the ultimate asymmetrical relationship: with God. Ideally, this potential for relationships recognizes the cosmic order of all creation as expressing the fecundity of different creatures as the intention of the Creator.[35] "By participating in the creatureliness of each other and of the cosmos, the human creature discovers who he or she is, because the Creator of the human creature is also the One who created the cosmos."[36]

Second, an anthropology of creatureliness bears resonance with eschatological hope in that it recognizes a divine coherency expressed in every aspect of the universe that is all-encompassing, a divine coherency that certainly includes our consciousness and intelligence yet extends far beyond embracing all the natural world and more. While humans possess a tenacious drive to understand this coherency, expressed every time we seek to understand our world, it nonetheless develops beyond our very best attempts to understand. In Bernard Lonergan's words: "Does there or does there not necessarily exist a transcendent, intelligent ground of the universe? Is that ground or are we the primary instance of moral consciousness? Are cosmogenesis, biological evolution, historical progress basically cognate to us as moral beings or are they indifferent and so alien to us?"[37] The dynamism of our existence impels us not to rest content until we understand all that we can understand. As part of this same drive to understand, we discover that, as Anthony Kelly has argued, "an anticipation of a final homecoming is built into conscious existence."[38] Affirming creaturehood before other forms of naming the human condition opens up a more holistic understanding of God's creative impulse expressed in the entire community of creation. When the God-human relationship is in focus in a manner that renders the rest of

34. Karl Rahner, "Theology of Freedom," in *Theological Investigations*, vol. 6, *Concerning Vatican Council II*, trans. Karl H. Kruger and Boniface Kruger (London: Darton, Longman & Todd, 1969), 183–86.
35. García-Rivera, *St. Martín de Porras*, 100–101.
36. Ibid., 102.
37. Bernard J. F. Lonergan, *Method in Theology* (London: Darton, Longman & Todd, 1972), 103, as quoted in Kelly, *Eschatology and Hope*, 203–4.
38. Kelly, *Eschatology and Hope*, 204.

the community of creation a mere backdrop, what results is a distorted theological anthropology flawed by its narrow bandwidth.

Third, an anthropology of creatureliness invites conversion by means of the enjoyment of life abundant known in the splendorous beauty of the community of creation. The Holy Spirit incessantly draws human souls to God most ardently (anagoge) by means of the glory of creation. Christian hope, which necessarily means hope in an eschatological key, requires a continual process of conversion toward seeing the integral relation of self, others, the universe, and God ever more transparently. This turning continuously transforms us in every dimension of our being and, most certainly, in terms of deepening our desire for God. The whole of the natural world, of which human beings are a part, is gifted with freedom "in and thorough which the Creator Spirit's gracious purpose is accomplished."[39] Johnson has rightly called for "a pneumatological interpretation of continuous creation," one that recognizes the open-ended evolutionary process of creation in which the Spirit is constantly moving (Romans 8). This journey is mirrored in the human. "Beauty enjoyed [appreciated] and en-joyed [created], at its most profound, is also the taste and the partial realization of a cosmos about to be transformed. In other words, Beauty has an eschatological dimension. We taste the world-to-come in the en-joying of the world-that-is. We become part of the world-to-come by imagining it into being."[40]

* * *

The creatureliness of human beings must command the first and most prominent word in our self-understanding, particularly in our understanding of our place in the community of creatures and in the cosmos. Only this kind of model has the possibility of consistently keeping at the forefront both the ultimate origins of all creatures as well as the final end for which God ordained them—in other words, a robust eschatological hope. If, as people of faith, we turn away from this view, then we limit our capacity to resist the environmental destruction affecting our generation and future generations. Appreciating our creaturehood and cultivating our anagogical imagination sets us on a path of discerning and orienting our vision toward the greatest good, truth, and beauty: God.

39. Johnson, *Ask the Beasts*, 179.
40. García-Rivera, *Garden of God*, 103.

18

Reimagining Eschatology: Toward Healing and Hope for a World at the *Eschatos*

Barbara R. Rossing

My little daughter is at the *eschatos*. Come lay your hands on her, in order that she may be healed and live.

—Mark 5:23

On either side of the river is the tree of life . . . and the leaves of the tree are for the healing of the nations.

—Revelation 22:2

"Why has faith for most Christians through most of their history come down simply to this: the hope for an *after*life rather than for *life itself*?"[1] This question posed by Catherine Keller sets the direction for eschatology in the face of global climate injustice.

We can employ a feminist liberation lens of hope and healing in

---

1. Catherine Keller, "Eschatology, Ecology, and a Green Ecumenacy," in *Reconstructing Christian Theology*, ed. Rebecca S. Chopp and Mark Lewis Taylor (Minneapolis: Fortress, 1994), 331.

order to reimagine the constellation of doctrines that has come to be labeled eschatology. Two Scripture verses—Mark 5:23 and Revelation 22:2—suggest a possible trajectory that has been largely overlooked in eschatological thinking: the trajectory of healing for our world. In our context of planetary crisis, when climate change represents the largest public health crisis humans have ever faced, the trajectory of healing becomes urgent.[2]

In the gospels, eschatology and healing are deeply connected in ways we have not always seen. "My daughter is at the *eschatos*," the synagogue leader Jairus implores Jesus (Mark 5:23). "Come heal her!" *Eschatos* means the "end" or "ultimate." It also means the edge, the brink. "At the point of death" is how English translations typically translate the reference in Mark 5:23 (RSV, NRSV). We and the biosphere, like the daughter, are at the point of death—the *eschatos*. We need healing! We need God to lay hands on us so that we might be saved. Come heal us.

Life on the Edge (*Eschatos*) of Climate Change

That *eschatos* or point of death became a reality for two native island villages in 2016—Isle de Jean Charles in the Gulf of Mexico and the Alaskan village of Shishmaref on the Chukchi Sea. Their inhabitants have officially become the United States' first "climate refugees." Isle de Jean Charles, home of the Biloxi-Chitimacha-Choctaw tribe, has lost more than 90 percent of its land due to sea-level rise. "Once our island goes, the core of our tribe is lost," says Chantel Comardelle, the deputy tribal chief's daughter. "We've lost our whole culture."[3]

Battered by catastrophic storm surges and erosion, the six-hundred member Inupiat village of Shishmaref, Alaska, voted in August 2016 to leave their ancestral island village and seek to relocate to safer ground. "Life on the edge of climate change" is how Esau Sinnok, a youth leader in Shishmaref Lutheran Church, describes his community's agonizing decision to relocate. Lives have been lost due to thin ice. Homes have fallen off cliffs. "It really hurts knowing that your only home is going to be gone," says Sinnok. "You won't hunt, fish, and carry on traditions

---

2. In 2009, the prestigious British medical journal *The Lancet* identified climate change as "the biggest global health threat in the 21st century." See Anthony Costello et al., "Managing the Health Effects of Climate Change," *The Lancet* 373 (2009): 1693–733. In 2014, the *Journal of the American Medical Association* made a similar point. See Howard Bauchner and Phil Fontanarosa, "Climate Change: A Continuing Threat to the Health of the World's Population," *Journal of the American Medical Association* 312, no. 15 (2014): 1519–77.
3. Carolyn Van Houten, "The First Official Climate Refugees in the U.S. Race against Time," *National Geographic*, May 25, 2016, http://tinyurl.com/lx5rswu.

the way that you're accustomed to and that your people have done for centuries."[4] The church's cemetery, with graves of hundreds of village ancestors, will likely not be moved.

The cruelest injustice for such communities of people living on the edge of climate change is this: The poorest and most vulnerable people of the world—people living near the tropics and polar regions—pay the highest price. Those who did the least to cause the crisis are its first victims.

The task of reimagining eschatology at the point of death must speak to those who have been displaced in our world, as Vítor Westhelle's *Eschatology and Space* insists.[5] It must speak to the people of Shishmaref and Isle de Jean Charles, to all who cry out for land and justice in this life. Reimagining eschatology must correct our tendency to discount this life on Earth in favor of an afterlife, as identified by Keller.

The world crossed an eschatological threshold in 2016: we became the final generation of humans to ever breathe air with concentrations of carbon dioxide under 400 parts per million. Carbon dioxide levels have increased by more than 40 percent since the advent of the Industrial Revolution, caused by the burning of fossil fuels. Now that the word "irreversible" begins to be used in scientific reports about climate change, science itself becomes eschatological.[6]

The *eschatos*, or "edge of the world," at which we are living is the subject of environmental scientist Gus Speth's sobering 2008 book, *The Bridge at the Edge of the World*. With stark graphs, Speth illustrates that "edge" of the world as the unsustainable growth from the beginning of the Industrial Revolution until today of sixteen indicators, including carbon dioxide concentration, water use, species extinction, fisheries exhaustion, fertilizer consumption, loss of tropical forests, and population growth. We are at "peak everything." What we need is a "bridge" that will safely help us cross over from crisis to sustainability. My thesis is that eschatology, reimagined, can help us find that bridge. It can help us cross over to healing for ourselves and our world.

---

4. Esau Sinnok, "Life on the Edge of Climate Change," *Sierra Magazine*, November/December 2015.

5. Vítor Westhelle, *Eschatology and Space: The Lost Dimension in Theology Past and Present* (New York: Palgrave/Macmillan, 2012).

6. Joby Warrick and Chris Mooney, "Effects of Climate Change 'Irreversible,' U.N. Panel Warns in Report," *Washington Post*, November 2, 2014. "'Continued emission of greenhouse gases will cause further warming and long-lasting changes in all components of the climate system, increasing the likelihood of severe, pervasive and irreversible impacts,' concluded the report by the United Nations' Intergovernmental Panel on Climate Change (IPCC)."

Eschatological Imagination: Hope

Eschatology speaks about hope. The term "eschatology" is itself a recent theological term, as Antje Jackelén notes.[7] Eschatological language is fundamentally "playful language," Krister Stendahl underscores.[8] It is metaphorical language, full of images, unlike abstract language. While eschatologies can be classified according to multiple types—whether realized, inaugurated, or consistent eschatology; premillennialist or postmillennialist; transcendental, process, liberationist, apocalyptic, and more—such efforts to categorize also founder. Too much systematizing of eschatologies runs the risk of "cutting Christian eschatology off from its imaginative roots, from its links to the past, and from its relevance to popular religious longings."[9]

Eschatological imagination draws on visual images. We are an image-driven culture, as was the ancient Roman world in which Jesus and the earliest communities of his followers lived. Visual images—both problematic and positive—have dominated Western Christian eschatology.

Eschatology speaks about imagined futures. The question of eschatology is so critical for spiritual life because it gives people a sense of hope for the future. Our eschatologies—conscious or unconscious—shape how we live our lives in the present. Yet our culture's multiple competing eschatologies no longer work for us. The so-called escapist rapture is one problematic eschatology today.[10] Even more problematic is the economic eschatology of endless growth, what Naomi Klein calls "winner-take-all capitalism."[11] Dystopic eschatological story lines such as *The Hunger Games* and zombie narratives reveal the depth of young people's despair for the future. We need positive, constructive eschatological visions of shared futures, so that we can move toward the future with hope.

Christian eschatology must speak of a new creation that is "both transcendently new and yet in continuity with this creation, since it

---

7. The term eschatology has been in use in Protestant dogmatics only since the seventeenth century, and in the English language only since the nineteenth century. For Catholics and Orthodox, the term is even more recent. See Antje Jackelén, *Time and Eternity: The Question of Time in Church, Science, and Theology* (Philadelphia: Templeton Foundation, 2005), 198–203. Jackelén, the first female archbishop of the Church of Sweden, coauthored the *Bishops Letter on the Climate* and advocates for climate justice through the World Council of Churches and Lutheran World Federation.
8. Krister Stendahl, "On Earth as It Is in Heaven—Dynamics in Christian Eschatology," in *The Eschaton: A Community of Love*, ed. Joseph Papin (Villanova, PA: Villanova University Press, 1971), 62.
9. Carol Zaleski, *The Life of the World to Come: Near-Death Experience and Christian Hope* (New York: Oxford University Press, 1996), 13.
10. Barbara Rossing, *The Rapture Exposed: The Message of Hope in the Book of Revelation* (Boulder, CO: Westview, 2004).
11. Sam Mowe, "Capitalism vs. the Climate," *Tricycle*, Fall 2015, http://tinyurl.com/lukx5el.

is the renewal of this world."[12] For this we need imagination. Visionaries and dreamers employ images that point beyond literal meanings. The Rev. Dr. Martin Luther King Jr., for example, drew on Revelation's vision of the New Jerusalem to inspire hope among poor people in American cities in the 1960s.

Eschatological imagination creates a counterworld, because "hope's greatest power is to negate the negatives of present experience," as Richard Bauckham notes. New Testament authors drew on images to confront the "negatives" of the Roman imperial narrative, boldly declaring an imminent "end" to this present evil age. So too, for us today, the Bible can offer positive alternatives to our own cultures' multiple "negatives"—whether to the religion of unfettered economic growth or to other eschatological narratives.

In employing the term "reimagining," I situate this essay in the trajectory of global feminist theologians, including Grace Ji-Sun Kim's challenge that "reimagining is not a one-time act but a continuous process." I work with the idea of "eschatological imagination" as described by Andrea Bieler and Luise Schottroff in their work on eucharistic imagination.[13] Such a practice of eschatological imagination can also be developed ecologically. As Sallie McFague underscores in her essay in this collection, imagination is "critical to changing the world." It is our human faculty of imagination that "helps us think in new ways."[14] This is important because the planetary crisis we face is not primarily a scientific crisis, nor even a moral crisis. Rather, as Naomi Klein describes it, our crisis is a narrative crisis: it is a crisis of imagination.

I will begin by exploring the diversity of New Testament and early Christian eschatologies, seeking especially the imagery and voices of women, where echoes might be retrieved. I will then address the question of how the wonderfully diverse landscape of New Testament eschatologies came to be reduced for much of Christian history to the last judgment, a problematic image for today. I will contextualize the first-century background of New Testament eschatologies—including the last judgment throne image—as resistance to the Roman Empire's eschatological propaganda. Finally, I will propose how broadening the

---

12. Richard Bauckham, "Conclusion: Emerging Issues in Eschatology in the Twenty-First Century," in *Oxford Handbook of Eschatology*, ed. Jerry Walls (Oxford: Oxford University Press, 2008), 681.

13. Andrea Bieler and Luise Schottroff, *The Eucharist: Bodies, Bread, and Resurrection* (Minneapolis: Fortress, 2007), esp. 15–48. See also Luise Schottroff, "Celebrating God's Future: Feminist Reflections on the Eschatology of Jesus," in *Time—Utopia—Eschatology*, ed. Charlotte Methuen, Yearbook of the European Society of Women in Theological Research (Leuven: Peeters, 1999), 7–15.

14. Sallie McFague, "Reimagining the Triune God for a Time of Global Climate Change," chapter 5 in this book.

landscape of eschatology to include traditions of paradise and healing can help us face the crisis of climate change today. My goal is to reclaim overlooked, sometimes subverted biblical texts and images that may serve us in new ways.

The Diverse Landscape of Biblical
and Early Christian Eschatologies

The New Testament offers a huge diversity of voices and ways early Christian communities worked out their vision of the future, of the reign of God and salvation. We do not need to try to harmonize the diverse views. Nor should we posit any "opposition between creation and eschatology, as though the eschatological kingdom comes to abolish and replace creation."[15] New Testament eschatologies are diverse, and all of them ground their eschatology in the Hebrew Bible's affirmation of the world as God's good creation.

The eschatological imagery of birthing and labor pains (ōdinō, Rev 12:2) figures prominently in Hebrew Bible and New Testament apocalyptic texts, as imagery of vulnerability and hope. The world is about to turn. We and the whole creation participate in this birth together. God co-groans and co-labors with us and with creation (Rom 8:22), the apostle Paul writes, using the Greek prefix syn to underscore solidarity. In the gospels, Jesus likewise uses feminine birth pain imagery to portray the urgent end of the unjust system and the turning of the world (Mark 13:8; Matt 24:8). The image of the pregnant woman connotes a "space and time of active waiting."[16] Revelation 12 gives us the most dramatic eschatological picture of the world's liberation portrayed as a woman laboring to give birth. The heavenly woman gives birth to the Messiah, who is rescued from the dragon by the female figure of Earth. Ecologically, we can draw on such biblical imagery of new birth and the agony of labor pains to frame our own painful experiences of crossing over from crisis to sustainability. Birth imagery proclaims rescue and new life, in the face of danger and death.

The Gospel of John, like Colossians, proclaims a more "realized eschatology," in contrast to the earliest Pauline letters that emphasize

---

15. See Richard Bauckham, *Living with Other Creatures: Green Exegesis and Theology* (Waco, TX: Baylor University Press, 2011), 72. "The kingdom of God in the teaching of Jesus represents not the abolition but the renewal of creation."

16. See Anne Elvey, *An Ecological Feminist Reading of the Gospel of Luke: A Gestational Paradigm* (Studies in Women and Religion; Lewiston, NY: Edwin Mellen, 2005), 112. On pregnant body imagery informing an ecological reading of eschatology see also Elaine Wainwright, *Habitat, Human, and Holy: An Eco-Rhetorical Reading of the Gospel of Matthew* (The Earth Bible Commentary Series; Norman Habel, ed., Sheffield: Sheffield Phoenix, 2016).

"not yet." Second- and third-generation followers of Jesus began to think that they were already living in eternal life. The Gospel of John says that knowing Jesus is to already have eternal life (John 17:3). The way the Gospel of John transforms future-oriented eschatology into a more present or realized understanding of resurrection is articulated in Martha's conversation with Jesus about resurrection (John 11). Eternal life in the Gospel of John is not life after death but rather a quality of life, something we can experience already now through relationships. Jesus himself becomes the resurrection and the life.

Closely related to eternal life in John's Gospel is abundant life. Jesus's promise in the Shepherd Discourse, "I came that they might have life, and have it abundantly" (John 10:10), may represent the most ecologically wonderful biblical promise for us today.[17] The key question becomes how to understand abundance. In John's Gospel, abundance is very different from our culture's model of abundance. We must look to the story of the feeding of the five thousand, where the same word "abundant" (*perisseusonta*) describes the overflowing baskets of bread (John 6:12). Abundance counters hungry people's perceptions of scarcity with God's generosity and sharing. The Gospel of John can help us reimagine abundant life economically and ecologically as an eschatology for all, replenishing us and the creation, rather than hoarding and insatiably consuming the planet's resources.[18]

Matthew's eschatology, different from John's Gospel, has sometimes been viewed as heaven-focused, since the phrase "kingdom of heaven" replaces Mark's "kingdom of God." As in all the Synoptic Gospels, Jesus's teaching about the kingdom represents the renewal of creation, not its abolition. Matthew's Gospel reflects a strikingly Earth-focused future vision, with the promise to the women that Jesus "goes ahead of" them into Galilee (Matt 28:7), and that "I am with you always" (Matt 28:20). Unlike the ascension trajectory of Luke-Acts, Matthew's Jesus does not ascend from Earth to heaven. "Jesus is going ahead—not going away," notes Elisabeth Schüssler Fiorenza about Matthew's Gospel. The "empty tomb does not signify absence but presence: It announces the Resurrected One's presence on the road ahead, in a particular space

---

17. For ecological readings of John's Gospel, see for example Susan Miller, "'I Came That They May Have Life and Have It Abundantly' (John 10:10): An Ecological Reading of John's Gospel," *Expository Times* 124, no. 2 (2012): 64–71; Celia Deane-Drummond and Barbara Rossing, "The Eco-Theological Significance of John 10:10: Abundant Life through the Sabbath, Trinitarian Vestiges, and the Tree of Life," *Ecumenical Review* 65, no. 1 (2013): 83–97; Margaret M. Daly-Denton, *John: An Earth Bible Commentary: Supposing Him to Be the Gardener* (London: Bloomsbury, 2017).

18. Economists Raj Patel and Tim Jackson help frame abundant life in terms of economic and environmental sustainability. Raj Patel, *The Value of Nothing: How to Reshape Market Society and Redefine Democracy* (New York: Picador, 2010); Tim Jackson, *Prosperity without Growth: Economics for a Finite Planet* (London: Earthscan, 2009).

of struggle and recognition."[19] Matthew's Gospel also gives an ethical focus to eschatology, especially with the parables. Process theologian Seung Gap Lee proposes that we include the creation itself among "the least of these" in the parable of the sheep and goats in Matthew 25, to expand this parable for "ecoeschatology."[20] Most important is Matthew's urgent prayer for God's reign "on Earth as in Heaven," over-coming any dualism between heaven and Earth.[21]

Luke's Gospel expands eschatology with wonderful imagery: feasting together in the kingdom of God (Luke 13:29) and dwelling in the bosom of Abraham (Luke 16:22). Along with Jesus's promise to the thief on the cross, "Today you will be with me in paradise" (Luke 23:43), these images fueled much eschatological speculation in medieval and Refor-mation theology, including whether purgatory was a temporary rest-ing place and whether there really would be eating in heaven. For planetary solidarity, we need both the promise of paradise for "today" and also the ethical urgency of seeing the hungry neighbor at the gate.

The eschatology of Revelation is both ecologically rich and challeng-ing. Waters and other natural elements speak, represented by angels or messengers, participating in judgment and salvation. The Earth her-self, imagined as a female figure, comes to the rescue of the woman (Rev 12:16). Yet, scenes of ecological destruction and cosmic catastro-phe fill this book. The key is to remember that violence against cre-ation represents not God's violence but Rome's violence, the conse-quences of the empire's rapacious system spinning out of control. The New Jerusalem vision of Revelation 21–22 brings heaven down to Earth, making all things "new," in the most expansive eschatological vision of the entire New Testament.[22] The healing leaves of the tree of life give us the core image for reimagining eschatology as healing.

The question of the specific role of women in the development of early Christian eschatology poses an intriguing problem. Women were

19. Elisabeth Schüssler Fiorenza, *Jesus: Miriam's Child, Sophia's Prophet* (New York: Continuum, 1995), 126.
20. Seung Gap Lee, "The Hope of the Earth: A Process Ecoeschatology for South Korea," in *Ecospirit: Religions and Philosophies for the Earth*, ed. Laurel Kearns and Catherine Keller (New York: Fordham University Press, 2007), 406. Lee cites David Ray Griffin, "A Process Theology of Creation," *Mid-Stream* 1–2 (Fall–Winter 1973–74): 70.
21. Vicki Balabanski, "An Earth Bible Reading of the Lord's Prayer: Matthew 6:9–13," in Norman Habel, ed., *Readings from the Perspective of Earth* (The Earth Bible 1; Sheffield: Sheffield Phoenix, 2000), 151–61.
22. New creation is a theme in Paul's letters to Galatians (Gal 6:15) and 2 Corinthians that holds promise for ecological eschatology. See David G. Horrell, Cherryl Hunt, and Christopher South-gate, *Greening Paul: Rereading the Apostle in a Time of Ecological Crisis* (Waco, TX: Baylor University Press, 2010). For the new creation image of 2 Corinthians in preaching, see Jan Schnell Rippentrop, "Reconciliation—The Love of Christ Compels Us: 2 Corinthians 5:14–20," *Ecumenical Trends* 45, no. 9 (2016): 10.

central in prophetic movements.[23] The book of Acts includes women in the prophetic succession of the "last" (*eschatai*) days: "In the last days . . . your sons and your daughters shall prophesy" (Acts 2:17; quoting from Joel 2:28–29). The four prophesying daughters of Philip gave prophetic leadership to the community in Caesarea (Acts 21:9). The ecstatic prophets in the Corinthian assembly were likely women (1 Cor 12–14), representing a more mystical eschatology in which resurrection was experienced as already present.[24] Yet, it is difficult to identify specific women's eschatological voices in the New Testament. Beginning in the second century, the grassroots New Prophecy movement (Montanism) was led by two women prophets, Maximilla and Priscilla.[25] Their prophecies took the form of oracular eschatological visions, proclaiming that God was acting on behalf of suffering people and that New Jerusalem would descend to Earth. In the third century, Perpetua and Felicity, perhaps the most famous of Christian martyrs, narrated prophetic visions of heaven, articulating a strong visionary trajectory of eschatology in the face of persecution.

Within the huge range of New Testament and early Christian eschatologies, we also note several striking absences. Nowhere do we find the idea that the purpose of life is to go to heaven after death. That idea of leaving Earth to go to heaven after death, which has become so prevalent in the popular mind-set, is rather a Platonist eschatology, as the New Testament scholar N. T. Wright has pointed out.[26] Similarly, the supposed delay of the parousia was not a primary focus of eschatology,[27] nor do we find the idea that the Earth as God's creation must be destroyed.[28] "Second coming" is not a term found anywhere in the New Testament.

---

23. Anne Jensen, *God's Self-Confident Daughters: Early Christianity and the Liberation of Women* (Louisville: Westminster John Knox, 2006), 127; Barbara Rossing, "Prophets, Prophetic Movements, and the Voices of Women," in *Christian Origins*, ed. Richard Horsley, vol. 1 of *A People's History of Christianity* (Minneapolis: Fortress, 2005), 261–86.

24. Antoinette Clark Wire, *The Corinthian Women Prophets: A Reconstruction Through Paul's Rhetoric* (Minneapolis: Fortress, 1990); Laura Nasrallah, *An Ecstasy of Folly: Prophecy and Authority in Early Christianity*, Harvard Theological Studies 52 (Cambridge, MA: Harvard Divinity School, 2003).

25. See Christine Trevett, *Montanism: Gender, Authority, and the New Prophecy* (Cambridge: Cambridge University Press, 1996).

26. See N. T. Wright, *Surprised by Hope: Rethinking Heaven, the Resurrection, and the Mission of the Church* (New York: HarperOne, 2008), 18–19; see also N. T. Wright, "Jesus Is Coming—Plant a Tree!," in *The Green Bible*, ed. Michael G. Maudlin and Marlene Baer (New York: HarperOne, 2008), 1–72.

27. See Vicky Balabanski, *Eschatology in the Making: Mark, Matthew and the Didache* (Cambridge: Cambridge University Press, 1997), esp. 4–10, "The Problem of the Delay of the Parousia: A Modern Construct?," for a review of the history of eschatological scholarship on this question.

28. The one exception is 2 Peter 3. Otherwise, the New Testament references destruction not of the Earth itself but of evildoers. See Barbara Rossing, "Hastening the Day When the Earth Will Burn? Global Warming, 2 Peter 3 and Revelation," in *The Bible in the Public Square: Reading the Signs of the Times*, ed. Cynthia Briggs Kittredge, Ellen Aitken, and Jonathan Draper (Minneapolis: Fortress, 2008), 25–38.

My point is this: We do not need to try to systematize or harmonize the various biblical eschatologies. Multiple eschatologies can all be "true," and indeed, like biodiversity, we may need the rich diversity of all the different perspectives to face our own future.

The Last Judgment, Hell, Heaven, and Threats of Punishment: Patriarchal Eschatological Imagination

Since the Middle Ages, however, the diversity of biblical imagination about eschatology has been collapsed into the single dominant end-times imagery of the last judgment. The focus has become the individual's afterlife—hell or heaven—with the individual's soul leaving Earth to go up to heaven or descend into hell.

The last judgment portrays God's great white throne of judgment from Revelation 20:11, combined with the judgment imagery of the sheep and goats from Matthew 25:31–46. The throne scene of Revelation 20 is by no means the central scene of judgment in Revelation, yet medieval theology made it the focus. Church art and sculpture portrayed this scene, visually threatening people with eternal hellfire. Above the entrance door to the twelfth-century Cathedral of St. Lazare in Autun, France, for example, a terrified crowd waits before God's throne, with tiers of graphic punishments for the damned on Christ's left side and the blessings of eternal life for those on his right side. Michelangelo's painting of the last judgment, influenced by Dante's *The Inferno*, occupies the most prominent wall in the Sistine Chapel at the Vatican in Rome.[29]

Paintings of the last judgment, known as "doom" paintings, became especially popular in England in the thirteenth century. In J. L. Carr's novel *A Month in the Country*, a young art conservationist hired to uncover a painting in the back of the country church knew even before he removed the whitewash that the painting was likely a last judgment: "It was bound to be a Judgment because they always got the plum spot where parishes couldn't avoid seeing the God-awe-full things that would happen to them."[30] Last judgment or "doom" scenes show "Christ in Majesty refereeing and, down below, the Fire that flameth evermore."[31]

As feminists note, the medieval image of the last judgment represents pure patriarchy, a vengeful Jesus sitting on the throne with God,

---

29. For the influence of Dante's *Inferno* on Michelangelo's *The Last Judgment*, see Paul Barolsky, "The Visionary Art of Michelangelo in the Light of Dante," *Dante Studies* 114 (1996): 1–14.
30. J. L. Carr, *A Month in the Country* (New York: New York Review Books, 2000), 17.
31. Ibid.

portrayed as an old white man. Healing, restoration, and renewal have no part in this picture. The function of the eschatological image of the judge on the throne was to terrify individuals into good behavior, like the dreadful Christmas song "Santa Claus is coming to town." Jesus is coming, and "He knows if you've been bad or good, so be good for goodness' sake." Schüssler Fiorenza gives a helpful analysis of the dual use of apocalyptic imagery in early Christian texts. Rhetorically, such imagery could function in either of two different ways: on the one hand, to use fear to control the behavior of individuals (as with the apocryphal Apocalypse of Peter and Apocalypse of Paul), on the other hand, to provide an alternative vision and promote community solidarity in the face of oppression (as with Revelation).[32] Unfortunately, the individualistic, moralistic function came to prevail in later patristic and medieval texts.

Political rulers, too, overtly used the last judgment to control the behavior of their subjects. In Venice, for example, a painting in the ruler's palace depicts scenes of military battles and victories, as well as the pope, culminating with the last judgment. The threatening message is clear: in order to avoid punishment in this life and the fires of hell in the afterlife, people must obey the church and the government.

No wonder that many feminist theologians express unease about the whole doctrine of eschatology, with such a focus on judgment and coercive fear. This system of eschatology is fraught with problems.

Heavenism

Eschatology that fixates on the last judgment and the afterlife is especially problematic in the face of the planetary crisis we face today. The visual picture of individuals being judged for their individual sins *cannot account for structural sin*. Conceptually, it fails to speak to the cruel structural injustice of climate change: that judgment falls not on those who sinned or caused the problem but on the poorest and most vulnerable people of our world.

Moreover, when salvation is imaged as the soul going to heaven after death, this can lead to the escapist eschatological thinking of "this world is not my home." "Heavenism" is a term coined by one biblical scholar to critique this view.[33]

---

32. See Elisabeth Schüssler Fiorenza, "The Phenomena of Early Christian Apocalyptic: Some Reflections on Method," in *Apocalypticism in the Mediterranean World and the Near East: Proceedings of the International Colloquium on Apocalypticism, Uppsala, August 12–17, 1979*, ed. David Hellholm (Tübingen: Mohr, 1989), 313.

33. Norman Habel defines "Heavenism" as "the belief that heaven, as God's home, is also the true home of Christians. . . . Earth, by contrast, is only a temporary 'stopping place' for Christians en

A T-shirt I saw in an airport with the acronym "BIBLE" endorses this problematic theology: "Basic Information Before Leaving Earth." The most extreme version of this theology is the fundamentalist embrace of the so-called "rapture," as embodied in the Left Behind novels and Hal Lindsey's *The Late, Great Planet Earth*. But even some traditional, non-rapture theology inscribes a kind of escapism that could be characterized as a kind of "Left Behind Lite." Wangari Maathai, Nobel Prize winner and founder of the tree-planting Green Belt movement, laments the damage that the idea of a future escape from Earth has caused:

> One song that is very popular for funerals in Kenya is "This World Is Not My Home," by the American Gospel music composer Albert E. Brumley. . . . While the vision of a better world beyond this one espoused in "This World Is Not My Home" might provide comfort to those who have lost someone they love . . . this song and some scriptures like it have been misused.[34]

Maathai adds, "The faithful would help themselves if they were to sing: 'This world *is definitely* my home,' and 'I'm *not* just passing through.'"[35]

Countering Rome's Eschatology of "Empire without End"

How did the patriarchal, white, throne image of the last judgment come to so dominate Western eschatology? And what alternative images can we lift up instead, to bring our eschatological focus from heaven and hell back to Earth?

First, it is important to say that Revelation's heavenly throne imagery originated as liberating imagery—as a daring counterimage to the Roman emperor's throne. The Hebrew prophets' scenes of God seated on the throne (Isa 6:1; Ezek 1:26; Dan 7:9) furnish the foundational biblical imagery, which Revelation shapes in deliberately anti-Roman ways, in a critique people would recognize.[36] Official Roman eschatology imaged the emperor sitting on the throne, ruling over the world forever. To that image, New Testament communities said "no." Only God is to be worshiped; only God sits on the throne, ruling the

route to heaven." See "Ecojustice Hermeneutics: Reflections and Challenges," in *The Earth Story in the New Testament*, ed. Norman C. Habel and Vicky Balabanski, Earth Bible 5 (London: Sheffield Academic Press, 2002), 3–4.

34. Wangari Maathai, *Replenishing the Earth: Spiritual Values for Healing Ourselves and the World* (New York: Doubleday, 2010), 122–23.

35. Ibid.

36. David Aune, "The Influence of Roman Imperial Court Ceremonial on the Apocalypse of John," *Biblical Research* 28 (1983): 5–26.

world. Questions of power and eschatology—"Who is the true Lord of this world? To whom does this earth belong?"—lie at the heart of Revelation, as Elisabeth Schüssler Fiorenza explains. "The book's central theological symbol is . . . the *throne*, signifying either *divine* and liberating power, or demonic and death-dealing power."[37]

Empire-critical interpretation of the Bible, one of the most important new approaches in biblical studies in the past thirty years, helps us see how early Christian communities critiqued the dominant Roman narrative. We now see that Jesus proclaimed the kingdom of God *over against the Roman imperial kingdom and its claims*. This includes Rome's eschatological claims. The Roman Empire promoted a vigorous political eschatology of *Roma Aeterna* (Rome as eternal), evidenced in its sculptures and art, religion, and official patriotic stories.

I saw this Roman eschatology firsthand my first year of graduate school on an archeological trip to Greece and Turkey. Everywhere we went we saw statues of Nike, the winged goddess of military victory. Shockingly brutal sculptures depict personified figures of captive nations, and even the Earth itself, being subjugated by Roman emperors. We saw inscriptions proclaiming Roman emperors as divine savior (*sotēr*), announcing the "good news" of Rome's "gospel" (*euangelion*), using the very same words as the birth of a savior, Jesus, in the Gospel of Luke—but for the birth of the emperor Augustus.

"World without end" for Rome meant "empire without end," in both the spatial sense of conquering the "ends of the earth" geographically and the temporal sense of lasting forever.[38] New Testament eschatological proclamations challenge head-on these Roman imperial eschatological claims. New Testament authors pronounce a "no" to the entire Roman eschatological narrative of eternal conquest and subjugation.

Pauline communities understood the time in which they were living to be the "end of the age." Such pronouncements about the "end of the age" (1 Cor 10:11) are not just vague end-of-the-world reminiscences that many of us grew up learning in Sunday school. Nor are they about going to heaven after you die. Paul and his coworkers are making daring anti-imperial pronouncements, undercutting the empire's eschatological propaganda of the "golden age" and "world without end." To understand Pauline eschatology, we must "recognize the ways in which Paul inserts many of the elements of his vivid eschatology within the larger domain of Roman rule and an imperial imagination."[39] Phrases such as "the rulers of this age who are doomed to per-

---

37. Elisabeth Schüssler Fiorenza, *Revelation: Vision of a Just World* (Minneapolis: Fortress, 1991), 58, 120.
38. Dieter Georgi, "Who Is the True Prophet?" *Harvard Theological Review* 79 (1986), 100–126.

ish" (1 Cor 2:6) referred the Roman political powers—as seen by the reference two verses later to the rulers' having crucified Jesus. Christ delivers us from "this evil age" (Gal 1:4), a not so veiled criticism of the Roman imperial order.

Similarly, the eschatology of Luke and the other Gospels is more anti-imperial than we have realized. In Jesus's apocalyptic discourse, and throughout all of Luke-Acts, the Greek word *oikoumenē*, often translated as "world," should be translated as "empire," making clear the anti-Roman echoes of the trauma of the Roman-Jewish war: "people will faint from fear and foreboding at what is coming upon the empire" (Luke 21:26). This translation shifts the end-times understanding to refer more to the end of the system of empire than to the end of the cosmos or the physical world. Similarly, in Acts, the "world" that is being turned upside down by Christ followers' mission is not the physical cosmos but rather the empire (*oikoumenē*, Acts 17:6).

While Revelation is the most overtly anti-Roman biblical text, the entire New Testament was written in a context where images of Roman imperial violence and propaganda of victory were all-pervasive, especially after the Jewish War and the reconquest of Jerusalem by Titus in 70 CE.

Rome's armies conquered other nations not only in order to take peoples captive but to take their lands and resources—their forests, farms, and minerals. Deforestation, extinctions, and environmental disaster were the result.[40] A text from 1 Maccabees about the conquest of Gaul (France) and Spain underscores the logic of Roman conquest in terms of natural resources and paying tribute:

> Judas heard of the fame of the Romans. . . . He had been told of their wars . . . among the Gauls, how they had defeated them and forced them to pay tribute, and what they had done in the land of Spain to get control of the silver and gold mines there. . . . They also subdued the kings who came against them from the ends of the earth, until they crushed them and inflicted great disaster on them; the rest paid them tribute every year. (1 Macc 8:1–4)

Roman eschatological rhetoric of eternal conquest and intimidation intensified after the destruction of Jerusalem in 70 CE. Outside the city gate of Antioch, Syria, for example,—the city where Matthew's Gospel may have been written—Emperor Titus set up bronze figures of cheru-

---

39. Harry O. Maier, *Picturing Paul in Empire: Imperial Image, Text and Persuasion in Colossians, Ephesians and the Pastoral Epistles* (London: Bloomsbury, 2013), 52.

40. J. Donald Hughes, *Pan's Travail: Environmental Problems of the Ancient Greeks and Romans* (Baltimore: Johns Hopkins University Press, 1996).

bim captured from the Jerusalem temple. On the gate facing toward Jerusalem, he now displayed a bronze figure of the moon and four bulls, a symbol of *Aeternitas*, making visual Rome's boast that it would rule forever.[41]

Imagine being a being a member of Matthew's community of Antioch after the war, looking each day at such blatant imperial propaganda proclaiming Roman eternity. At a time when Rome claimed eternal dominance over the whole world with slogans such as *Roma Aeterna,* the eschatological focus of the Gospels and other post-70 CE New Testament literature— including the heavenly throne imagery of Matthew 25 and Revelation 20—was aimed at giving people hope for a different future.

Visualizing Gender and Roman Imperial Eschatology of "World without End"

Davina Lopez and others analyze the iconography of one of the potent monuments of this eschatological ideology of eternal conquest from the first century, the Sebasteion of Aphrodisias in Asia Minor (Turkey), and its implications for interpreting the New Testament.[42] The sculptures of the Sebasteion vividly portray the gendered and sexualized dimensions of Roman conquest. Women's bodies represent enslaved nations; spectacular marble sculptures personify conquered lands as feminine bodies, showing graphic scenes of brutal rape and torture. To depict the conquest of Britain, the sculptor portrays Emperor Claudius holding down a half-naked woman with his knee, while pulling her head upwards so he can kill her. Similarly, the conquest of Armenia by Emperor Nero is represented by dragging an unconscious naked woman. "Personified Roma stands over a reclining *Ge* [Earth] and receives her bounty, indicating that the abundance of the land belongs to the victorious city of Rome."[43]

The Sebasteion monument is "deeply eschatological. The sun illuminated images of victory on its north side as it rose and set, and communicated a reign without end to the ends of the earth."[44]

The most overtly eschatological Roman monument may be Emperor

41. Glanville Downey, *A History of Antioch in Syria: From Seleucus to the Arab Conquest* (Princeton: Princeton University Press, 1961), 206; citing the sixth-century CE traveler Malalas.
42. Davina Lopez, *Apostle to the Conquered: Reimagining Paul's Mission* (Minneapolis: Fortress, 2008). See also Barbara Rossing, "Alas for the Earth: Lament and Resistance in Revelation 12," in Norman Habel and Shirley Wurst, eds., *The Earth Story in the New Testament* (*The Earth Bible*, vol. 5; Sheffield: Sheffield Academic Press, 2002).
43. Ibid., 46.
44. Maier, *Picturing Paul in Empire*, 52.

Trajan's Column in Rome, with its spiraling narrative that "reads like a modern-day comic strip," narrating the conquest of Romania (Dacia).[45] A kind of Tower of Babel, it makes a claim for Rome's rule extending upward toward the heavens, a vision of an eternal empire, "world without end." Scenes include graphic depictions of the conquest and cutting of forests, assaults on rivers, construction of bridges and siege works, mining of resources, looting of treasure, and overall, conquest of the Dacian landscape as part of the sequence of battles against the Dacian (Romanian) peoples. Erected in the center of Rome in 113 CE to celebrate the Dacian Wars of 101–2 and 105–6 CE, Trajan's Column was "a propaganda piece intended to be noticed and 'read' by the public."[46] Its 190-meter frieze of spiraling panels leads the viewer's gaze upward, unfolding the narrative of conquest. The statue of Emperor Trajan on top of the column, as well as explicitly religious aspects of the iconography, makes an eschatological claim for Rome's eternal conquest of the whole world. But biblical authors said "no" to those claims.

As Jürgen Moltmann reminds us, eschatology announces not the end of the world but "the end of the system of this world."[47] In order to reclaim the subversive power of New Testament eschatologies, and to reimagine eschatology today, we can learn from New Testament authors' critique of Rome's own eschatological propaganda. The stunning iconography of Roman conquest as proclaimed at the Sebasteion of Aphrodisias in Asia and on Trajan's Column in Rome can help us diagnose and respond to climate change and the "system of this world" that must come to an end. Today, similar ideologies of domination over the Earth's resources make claims that have eschatological ramifications for our world's future. Such a critique can guide us today, in the face of our own culture's multiple problematic imperial eschatologies, to announce "the end of the system of this world."

Eschatology as Resistance and Healing: The World Is About to Turn

The element of critique points us to an important dimension of eschatology so central also for the earliest Christians that we must reclaim today: eschatology is resistance. Eschatology—especially for women,

---

45. Andrew Curry, "Trajan's Amazing Column," *National Geographic*, April 2015, 121.

46. Arthur Dewey, "The Gospel of Trajan," in *Jesus, the Voice, and the Text: Beyond the Oral and the Written Gospels*, ed. Tom Thatcher (Waco, TX: Baylor University Press, 2008), 183.

47. Jürgen Moltmann, "Liberating and Anticipating the Future," in *Liberating Eschatology: Essays in Honor of Letty M. Russell*, ed. Margaret A. Farley and Serene Jones (Louisville: Westminster John Knox, 1999), 189.

and for enslaved and colonized peoples—is grounded in "struggle and resistance."[48] Eschatology recognizes that things are not how they are meant to be. The current situation is one in which unjust structures of power have temporarily taken over the world and its life—but this system will not last forever. As Mary's Magnificat sings, "the world is about to turn."[49]

The crisis of climate change is perhaps the most important reason we need an eschatology of resistance and healing today: because more and more people despair of all hope for the future. We live at an urgent "kairos moment," as Greek Orthodox Patriarch Archbishop Bartholomew describes. But it is not too late. Like the little daughter who is ill, who is at the *eschatos*, in Mark 5, we need healing.

There are multiple ways we could "frame" the climate crisis theologically. In terms of sin and forgiveness, we could frame climate change as a sin against the poor and against future generations for which we need to repent. Or we could talk about climate change as idolatry, the dangerous ways humans are "playing God" by altering the climate.[50] Both these frames are true. But I find that what best reaches people today is to frame the issues of climate in terms of sickness and healing. The world is ill; we are making ourselves sick. We need healing.

This coheres also with Yale 350 climate communication research by Anthony Leiserowitz and others about what persuades Americans to take action: framing of climate change in terms of health is more effective than guilt. When "climate change is introduced as a human health issue, a broad cross-section of audiences—even segments otherwise sceptical of climate science—find the information to be compelling and useful."[51] It also coheres with research about the devastating toll of climate change on human health. People are already getting sick and dying from climate change—whether from vector-borne pests such as zika and chikungunya, from cholera-contaminated water from floods,

---

48. Kwok Pui-lan, "Mending of Creation: Women, Nature, and Eschatological Hope," in Farley and Jones, *Liberating Eschatology*, 152.
49. Rory Cooney, "Canticle of the Turning," in *Evangelical Lutheran Worship* (Chicago: GIA Publications, 1980), hymn 723: "My heart shall sing of the day you bring, let the fires of your justice burn. Wipe away all tears, for the dawn draws near, and the world is about to turn."
50. See Bill McKibben, *The Comforting Whirlwind: God, Job, and the Scale of Creation* (Grand Rapids; Eerdmans, 1994).
51. Teresa A. Myers, Matthew C. Nisbet, Edward W. Maibach, and Anthony A. Leiserowitz, "A Public Health Frame Arouses Hopeful Emotions about Climate Change," *Climatic Change* 113, no. 3 (August 2012): 1105.

from heat stroke, or from drought-caused hunger.[52] The health effects will continue to become more devastating.

Health encompasses multiple dimensions of our lives. It is "not simply the absence of disease—it comprises a wide range of activities that foster healing and wholeness."[53] Public health and pastoral care practitioners describe health as something that embraces spiritual, physical, and environmental dimensions. This is the vision of Vergel Lattimore, an African American pastoral care professor and seminary president, who extends pastoral care insights on healing to creation care. What we need now, he says, is not just healing for our bodies and souls but also healing for the biosphere.[54]

As a biblical scholar, I find the framework of illness and healing helpful for addressing climate change because the Bible provides so many wonderful stories of healing—stories of Jesus who reaches out to sick people and heals them and stories of a God who wants to heal Israel's wounds. "I am the Lord your healer" (Exod 15:26) is a promise that permeates the entire Bible. The world is ill. But this is not the sickness unto death, as Jesus told Mary, Martha, and Lazarus (John 11). What Jesus does is help us both diagnose the world's ills and bring a message of healing and hope to these crises.

The framework of healing also coheres with recent research in the scientific fields of evolutionary anthropology and neuroscience. Compassion, cooperation, and altruism are attested in the human fossil record dating back at least 300,000 years, and perhaps much longer. Early humans cared for those who were disabled, as evolutionary anthropologist Penny Spikins's research has shown.[55] As early as 1.5 million years ago, skeletal remains of an archaic female suffering from hypervitaminosis suggest that "someone took care of her." Healed broken bones from many archaic human fossils in the Upper Palaeolithic record shows "extensive care of injured or incapacitated individuals."[56] The wisdom and imagination that evolved to draw on compassion's spiritual power for healing, and for becoming communities of healing,

52. See Aana Marie Vigen, "Living Advent and Lent: A Call to Embody Reformation for the Sake of Human and Planetary Health," in Eco-Reformation: Grace and Hope for a Planet in Peril, ed. Lisa E. Dahill and James B. Martin-Schramm (Eugene, OR: Wipf & Stock, 2016), 234–51. Vigen describes the three basic threats climate change poses to human health as "thirst, hunger, and bugs."

53. Emilie M. Townes, Breaking the Fine Rain of Death: African American Health Issues and a Womanist Ethics of Care (Eugene, OR: Wipf & Stock, 2006), 2.

54. Vergel Lattimore, "Pastoral Care Perspective" (Seminary Stewardship Alliance conference, September 12, 2014).

55. P.A. Spikins, H.E. Rutherford, A.P. Needham, "From Homininity to Humanity: Compassion from the Earlierst Archaics to Modern Humans," Time and Mind 32 (2010): 303–25.

56. Ibid, 311.

may be an important element of the evolution of human distinctiveness that can also help us respond to our current situation.

Reclaiming Paradise and Healing: Early Christian Eschatological Images

Early Christianity offers other eschatological images that can point us to healing today. In a remarkable reclaiming of eschatology, Rita Nakashima Brock and Rebecca Ann Parker in *Saving Paradise* explore the eschatology of Christian art, examining mosaics, catacomb paintings, frescoes, and sculptures. What they discover is the overwhelming representation of paradise traditions and healing. Not until the Middle Ages does the visual world of Christianity take up the scene of the last judgment. "In catacomb paintings, Jesus is never imaged as judge. A divide of the afterlife into heaven and hell is absent from Christianity's visual world until the medieval period."[57]

Catacomb paintings depict Jesus as healer and shepherd, as giving water of life to the Samaritan woman, and as healing the woman with the hemorrhage who touches his garments. Early Christian art loved scenes of baptism and Eucharist, loaves and fishes, vines and fruit, the Shepherd and Lamb, and Old Testament stories of Abraham, of Jonah and the fish. Sacramental "feasting in paradise" transformed early Christians' vision. As Brock and Parker observe:

> The assurance of paradise was an inebriating grace. . . . This assurance of salvation fueled Christian resistance to Roman oppression and sustained love for the world, despite its many difficulties. When Christians gathered to share of the bread of heaven, partaking the Eucharist feast, they entered the most concentrated form of paradise on earth, where living and dead communed with the risen Christ, and the banquet of abundance was spread for all. From feasting in paradise, they took strength to embody ethical grace in the world—the world that God so generously loved.[58]

Admittedly, in most studies of eschatology, healing is not a central concept. The index to *The Oxford Handbook of Eschatology* contains entries for heaven, paradise, and hell, but none for healing.[59] But "salvation" is certainly a word that has been central to studies of eschatology—and

57. Rita Nakashima Brock and Rebecca Ann Parker, *Saving Paradise: How Christianity Traded Love of this World for Crucifixion and Empire* (Boston: Beacon, 2009), 13.
58. Ibid., 55.
59. Similarly, neither Markus Mühling's *T&T Clark Handbook of Christian Eschatology* nor Brian Daley's *The Hope of the Early Church: A Handbook of Patristic Eschatology* include *healing* in the index.

salvation includes healing. The Greek word *sōzō*, often translated "save," first of all means "heal" or "make whole." My Greek students find this astounding. *Sōzō* characterizes the healing of the woman with the hemorrhage in Mark 5, as well as Jairus's daughter, in addition to passages about salvation. What we miss in English translations is that salvation includes healing. John 3:17, for example, could be translated as "For God did not send the Son to condemn the world, but in order that the world might be *healed* through him." Aana Vigen makes a similar argument about the Latin word *salus* and for the German *Heilung*, both important for Luther's understanding of salvation. "The Latin noun *salus* originally meant 'safety, welfare, health' before it came to denote 'salvation.' . . . The point is that in Reformation theology, *Heil*/salvation is intrinsically bound up with healing."[60]

Eschatological reimagining seeks to bring together the multiple dimensions of *sōzō* to encompass healing beyond physical healing. We can draw on a sometimes-overlooked tradition dear to Patristic theology and also to the Reformers, the tradition of *Christus Medicus* (Christ the Healer).[61] Augustine and the *Christus Medicus* tradition make the move in speaking of Christ's healing for the soul as well as the body. We must now add healing for the planet. What I propose is to take this biblical trajectory of salvation as healing in more eschatological, ecological, and social directions.

Feminist scholarship on healing in early Christianity can help. Elaine Wainwright suggests viewing Jesus as a healer within a broader movement of healing. People around Jesus shared a common spirit of prophecy and also "a common spirit of healing."[62] Today, eschatological imagination needs to lift up circles of healers who are renewing our world, embodying "a common spirit of healing."

Visualizing the Tree of Life for Healing Our World

Revelation's final vision of New Jerusalem is the Bible's most concrete eschatological vision, foundational for shaping hopes for a shared future that include renewal and healing. Revelation's tree of life, whose leaves are for the healing, can heal our world. The biblical tree of life

---

60. Vigen, "Living Advent and Lent," 240.
61. The identification of Christ as physician begins with Ignatius of Antioch ("For there is one physician . . . Jesus Christ, our Lord," Ignatius *Eph.* 7.2) and comes to the fore with Augustine. (See Rudolph Arbesmann, "The Concept of 'Christus Medicus' in St. Augustine," *Traditio* 10 [1954]: 1–28). Luther also loved the *Christus Medicus* metaphor. See Johann Anselm Steiger, *Medizinische Theologie: Christus medicus und theologia medicinalis bei Martin Luther und im Luthertum der Barockzeit*, SHCT 121 (Leiden: Brill, 2005).
62. Elaine M. Wainwright, *Women Healing/Healing Women: The Genderization of Healing in Early Christianity* (London: Equinox, 2006), 100.

first appears in Genesis, in the garden, and recurs in prophetic and apocalyptic literature and in wisdom literature. "Wisdom is a tree of life" in Proverbs. In Ezekiel 47, trees have leaves for healing, but the trees are not yet trees of life. It is Revelation that makes the crucial move to bring together Ezekiel's healing leaves with the tree of life in paradise.

Similarly, 4 Ezra, a Jewish apocalypse from the same time as Revelation: "For you is opened Paradise, planted the tree of life, the future Age prepared" (4 Ezra 8:52). And that tree brings healing: "Paradise, whose fruit endures incorruptible, wherein is delight and healing shall be made manifest" (4 Ezra 7:123). The imagery of healing draws from an earlier Jewish apocalypse, 1 Enoch's Book of the Watchers, where God sends the angel Raphael—whose name means "God has healed"—to heal the Earth: "And heal the earth, which the waters have desolated; and announce the healing of the earth, that the plagues may be healed" (1 Enoch 10:7).[63]

The tree of life became a multivalent symbol, combined with the cross of Christ in a number of patristic texts. Ephrem's *Hymns on Paradise*, a fourth-century collection of hymns, projects the paradise of Genesis into a future paradise, combining vine imagery as well as healing imagery: "The assembly of saints bears resemblance to Paradise: In it each day is plucked the fruit of Him who gives life to all; in it is trodden the cluster of grapes, to be the Medicine of life."[64]

Frances Young draws on art and images in her *Construing the Cross: Type, Sign, Symbol, Word, Action* to analyze early Christian understandings of the cross before atonement theories. Using a method she calls "theoria," or "seeing through," Young takes her cue from the poetic theology of fourth-century writer Ephrem the Syrian. She works through "imaginative engagement or storytelling rather than literalizing exegesis."[65] Especially helpful is the chapter on the image of the tree of life. Young traces what she calls "tree mania" in the twelfth and thirteenth centuries, as the tree of life became a medieval image for structuring the believer's contemplation of Christ's life, using the framework of Bonaventure's *Tree of Life* with its fruits. Healing is part of Bonaventure's understanding of the tree: "Picture in your mind a tree whose roots are watered by an ever-flowing fountain.... Imagine that the leaves are a most effective medicine to prevent and cure every kind

---

63. George W. E. Nickelsburg and James C. VanderKam, *1 Enoch: A New Translation Based on the Hermeneia Commentary* (Minneapolis: Fortress, 2004), 28.
64. St. Ephrem the Syrian, *Hymns on Paradise*, trans. Sebastian Brock (Crestwood, NY: St. Vladimir's Seminary Press, 1990), 6.8.111.
65. Frances Young, *Construing the Cross: Type, Sign, Symbol, Word, Action* (Eugene, OR: Cascade, 2015) p. xvii.

of sickness, because the word of the cross is the power of God for salvation."[66]

This is eschatology that can help us today. Wangari Maathai describes the power of trees to reveal both the eschatological wounds of our world and also the power of healing. Prophets today, in the tradition of John of Patmos, depict "an alternative to the degradation of the environment that has turned waters of life here and earth that were 'bright as crystal' into mud and silt, and the 'tree of life with its twelve kinds of fruit' into stumps and charcoal, and has led to nations not being healed but rather fighting one another for access to the remaining clean water and food supplies.... These prophets are asking why we do this to the earth, and they are commanding us to heal and replenish it now."[67]

Eschatology of Gratitude and Beauty: Healing for Ourselves

Eschatology must include justice, God's vindication for innocent sufferers. The waters in Revelation cry out for justice, and the martyrs cry out "How Long O Lord?" In formulating an eschatology of healing that can help us in a time of climate injustice and planetary solidarity, we need to broaden our images of justice and judgment to foreground scenes of judgment that can address structural sin. More central in Revelation than the throne judgment in Revelation 20 is the judgment of Babylon in Revelation 17–18, the fall of the entire Roman Empire imaged through an anticipatory funeral for the unjust economy. The three-fold laments for the rulers, the merchants, and the mariners (Rev 18:9–20) show a model we can emulate. Revelation draws the imagery of a funeral in advance from Isaiah 14, performatively enacting the end of the Roman economic system via satirical dirge songs, "Alas, alas, alas" (Rev 18:10, 16, 19). Revelation's funeral liturgy for Babylon/Rome is a funeral we also can perform to announce the "end of the system of this world" today, the fossil-fuel economy that devours lands and peoples.

But most of all, we need to find ourselves again in God's beauty. What Sally McFague wrote in 1993 about her own life is something I experience as well: "wonder helps sustain me."[68] Eschatology is about "hoping for more," as Deanna Thompson describes of her own cancer journey.[69] It is about luminous presence, mystical moments of the divine

---

66. Bonaventure, *The Tree of Life*, in *Bonaventure: The Soul's Journey into God, The Tree of Life, the Life of St. Francis*, trans. Ewert Cousins (New York: Paulist, 1978), 120.

67. Maathai, *Replenishing the Earth*, 125.

68. Sallie McFague, *The Body of God: An Ecological Theology* (Minneapolis: Fortress, 1993), 210.

breaking into our world. It is about apocalyptic ruptures in this world that reveal another world, God's world: world within world. It is about seeing God's *doxa* or glory as a radiant presence in our lives. Annie Dillard uses the word "transfigured." Richard Kearney call this sight "micro-eschatologies," drawing on the poetry of Gerard Manley Hopkins. Poets help us experience what Kearney calls "sundering," breaking open our sight so that we can see the "*eschaton* at the heart of things."[70]

World healing needs eschatological imagination that sees beauty and healing. When we can imagine our future healing, then we are able to move toward it. In Revelation, the future healing is imaged as New Jerusalem, with its world-healing tree of life. The goal is to see the future as "friend," as suggested by the subtitle of the Compassionate Eschatology Project of which I was a part.[71]

Maathai keeps our eschatology focused on the Earth God loves:

> I would hope that every preacher, imam, rabbi, guru, sensei, and priest would balance making sure we gain some surety over what happens after we die with an equal insistence on the preservation of the earth and our particular accountability for the survival of the planet's ecosystems: that we are not simply "passing through," as the Jim Reeves song states. When we do pass, we shall leave the planet to our children and our grandchildren.[72]

69. Deanna Thompson, "Hoping for More: How Eschatology Matters for Lutheran Feminist Theologies," in *Transformative Lutheran Theologies: Feminist, Womanist, and Mujerista Perspectives*, ed. Mary J. Streufert (Minneapolis: Fortress, 2010), 225–36.
70. Richard Kearney, "Epiphanies of the Everyday: Toward a Micro-Eschatology," in *After God: Richard Kearney and the Religious Turn in Continental Philosophy*, ed. John Panteleimon Manoussakis (New York: Fordham University Press, 2006), 18.
71. See Ted Grimsrud and Michael Hardin, eds., *Compassionate Eschatology: The Future as Friend* (Eugene, OR: Cascade, 2011).
72. Maathai, *Replenishing the Earth*, 147.

Select Bibliography

Alam, Mayesha, Rukmani Bhatia, and Briana Mawby. *Women and Climate Change: Impact and Agency in Human Rights, Security, and Economic Development*. Washington, DC: Georgetown Institute for Women, Peace and Security, 2015.

Amanze, James. *African Traditional Religion in Malawi: The Case of Bimbi Cult*. Blantyre: Christian Literature Association in Malawi, 2002.

Balabanski, Vicky. *Eschatology in the Making: Mark, Matthew and the Didache*. Cambridge: Cambridge University Press, 1997.

Bauckham, Richard. "Conclusion: Emerging Issues in Eschatology in the Twenty-First Century." In *The Oxford Handbook of Eschatology*, edited by Jerry L. Wallis, 680–81. Oxford: Oxford University Press, 2008.

_____. *Living with Other Creatures: Green Exegesis and Theology*. Waco, TX: Baylor University Press, 2011.

Bennett, Jane. *The Enchantment of Modern Life: Attachments, Crossings, and Ethics*. Princeton: Princeton University Press, 2001.

_____. *Vibrant Matter: A Political Ecology of Things*. Durham, NC: Duke University Press, 2010.

Bieler, Andrea, and Luise Schottroff. *The Eucharist: Bodies, Bread, and Resurrection*. Minneapolis: Fortress, 2007.

Boff, Leonardo. *Cry of the Earth, Cry of the Poor*. Maryknoll, NY: Orbis, 1997.

Brazal, Agnes, and Kochurani Abraham, eds. *Feminist Cyberethics in Asia: Religious Discourses on Human Connectivity*. New York: Palgrave Macmillan, 2014.

Briggman, Anthony. *Irenaeus of Lyons and the Theology of the Holy Spirit*. Oxford: Oxford University Press, 2012.

Brock, Rita Nakashima, and Rebecca Ann Parker. *Saving Paradise: How Christianity Traded Love of This World for Crucifixion and Empire*. Boston: Beacon, 2009.

Brock, Rita Nakashima, and Susan Brooks Thistlethwaite. *Casting Stones: Prostitution and Liberation in Asia and the United States*. Minneapolis: Fortress, 1996.

Brorby, Taylor, and Stefanie Brook Trout, eds. *Fracture: Essays, Poems and Stories on Fracking in America*. North Liberty, IA: Ice Cube, 2016.

Butler, Judith. *Giving an Account of Oneself.* New York: Fordham University Press, 2005.

Caputo, John D. *Hoping against Hope: Confessions of a Postmodern Pilgrim.* Minneapolis: Fortress, 2015.

_____. *The Weakness of God: A Theology of the Event.* Bloomington: Indiana University Press, 2006.

Caraher, William, and Kyle Conway. *The Bakken Goes Boom: Oil and the Changing Geographies of Western North Dakota.* Grand Forks: Digital Press at the University of North Dakota, 2016.

Carbine, Rosemary P., and Hilda P. Koster, eds. *The Gift of Theology: The Contribution of Kathryn Tanner.* Minneapolis: Fortress, 2015.

Carrasco, Davíd. *Religions of Mesoamerica: Cosmovision and Ceremonial Centers.* San Francisco: HarperSanFrancisco, 1990.

Christ, Carol P., and Judith Plaskow. *Womanspirit Rising: A Feminist Reader in Religion.* New York: HarperOne, 1992.

Chung, Meehyun. "Seeking the Lost Threefold Thoughts: Relationships with God, Earth and Human Beings." *Madang* 22 (December 2014): 115–36.

Cobb, John B. Jr., and Ignacio Castuera, eds. *For Our Common Home: Process-Relational Responses to* Laudato Si'. Anoka, MN: Process Century, 2015.

Conradie, Ernst M., Sigurd Bergmann, Celia Deane-Drummond, and Denis Edwards, eds. *Christian Faith and the Earth: Current Paths and Emerging Horizons in Ecotheology.* London: Bloomsbury, 2014.

Congar, Yves. *I Believe in the Holy Spirit: The Complete Three Volume Work in One Volume.* New York: Crossroads, 1997.

Coole, Diana, and Samantha Frost, eds. *New Materialisms: Ontology, Agency, and Politics.* Durham, NC: Duke University Press, 2010.

Daggers, Jenny, and Grace Ji-Sun Kim, eds. *Christian Doctrines for Global Gender Justice.* New York: Palgrave Macmillan, 2015.

Dahill, Lisa E., and James B. Martin-Schramm. *Eco-Reformation: Grace and Hope for a Planet in Peril.* Eugene, OR: Wipf & Stock, 2016.

Daneel, M. L. *The God of the Matopo Hills: An Essay on the Mwari Cult in Rhodesia.* The Hague: Mouton, 1970.

Dankelman, Irene. *Gender and Climate Change: An Introduction.* London: Earthscan, 2010.

Dozier, Verna J. *The Dream of God: A Call to Return.* Cambridge, MA: Cowley, 1991.

Eaton, Heather. *Introducing Ecofeminist Theologies.* London: T&T Clark, 2005.

Elmhirst, Rebecca. "Gender and Sustainability: Lessons from Asia and Latin America." *Gender & Development* 21, no. 2 (2013): 413–15.

Engelke, Matthew Eric. *A Problem of Presence: Beyond Scripture in an African Church.* Berkeley: University of California Press, 2007.

Farley, Margaret A., and Serene Jones, eds. *Liberating Eschatology: Essays in Honor of Letty M. Russell.* Louisville: Westminster John Knox, 1999.

Foucault, Michel. *The History of Sexuality Vol. I: An Introduction.* Translated by Robert Hurley. New York: Vintage, 1978.

Francis. *Laudato Si': On Care for Our Common Home.* Huntington, IN: Our Sunday Visitor, 2015.

Francis, and Sean McDonagh. *On Care for Our Common Home "Laudato Si'": The Encyclical of Pope Francis on the Environment.* Maryknoll, NY: Orbis, 2016.

Gallares, Judette A., and Astrid Lobo-Gajiwala, eds. *Practicing Peace: Feminist Theology of Liberation Asian Perspectives.* Quezon City, PHL: Claretian, 2011.

García-Rivera, Alejandro. *The Community of the Beautiful: A Theological Aesthetics.* Collegeville, MN: Liturgical, 1999.

———. *The Garden of God: A Theological Cosmology.* Minneapolis: Fortress, 2009.

———. *St. Martín de Porres: The "Little Stories" and the Semiotics of Culture.* Maryknoll, NY: Orbis, 1995.

Gebara, Ivone. *Longing for Running Water: Ecofeminism and Liberation.* Minneapolis: Fortress, 1999.

———. *Out of the Depths: Women's Experience of Evil and Salvation.* Translated by Ann Patrick Ware. Minneapolis: Fortress, 2002.

Gnanadason, Aruna. "Women, Economy and Ecology." In *Ecotheology: Voices from South and North,* edited by David G. Hallman, 179–85. Eugene, OR: Wipf & Stock, 2009.

Grey, Mary C. *Sacred Longings: The Ecological Spirit and Global Culture.* Minneapolis: Fortress, 2004.

Grosz, Elizabeth. *Space, Time, and Perversion: Essays on the Politics of Bodies.* New York: Routledge, 1995.

———. *Time Travels: Feminism, Nature, Power.* Durham, NC: Duke University Press, 2005.

Haraway, Donna J. *Simians, Cyborgs and Women: The Reinvention of Nature.* London: Free Association Books, 1991.

Harding, Sandra. *The Science Question in Feminism.* Milton Keynes, UK: Open University Press, 1986.

———. *Whose Science? Whose Knowledge? Thinking from Women's Lives.* Milton Keyes, UK: Open University Press, 1991.

Hartsock, Nancy C. M. *The Feminist Standpoint Revisited and Other Essays.* Boulder, CO: Westview, 1998.

Haught, John F. *God after Darwin: A Theology of Evolution.* Boulder, CO: Westview, 2000.

Heron, Alasdair I. C. *The Holy Spirit.* Philadelphia: Westminster, 1983.

Hessel, Dieter T., and Rosemary Radford Ruether, eds. *Christianity and Ecology: Seeking the Well-Being of Earth and Humans.* Cambridge, MA: Harvard University Press, 2000.

Horrell, David G., Cherryl Hunt, and Christopher Southgate. *Greening Paul:*

Rereading the Apostle in a Time of Ecological Crisis. Waco, TX: Baylor University Press, 2010.

Hughes, J. Donald. *Pan's Travail: Environmental Problems of the Ancient Greeks and Romans*. Ancient Society and History. Baltimore: Johns Hopkins University Press, 1996.

Irenaeus of Lyons. *Against Heresies*. Whitefish, MT: Kessinger, 2007.

Isherwood, Lisa, and Elizabeth Stuart. *Introducing Body Theology*. Cleveland: Pilgrim, 1998.

Jagose, Annamarie. *Queer Theory: An Introduction*. New York: New York University Press, 1996.

Jantzen, Grace M. *Julian of Norwich: Mystic and Theologian*. London: SPCK, 1987.

Jenkins, Katy. "Women, Mining, and Development: An Emerging Research Agenda." *The Extractive Industries and Society* 1, no. 2 (2014): 329–39.

Jensen, Anne. *God's Self-Confident Daughters: Early Christianity and the Liberation of Women*. Louisville: Westminster John Knox, 1996.

Joh, Wonhee Anne. *Heart of the Cross: A Postcolonial Christology*. Louisville: Westminster John Knox, 2006.

Johnson, Elizabeth A. *Ask the Beasts: Darwin and the God of Love*. London: Bloomsbury, 2014.

_____. *She Who Is: The Mystery of God in Feminist Theological Discourse*. New York: Crossroad, 1992.

Jones, Serene. *Feminist Theory and Christian Theology: Cartographies of Grace*. Minneapolis: Fortress, 2000.

Kärkkäinen, Veli-Matti. *Pneumatology: The Holy Spirit in Ecumenical, International and Contextual Perspective*. Grand Rapids: Baker Academic, 2002.

Kearns, Laurel, and Catherine Keller, eds. *Ecosprit: Religions and Philosophies for the Earth*. New York: Fordham University Press, 2007.

Keim, Christine. *Frauenmission und Frauenemanzipation: eine Diskussion in der Basler Mission im Kontext der frühen ökumenischen Bewegung 1901-1928*. Münster: Lit, 2005.

Keller, Catherine. *Cloud of the Impossible, Negative Theology and Planetary Entanglement*. Insurrections: Critical Studies in Religion, Politics, and Culture. New York: Columbia University Press, 2014.

_____. "Eschatology, Ecology, and a Green Ecumenacy." In *Reconstructing Christian Theology*, edited by Rebecca S. Chopp and Mark Lewis Taylor, 326–45. Minneapolis, Fortress, 1994.

_____. "Power Lines." In *Power, Powerlessness, and the Divine: New Inquiries in Bible and Theology*, edited by Cynthia L. Rigby, 59. Atlanta: Scholars Press, 1997.

_____. *On the Mystery: Discerning Divinity in Process*. Minneapolis: Fortress, 2008.

Kelly, Anthony. *Eschatology and Hope*. Theology in Global Perspectives. Maryknoll, NY: Orbis, 2006.

Keum, Jooseop, ed. *Together towards Life: Mission and Evangelism in Changing Land-scapes.* Geneva: World Council of Churches, 2013.

Kim, Grace Ji-Sun, ed. *Making Peace with the Earth: Action and Activism for Climate Justice.* Geneva: World Council of Churches, 2016.

Kim, Grace Ji-Sun, and Jenny Daggers, eds. *Reimagining with Christian Doctrines: Responding to Global Gender Injustices.* New York: Palgrave Macmillan, 2014.

Kolbert, Elizabeth. *The Sixth Extinction: An Unnatural History.* New York: Henry Holt, 2014.

LaDuke, Winona. *The Winona LaDuke Chronicles: Stories from the Front Lines in the Battle for Environmental Justice.* Edited by Sean Aaron Cruz. Ponsford, MN: Spotted Horse, 2016.

Leach, Melissa. "Earth Mother Myths and Other Ecofeminist Fables: How a Strategic Notion Rose and Fell." *Development and Change* 38, no. 1 (2007): 67–85.

Maathai, Wangari. *Replenishing the Earth: Spiritual Values for Healing Ourselves and the World.* New York: Doubleday, 2010.

McFague, Sallie. *Blessed Are the Consumers: Climate Change and the Practice of Restraint.* Minneapolis: Fortress, 2013.

———. *The Body of God: An Ecological Theology.* Minneapolis: Fortress, 1993.

———. *Models of God: Theology for an Ecological, Nuclear Age.* Philadelphia: Fortress, 1987.

———. *A New Climate for Theology: God, the World, and Global Warming.* Minneapolis: Fortress, 2008.

———. *Super, Natural Christians: How We Should Love Nature.* Minneapolis: Fortress, 1997.

McGuckin, John Anthony. *The Westminster Handbook to Patristic Theology.* Louisville: Westminster John Knox, 2004.

McKibben, Bill. *The Comforting Whirlwind: God, Job, and the Scale of Creation.* Grand Rapids; Eerdmans, 1994.

Mercer, Joyce Ann. "A Practical Theological Approach to Ecofeminism: Story of Women, Faith, and Earth Advocacy." In *Body Memories: Goddesses of Nusantara, Rings of Fire, and Narratives of Myth,* edited by Dewi Candraningrum, 93–106. Jakarta, IDN: Yayasan Jurnal Perempuan Press, 2014.

Merchant, Carolyn. *Reinventing Eden: The Fate of Nature in Western Culture.* New York: Routledge, 2004.

Miles, Margaret R. *The Word Made Flesh: A History of Christian Thought.* Malden, MA: Blackwell, 2005.

Min, Anselm. *The Solidarity of Others in a Divided World: A Postmodern Theology after Postmodernism.* New York: T&T Clark, 2004.

Moe-Lobeda, Cynthia D. *Resisting Structural Evil: Love as Ecological-Economic Vocation.* Minneapolis: Fortress, 2013.

Moltmann, Jürgen. *The Crucified God: The Cross of Christ as the Foundation and Criticism of Christian Theology.* Translated by R. A. Wilson and John Bowden. New York: Harper & Row, 1974.

_____. *God in Creation: An Ecological Doctrine of Creation.* Translated by M. Kohl. London: SCM, 1985.

Morton, Timothy. *The Ecological Thought.* Cambridge, MA: Harvard University Press, 2010.

_____. *Ecology without Nature: Rethinking Environmental Aesthetics.* Cambridge, MA: Harvard University Press, 2007.

Mukonyora, Isabel. *Wandering a Gendered Wilderness: Suffering and Healing in an African Initiated Church.* New York: Peter Lang, 2007.

Oduyoye, Mercy Amba. *Daughters of Anowa: African Women and Patriarchy.* Maryknoll, NY: Orbis, 2005.

Oh, Jea Sophia. *A Postcolonial Theology of Life: Planetarity East and West.* Upland, CA: Sopher, 2011.

Ott, Martin. *African Theology in Images.* Blantyre: Christian Literature Association in Malawi, 2000.

Pannenberg, Wolfhart. *The Apostles Creed in the Light of Today's Questions.* Translated by Margaret Kohl. Philadelphia: Westminster, 1972.

Phiri, Isabel Apawo. *Women, Presbyterianism and Patriarchy: Religious Experience of Chewa Women in Central Malawi.* Blantyre: Christian Literature Association in Malawi, 1997.

Phiri, Isabel Apawo, and Nada Sarojini, eds. *African Women, Religion, and Health: Essays in Honor of Mercy Amba Oduyoye.* Maryknoll, NY: Orbis, 2006.

Pöntinen, Mari-Anna. *African Theology as Liberating Wisdom: Celebrating Life and Harmony in the Evangelical Lutheran Church in Botswana.* Leiden: Brill, 2013.

Ranger, Shelagh. *The Word of Wisdom and the Creation of Animals in Africa.* Cambridge: James Clarke, 2007.

Rasmussen, Larry L. *Earth-Honoring Faith: Religious Ethics in a New Key.* Oxford: Oxford University Press, 2013.

Rossing, Barbara. "Hastening the Day When the Earth Will Burn? Global Warming, 2 Peter 3 and Revelation." In *The Bible in the Public Square: Reading the Signs of the Times,* edited by Cynthia Briggs Kittredge, Ellen Bradshaw Aitken, and Jonathan A. Draper, 25–38. Minneapolis: Fortress, 2008.

_____. "Prophets, Prophetic Movements, and the Voices of Women." In *Christian Origins,* edited by Richard Horsley, 261–86. Vol. 1 of *A People's History of Christianity.* Minneapolis: Fortress, 2005.

_____. *The Rapture Exposed: The Message of Hope in the Book of Revelation.* Boulder, CO: Westview, 2004.

Ruether, Rosemary Radford. *Sexism and God-Talk: Toward a Feminist Theology.* Boston: Beacon, 1983.

_____. *Womanguides: Readings toward a Feminist Theology*. Boston: Beacon, 1985.

_____, ed. *Women Healing Earth: Third World Women on Ecology, Feminism, and Religion*. Maryknoll, NY: Orbis, 1996.

Said, Edward W. *Orientalism*. New York: Vintage, 1994.

Schmidt, Elizabeth. *Peasant, Traders, and Wives: Shona Women in the History of Zimbabwe, 1870-1939*. Social History of Africa. Portsmouth, NH: Heinemann, 1992.

Schottroff, Luise. "Celebrating God's Future: Feminist Reflections on the Eschatology of Jesus." In *Time—Utopia—Eschatology*, edited by Charlotte Methuen, 7–15. Yearbook of the European Society of Women in Theological Research 7. Leuven: Peeters, 1999.

Schüssler Fiorenza, Elisabeth. *But She Said: Feminist Practices of Biblical Interpretation*. Boston: Beacon, 1992.

_____. *Jesus: Miriam's Child, Sophia's Prophet; Critical Issues in Feminist Christology*. New York: Continuum, 1995.

_____. *Revelation: Vision of a Just World*. Minneapolis: Fortress, 1991.

Shiva, Vandana. *Biopiracy: The Plunder of Nature and Knowledge*. Boston: South End, 2000.

_____, ed. *Manifestos on the Future of Food and Seed*. Cambridge, MA: South End, 2007.

_____. *Staying Alive: Women, Ecology and Development*. London: Zed, 2002.

Spivak, Gayatri Chakravorty. "Can the Subaltern Speak?" In *Marxism and the Interpretation of Culture*, edited by Cary Nelson and Lawrence Grossberg, 271–315. Urbana: University of Illinois Press, 1988.

Stanton, Elizabeth Cady. *The Woman's Bible*. Seattle: Coalition Task Force on Women and Religion, 1974.

Suchocki, Marjorie Hewitt. *The Fall to Violence: Original Sin in Relational Theology*. New York: Continuum, 1994.

Tauli-Corpuz, Victoria. "Reclaiming Earth-Based Spirituality: Indigenous Women in the Cordillera." In *Women Healing Earth: Third World Women on Ecology, Feminism, and Religion*, edited by Rosemary Radford Ruether, 99–106. Maryknoll, NY: Orbis, 1996.

Taylor, Barbara Brown. *Speaking of Sin: The Lost Language of Salvation*. Cambridge, MA: Cowley, 2000.

Thistlethwaite, Susan Brooks. *Women's Bodies as Battlefield: Christian Theology and the Global War on Women*. New York: Palgrave Macmillan, 2015.

Townes, Emilie M. *Breaking the Fine Rain of Death: African American Health Issues and a Womanist Ethics of Care*. Eugene, OR: Wipf & Stock, 2006.

Trible, Phyllis. *God and the Rhetoric of Sexuality*. Philadelphia: Fortress, 1985.

Tripathy, Jyotirmaya. "Indian Environmentalism, and Its Fragments." In *Ecoambiguity, Community, and Development: Toward a Politicized Ecocriticism*, edited by Scott Slovic, Swarnalatha Rangarajan, and Vidya Sarveswaran, 71–84. Lanham, MD: Lexington, 2014.

Waal, Frans B. M. de. *Primates and Philosophers: How Morality Evolved.* Edited by Stephen Macedo and Josiah Ober. Princeton: Princeton University Press, 2006.

Waal, Frans B. M. de, Patricia Smith Churchland, Telmo Pievani, and Stefano Parmigiani, eds. *Evolved Morality: The Biology and Philosophy of Human Conscience.* Leiden: Brill, 2014.

Wainwright, Elaine M. *Women Healing/Healing Women: The Genderization of Healing in Early Christianity.* London: Equinox, 2006.

Wallace, Mark I. *Finding God in the Singing River: Christianity, Spirit, Nature.* Minneapolis: Fortress, 2005.

_____. *Fragments of the Spirit: Nature, Violence, and the Renewal of Creation.* New York: Continuum, 1996.

Welker, Michael. *God the Spirit.* Translated by John F. Hoffmeyer. Minneapolis: Fortress, 1994.

Westhelle, Vítor. *Eschatology and Space: The Lost Dimension in Theology Past and Present.* New York: Palgrave/Macmillan, 2012.

White, Lynn. "The Historical Roots of Our Ecologic Crisis." *Science* 155 (March 1967): 1203–7.

_____. *Medieval Technology and Social Change.* London: Oxford University Press, 1964.

Wright, N. T. *Surprised by Hope: Rethinking Heaven, the Resurrection, and the Mission of the Church.* New York: HarperOne, 2008.

Zizioulas, John D. *Being as Communion: Studies in Personhood and the Church.* London: Darton, Longman & Todd, 1985.

_____. *Communion and Otherness: Further Studies in Personhood and the Church.* Edited by Paul McPartlan. London: T&T Clark, 2006.

Index

www.ingramcontent.com/pod-product-compliance
Lightning Source LLC
Chambersburg PA
CBHW071855090426
42811CB00004B/612